Anna Jameson, Elizabeth Eastlake

The history of our Lord as in works of art

with that of his types; St. John the Baptist and other persons of the Old and New

Testament, Volume 1

Anna Jameson, Elizabeth Eastlake

The history of our Lord as in works of art
with that of his types; St. John the Baptist and other persons of the Old and New Testament, Volume 1

ISBN/EAN: 9783742860484

Manufactured in Europe, USA, Canada, Australia, Japa

Cover: Foto ©Lupo / pixelio.de

Manufactured and distributed by brebook publishing software (www.brebook.com)

Anna Jameson, Elizabeth Eastlake

The history of our Lord as in works of art

THE
History of Our Lord

AS EXEMPLIFIED IN WORKS OF ART:

WITH THAT OF

HIS TYPES; ST. JOHN THE BAPTIST; AND OTHER PERSONS
OF THE OLD AND NEW TESTAMENT.

COMMENCED BY THE LATE
MRS. JAMESON.

CONTINUED AND COMPLETED BY
LADY EASTLAKE.

IN TWO VOLUMES.—VOLUME I.

FOURTH EDITION.

LONDON:
LONGMANS, GREEN, AND CO.
1881.

PREFACE.

THE VOLUMES now before the reader—'The History of Our Lord, as Exemplified in Works of Art'—were reserved by the late Mrs. Jameson as the more important section, as well as the natural completion, of the series already contributed by her to the literature of Christian Art. This Work, of which she had written a portion, was cut short by her death in the spring of 1860. I was requested by her publisher and by her family to continue and complete it. For this task I was fitted in no other way than by a desire, to the best of my power, to do homage to her memory. The interval has since been devoted by me to a special study of the subjects here treated, during which time I have enjoyed every possible advantage, at home and abroad, that could facilitate my labours, excepting that of uninterrupted leisure. To this latter circumstance, therefore, the delay in the appearance of the Work is to be attributed. At the same time those at all conversant with the extent, interest, and comparative obscurity of this study, are aware that the devotion of a life would have only sufficed to do it justice. As it is, these Volumes serve little more than to indicate those accumulated results of the piety and industry of ages, and the laws, moral, historical, and pictorial, connected with them, which have created a realm of Art almost kindred in amount to a kingdom of Nature.

I must now explain the condition of Mrs. Jameson's MS. when first entrusted to me. I found a programme—contained on one sheet of paper—of the titles and sequence of the different parts of the subject; also a portion of the manuscript in a completed state, though without the indication of a single illustration. For what was still unwritten, no materials whatever were left. By her sisters—the Misses Murphy—who have shown the utmost desire to assist me, I was furnished with many note-books and journals.

These, however, threw no light on Mrs. Jameson's intentions as regards the treatment of the large portion still unexecuted; it was evident that she was accustomed to trust to the stores of her rich mind, and to her clear memory, for an index to them. Under these circumstances, I was left to do the work in my own way. How inferior that way has been to Mrs. Jameson's, I wish to be the first to point out.

A few words must especially be said upon the order of the Work. In the short programme left by Mrs. Jameson, the ideal and devotional subjects, such as the Good Shepherd, the Lamb, the Second Person of the Trinity, were placed first; the Scriptural history of our Lord's life on earth next; and, lastly, the Types from the Old Testament. There is reason, however, to believe, from the evidence of what she had already written, that she would have departed from this arrangement. After much deliberation, I have ventured to do so, and to place the subjects chronologically. The Work commences, therefore, with that which heads most systems of Christian Art—the Fall of Lucifer and creation of the World—followed by the Types and Prophets of the Old Testament. Next comes the history of the Innocents and of John the Baptist, written by her own hand, and leading to the Life and Passion of our Lord. The abstract and devotional subjects, as growing out of these materials, then follow, and the Work terminates with the Last Judgment.

In the number of subjects treated, also, I have deviated from the programme, though chiefly in adding to them. My excuse, if needful, is, that having taken monuments of Art for my guidance, I have simply followed their teaching. Still, I am desirous to explain that this Work comes before the Public with no pretension to completeness, but, rather, with the avowal of very great inequality of description and illustration. One deficiency, of which I may anticipate the notice, consists in the comparative omission of the mosaics in the early Roman churches, the history and representation of which have been so thoroughly given by well-known writers as to induce me to seek my examples in less-worked mines of Art.

I take this opportunity of expressing my obligations to the gentlemen in various Art departments of the British Museum, especially to Mr. Carpenter, Mr. Holmes, and Mr. Franks; also to the Hon. Robert Curzon, Dr. Rock, Mr. Robinson, and Mr. George Scharf; and to Mr. Stewart, of King William Street, to whom I am specially indebted for the assistance afforded me in the use of early and valuable works.

As regards the numerous Illustrations, many of which have the recommendation of being new to the Public, I am anxious to add that I owe the execution of the etchings, with the exception of two, to Mr. Edward Poynter, that of by far the larger number and more important of the drawings on wood to Miss Clara Lane, and the engraving of the blocks to the labours of Miss Matéaux and Mr. Cooper.

It only remains to explain that the portion of the Work which, to a large circle of readers, will have a twofold interest, will be found to be strictly separated from that supplied by myself. Mrs. Jameson's text will be at once recognised by the insertion of the initials, *A. J.* at the top of every page, and at the beginning of any interpolated paragraph.

E. E.

7 FITZROY SQUARE,
March 26, 1864.

CONTENTS

OF

THE FIRST VOLUME

INTRODUCTION.

	PAGE
Early Symbolical Forms of Christian Art	10
Christian Sarcophagi	13
Mural Paintings in Catacombs	16
Mosaics	18
Doors of Churches	20
Ivories	21
Enamels	25
Miniatures and early Block Books	25
Portraits of Christ	31

The Fall of Lucifer and of the Rebel Angels	54
The Creation of Angels	62
The Creation of the World	66
The Days of Creation	75
The Creation of Adam	86
The Sleep of Adam, and the Creation of Eve	93
The Marriage of Adam and Eve	98
Eve listening to the Serpent	100
The Fall	102
Adam and Eve hiding in the Garden	109
The Lord accusing Adam and Eve	109
The Coats of Skins	111
Giving Adam a Spade, and Eve a Spindle	111
The Expulsion	112
Adam and Eve in their Fallen Condition	115
Abel	118

	PAGE
Adam and Eve lamenting over the Body of Abel	121
Lamech kills Cain	123
Enos	124
Enoch	124
Noah	126
Abraham and Isaac	133
Lot	139
Hagar	141
Rebekah	143
Isaac receives his Bride Rebekah	145
Abraham	147
Jacob	149
Joseph	156
Moses	171
Joshua	187
Judges	192
Gideon	192
Jephthah	194
Samson	195
Samuel	199
David	201
Solomon	216
Elijah and Elisha	220
Job	225
Daniel and the Three Children	232
Nebuchadnezzar's Dream	235
Bel and the Dragon	237
Jonah	238
The Prophets	240
The Sibyls	245
The Murder of the Innocents	259
Joseph the Husband of the Virgin	273
Christ disputing with the Doctors	277
John the Baptist	281
The Temptation in the Wilderness	310
Angels minister to our Lord in the Wilderness	315
The Money-Changers expelled from the Temple	316
Christ as Teacher	318
Christ teaches in the Temple (or the Synagogue)	321
Christ preaching from the Ship	322
The Tribute Money	323
Christ in the House of Martha and Mary	325
Christ blesses little Children	328
The Woman taken in Adultery	332
Christ and the Woman of Samaria	337

CONTENTS OF THE FIRST VOLUME.

	PAGE
The Transfiguration	340
The Miracles	347
The Marriage at Cana of Galilee	354
The Raising of Lazarus	356
The Raising the Widow's Son	361
Jesus heals the Daughter of the Woman of Canaan	363
Christ heals the Centurion's Servant	364
The Pool at Bethesda	367
The Blind are healed	370
Miracle of the Loaves and Fishes	370
The Miraculous Draught of Fishes	372
The Calling of the two first Apostles, Peter and Andrew	374
The Parables of our Lord	375
The Rich Man and Lazarus	379
The Doom of the Wicked Rich Man	380
The Prodigal Son	382
The Good Samaritan	388
The Wise and the Foolish Virgins	390
The Householder who hired Labourers for his Vineyard	394
The Unmerciful Servant	395
The Blind leading the Blind	396
The Tree which bore Good Fruit and the Tree which was Barren	396
The Pearl of great Price	396
The Lost Drachm	397

LIST OF ILLUSTRATIONS

IN

THE FIRST VOLUME.

Those marked with an asterisk have not been engraved before.

*1. Scutum Fidei, or Shield of Faith. *Ancient ivory.*
2. Emblem on early Christian Signet Ring.
3. Ceiling in Catacomb: *Bottari.*
4. Page from 'Biblia Pauperum.'
*5. Abgarus Portrait of Christ. *Prince Consort's Collection.*
*6. King Abgarus receiving miraculous Portrait. *Prince Consort's Collection.*
*7. Veronica before Emperor. *Biblioteca Ambrosiana, Milan.*
8. Classic Head of Christ.
9. Byzantine Head of Christ.
*10. Byzantine Head of Christ.
*11. Anglo-Saxon Head of Christ.
*12. Head of Christ.
*13. Head of Christ.
*14. Head of Christ.
*15. Head of Christ.
*16. Lucifer in Rebellion. *MS. Mr. Holford.*
17. Creation of Angels and Light. *Monreale.*
*18. Sol and Luna. *Bible de Noailles. Bibliothèque Impériale, Paris.*
*19. Diagram of Creation. *Anglo-Saxon MS. B. Museum.*
*20. First Day. Division of Light from Darkness. *Mosaics. St. Mark's, Venice.*
*21. Christ blessing Seventh Day. *Mosaics. St. Mark's, Venice.*
22. Spirit moving on Face of Waters. *Monreale.*
23. The Lord resting on the Seventh Day. *Monreale.*
24. Creation of Fishes and Birds. *Orvieto.*
25. Creation of Animals. *Orvieto.*
26. Creation of Light. *Raphael.*

27. Creation of Adam. *Orvieto.*
*28. The Living Soul. *Mosaics. St. Mark's, Venice.*
29. The Breath of Life. *Monreale.*
30. Creation of Adam. *Ghiberti. Bronze doors, Florence.*
*31. Christ giving Adam Spade and Keys. *Bible Historiée. Paris.*
32. Extracting Adam's Rib. *Orvieto.*
33. Creation of Eve. *Orvieto.*
34. Creation of Eve. *Ghiberti. Bronze doors, Florence.*
35. Marriage of Adam and Eve. *Speculum Salvationis.*
36. Eve listening to Serpent. *Speculum Salvationis.*
37. Christ giving Adam Wheatsheaf and Eve Lamb. *Sarcophagus.*
38. The Fall. *Raphael.*
39. The Temptation. *Lucas Cranach.*
40. Adam and Eve hiding. *N. Pisano. Orvieto.*
*41. The Lord accusing Adam and Eve. *Bible de Noailles, Paris.*
*42. Angel giving Spade and Spindle. *MS., B. Museum.*
43. Expulsion of Adam and Eve. *Raphael. Loggie.*
44. Adam and Eve. *Raphael. Loggie.*
*45. Adam. *Statue on Milan Cathedral.*
*46. Cain and Abel. *Bible Historiée. Paris.*
*47. The Lord accusing Cain. *Bible Historiée. Paris.*
*48. Adam and Eve lamenting over dead Body of Abel. *Mr. Boxall's Speculum.*
49. Lamech and Cain. *Lucas van Leyden.*
*50. Translation of Enoch. *Bible Historiée. Paris.*
51. God appearing to Noah. *Raphael. Loggie.*
52. Isaac carrying Wood. *MS., B. Museum.*
53. Abraham and Melchisedec. *Memling. Munich.*
54. Abraham entertaining Angels. *Benozzo Gozzoli. Campo Santo.*
55. Rebekah and Eleazar. *Benozzo Gozzoli. Campo Santo.*
56. Angels taking Leave of Abraham. *Benozzo Gozzoli. Campo Santo.*
57. Jacob's Dream. *Raphael. Loggie.*
*58. Jacob wrestling. *Bible Historiée. Paris.*
59. Joseph dropping Wheat in River. *MS., B. Museum.*
*60. Jacob receiving Joseph's Garment. *Mr. Boxall's Speculum.*
61. Joseph's Dream. *Raphael.*
62. Joseph recognised by his Brethren. *Ghiberti. Bronze doors.*
*63. Meeting of Jacob and Joseph. *Ancient ivory. Arundel Society.*
*64. Jacob blessing Joseph's Children. *Bible Historiée. Paris.*
*65. Finding of Moses. *Bible Historiée. Paris.*
*66. Sister watching Infant Moses. *Bible, B. Museum.*
67. Moses' Choice. *Giorgione. Uffizj.*
68. Moses untying Sandal. *Wall Painting, Catacomb.*
*69. Moses and Burning Bush. *MS., Liège Library.*
*70. Israelites striking the Doorposts. *Bible Historiée. Paris.*
71. Overthrow of Pharaoh. *Ancient sarcophagus.*

72. Moses striking Rock. *Ceiling in Catacomb.*
 73. Moses receiving the Law. *Ancient sarcophagus.*
*74. Burial of Moses. *Bible de Noailles. Paris.*
 75. Joshua's Vision. *MS., Vatican.*
 76. Joshua arresting Sun and Moon. *MS., Vatican.*
 77. Gideon and Fleece. *Speculum Salvationis. M. Berjeau.*
*78. Samson overcoming Lion. *Mr. Boxall's Speculum.*
 79. Samson drinking from Jaw-bone. *Guido. Gallery, Bologna.*
*80. Presentation of Infant Samuel. *Mr. Boxall's Speculum.*
 81. David with Sling. *Ceiling, Catacombs.*
*82. David with Harp. *Greek MS.*
 83. David between Knowledge and Prophecy. *Greek MS.*
 84. David and Head of Goliath. *Guido.*
*85. Triumph of David. *Pesellino. Marchese Torrigiano, Florence.*
 86. David's Triumph. *Matteo Rosselli. Pitti.*
*87. Nathan before David. *Mr. Boxall's Speculum.*
*88. David playing on the Bells. *MS. Mr. Holford.*
 89. Translation of Elijah. *Ancient sarcophagus.*
 90. Elisha. *Painted window. Lincoln College, Oxford.*
 91. Job. *Fra Bartolomeo. Uffizi.*
 92. Job. *Bellini. Belle Arti, Venice.*
 93. Almighty appearing to Job in Whirlwind. *Blake.*
 94. The Three Children in the Furnace. *Wall Painting, Catacombs.*
*95. The Three Children in the Furnace. *Mr. Boxall's Speculum.*
 96. Nebuchadnezzar's Dream. *Speculum. M. Berjeau.*
 97. The History of Jonah. *Ancient sarcophagus.*
 98. Prophet Isaiah. *Gaudenzio Ferrari.*
 99. Sibyl and Emperor. *Garofalo. Vatican.*
 100. Sibylla Cumana. *Baldini.*
 101. Sibylla Libyca. *Michael Angelo.*
 102. Prophet Jeremiah. *Michael Angelo.*
 103. Sibylla Cumana. *Raphael.*
 104. Sibylla Cumana. *Andrea del Castagno. Uffizi.*
*105. Innocents as Martyrs. *Choral Book. S. Ambrogio. Milan.*
*106. Massacre of the Innocents. *Fra Angelico. Choral Book. S. Marco.*
*107. Innocent. *Luca della Robbia. Florence.*
 108. Joseph and Infant Christ. *Guido.*
*109. Joseph's Dream. *Mr. Boxall's Speculum.*
 110. Christ disputing with the Doctors. *Spagnoletto. Vienna Gallery.*
 111. Virgin with Christ and Baptist. *Luini. Lugano.*
 112. John the Baptist. *Memling. Munich Gallery.*
*113. Baptist and Bishop. *Drawing by Bellini. B. Museum.*
*114. Infant Baptist on the Lap of Virgin Mary. *Brentano Miniature.*
 115. Baptist in the Wilderness. *Bugiardini. Bologna Gallery.*
*116. Baptism. *MS., 13th century. Bologna.*
 117. Baptism. *Verrocchio. Accademia, Florence.*

118. Burial of Baptist. *Andrea Pisano.* *Doors of Baptistery, Florence.*
119. Baptist taking Leave of Parents. *Fra F. Lippi.* *Prato.*
120. The Temptation. *Lucas van Leyden.*
121. Christ Teaching. *Luini.* *National Gallery.*
122. Christ in House of Martha and Mary. *Jouvenet.* *Louvre.*
123. Christ blessing little Children. *Rembrandt.*
124. The Woman taken in Adultery. *Mazzolino di Ferrara.* *Pitti.*
125. Christ and the Woman of Samaria. *Ancient sarcophagus.*
126. Transfiguration. *Fra Angelico.* *S. Marco. Florence.*
127. Conversion of Water into Wine. *Ancient sarcophagus.*
128. Miracle of Loaves and Fishes. *Ancient sarcophagus.*
*129. Miracle of Loaves and Fishes. *MS. Mr. Holford.*
130. Christ healing the Blind. *Ancient sarcophagus.*
131. Christ healing the Woman. *Ancient sarcophagus.*
132. Christ healing the Lame. *Ancient sarcophagus.*
133. Raising of Lazarus. *Fra Angelico.* *Accademia, Florence.*
134. Christ healing Woman. *Paul Veronese.*
*135. Prodigal Son. *Mr. Boxall's Speculum.*
136. Prodigal Son. *Guercino.*
137. The Wise and Foolish Virgins. *Speculum.* *M. Berjeau.*
138. Lost Drachm. *Domenico Feti.* *Pitti.*

Etchings.

Sarcophagus of Junius Bassus. 4th century . . . *to face page* 13
*Ivory Gospel Cover 22
*Ivory Diptych. 14th century 23
*Creation and Fall of Angels 62
*Diagram of the Universe. *English miniature.* 14th century . . 74
Moses striking Rock. *Poussin* 183
*David killing Lion. *Byzantine miniature.* 9th century . . 204
*Nathan before David. David Repentant. *Byzantine miniature.* 9th century . 212
*Innocents with Patron Saints. *Ghirlandajo.* *Church of the Innocents,*
Florence 364

Scutum Fidei, or Shield of Faith (ancient ivory).

Introduction.

SOURCES AND FORMS OF CHRISTIAN ART.

THE HISTORY of our Lord, as represented in Art, is essentially the history of Christian Art. Round His sacred head, encircled in early mediæval forms with the cruciform nimbus, all Christian Art revolves, as a system round a sun. He is always the great centre and object of the scene; since whether represented, according to the taste of the artist, or the requirements of the patron, as Infant, Youth, or Man—as Teacher, Physician, or Friend—as Victim and Sacrifice—as King or Judge—He is always intended, under every aspect, real or ideal, to be looked upon as God. For no philosophy, 'falsely so called,' intrudes into the domain of Christian Art—no subtleties on His human nature, no doubts of His Godhead, no rational interpretations of His miracles. Christian Art pre-eminently illustrates faith in Christ as 'God manifest in the flesh,' as 'the Lamb slain from the foundation of the world;' and without these great fundamental truths of Christianity there is no Christian Art, either in fact or in possibility.

In the history of Christ as traced in Art we have therefore primarily to look to those forms which are most Christian, or which, in other words, imply most faith and reverence in the mode of conception. For though Christ continued to be ostensibly the object represented in pictures executed for churches and chapels, yet there came a time when Art itself, rather than its divine theme, became evidently, both to artist and spectator, the centre of adoration. There are none who feel deeply the intention and power of Christian Art who will not confess, on looking at the works of the greatest masters of the 16th century, that the sense of religious edification keeps no pace with that of their technical beauties; but that, by a strange paradox, the excellence of the means has become apparently fatal to the sacredness of the end. We say apparently, for such a deduction would be as false in theory as unfair to Art. It is true, as we shall have abundant evidence to show in the course of this work, that the clumsy and ignorant efforts of early mediæval Art convey a far deeper spirituality and reverence of feeling than is shown in any *chef-d'œuvre* of the 16th century. But this proves only a fact, not a law. It would be indeed distressing to believe that earnestness of intention could only be combined with infant Art, and the reverse with Art full-grown; and all common sense protests against such a conclusion. It is doubtless legitimate matter of surprise that the ignorant artist should have done any justice to the faith that was in him; but it is self-evident that no hand can be too skilled for the service of the highest requirements and forms of expression. We must rather acknowledge the causes for such a seeming anomaly to lie in circumstances without, and not within, the artist's studio—in the history of Religion and her external forms, and in the morals and modes of thought which prevailed at given periods. To enter into so large a theme is, however, quite beyond the scope and purpose of this work, and we take this early opportunity of disclaiming all judgment except such as is suggested by Art itself. Art faithfully reflects all those outward influences which raise or debase her aim, sanctify or degrade her use. The student of history may trace these influences up to their various sources, and show us why it was that the artist might be expected to exhibit certain characteristics at certain epochs; but our business is to confine ourselves, as far as the necessary connection of all history with itself will allow, to the proof that he did exhibit such characteristics. If each explorer faithfully perform his part, they will converge at the same point, and scarcely lose sight of one another on the way.

The first object of Christian Art was to teach. St. Augustine called pictures and statues 'libri idiotarum,' or 'the books of the simple.'

Art. was then, like an alphabet, made use of as a sign, not as an ornament. In this form she was employed to set visibly forth the great rudimental facts of Christian doctrine. But it was far different when the multiplication of the means of teaching by a direct process superseded the primitive use of the picture. By that time also, in the providential fitness of all things, Art had outgrown her hieroglyphic state, and as she was no longer wanted, so she was no longer fitted for that phase of teaching. Her vocation had risen with her powers, and the far more intellectual task was opened to her of refreshing the perception of those truths which were already known. Properly speaking, the craft of the printer was the enfranchisement of the artist: it took all the previous mechanical drudgery from him, and set him free for the more congenial occupation of adorning that doctrine which he had before been required to teach. It must be owned that in this sense—the sense of Christian feeling—the Italian masters who flourished after the invention of printing did very inadequate justice to the greatness of the opportunity. We need to steal no glance at the student of history to convince ourselves that the real service of religion was not the aim of the southern artists of the 16th and 17th centuries. It is sufficient to state the mere fact, that the zenith of the powers of Art added scarcely a new subject to the repertory of the artist.

Before tracing the history of our Lord through monuments of Art bequeathed to us by the schools of various countries, and spreading over a space of time little short of the whole Christian Era, it must first be admitted that the materials for this history in Art are only properly derivable from Scripture, and therefore referable back to the same source for verification. In this respect the earlier works afford almost unalloyed interest to the Christian student. The early Fathers pored over the words of Scripture, and gathered from them every moral symbol and allusion that pious diligence could suggest. But they left the sacred text inviolate, even from devout speculation, according to the great rule afterwards laid down by the venerable Bede: 'We cannot know that on which Truth keeps silence.' The Art, therefore, which immediately succeeded the expiration of classic influences, viz., that of the 10th and 11th centuries, is so characterised by close adherence to the letter of

Scripture, as scarcely to be understood without the Bible in hand. But no student of Christian Art can proceed far without perceiving that whereas certain periods bear witness to generations of artists who followed the guidance of Holy Writ with implicit obedience, other periods as unmistakably show the addition of non-Scriptural materials, as well as the alteration of the Sacred Text itself. We come, in short, to the indications of Legend—always traceable from the picture to the opinions and writings current at the time. All legend concerning our Saviour is based, it may be observed, on the principle of filling up what the Gospels have left unsaid. Thus those portions of our Lord's life which the wisdom of Scripture leaves unaccounted for, are especially the objects of fabrication by the authors of the apocryphal Gospels. By these we mean certain spurious writings, not tending to edification, rejected by all Christian Churches; and, therefore, not admitted even among what our Church calls the apocryphal books. These were of ancient date, compiled in the first ages of Christianity, and revised and circulated from time to time in manuscript, and subsequently in print. Little, for instance, is said by the inspired writers of the infancy of our Lord, less of His boyhood, nothing of His childhood. The so-called 'Gospel of Infancy,' therefore, supplies an account of the Child while yet in the cradle, of His life in Egypt, of His boyhood in Judæa, and of His miracles throughout these different ages. This work has the negative merit of being neither directly grafted upon nor mixed with any portion of Holy Writ; though, like all the writings of this class, it is carefully interlarded with Scriptural passages and allusions, so as to increase the appearance of probability. The art, therefore, which illustrates it, and which is insignificant in character and amount, is, as we shall see, entirely distinct from the legitimate range of Christian subjects.

But it is different with the so-called 'Gospel of Nicodemus,' or 'Acts of Pilate'—purporting to have been found among the documents of the Roman governor—which, taking the main circumstances of our Lord's condemnation and crucifixion as a foundation, encumber the text with a large amount of extraneous matter, directly mingling with the sacred narrative. This forces its way in various forms on to the surface of Art, more especially in that mysterious fact of our Lord's mission to the spirits in prison (1 Peter iii. 19), largely dwelt upon in the Gospel of Nicodemus, and rendered by Art under the subject of Christ's descent into Limbus.

The writers, also, of scholastic history, such as Peter Comestor in the twelfth century, without precisely infringing upon the text, yet contribute, by their strained and whimsical commentaries and interpretations, to adulterate the sources to which the artist looked for guidance.

Again, as regards especially the sufferings, death, and interment of our Lord—of which Scripture, as if purposely to interdict the exercise of morbid imaginations, gives an outline unexampled in simplicity and reticence—the reveries and ecstacies of saints and nuns, as well as the sermons of preachers, have been directed to heighten the effect of some portions of the text, and to fill up supposed gaps in others. The Life of Christ, for example, by St. Bonaventura, in the 13th century, and the Revelations of St. Brigitta of Sweden in the 14th, which we shall have frequent occasion to refer to, with many others, have embodied this aim. Art bears, accordingly, witness to the currency of writings which, except for their impress thus retained, are, in great measure, consigned to oblivion. Even in the best and most legitimate examples of the class of literature which proceeded from the fervid minds of that time, anxious to stem the natural wickedness of man, the chief aim was to exhort the reader to look, not on the holy life and teaching of the Lord, but almost solely on His sufferings—to gaze upon them, to pause, to contemplate, to realise the dreadful truth, dressed up for him with every ingenuity of description, till he was told that his heart, unless of stone, would stream in torrents from his eyes. These were the contemplations by which devotion was to be stimulated, and which the painters were naturally required to translate into positive images. Far be it from us, in the self-glorification of our century, to despise the form in which these earnest appeals were made, or the means inculcated for a life of sanctity. Wisdom was justified of her children. These pious writers gave rules which to the world seem always foolishness, but which, if seriously followed, could but weaken the temptations of the flesh and create a spiritual element.

From the 13th to the 16th centuries, it may be observed, the inclination among southern races was to add to the text of Scripture;

from the 16th to the 19th century, with northern races, the inclination has been to take from it. The first fact may be characterised as the natural tendency to superstition; the latter as the natural tendency to infidelity. Between the two, Scripture stands firm, for Art as for morals. For without entering further into the merits or demerits of the writings to which we have alluded, it may be at once laid down as a principle that the interests of Christian Art and the integrity of Scripture are indissolubly united. Where superstition mingles, the quality of Christian Art suffers; where doubt enters, Christian Art has nothing to do. It may even be averred, that if a person could be imagined, deeply imbued with æsthetic instincts and knowledge, and utterly ignorant of Scripture, he would yet intuitively prefer, as Art, all those conceptions of our Lord's history which adhere to the simple text. He would shrink from exaggerated and degrading representations of His sufferings, as doing violence to the true principles of the artist. He would prefer to see the Blessed Virgin standing by the Cross in dutiful though agonised resignation, rather than sinking upon the ground, and thus diverting the attention both of the actors in the scene and the spectators of the picture from the one awful object. He would feel that St. Veronica, primly presenting her cloth to the overburdened Saviour, was peculiarly *de trop*—morally and pictorially. All preference for the simple narrative of Scripture he would arrive at through Art—all condemnation of the embroideries of legend through the same channel.

And if an unconcerned connoisseur would so judge merely in the interests of a favourite pursuit, how much more must a believer take umbrage at alterations in the text, which, however slight, affect the revealed character of our Lord! The circumstance, for example, of Christ's carrying His Cross on the way to Calvary, is not only a fact in that part of His history, but a moral which He thus illustrates for our example. An alteration of the text, therefore, which makes Him falling, sometimes even prone beneath it, as He is represented at certain periods, affects a vital point in our Lord's character, and invalidates an inestimable precept given for our daily encouragement.

On the other hand, additions to Scripture given in positive images, if neither prejudicial to Art nor inconsistent with our Lord's character, are not in themselves necessarily objectionable; but will, according to their merits, be looked upon with indulgence or admiration. The pictures, for instance, representing the disrobing of our Lord—a fact not told in Scripture, yet which must have happened—will be regarded with pathetic interest. The same will be felt of Paul de la Roche's exquisite little picture, where St. John is leading the Virgin home; for such works legitimately refresh and carry on the narrative in a Scriptural spirit. Nay, even episodes which are more purely invention—such as the ancient tradition of the Mother of Christ wrapping the cloth round her Son, previous to His crucifixion; or again, the picture by Paul de la Roche of the agony of her and of the disciples, represented as gathered together in a room while Christ passes with His Cross—even such imaginary episodes will silence the most arrant Protestant criticism, by their overpowering appeal to the feelings; since in neither case is the great duty of Art to itself or to its divine object tampered with.

The same holds good where symbolical forms, as in Christian Art of classic descent, are given, which embody the idea rather than the fact. For instance, where the Jordan is represented as a river god, with his urn under his arm, at the baptism of our Lord; or when, later, the same event is accompanied by the presence of angels, who hold the Saviour's garments. Such paraphrases and poetical imaginings in no way affect the truth of the facts they set forth, but rather, to mortal fancy, swell their pomp and dignity.

Still less need the lover of Art, and adorer of Christ, care about inconsistencies in minor matters. As, for example, that the entombment takes place in a renaissance monument, in the centre of a beautiful Italian landscape, and not in a cave in a rock in the arid scenery of Judæa. On the contrary, it is right that Art should exercise the utmost possible freedom in such circumstances, which are the signs and handwriting of different schools and times, and enrich a picture with sources of interest to the historian and the archæologist. It is the moral expression that touches the heart and adorns the tale, not the architecture or costume; and whether our Lord be in the garb of a Roman citizen or of a German burgher (though His dress is usually conventional in colour and form), it matters not, if He be but God in all.

One principle in Art, though apparently obvious, is yet so liable to be misunderstood by the general class of readers, to whom this work is addressed, as to excuse some explanation. All will agree that the duty of the Christian artist is to give not only the temporary fact, but the permanent truth. Yet this entails a discrepancy in which something must be sacrificed. For, in the scenes from our Lord's life, fact and truth are frequently at variance. That the Magdalene took our Lord for a gardener, was the fact; that He was the Christ, is the truth. That the Roman soldiers believed Him to be a criminal, and therefore mocked and buffeted Him without scruple, is the fact; that we know Him through all these scenes to be the Christ, is the truth. Nay, the very cruciform nimbus that encircles Christ's head is an assertion of this principle. As visible to us, it is true; as visible even to His disciples, it is false. There are, however, educated people so little versed in the conditions of Art, as to object even to the nimbus as a departure from fact, and, therefore, an offence to truth; preferring, they say, to see our Lord represented as He walked upon earth. But this is a fallacy in more than one sense. Our Lord, as He walked upon earth, was not known to be the Messiah. To give Him as He was seen by men who knew Him not, would be to give Him not as the Christ. It may be urged, that the cruciform nimbus is a mere arbitrary sign—nothing in itself, more than a combination of lines. This is true; but there *must* be something arbitrary in all human imaginings of the supernatural. It is like religion itself, where something also must be assumed, and something granted. Art, for ages, assumed this sign as that of the Godhead of Christ, and the world for ages granted it. It served various purposes; it hedged the rudest representations of Christ round with a divinity which kept them distinct from all others. It pointed Him out to the most ignorant spectator, and it identified the sacred head even at a distance.

Further, it is a mistake to suppose that a picture can convey the double sense of Christ as He appeared to those around Him, and as He is beheld through the eye of Belief. Art, by its essential conditions, has but one moment to speak, and one form of expression to utter. If, therefore, we require to see Christ 'without form or comeliness,' we cannot in the same picture behold Him as 'the express image of the Father, full of grace and truth.' The Eastern Church, as we shall see, is supposed to have maintained the first definition of our Lord's person—the Western the second; but neither of them imagined that, in the sense of Art, they could be given together. Thus there must be always a compromise, between what we have termed temporary fact and permanent truth, and that at the expense of the least important of the two. And this compromise, which is the soul of Christian Art, is not proper to that only. It is the soul also, in the strictest sense, of all Art. What is the Drama without it? There is always the fact for the actors, and the truth for the spectators. That Othello sees in Iago an honest man is the fact; that we see him to be a villain is the truth. The real object of the play is always outside the boards. The poorest romance recognises this necessity. This involves far greater skill in the dramatist or novel writer, for the spectator or reader has to be satisfied that the difference between his view and the actor's view is well accounted for. The painter has no such difficulty; he cannot, if he would, represent one image to the actor and another to the spectator, for he has but one image to give at all.

We must, therefore, in the task that is before us, keep in mind that the object of Christian Art is the instruction and edification of ourselves, not any abstract and impossible unity of ideas that cannot be joined together. Early Art never loses sight of this instinct. Pictures, as we have said, were the 'books of the simple.' The first condition, therefore, was that the books should be easily read.

Having thus seen certain moral excellences appertaining to early Christian Art—its faithful adherence to Scripture, and its true instinct as to its duty—we shall be the more justified in bringing it largely before the reader in a research intended to define the true standards of religious modes of representation. It is not only that from these simple and nameless artists have descended those Scriptural types and traditions which constitute the science of Christian Art, but that in them we find the subject, and not the art, the chief aim of their labours. Art was for many centuries, where not affected by classic influences, too undeveloped to allow its votary to expand and disport himself in the conscious exercise of mechanical skill. He therefore suited his art, such as it was, to his subject: later

painters may be said to have done the reverse. The transition
from the one to the other, considered in a general way, is a curious
scale, beginning with moral and ending with physical indications.
Thus reverence is seen first, endowing scenes devoid of almost
every other quality with a pious propriety, which, if not Art, is
its best foundation. Then came a certain stereotyped dignity of
forms, descended from Byzantine tradition; to this followed
expression of feeling and dramatic action, as with Duccio and
Giotto; next the true variety of the human countenance, as with
Fra Angelico; and then all these qualities together, heightened
by greater skill in each, as with the great Quattro-centisti of
Florence, Padua, and Venice. These found their height of
culmination in Leonardo da Vinci, and partially in Raphael, who
threw down the last barriers of difficulty between a painter's hand
and mind, and in whom, therefore, subject and Art may be said
to have had equal part. From this time commence the triumphs
of Art proper—the glories of colour, the feats of anatomical skill,
the charms of *chiaroscuro*, and the revels of free-handling; all
claiming to be admired for themselves, all requiring the subject to
bend to their individualities. Here, therefore, there is little to say,
however much to delight in. This is Art alone—as much as, in
another sense, the Dutch school is Art alone—taking its forms
from elevated or from homely nature, and accordingly producing
works before which, to use a too familiar phrase, the mouth of the
connoisseur waters, but, with very few exceptions, the eye of feeling
remains dry.

EARLY SYMBOLICAL FORMS OF CHRISTIAN ART.

Before entering more particularly into the great subject of our researches—the pictorial History of our Lord and His Types—we must
briefly point out some of the classes, cycles, and series of Art, through
which this subject has descended to us, and from which we have
derived most assistance in the course of these labours. It is by no
means, as we have hinted, in the works of what are called the old
masters only that the materials for study are to be found. The pith
of Christian Art lies rather in forms and objects far anterior in date
to any pictures now existing, and which, owing to the researches of

archæologists and the formation of museums, are daily being rescued from further destruction.

And first we must point out some of the minuter forms under which the desire to exhibit the ideas belonging to the new faith showed itself.

In the first centuries of Christianity, Art is supposed to have suffered complete suppression as regards all manifestation of Christian feeling. The early converts consisted of two races—of Jews, to whom every species of graven image was, by law and habit, an abomination; and of Roman Gentiles, who, with the old idolatry, necessarily abjured the forms that embodied it. So rigorously, for these double reasons, was the abstinence from Art enforced, that, like as with other commodities forbidden by policy or religion, the strictest measures were enacted against the producers. Whatever convert to Christianity, originally an artist, returned to his former craft, was considered an apostate, and denied the rite of baptism—a ceremony not partaken of, in the first ages of the Church, until after years of conformity. It was not, however, in the nature of a people who lived in the atmosphere of beautiful and ideal forms, to close their minds longer than was absolutely necessary against them. The first signs of life given by the fettered but never extinguished element, and exhibited cautiously and timidly, were seen in small objects, such as incised gems and signet rings. These bore the mask of a symbolism intelligible to a race accustomed to decipher ideas under the most abstract forms. In many instances a familiar Pagan image was even permitted under the sanction of a new and higher meaning.

The symbol of the Fish, the most frequently seen, appears to be of strictly Christian origin. It had several homogeneous meanings. It alluded to the regenerating waters of baptism. It typified the believer as the 'little fish' caught by those whom Christ had appointed to be the fishers of men. It expressed also the person of Christ Himself, who is called 'the Fish' by early Christian writers; and it especially obtained favour from the mystical combination of letters forming the Greek word for fish, which represented in an acrostic form the Greek sentence, 'Jesus

² Emblem on early Christian signet ring

Christ, Son of God, Saviour.' Accordingly, the symbol and the anagram are sometimes given separate, oftener together, as in our illustration.

The Ship was another purely Christian symbol, indicating the Church, in allusion to Noah's Ark. Instances occur where the symbol of the ship is seen resting on that of the fish—the Church on its head. The Papal signet ring, called the 'Ring of the Fisherman,' preserves in part this allusion, the Pope being seen in a boat, drawing a net from the waters. This is, however, as may be supposed, of a far later date.

The Dove was an antique symbol of innocence, adopted by our Lord in the text, 'Be ye wise as serpents and harmless as doves.' It may therefore be supposed to have been used by Christians in the same sense. It was also the Scriptural sign of the Holy Spirit.

The Anchor was a well-known antique civic emblem, originally understood to signify a safe harbour, and therefore, later, a flourishing city. With the Christians it set forth one of the great evangelical virtues—Hope.

The Lyre was the attribute of Apollo and the Muses. It is easy to see how it passed into the service of the Christian under the ideas of praise and thanksgiving to God, and of persuasion to man. In this sense Orpheus and his lyre are both retained in Christian classic Art as the symbol of our Lord, and of the power of the Gospel.

We have mentioned these symbols first, their early date being ascertained by an epistle from Clement of Alexandria (died 216), in which he prescribes all these images as proper and decorous to be worn in rings by the Christians. Many others may be enumerated, such as the Palm-branch, the Peacock, the Phœnix, the Crown—all symbols of Pagan origin; the Monogram, and the Cross, of which further; and also, and principally, the Scriptural symbols of our Lord—the Lamb, and the Good Shepherd—which will be separately described.

History as yet has failed to define the precise dates of objects on which these last-mentioned symbols appear—such as monumental slabs, lamps, glass drinking-vessels. But it may be safely assumed that the increase of Art, especially in the shape of luxurious drink-

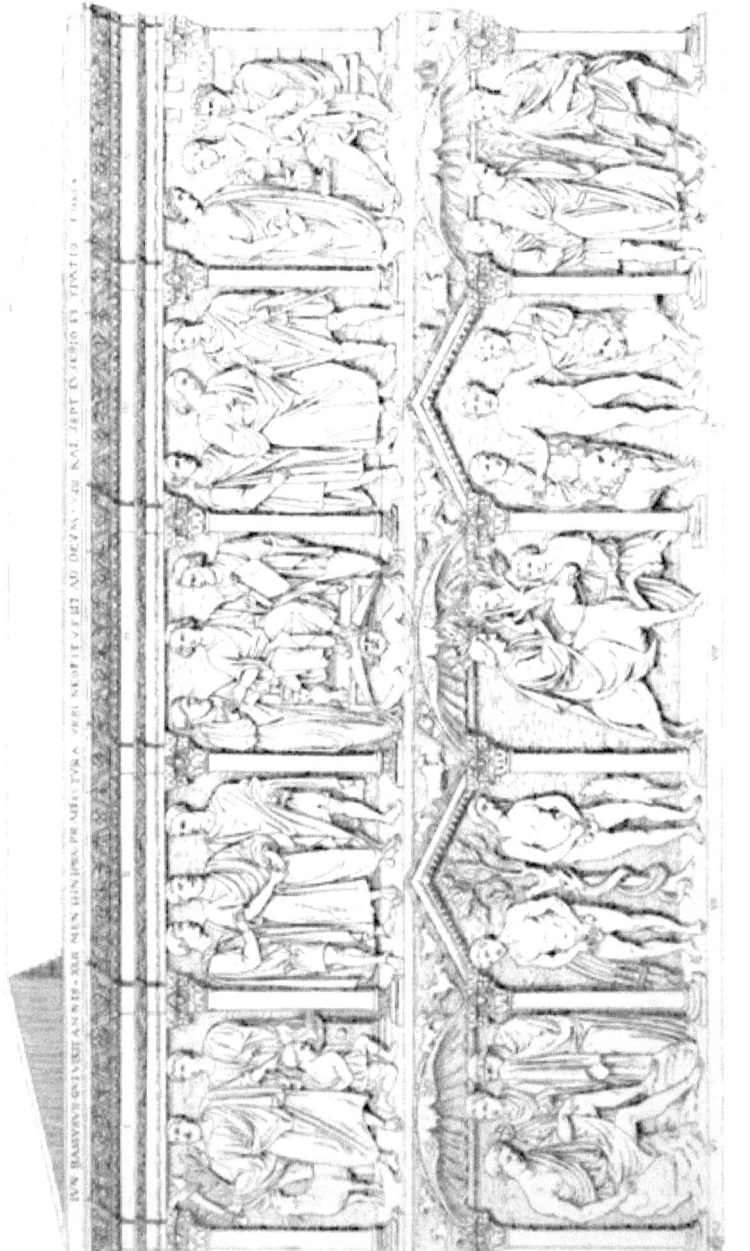

ing-vessels, points to a proportionate increase of security, and also to a growing relaxation of discipline, in favour of Pagan habits and images, where such could be indulged without any dereliction of Christian principle.

CHRISTIAN SARCOPHAGI.

This brings us to the first regular cycles of Christian Art, embodied in larger forms, and discovered upon the exploring of the Catacombs of Rome, which are believed to have been reopened, after the lapse of ages, in the 16th century. They consist of white marble sarcophagi, richly decorated with bas-reliefs—now forming a part of the Christian Museum of the Vatican—and of paintings still existing on the walls and ceilings of these subterranean chambers. The subjects here delineated, especially those of an earlier date, represent scenes from the history of our Lord, His miracles, and the great doctrines of the Christian religion—Faith, Atonement, Resurrection—set forth by biblical types, or, in other words, by events taken from the Old Testament, illustrating the chief truths contained in the New. Here the genius of Pagan or classic Art reigns without restraint, showing an elaboration and beauty of design and execution only compatible with periods of perfect security. For there is no difference, except in the choice of subjects, between the general form and mode of decoration of the earlier sarcophagi commemorating the death of a Christian, and those devoted to the Pagan dead. Accordingly, a sarcophagus, believed to be one of the first examples, and of which the date is ascertainable, is that of a proconsul of the name of Junius Bassus, known to have died in 359, or thirty-four years after the Council of Nice.

We give an etching of the whole monument (Bottari, vol. ii. tab. xxviii.), and a merely general explanation, for each subject will find a more particular description in its place. Our Lord is here seen in the centre of the lower range celebrating His one earthly triumph as He entered Jerusalem. Above, He sits enthroned in heavenly state, for His feet are upon Earth as His footstool, which is represented under the form of

Tellus, with the firmament symbolised by an arch of drapery above him. The volumen, or book of Wisdom, is in Christ's hand. Two figures, probably Apostles, are at His side. The learned are much divided on the precise meaning of this subject, some having maintained it to be Christ disputing with the Doctors—an idea which the symbolism of the Earth quite refutes. May it not possibly mean the Transfiguration?—our Lord's other triumph on earth—with Moses and Elijah on each side, and the Earth, on which they are supported, typifying the 'high mountain' on which the scene occurred.

On one side of this, a subject extending through two compartments, is Christ before Pilate, who is preparing to wash his hands. This is a very beautiful composition.

On the other side is a scene called the Repentance of Peter, supposed to be represented by that moment when they say unto him, 'Surely thou also art one of them; for thy speech bewrayeth thee' (Matt. xxvi. 73).

Farther on is the Sacrifice of Isaac, always typifying in himself the willingness, and in the lamb the fact, of the sacrifice of Christ.

Below this is Job; according to St. Jerome, a figure of the suffering of Christ. Next to him our First Parents, after the Fall —being the sin which points to the Atonement. Then Daniel in the Lion's Den—a type of Faith, and also of the Resurrection; and, finally, a man bound and led by two men, supposed to be Peter going to prison, or a figure of the persecution suffered by the Christian Church. This subject, however, may be considered as still unexplained.

Thus we have here a cycle of consecutive ideas, all centering in Christ, as the great Author and Finisher of our faith, and expressing trials and tribulations—overcome, repented of, and atoned for —from the fall of Adam and Eve to the denial of our Lord by St. Peter.

Nor must we omit the sheep, minutely sculptured on the pediments and flat arches of the lower range, which most curiously set forth our Lord and His types in a form not seen elsewhere. For though both Shepherd and flock are, as we shall see, frequently given under the form of sheep, yet nowhere have we seen such a series of literal acts and figurative forms. These will immediately explain themselves to the reader on reference to the etching.

On the one hand is a sheep striking a rock with a rod, whence flows water; another sheep prepares to drink from it. On the opposite corresponding arch is the same animal receiving the table of the Law from a hand in the clouds, an attendant sheep, meant for Joshua, standing at a distance. Nearer the centre is the Miracle of the Loaves—a sheep, also with a staff or rod, as the symbol of power, striking baskets in which are loaves. Opposite this is the Baptism, most curiously given—one sheep standing with its foreleg on the head of another, who is half immersed in a stream, while above is a bird, with a ray of light reaching from its beak to the head of the animal personifying the Saviour. On the extreme right of the spectator is the raising of Lazarus—a sheep touching with a staff the upright figure of a mummy; on the extreme left are the remains of a scene supposed to represent the Three Children in the Furnace. Such a series as this characteristically sets forth the mental as well as visual habits of those to whom such art was addressed, and who preferred to perceive the idea through a symbolical rather than actual form; for the evidence of other sarcophagi, in which most of the same episodes are given under more natural conditions, shows that only the love and habit of the ideal suggested these.

To return to the larger subjects. Many of them are frequently repeated, with slight variations, in the art of the Catacombs: some sarcophagi show only the miracles; others, Christ sending forth His disciples. Some are adorned with branches of vine and clusters of grapes, in allusion to our Lord's words, 'I am the true vine.' In many, the classic impersonation of natural objects is seen, such as the figure of Tellus in our etching, or that of the Jordan represented as a river god in the ascension of Elijah. Some writers have believed that the application of such symbolism marks the monuments of Gnostic Christians, known to have been more lenient in their feelings towards Heathendom.

MURAL PAINTINGS IN CATACOMBS.

The ceilings of the Catacombs also afford cycles of very remarkable character. We give an illustration of one, in which numerous

Ceiling in Catacomb. (Bottari, vol. ii. tab. cxviii.)

events from the Old and New Testament are given, all pointing to the ideas of Pardon, Regeneration, and Resurrection, to the power of

Christ to feed the hungry, heal the sick, and raise the dead, and all centering in the figure of the Good Shepherd carrying His sheep, with other sheep resting round Him in the centre. Five of the subjects are from the Old Testament, and three from the New. They are as follows:—

Noah in the Ark with arms extended, welcoming the Dove which bears the Olive-branch of Peace; the Ark being generally a mere box floating on the water, but here floating in a boat.

Moses striking the Rock.

Jonah in the act of being swallowed by the Fish—here a great dragon of fabulous character.

Jonah ejected from the Fish's Mouth.

Daniel between the Lions. Some have interpreted his figure as intended for the form of a cross, and thus holding the lions at bay; but this idea belongs to a later period of symbolism. Here the figure was probably only dictated by the space, which is a despotic ruler in all Art.

Christ restoring Lazarus to life—a subject always given in this form in classic Christian Art.

The Miracle of the Loaves.

The Lame Man taking up his Bed and walking.

The birds may be interpreted as symbols of the human soul, feeding on fruits of Paradise.

The ceilings of the Catacombs are varied in form, but not much in subject. The walls show a more gradual change of representation.

The cycles we have described contain, as we see, no indications of our Lord's sufferings. There are no mockings, or flagellations, or crucifixions, hitherto seen; nay, no weariness of body or sorrow of mind—facts for which we must forbear to seek causes in the fear of enemies to the faith, the period for which was past, but only in the inherent conditions of classic Art, which interdicted scenes of terror, pain, or distress. Thus even in forms, no longer timid, and not always symbolical, Christianity was seen under a mask; for no one will believe that these gentle and serene images really reflected the state of the Christian's course, or that of the social world around. But the Art of which Christians availed themselves had been developed by a race, of whose gods, dignity and repose, beauty and youth, were the highest attributes. And there is no doubt that these long-descended ideas harmonised too well with the ineradicable art-instincts of the Gentile Christians not to have contributed to that sentiment of reverence towards the Saviour's person which is the refreshing distinction between early and later Art. It is assumed also, and with great appearance of probability, that this category of subjects, restricted chiefly to signs of our Lord's beneficence, and of the earthly rescue of His chosen servants in the Old Testament, were the more welcome as contributing to reconcile new converts to a scheme of religion, otherwise too self-sacrificing in its main features for those who were still babes in doctrine.

The date of the Art of the Catacombs, commencing, at all events, as we have seen, with the 4th century, is supposed to spread over a space extending to the 11th. A corresponding addition and change of subjects, tending to the more purely historical, is visible, which is chiefly seen on the walls. The Adoration of the Magi appears, the literal scene of the Baptism, one example of the Crucifixion (of which more in its place), and the introduction of saints. These continue to bear more or less the impress of classic Art—which is indeed traceable outside the Catacombs up to the 12th century, and which, having given its strength and its prime to glorify the deities of the Pantheon, thus fittingly expired in the service of the one true God.

MOSAICS.

The workers in mosaic took up the same class of subjects in the light of day which were being carried on in the darkness of the Catacombs, and continued and developed them long after those pious and mysterious underground labours had ceased. With these minute and durable materials, composed of cubes of various-coloured stones, terra cotta, and vitrified substances, the walls and cupolas of ancient basilicas and churches were covered, offering the largest and most monumental forms in which Christian Art*has ever been embodied. These materials, as we know from many an ancient pavement left by the Romans in this country, were, as well as the rules of style, derived from antique practice, though it is certain that their larger use, for walls and historical subjects, belongs entirely to the Christian epoch. Christian mosaics of a decorative and symbolical character, such as the vine and the grape, in S. Costanza, near Rome, are traceable back to the 4th century, but their complete application to figures and groups, and their technical splendour, burst forth first, both in Ravenna and in Rome, in the 5th century. These continue the cycles of typical incidents, differing in choice though not in kind. For to the Sacrifice of Isaac are added the Offerings of Abel and Melchisedec, Abraham entertaining the Angels, Moses and the Burning Bush, and single figures of Prophets and Evangelists. The Baptism, also, with the Jordan as a river god, takes its place in the separate baptistries then erected.

The basilica form of early churches, the long nave, the grand arch terminating it, and the semi-domed tribune or apse, into which this arch conducted, greatly contributed to dictate the subjects. On each wall above the arches of the nave are seen, as in S. Apollinare Nuovo, at Ravenna, processions, on the one side, of the male figures of confessors and martyrs; on the other, of the female. The Arch of Triumph shows above, the Agnus Dei, or the head of Christ, with the symbols of the Evangelists, or the four rivers of Paradise, and in the spandrels—for instance, on the arch of S. Paolo-fuori-le-Mura, at Rome, partially rescued from the fire of 1823—the twenty-four elders offering crowns. The twelve on the one side have their heads covered, the twelve on the other are bareheaded; signifying, the first, the Prophets of the Old Covenant, who saw the truth as through a veil; the second, the Apostles to whom, in the New Covenant, it was clearly revealed. Finally, the dome of the apse exhibits the Saviour standing in glory, with the founders of the Church, or patron saints, in adoration on each side. Above, the hand of the Father is holding a crown, while a bird like a phœnix, as in the churches of S. Cosmo and Damian, and S. Prassede, at Rome, on a palm-tree, denotes the Holy Spirit. Thus the whole imagery of the Church may be said to have flowed towards this culminating idea of Christ in glory; beginning with the records of the faithful, on the walls of the nave, passing through the apocalyptic vision, or the second coming of Christ, on the Arch of Triumph, and ending with the largest idea of the Godhead, the fulness of the Trinity itself, on the most sacred part, the dome of the apse.

To the Art of the mosaicists, also, we are indebted for the preservation of some of the earliest conceptions of the first chapters in Genesis. The Fall of our First Parents had been given with ideal simplicity on Christian sarcophagi, and on the walls of the Catacombs; but it needed that infusion of various elements consequent on the overthrow of empires—which counterbalanced the rudeness of their forms by the larger play of the imagination—to represent the more indefinable ideas of the first acts of Creation. We see these given in series in the vestibule cupolas of St. Mark's at Venice, and on the walls of the Cathedral of Monreale; the one believed to belong to the 11th, the other to the 12th century. In these there is a harmony between subjects and materials, as respects a certain rudeness and grandeur, which totally vanishes in the flowing lines and more pretentious colouring of the later examples of mosaic work. For after the restriction which the dignity and repose of classic feeling had imposed upon the mosaicist had passed away, it needed the very deficiencies of early mediæval Art to replace them. The incongruity between the later development of the Picturesque, and these stern rudimental materials, is at once felt in the unsatisfactory impression produced by modern examples of mosaics; as in other parts of St. Mark's at Venice, which were restored in the 17th century. A late Venetian picture, given in mosaic work, is like a rope-dancer in a suit of armour. On this account it is that the stiffness and immobility of Byzantine Art are more tolerable in this garb than in any other.

Doors of Churches.

The doors of ancient churches, cast in bronze or brass, or carved in wood, offer pages of curious interest to the student of Christian Art. On one door are the chief typical events of the Old Testament, on the other the actual incidents of the New. Such doors are traceable chiefly to the 11th century, when, the expectation of the millennium having passed away, churches were extensively built or repaired. Of such age and class are the brazen doors at Benevento in the Neapolitan territory, the bronze doors of S. Zeno at Verona, and the old oak doors of S. Maria in Capitolio at Cologne; to all of which we shall have occasion to refer. In each of these, the sufferings of our Lord—His capture, flagellation, and crucifixion—are rendered; events which had obtained a footing in Art by that time.

The ancient church of S. Paolo-fuori-le-Mura, at Rome, destroyed by fire in 1823, possessed doors of the 11th century, of a curious workmanship called *Agemina*, consisting of bronze tablets inlaid with silver wire. Engravings of these, taken before the fire, fortunately exist.[1] These doors were executed by Byzantine artists, and it is curious to compare them with the rude forms of those in the north of Italy, and still more with those on the other side of the Alps.

IVORIES.

We now come to a smaller department of materials. From an early date in Christian history, a class of objects, also of classic origin and treatment, was preparing invaluable stores for the future student of Christian iconography. The application of ivory to purposes of flat sculpture, known even in Nineveh, was familiar to the Romans. These served to portray, in delicate forms and portable sizes, subjects of mythological and historical import, and consisted generally of two tablets, which opened and folded together by hinges, and were carved in low relief on the outer sides. In the 4th and 5th centuries, the use of these double tablets, or diptychs, was generally appropriated to the portraits of Roman consuls, who presented them as gifts to their friends and patrons; hence the name of consular diptychs, by which such ancient specimens as still survive are known. About the same time the Christian Church appears to have availed itself of the same forms in ivory, for ecclesiastical purposes; the inside surface being inscribed with the names of eminent individuals, and the outside sculptured with religious subjects.

On some occasions the consular diptych appears to have been transformed into an ecclesiastical diptych, the portrait of the consul being converted by slight changes into that of King David, and the inscription, by a palimpsest process, altered to correspond. But

[1] D'Agincourt's Storia dell' Arte. Sculpture.

whether originally consular or ecclesiastical, these objects, from their detached nature, have rarely survived, or one leaf has been preserved and the other lost.

It was different with another class of ivory objects of Christian use, namely, the sculptured tablets applied as book-covers to the Sacred Volumes. Their purpose, as a material safeguard to early manuscripts of the Scriptures, contributed, doubtless, in turn, to their own protection; for the larger number of the earliest specimens of ivories now existing are of this class. We give an etching of one of a magnificent pair of Gospel covers, preserved in the Treasury at Milan, and belonging, it is supposed, to the 6th century. The subjects show, in some respects, an independence of the Art of the Catacombs, which points, perhaps, to a different part of the Roman Empire for their source. Some of them will be difficult of interpretation to an inexperienced eye. We therefore give the general meaning, reserving description of particular subjects for their respective places in this work.

In the corners above are the angel of St. Matthew, and the bull of St. Luke, each, seraph-like, with six wings. In the corners below, the busts of those Evangelists. The two others are on the reverse cover. In the centre is the Agnus Dei.

Above the centre, the Nativity. The ox and the ass admirable, and Joseph with a carpenter's saw, scarcely differing from those now in use.

In the centre below, the Massacre of the Innocents. The other subjects commence at the left hand above, and terminate on the right hand above.

The Annunciation. The Virgin drawing water—a tradition of which signs occur in other early representations.

The Three Kings seeing the Star—which is above, on the border.

The Baptism.

The Entry into Jerusalem.

Christ before Pilate.

The Magdalene with the Angel at the Sepulchre.

The use of ivory book-covers continues all through the mediæval ages. They embody gradually the scenes of our Lord's suffering, and represent, as we shall see, some of the earliest specimens of the Crucifixion. We refer the reader to the etching.

IVORY BOOK COVER.
9th century Milan Cathedral.

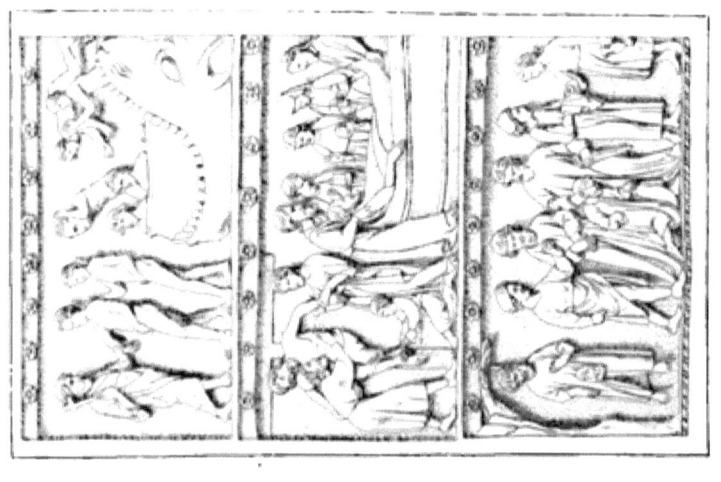

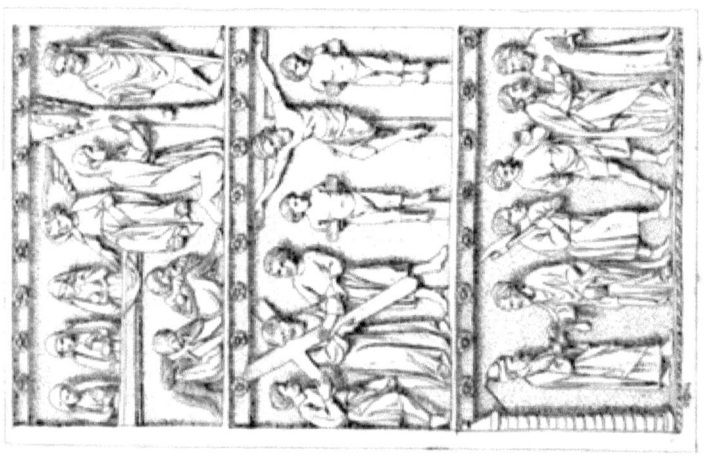

FIGUR TRETTE.

Meanwhile the ecclesiastical diptych reappears in the field with some alteration of feature. For, for obvious reasons, the bas-reliefs, which are much more deeply cut than those of the early time, are on the inner sides, and thus, when closed together, protected from injury. These took their place on the altar, in the early part of the 14th century, and are chiefly devoted to cycles of the Passion. The scheme of these cycles is traceable originally to the Life of Christ, by S. Bonaventura, a Franciscan monk of the 13th century, which was afterwards divided under seven heads, according to the hours of our Lord's Passion as solemnised by the Church. Thus Vespers are represented, according to some versions, by the Last Supper; Compline, by the Agony in the Garden; Matins, by Christ before Caiaphas; Prime, or the first hour, by Christ before Pilate; Tierce, or third hour, by Christ crowned with Thorns; Sext, or sixth hour, by Pilate washing his Hands; and None, or the ninth hour, by the Crucifixion.

Great latitude, however, was taken in the arrangement, and any choice, and any number of subjects, seem to have been permitted, provided they belonged to the category of the Passion, which extended, as will be seen, from the Entry into Jerusalem to the Ascension.

We give an etching of a beautiful Italian diptych with the following range of subjects, beginning, be it observed, from the left hand below: —

1. Judas receiving the Money.
2. Judas pointing out Christ.
3. Judas drawing near to kiss Him.
4. Judas hanging, with his Bowels out.
5. Christ in the Grasp of a Soldier.
6. Peter cutting off Malchus' Ear.
7. Pilate wiping his Hands. His attendant with a jug.
8. Christ bearing His Cross. Simon helping.
9. Crucifixion.
10. Descent from Cross.
11. Entombment.
12. Maries at Tomb. Angel seated on it. Guards asleep.
13. Christ appearing to Magdalen.
14. Christ delivering Souls from Limbus.

Ivories of this description are comparatively numerous, and are met with of Italian, French, and German origin.

The ivory triptych was another form of Art which also took its place on the altar. It answered, indeed, the purpose of an altar picture, having a centre, with two wings which closed over it. The centre sometimes contains the Crucifixion; the wings, other scenes from the Passion, or the figures of Prophets.

This class led naturally to an amplification of the same form. Large altar-pieces, occupying the whole width of the altar, and composed of numerous parts, like the complicated pictures of the same class, were formed entirely of sculptured ivory, or bone, divided by architectural features, and surmounted with canopies. A magnificent specimen, of the latter part of the 14th century, executed by the monks of Poissy for Jean de Berry, brother of Charles V. of France, and for Jeanne de Boulogne, his wife, is in the Louvre. It contains the history of our Lord from the Annunciation, and that of John the Baptist, in forty-four compartments.

The largest and one of the most ancient forms of ivory, applied to Christian Art, is the throne or chair of S. Maximian, Archbishop of Ravenna from 546 to 556, preserved in the Cathedral of Ravenna. The back and sides are covered with reliefs, inside and out, giving the history of Christ, and that of one of His chief types, the Patriarch Joseph.

Caskets in ivory also furnished occasion for Christian Art. A circular box in the Berlin Museum points to an origin not far removed in time from the sarcophagus of Junius Bassus in the Catacombs.

Another casket in the treasury of the Cathedral of Sens, of which a fac-simile exists in the Arundel collection, bears also the stamp of the earliest classic Christian character. It sets forth the lives of the two great types of Christ, Joseph and David.

Other objects in ivory which contribute to Christian Art will be referred to in this work.

ENAMELS.

Enamels are another class of materials in which Christian Art has found means of expression. We only allude to that form of enamels which are applied, mosaic-like, to metals, not to such as are spread smoothly on the surface of porcelain, which are of too late a date to be valuable in the sense of subjects. Both descriptions were manufactured at Limoges: those applied to metals, in the 12th and 13th centuries; those executed like paintings, from the 16th century. The art of the first-mentioned kind has no antique traditions, not having been discovered until an early period of Christianity, when it was largely practised by Byzantine artists. Objects decorated with this kind of enamel have taken similar forms, and set forth much the same class of subjects as the ivories. Covers of the Sacred Books, consisting of metal, generally copper gilt, are frequent. Shrines and reliquaries are also numerously found in treasuries of churches—or in their present next best asylum, museums—encrusted with enamels of figures of prophets, apostles, and saints. Altarpieces exist of elaborate designs, the Crucifixion in the centre and scenes from the Passion around. The forms of Art, owing to the rigid conditions of the materials, have a certain stiffness, sometimes conducive, as in mosaics, to grandeur, and, from the same cause, are limited in detail and variety. The special beauty, however, of enamels lies in their colours, which rival those of jewellery. Every kind of ecclesiastical ornament and utensil has derived colour and lustre from the application of this Art, and in many instances enamels of an early and unknown date are found preserved and reset in goldsmith work of a later and certain period.

MINIATURES [1] AND EARLY BLOCK BOOKS.

Richer than any other source hitherto considered, and almost as ancient, we may now advert to the so-called miniatures, or illu-

[1] We remind the reader that it is principally by the labours of Dr. Waagen that attention has been called to the department of miniatures. We owe frequent obligations to him in the course of this work.

minations, of the Scriptures and ancient religious books, which literally supply galleries of curious and beautiful conceptions, often within the compass of a few inches, and for the most part the work of unknown minds and hands. Even after the varied and accumulated forms of destruction, common to all things, and more especially to monuments of religious Art—ignorance, neglect, and cupidity, war, fire, and time—have done their worst, the number of these books is still fortunately Legion. For no church treasury, or convent choir of any pretensions to wealth—no royal or noble personages of piety, pride, or taste—failed to reckon these precious volumes among their choicest possessions. Here, on these solid and well-nigh indestructible parchment folios, where text and picture alternately take up the sacred tale—the text itself a picture, the picture a homily—the skill of the artist has exhausted itself in setting forth in positive images the great scheme of salvation. Sometimes these miniatures spread in solemn hierarchy over a whole page; oftener, and truer to their name, they nestle in the spaces of initials, or capital letters, and in the medallions of intricate borders. Now they look upon us with the forms, costumes, and even the countenances as of another world; then again they claim affinity by some touch of that common nature which makes all men kin. Nowhere is space lost, either within or without these venerable, silver-clasped and jewel-embossed volumes, whose very covers, as we have seen, afforded a field for special branches of artistic handicraft. Nor was all this labour spent in vain: their homes for centuries were in the silence of the sanctuary; their authors have mingled with the dust of the convent cemetery; over them have passed the rise and fall of the kingdoms of this world; but through them history has been transmitted with a continuity and fulness not to be found in any other forms of Art, or, it may be said, in any form of literature. For pictures have speech and meaning where text is obsolete or obscure. 'The pencil speaks the tongue of every land.'

The very variety of these volumes permits of only general mention. Singly or collectively the canonical books of Scripture have been the main object of the work of the miniaturist: Genesis, Joshua, the Psalter, the Apocalypse, the Pentateuch, the Gospels, separately or together; the whole Bible; later, the Missal and the Breviary;

the Office of the Virgin, and Books of Prayer. These spread over a space of time extending from the 5th to the 15th century, while every race, Greek and Latin, Byzantine and Carlovingian, French, Netherlandish, Anglo-Saxon, Irish, English, German, and Italian, who have acknowledged the Cross and felt after Art, have set their individual mark on these monuments of devotional labour. Accordingly, for the antiquary and connoisseur, seeking to unravel the intricate threads of national character, there is no such help as that afforded by ancient miniatures, while to the student of Christian Art they are indispensable. For in them are found the great centres of harmony with modes of Art of shorter duration, more limited range, and more perishable nature; from the types which emerge from the darkness of the Catacombs, as from the womb of the earth, through the abstract conceptions of a profounder, though outwardly ruder time, to the more strictly historical scenes of our Lord's Life and Passion; the interstices between each class, as well as each class itself, being filled up and enriched with a closeness and abundance only possible under the conditions of this more manageable form of illustration. Thus here may be traced, with peculiar accuracy, where old traditions cease and new ones start into life—when a fresh subject takes timid root—how adherence to Scripture slackens, and legend and heresy creep in—till these in themselves become, to a practised eye, the landmarks of certain periods and races.

To enumerate the subjects, though not without a plan, would be impossible: our frequent allusions to them in the coming pages will, however, give some idea of their variety. But out of these more definite religious books grew a number of others of a more fanciful class, in which a succession of subjects and types was laid down on the same principle of correspondence between Old and New Testament, and with a conventional precision never departed from. We mean such works as the 'Stories from the Old and New Testament,' or 'Biblia Pauperum,' and the 'Speculum humanæ Salvationis' —the latter supposed to have proceeded from the Order of the Benedictines. These, having employed the patient scribe and miniaturist during the 14th century, were in the 15th taken up and multiplied, both text and pictures, by those great new powers of type and block printing of which they are some of the most conspicuous first fruits. Curious and interesting as these works are, they were not, as our readers will often have occasion to see, best calculated to recommend the edifying purpose of a series of Christian illustrations. As the invention of printing drew near, the deterioration of pictures as the 'books of the simple' as gradually proclaimed its necessity. Embodying, as they do, the whimsical and artificial interpretations of scholastic history, their types, while far more numerous, are nowhere so faithful and impressive as when they adhere to the early traditions. Otherwise the allusions

Page from 'Biblia Pauperum.' (14th century.)

are often of a strained and far-fetched character, gathered at all hazards from the apposition of various parts of Scripture, and dictated, it would seem, occasionally, by no other rule than the jingle of words, the coincidence of numbers, and the likeness of locality. Thus the wicked and unfilial Absalom, hanging on the tree, becomes the type of the Saviour on the Cross. The King of Ai, taken from the tree where Joshua had hung him, represents the Descent from the Cross. Reuben searching for Joseph in the well is a type of the Maries at the Sepulchre; the death of the sons of Eli, that of the Murder of the Innocents, &c. Legend also is introduced, the sources of which it would be difficult to trace, and great repetition occurs, the same plate sometimes serving for opposite purposes. As Heinecken[1] says, 'These books were the fashion of the day, and provided there were but pictures, no one cared whether they squared with the subject or not.' Nevertheless there is a certain completeness of principle as regards Art, which renders the study of these volumes conducive to the understanding of more fragmentary representations—the text and scroll (or Legend, as it is technically called) preventing all ambiguity as to meaning. We give a page from the 'Biblia Pauperum' (see woodcut, No. 4). The figures of the prophets—in each case intended to represent those who foretold the particular event in the centre—point forward to the scheme of the Van Eyck altarpiece, and forwarder still to the traditions that guided even Michael Angelo in his Sistine ceiling.

In this plate we see Isaiah above, on the right hand, holding the legend (thus translated): 'He was opprest . . . yet He opened not His mouth' (liii. 7). Opposite to him David: 'They pierced my hands and my feet' (Ps. xxii. 16). Below, on the right, Habakkuk: 'He had horns coming out of His hand: and there was the hiding of His power' (iii. 4). Opposite to Habakkuk, Job: 'Canst thou draw out Leviathan with an hook?' (xli. 1).

The 'Speculum Salvationis' has two subjects on each page, with a Latin or German text in blank verse below. We refer our readers to the end of this work for a complete list of the plates in each of these books.

In the different classes of Art enumerated in this short survey, we have restricted ourselves to those which are principally referred to in the coming pages. To attempt to instance or describe all that exist would be far beyond our limit, where each class in turn might fill, and has filled, volumes of separate study. The sculpture attached to church architecture has its peculiar cycles: ancient painted glass is rich in the same. Embroidered vestments transmit the sacred story. Every crozier, candelabrum, foot of crucifix, and ecclesiastical utensil, however small, gives opportunity for Christian Art; and even a series of our Lord's Passion has found place within the compass of a walnut-shell. We therefore only point out the connection of subjects between all forms of

[1] Idée d'une Collection d'Estampes.

Art, which can only be understood by the thorough knowledge of a few. After the invention of printing, also, few new classes arose. The series by the German engravers—headed by Martin Schön and Albert Dürer—we shall have frequent occasion to speak of. As to the great series of fresco paintings, the grandest form, in some respects, in which pictorial Art has ever appeared, they are devoted far less to the Life of our Lord than to the Legends of the Saints; in which character they have been fully treated in the admirable series of works by the late Mrs. Jameson, of which these are intended to be the concluding volumes.

It is no object of this work to give a history of Greek or Byzantine Art, though there will be many occasions on which we shall require to define the difference between Eastern and Western schools. For this purpose we refer to the Manual of Byzantine Art discovered at Mount Athos by M. Didron, and edited by him under the title of 'Guide de la Peinture Grecque.'

PORTRAITS OF CHRIST.

DESCRIPTIONS of our Lord's outward appearance, as given in the Old Testament, whether figuring His sorrows and sufferings, or His glory and majesty, are all of a moral and symbolical kind. Allusions of a more positive nature could only be expected in the sacred record of that time when He dwelt among men. We search, however, in vain for the slightest evidence of His human, individual semblance in the writings of those disciples who knew Him so well. In this instance the instincts of earthly affection seem to have been mysteriously overruled. He whom all races of men were to call brother, was not to be too closely associated with the particular lineaments of any one. St. John, the beloved disciple, could lie on the breast of Jesus with all the freedom of friendship, but not even he has left a word to indicate what manner of man was that Divine Master after the flesh.

Nevertheless, one of the first thoughts that suggest themselves in the study of the History of our Lord in Art is the devout and pardonable speculation as to the character of His human person; and the possibility of His features having been in some way handed down through intervening centuries is a vision which a pious mind unwillingly relinquishes. Legend has, in various forms, supplied this natural craving, but it is hardly necessary to add, that all accounts of pictures of our Lord taken from Himself are without historical foundation. We are therefore left to imagine the expression most befitting the character of Him who took upon Himself our likeness, and looked at the woes and sins of mankind through the eyes of our mortality. And we best arrive at the solution by considering what expression is that which was never believed to belong to Deity before. It is in vain, therefore, to impute to our Lord, as His chief physiognomical distinction, the expression of grandeur, for this was possessed by the gods of the Pantheon in the highest form of human conception; or of dignity, for the same reason; or of power, beauty, or grace. But one thing those gods lacked—being only the work of men's hands, and the images of their fancy—and that was the expression which the natural man, in the awful distance between himself and a supreme and unapproachable Being, can never, untaught, attribute to Deity. That very quality it was which our Lord came down to make manifest. And accordingly, while He is depicted as on earth, the expression of *sympathy*, however blended with grandeur, dignity, power, beauty, and grace, becomes the leading characteristic which we are bound to demand at the hands of Christian Art. It must be owned that the fulfilment of this demand requires gifts of a class seldom possessed by man. The pictures of Christ, therefore, seldom satisfy the eye equally of taste and faith.

Great pains have been taken by modern investigators to elucidate the question of the portraits of Christ, and all that it will ever be possible to elicit on the subject is probably known. The first representations which are mentioned appear to have been executed in gold and silver, and to have been placed in the houses of the heathen, where they were regarded on the same footing as those of other wise and good men. Thus the images of Abraham, Orpheus, and Christ, as founders of different religions, were placed by Alexander Severus (died 210) in what Gibbon calls his 'private chapel,' where he is said to have propitiated them with incense and sacrifices. Also Marcellina, a woman of the Gnostic sect, who are believed to have united heathen and Christian tenets, is related by St. Augustine to have worshipped the images of Homer, Pythagoras, Christ, and St. Paul. In neither case are these images described.

But we hear more particulars of a bronze group formerly at Cæsarea, which consisted of a male figure standing and extending the hand to a female kneeling before him. This was seen and described by Eusebius (died 340), who adds that it was reported to represent the figure of our Lord, with that of the woman healed by touching the hem of His garment. Later writers added weight to this supposition by asserting that Julian the apostate, from contempt for the Christians, overthrew the figure of Christ, and erected his own in its stead, which, in the vengeance of Heaven, was immediately destroyed by lightning. But the fact of the intention of the group, and with it, therefore, the act of Julian, is contradicted by internal evidence of a far more reliable nature. For had such a statue of our Lord been known to exist, there is no doubt that in the intimate union which prevailed among the early Christian converts, mention would have been made of it in the writings of the Fathers of the first three centuries. That a group of this form was seen by Eusebius is undeniable; also, that his description should, in after times—when the subject of Christ and the same woman was represented in the Art of the Catacombs—be so interpreted, is quite to be comprehended. But the more likely hypothesis as to the original intention of a group, executed at that early time, is that it represented the city or province of Cæsarea under the allegorical figure of a female kneeling, and doing homage to the emperor of the time. This was a usual form of respect under the Roman sway, and groups tallying in every way with the description given by Eusebius are found on coins, especially on those of the Emperor Adrian, elected emperor A.D. 117. At all events, neither this statue nor the images related to have been reverenced by the heathen were reputed to have been taken from Christ himself, or from any traditional descriptions of Him. Otherwise, with such to refer to, no controversy could have arisen as to which of the Scriptural allusions to His person were most literally to be understood. The fact, however, of such a controversy between the early Greek and Latin Fathers has been magnified by later writers into dimensions which Art by no means corroborates. That opposite opinions did exist there is no question; but these seem rather to have resulted from the opposite circumstances of succeeding epochs than from any actual difference in contemporaneous ideas. Two apparently opposite views might be gathered from Scripture. There were the pathetic words of Isaiah: 'Who hath believed our report? and to whom is the arm of the Lord revealed? For He shall grow up before Him as a tender plant, and as a root out of a dry ground: He hath no form nor comeliness; and when we shall see Him, there is no beauty that we should desire Him' (liii. 1, 2). And there were the exulting words of the Psalmist: 'Thou art fairer than the children of men: grace is poured into Thy lips: therefore God hath blessed Thee for ever. Gird Thy sword upon Thy thigh, O most mighty, with Thy glory and Thy majesty' (Ps. xlv. 2, 3).

In the 2nd and 3rd centuries it was natural that the humble and persecuted followers of Christ should attach themselves most to the passages which describe Him to be, as they then were, poor and miserable, and bearing outward signs calculated rather to avert than to attract the attention of the world. An Epicurean philosopher, Celsus—of the time of Adrian and Antoninus Pius—went even so far as to deride the Christians for maintaining their God to be small, ill-formed, and of a mean aspect. There is, however, no evidence that they carried their self-abasing ideas of Christ to this extreme, though Origen (born A.D. 186) and others openly affirm that He was devoid of all external beauty.

But in the 4th century, the triumph of Christianity over its enemies brought an equally natural change of feeling. In proportion as they ceased to be oppressed and despised, the image of their Founder increased in loftiness and beauty. When Christendom was represented by one of the most powerful monarchs that ever sat on a throne, Christ was no longer the type for misery and worldly insignificance. The words of the Psalmist were now felt to supply the right ideal of One no longer despised on earth, but exalted in heaven. St. Jerome, especially, inveighs against the earlier view, not only basing his argument on the words of the Psalmist, but contending that had our Lord not possessed something divine in His face and eyes, the Apostles would never have followed Him so readily as they did. Above all, Art began then to exercise her irresistible arguments, filling the eye with a standard of youth and beauty as regards the person of Christ, in which classic Christian Art stands alone. It appears that this view was even shared by the Jews, and curiously used against us; for Bishop Münter[1] quotes a learned Rabbi of the 15th century, who, resting on the tradition of his people, maintains that the Messiah mentioned by Isaiah could not be the Christian's Christ, for He was known to have been a beautiful and blooming youth.

Thus the so-called controversy between the East and the West as regards the Person of Christ may be rather looked upon as the different opinions unanimously entertained at different epochs,— those of the earlier time being, as it happened, expressed chiefly by Greek writers, those of the later time by Latin.

How soon reputed traditions of our Lord's outward appearance began to prevail, it would be impossible to define. That description

---

[1] Münter, Sinnbilder. See vol. ii., 'Christus-Bilder,' from which learned and lucid essay we have chiefly taken our authority on this subject.

to which most importance is attached was not discovered earlier than in the writings of Anselm, Archbishop of Canterbury, who lived in the 11th century. It consists in a letter purporting to have been addressed to the Senate of Rome, and describing Christ, by one Publius Lentulus, friend of Pilate, and his predecessor in the government of Judæa. The list of the Roman procurators proves this last assertion to be false, and history has passed the same verdict on the letter itself. It is admitted, however, to have been possibly fabricated as early as the 3rd century, and from its tenor there is no doubt of its having proceeded from a Christian source. We translate it in full from the Latin, in which form the archbishop had preserved it. 'In this time appeared a man, who lives till now, a man endowed with great powers. Men call Him a great prophet; His own disciples term Him the Son of God. His name is Jesus Christ. He restores the dead to life, and cures the sick of all manner of diseases. This man is of noble and well-proportioned stature, with a face full of kindness and yet firmness, so that the beholders both love Him and fear Him. His hair is the colour of wine, and golden at the root—straight, and without lustre—but from the level of the ears curling and glossy, and divided down the centre after the fashion of the Nazarenes.[1] His forehead is even and smooth, His face without blemish, and enhanced by a tempered bloom; His countenance ingenuous and kind. Nose and mouth are in no way faulty. His beard is full, of the same colour as His hair, and forked in form; His eyes blue, and extremely brilliant. In reproof and rebuke He is formidable; in exhortation and teaching, gentle and amiable of tongue. None have seen Him to laugh; but many, on the contrary, to weep. His person is tall; His hands beautiful and straight. In speaking He is deliberate and grave, and little given to loquacity. In beauty surpassing most men.'

Another description is found in the writings of St. John of Damascus, a Greek theologian, who flourished in the 8th century, and warmly espoused the cause of images during the iconoclastic struggle. This is also taken from earlier writings, though it is probably of later date than the letter of Lentulus. He says that Jesus was of stately growth, 'with eyebrows that joined together,

[1] Put for Nazarites.

beautiful eyes, curly hair, in the prime of life, with black beard, and with a yellow complexion and long fingers, like His mother.'

Though there is little to supply a portrait in either of these somewhat differing descriptions, which are probably only examples of others of the same class, yet they seem to have been soon and not unnaturally followed by pictures, for the credibility of which various evidence was resorted to. St. Luke was asserted to have been a painter, and to have taken our Lord from life—St. Peter to have drawn Him from memory—and Nicodemus, though a ruler of the Jews, with whom graven images were forbidden, was pronounced to have been a sculptor, and to have carved the Holy Image at Lucca. Pilate also was declared to have secretly taken a portrait of Christ. A vision of our Lord himself is believed to have appeared at the consecration of the ancient church of St. John Lateran, which gave rise to the mosaic there preserved; and miraculous portraits—or, as the expression is, 'pictures of Christ made without hands'—such as the impression of His divine countenance upon the winding-sheet, or upon His robe, or other textures, appeared, duly attested, in various parts of Christendom. By the 6th century every principal Christian community had some sacred image of this kind to show, till, at the time of the iconoclastic feud, their very number and variety became an evidence against them. For which, it was asked, was the true portrait among so many?—that possessed by the Romans? or that represented by the Hebrews? or that treasured by the Greeks? or that worshipped by the Ethiopians?—since all in turn maintain that Christ had borne the features of their particular race! Thus it need only be observed, that at the seventh General Council held at Constantinople in 754, all the pictures purporting to have descended direct from Christ or His Apostles were condemned.

On the score of Art, the stories of the portraits of our Lord produced by the impression of His features upon cloth require more particular attention. That connected with King Abgarus of Edessa is by far the earliest.

The short apocryphal Gospel, entitled 'Christ and Abgarus,' is mentioned by Eusebius, and is still extant. It is headed, 'A Copy of a Letter written by King Abgarus to Jesus, and sent to Him by Ananias, his Footman, to Jerusalem, inviting Him to Edessa.' It begins with greetings from Abgarus to Jesus, 'the good Saviour,' of whose cures, without the use of medicine or herbs, the king has heard. He therefore earnestly begs Him to make a journey to Edessa, to cure him of a disease under which he is suffering; adding, 'My city is indeed small, but neat, and large enough for us both.'

Our Lord replies that He cannot come, for that He must fulfil the ends of His mission amongst the Jews; but adds, that, after His Ascension, He will send one of His disciples, 'who will cure your disease, give life to you, and all that are with you.' This is the end of the story, in which no mention is made of any picture. The date of this version is the fourth century. In the 8th century, St. John of Damascus alludes to a further tradition, that Abgarus, out of pure love to our Lord, had desired to possess His picture; and by the 10th century, the request for the picture is connected with the disease of the king, and desired as a means of cure.[1] In all dates the legend has many forms. According to one, Abgarus, instead of a messenger to invite, sends a painter to portray Christ. But the painter finds an insurmountable difficulty in the light which beams from the Lord's countenance. Christ, knowing the thoughts of the messenger, takes His robe, and pressing it to His countenance, leaves a perfect portrait upon it. This He sends to King Abgarus, who is cured thereby.

Another version of greater circumstantiality and variety is edited by the Emperor Constantine Porphyrogenitus (died 959), who states his materials to have been derived from written documents and from oral tradition. It is as follows:—

'Abgarus, King of Edessa, suffering from the twofold infliction of gout and leprosy, withdrew from the sight of men. Ananias, one of his servants, returning from a journey to Egypt, tells him of the wonderful cures by Christ, of which he had heard in Palestine. In the hope of obtaining relief, Abgarus writes to Christ, and charges Ananias, who was not only a good traveller but a skilful painter, that if Christ should not be able to come, He should at all events send him His portrait. Ananias finds Christ, as He is in the act of performing miracles and teaching the multitude, in the open air. As he is not able to approach Him for the crowd, he mounts a rock

---

[1] Die Sage vom Ursprung der Christus-Bilder, von Wilhelm Grimm, p. 32. We take our sketch of the Abgarus and St. Veronica legends chiefly from this learned source.

not far off. Thence, he fixes his eyes upon Christ, and begins to take His likeness. Jesus, who sees him, and also knows in spirit the contents of the letter, sends Thomas to bring him to Him, writes His answer to Abgarus, and gives it to him. But seeing that Ananias still lingers, Jesus calls for water, and having washed His face, He wipes it on a cloth, on which, by His divine power, there remains a perfect portrait of His features. This He gives to Ananias, charging him to take it to Abgarus, so that his longing may be satisfied, and his disease cured. On the way Ananias passes by the city of Hierapolis, but remains outside the gates, and hides the holy cloth in a heap of freshly made bricks. At midnight the inhabitants of Hierapolis perceive that this heap of bricks is surrounded with fire. They discover Ananias, and he owns the supernatural character of the object hidden among the bricks. They find, not only the miraculous cloth, but more still; for, by a mysterious virtue, a brick that lay near the cloth has received a second impress of the divine image. And, as no fire was discoverable except the light that proceeded from the picture, the inhabitants kept the brick as a sacred treasure, and let Ananias go on his way. He gives King Abgarus the letter and the cloth, who is immediately cured.'

A picture in the collection of the late Prince Consort, formerly at Kensington Palace (the choicest works of which have now, in fulfilment of His Royal Highness's wish, been presented by Her Majesty to the National Gallery), shows a curious series of this legend, by a late Byzantine hand, though probably, in the unchangeableness of all subjects belonging to the Greek Church, taken from a much earlier work. This points to further variations of the same theme.

In the centre is the head of our Lord on a cloth (see woodcut, No. 5), the hair divided in the middle, and the beard forked, so far agreeing with the description by Lentulus. Within the cruciform spaces of the glory are three letters—intended to represent $O\ \Omega N$, the Being—often introduced, in Greek Art, round the head of our Saviour. The inscription below the head, in the faulty Greek common to works of this class, represents the words τὸ ἅγιον μανδύλιον (the holy cloth). Around this are ten small pictures representing the legend. These are of no merit, and very obscure in meaning, but one of them, of which we give an illus-

Abgarus Portrait of Christ. (Prince Consort's Collection.)

tration the size of the original (see woodcut, No. 6), represents King Abgarus in bed, receiving the miraculous picture from the hands of the messenger.

In the time of the Imperial editor of this last story, the original cloth was at Constantinople; another at Rome, in the church of S. Sylvestro; a third at Genoa; a purposely contrived false copy in the hands of King Chosroes of Persia, who requested it for the healing of his possessed daughter; while the brick also, which possessed the photographic power of impressing its image on the nearest object, was still at Hierapolis, whence it had furnished

King Abgarus receiving miraculous Portrait. (Prince Consort's Collection.)

fresh images to other cities. It may be added, that the *replica* of the cloth still exists in S. Sylvestro at Rome, and has had copies taken from it in the more common way, one of which forms the frontispiece of Grimm's essay. Here Art, as in many cases, upsets all tradition by incontrovertible evidence of her own, and proclaims this sacred picture to be a weak and ill-drawn work of the 16th century.

Before quitting the subject, the Emperor Constantine adds another version, which connects the legend of Abgarus with that, better known, of St. Veronica, who was destined to carry the subject over from the schools of the East to those of the later West. We give it.

As Christ was proceeding on His weary way to Calvary, and the sweat running down in bloody drops from His face, He took a piece of linen from one of His disciples, and having wiped His face, the divine image was found impressed upon it. Thomas kept the cloth, and, after the Ascension of Christ, made it over, as he had been ordered, to Thaddeus, who was instructed to bring this picture, not painted with hands, to King Abgarus, so as to fulfil the words of Christ. But Thaddeus lingers first in Edessa, in the house of a Jew of the name of Tobias, with the view of making himself first known to Abgarus by his miracles. Accordingly he heals the sick by calling on the name of Christ. Abgarus hears of him, and hoping that he is the disciple whom Jesus had promised to send, summons him to his presence. As Thomas enters, he lifts the picture to his forehead, and so bright a light proceeds from it that Abgarus, terrified, and not thinking of his lameness, leaps from his bed, and goes to meet him. He takes the cloth, presses it upon his head and his limbs, and feels himself strengthened. The leprosy begins to disappear, only upon the king's forehead do a few marks remain. As Thaddeus converts him to the truth, he becomes stronger and stronger, and when he is baptized, the last marks disappear from his forehead. Abgarus is only prevented by the Roman domination from making war upon the Jews.

In every way this edition of the legend leads us to that of St. Veronica, always connected in the earlier times with the destruction of Jerusalem. Many versions of this also exist, all bearing the same general features, which we may condense in the following form.

Veronica was the woman who had been healed by touching the hem of Christ's garment. She greatly longed for a picture of Him. She therefore brought a cloth to Luke, who was a painter. When the picture was finished, both thought it very like, but when they next saw Christ, they found that His face was quite different. Veronica wept, and Luke painted another picture, and then a third, but both were less like than the first. Then God heard the prayers of Veronica, and Christ said to her, 'Unless I come to your help, all Luke's art is in vain, for my face is only known to Him who sent me.' Then He said to the woman, 'Go home and prepare me a meal; before the day is over, I will come to you.' Veronica joyfully hastened home and prepared the meal. Soon Christ arrived, and asked for water to wash. She gave it Him, and also a cloth to wipe with: He pressed it to His face, and it received a miraculous portrait of His features. 'This is like me,' He said, 'and will do great things,' and He gave it to her. Meanwhile Cæsar reigned at Rome in great majesty. Sometimes the tale makes it the Emperor Tiberius, sometimes the Emperor Vespasian. Whichever it was, each was afflicted with a dreadful malady. Tiberius had worms in his head; Vespasian, a wasp's nest in his nose. It was an awful sight. The emperor hears of a Great Physician in Judæa, who heals every sickness. He sends a messenger to Jerusalem, who finds that the Jews have killed the Physician three years before. The messenger questions Pilate, who is greatly alarmed, and he and the Jews mutually accuse each other. Then the messenger inquires for Christ's followers: they bring him Joseph of Arimathea, and Nicodemus, and, lastly, Veronica. He demands to see the portrait of Christ. She first denies that she has it, then owns that she keeps it locked up, and afterwards fetches it. The messenger adores it, and begs her to lend it to him to take to the emperor. She consents on the condition of going with it herself. They therefore depart by sea for Rome, and have a marvellously short passage. Veronica is received with honour, and taken before the emperor. The messenger explains that the Great Physician has been killed by Pilate and the Jews, and that he has brought a woman who possesses a miraculous portrait of Him. She holds up the cloth, the emperor believes, and is immediately cured.

We give an illustration from a book of pen-drawings of the

14th century at the Ambrosian Library at Milan, which contains a complete series of this legend (woodcut, No. 7).

In the next picture the same subject is repeated, but wasps are falling, as big as pigeons, from the emperor's head, and going into a hole by the side of the throne. With this miracle the cure

Veronica before Emperor. (Biblioteca Ambrosiana, Milan.)

is complete. Pilate is then cast into a dungeon, where he kills himself, and his dead body is thrown into the Tiber, where it is attacked by horrible demons.

Vespasian, being perfectly recovered, determines with his son Titus to revenge the death of Christ upon the Jews. They take a great army and besiege Jerusalem. The Jews are slain by thousands, till the bodies cannot be buried. At length Jerusalem is taken, and vengeance follows. The captives are crucified, the four soldiers who divided the robe are each cut in four quarters, and the rest are sold for thirty pence apiece.

This is the substance of the earlier Veronica legend, in which the miraculous picture is properly the 'volto santo' (a well-known form of imprecation in the Middle Ages—'God's image'), and not the 'sudarium,' which is the name proper only to the later version. Representations even of this earlier legend do not begin before the 14th century, which makes it probable that the story was not known until that time, when the apocryphal Gospels came again into repute. For the Greek name of Bernice (*latiné* Veronica) is given in the apocryphal Gospel of Nicodemus to the woman who was cured by the touch of Christ's garment. The etymology of the word probably supplied the idea of the transfer of the long-known Abgarus story to this female saint, called indiscriminately Bernice, Beronica, and Veronica—*Vera Icon* signifying in hybrid Greek the sacred picture.[1] The picture itself is called also 'a Veronica.' The earlier story may be always recognised in Art by the less suffering look of the head, and also by the absence of the crown of thorns, which has no business to be seen when the occasion is not connected with the procession to Calvary. The cloth is sometimes held by the saint herself, as in the Cologne picture, No. 687 in the National Gallery, or by angels.

The later story is of more meagre character. Veronica is no longer the woman who was cured, but simply a daughter of Jerusalem, whose house stood on the way to Calvary. Seeing our Lord pass, on His way to be crucified, she compassionated Him, and taking her veil from her head gave it Him to wipe His distressed face. He returned it to her with the sacred image impressed upon it. This version is recognised by the Roman Church, and is related in the 'Acta Sanctorum.' Her house is also shown in the Via Dolorosa at Jerusalem. The history of this saint as regards this simpler legend has been given by Mrs. Jameson.

We may also allude here to a carved image of our Lord, long worshipped at Lucca, where it still exists,—attributed to the hand of Nicodemus. Dante alludes to it in his twenty-first Canto, where, in the fifth circle of Malebolge, the public peculators are punished:—

> Here the hallowed visage saves not (Qui non ha luogo il santo volto).

---

[1] By the same rule, *vespa*, a wasp, indicates the origin of Vespasian's terrible complaint.

As far as respects Art, a reference to the image shows it to be a work possibly of the 14th century.

A picture of Christ as dark as a Moor—from Canticles, 'I am dark but comely,' a verse applied to the Church—is sometimes seen on a Veronica cloth. It appears to be strictly of modern origin, and was probably taken from the much-darkened Byzantine representations. No legend of a black face as associated with Christ exists.

In considering the points of divergence between the earlier and the later character of these legends, we can but be struck by the consistency, even in their difference, with the source and history of Art. The desire for a portrait of the Redeemer, and its miraculous powers, are the same with each; but in the Abgarus and early Veronica stories these powers are applied to the gifts of healing; being thus in strict keeping with the Art of the Catacombs, where our Lord's beneficent miracles are the main subjects. On the other hand, in the later Veronica legend, this purpose is entirely dropped, and the tale is only calculated to bring into strong view the sufferings of our Lord, which, by the 15th century, had almost superseded every other historical illustration of His life. Indeed the more exaggeration is given to the subject of the Passion, the more sure, as we shall have occasion to see, are we to find St. Veronica and her veil present.

We have not hitherto mentioned the character and physiognomy given to Christ. It is usual to dwell upon a so-called type of our Lord's head, derived from remotest antiquity, and continued in one unbroken descent to the masters of Italy and Northern Europe. But this idea has obtained a prominence not sufficiently warranted, to our view, by the only authorities on which it can rest, namely, by works of Art. At all events, if we seek to establish the theory of a type of Christ, it must be admitted with very great limitations; such as being confined to the Byzantine school only, and as consisting even there of nothing more than the division of the hair down the centre of the head—and that feature sometimes failing—and of the long curls on the shoulders; these last being doubtless in allusion to Jesus as the true Nazarite. And even this distinction loses its meaning by being extended in great measure to all heads alike —to Adam and Eve, to patriarchs and prophets, to disciples and apostles—except where, as in the case of Peter and Paul, they possessed far more marked types of their own—to John the Baptist, and to angels and archangels. Not even the pointed beard —*bifurcata*, mentioned in Lentulus' letter—is by any means a constant feature. In the miraculous picture impressed on cloth, and preserved in the sacristy of St. Peter's, at Rome, and in another, professing equal antiquity and supernatural origin, to which we have alluded, in S. Bartolomeo, at Genoa, of both of which careful drawings have been recently made,[1] the beard is scrupulously and strongly divided into three points, one on each side and one in the centre.

Let us here retrace our steps a little, and glance at the more prominent classes of physiognomy given to Christ in the strivings of early Christian Art.

The first known conception of the Saviour's features (there were, as we have seen, no portraits) was inspired by the lingering feeling for classic forms, and is found in the earlier monuments of the Roman Catacombs. Here the type of Christ (woodcut, No. 8, over leaf) is simply that of youth, and of the expression proper to that period. Christ accordingly appears before us clad in that tender sweetness of unsuffering and unforeboding youthfulness, which only gains pathos from our sense of its ideal untruth. Here we seek for no expression of sympathy, for sorrow has not been known, nor even for that of sanctity, where innocence is paramount. Still in the well-nigh impossibility of duly embodying the double idea of the Godhead and the Manhood, we look the more approvingly on these early representations which only attempt the first. For classic Art gave young and beautiful forms to Christ, as she had before given them to the pagan gods, such being the highest conception she possessed of divine purity; as we give them still and have given them throughout all Christian ages to angels. It is thought, too, that the title of 'Son of God,' acting upon minds accustomed to associate this relationship with the great and ever-juvenile demigods of antiquity, conduced at first to invest our Lord with the attributes of youth. However this may be, that, again, cannot be strictly called a type of Christ which is not confined to Him. The youthful being who stands touching an upright mummy with his staff, or gently smiling before the judgment-seat of Pilate, is known to be the Lord by his act and

[1] See Art Journal, No. 77, May 1861.

position; but the figure of Moses unloosening his sandals, or Daniel, erect between two lions, or David holding a sling—and here more rightfully—is in many instances equally as young. Admitting, however, the type of the Christ in the earlier examples of the Catacombs to consist in youth, there fails even that very slender sign, supposed to be the indispensable distinction—the divided hair. Here, like the heads of Bacchus or Apollo, the hair is short, clustering and united in front, though somewhat longer behind. We give an illustration from an early sarcophagus in the Catacombs. Even as time advanced, and the apparent years of our Lord advanced with it (for in the first centuries of Art the age given to Christ becomes a date), the head of Christ, though bearded and furrowed, keeps its undivided hair.

8 Classic Head of Christ.

We abstain from instancing here those two so-called portraits of Christ, existing on the walls of the Catacombs of Rome—and curiously distinct from all other representations of Him there—which are generally cited as fixed points from which all heads of Christ diverge. Investigation shows both these pictures to be surrounded with too much obscurity, as to intention and period, to be taken as any safe data. The first, forming the centre of a ceiling in the catacomb of St. Calixtus, is, in the absence of all nimbus, only conjectured to be Christ; the second, on a wall in the catacomb of S. Ponziano, is an example of the mechanical and forbidding, and decidedly later phase of the Byzantine conception: both, excepting the one distinction of the divided hair, are too widely different in feature and expression to allow of any theory of a common origin. Little, therefore, can be gathered from heads thus uncertain in intention, vague in date, opposite in character, and, above all, in the ruined state to which time and injury have reduced them.

In the wide realm and long reign of Byzantine Art—though in many respects allied with classic traditions—we enter into another distinct form of the human countenance, and therefore of that of the Lord. The hair divided in the centre of the forehead may here be said to constitute an unfailing sign of identity. At the same time there was nothing in this feature to prevent the utmost possible difference in every other. We find, accordingly, in the works of Byzantine origin, as much diversity as might be expected from the differing conditions to which Art was subjected—from the mere mechanical reproduction of the same ever-copied and ever-deteriorating pattern, to the work of such artists who, though conforming in treatment of subject to the overruling laws of the Greek Church, yet infused into it a feeling for beauty and elevation of character. That the first-named class of works should exist in far greater abundance than the latter is only natural, and it is to them that the so-called type of Christ's head in Byzantine Art is traceable. We see, therefore, our Lord, as in our illustration (No. 9), invested with the harshest features, and the meanest and most forbidding expression —with His face furrowed with lines of age rather than thought, and of sourness rather than sorrow—a conception, in short, directly opposed to any view of His nature, and which may be partially ascribed to the obdurate materials, such as mosaic and enamel work, in which the head of Christ was often rendered.

9   Byzantine Head of Christ.

On the other hand, however, and though not often, yet frequently enough to raise a strong protest against the general condemnation passed by some authors on Byzantine Art,[1] we meet with examples of Eastern conceptions of the head of the Saviour, which, for beauty and grandeur, are unequalled, perhaps, by the efforts of any time. We take an illustration (No. 10, over leaf), to which, however, no woodcut can do justice—from a MS. in the British Museum (Harleian, 1810) of the 12th century, contemporary, it is believed, with the head given above. Here Christ has assumed a solemn and stern aspect, always more or less characteristic of the Art of the Greek Church. He is no longer, as in our classic illustration, the God of a race who deified the pleasures of this life, or the expression of an Art whose highest principle was

[1] For example, by M. Rio.

the sense of repose, but He is a Being so far fitted for Christian worship as embodying the great fact of Sacrifice and Suffering, though combined with a sternness which forbids all thought of sympathy. But whether this sternness rises into beauty or sinks into ugliness, the same form and expression will be found more or less to pervade every other head accompanying that of Christ, thus showing that the type was that given to the general human physiognomy in that particular school and period, and not to the separate person of our Saviour. This diversity also bears witness against the supposed principle, too sweepingly assigned to the Greek Church, of representing Christ as devoid of all beauty.

10 Byzantine Head of Christ.

It would be impossible to follow with any accuracy the complicated history of the Art which proceeded from Byzantium. In the refuge and encouragement afforded by Rome at different times to schools of Greek artists, from the iconoclastic period—the early part of the 8th century—to the conquest of Constantinople by the Turks in 1206, the cards of Art were too intricately shuffled to be, perhaps, ever clearly sorted out. Perhaps the broadest definition of the beginnings of Western Art, as opposed to Eastern, may be said to consist in its unmitigated rudeness. The time of Charlemagne and his dynasty—what is called the Carlovingian period—offers little that is not equally barbaric in design and execution. In the convulsions of kingdoms, Art had returned to the quarry whence she had sprung, and had to be hewn out afresh, and by very different hands. Here Christ, like all around Him, is a mere grotesque deformity in shape and expression; or if the head occasionally rises into a kind of stony solemnity from the negation of all expression, the effect may be traced in part to some Byzantine influence.

The Anglo-Saxon period, which, in respect of Art, seems to mingle both classical reminiscences and Byzantine traditions with a grandly fantastic native element, offers more interest. Christ is here more strictly separate; the disciples have one class of features, being chiefly given with classically formed profiles, the angels and archangels another, and Christ a third. This is of an abstract and weird character, conveying a strange sense of the supernatural, perfectly in keeping with the abstract nature of the more general conception, which represents our Lord in glory. The head rises grandly above the stony stare, the divided hair is cinctured with a fillet and jewel, and the beard is formed into three points. The lines are few and equal, as if by a hand accustomed to incise them on a harder material. (See head in diagram of creation, woodcut No. 19.) Another form, with a bushy wig of hair, of which we annex an illustration (No. 11), is more fantastic, though not without a certain grandeur. This is taken from an Anglo-Saxon MS. in the British Museum, of the year 1000. (Biblia Cotton. Tiberius, C. VI.)

11 Anglo-Saxon Head of Christ.

We now enter streams of Art too numerous and self-intersecting to be pursued in this brief notice. The human head here serves of course, as in all Art, to distinguish one school from another, but it would be perilous to attempt any nicety of connoisseurship. We annex, however, a few illustrations of closely connected schools and times. The small illustration (No. 12) is from a French Bible of the 13th century, ornamented with above 1000 pen-drawings, in the British Museum. It represents the upper part of Christ's figure in the act of creation. The youthfulness of the conception renders it peculiar.

Our next specimen (No. 13, over leaf) is English in origin, taken from a psalter (Biblia Regia, 2 A. XXII, in the British Museum, of about the year 1250. This is reduced from a head half the size of life. Here the fact that the type of Christ's head is the same as that of contemporary persons is strikingly borne out, for

14. Head of Christ.

the head of Henry III. (1216-72), discovered on the wall of the Windsor cloisters, is curiously identical in form and expression, though more rude.

Our next woodcut (No. 14) is from a Belgian MS.—the Psalter and Offices—belonging to Mr. Holford—pronounced to be of about the year 1310. This is also simply the head, which serves as a frontispiece to the various events of the canonical hours. Our illustration is the size of the original, which, except as being larger, differs in no way from an also separate head of John the Baptist which precedes it by a few pages.

The fourth woodcut (No. 15) is from an English MS. belonging also to Mr. Holford, of the early part of the 14th century, in which Christ as Creator is reproving our disobedient parents. Other illustrations of Christ in this work will supply ample proof of the diversities of representation during this and previous centuries. Generally speaking, however, and without affecting any precision, there is a sort of analogy between the heads of Christ and the generally received characteristics of the principal

14   Head of Christ.

northern nations, even to this time. The conception of Christ's countenance in English miniatures has a certain earnest downrightness, in French works it is decidedly gay, while the German have an expression of thought.

With all alike, the person of our Lord, when represented in the act of ascension, or in glory, has a certain abstract countenance which gives elevation to the most diverse features; but when seen among men, there is nothing by which He can be so distinctly and certainly identified as by the necessary and seldom absent cruciform nimbus.

We seek, therefore, in vain for a sole and continuous type of our blessed Lord during those periods when the faculty of representing individual expression was yet undeveloped. As long as Christ was depicted like other men,

15   Head of Christ.

and other men like Him, He cannot be said to have had a character of His own. No type, strictly speaking, therefore, could begin till Christ stood isolated by the personal individualities of those around Him. This power was partially reserved for the Italian masters of the renaissance of Art, which began in the 13th century. That they should have reverentially retained the few characteristics transmitted through the Byzantine forms—the divided and falling hair, the forked beard, the somewhat lengthy face—was but natural: their business was to vary other faces, not that of our Lord. But even that cannot be said to have been successfully done until the true painter of the human soul arose. Fra Angelico is admitted to have been the first who attained the wondrous gift of expression, by which each individual received a separate existence. He therefore may be said to have been the first who isolated Christ. Whether the character given to the Lord rose in proportion with that of those around him, is another question. We need but to look at the picture by Fra Angelico in the National Gallery, to see that while surrounded with greater variety, and higher types of individual beauty, earnestness, and devotion, than almost any other known picture presents, the head of the Christ is negative and unmeaning. Other instances, however, show that while the Frate's pious hand seems lamed when addressing itself to that awful countenance, yet the expression at which he aimed was that most proper to Christ—the divine sympathy towards the human race.

It is to be regretted that the great painters of the beginning of the 15th century—Florentine, Paduan, Venetian—have left so few models of their conception of the Lord's head. The Madonna and the Infant reign supreme at this time; the Entombment and the Ascension also present His dead or His glorified features; but our Lord as He walked among men is scarcely seen. It would seem as if, in the first triumphs over the living face of one of the most powerful and beautiful races of men, they shrank from a head in which something better than the pride of the eye and the power of the brain was demanded. The great Florentine giants of the 15th century—Sandro Botticelli, Domenico Ghirlandajo, the Lippi—have hardly left a conception of Christ in His living manhood—nor Bellini, nor Mantegna. Nevertheless, the

15th century did not elapse without bequeathing the profoundest conception of the Son of Man which mortal hand has ever executed. Most of our readers will think of that dim ghost of a head, still lingering on the walls of an old refectory in Milan, which, like its divine original, has suffered the contempt and injury of man, yet still defies the world to produce its equal. Leonardo da Vinci's Cena is confessed to have been a culminating point in Art: in nothing does it show this more than in surrounding Christ with the highest forms of intelligence, earnestness, beauty, and individuality in male heads, and yet preserving the Divine Master's superiority to all. We will not attempt to analyse the causes for this, though perhaps the intense pathos of that sympathising look may give a clue. After this there are few heads of Christ, as living, on which we dwell with that sadness of admiration which is the evidence of their affinity to our higher part, though the utmost pathos has been given to the dead features; as, for instance, in the Christ in the large Pietà, by Perugino, in the Pitti, and that in the same subject by Francia, in the National Gallery, which are both of a very high order. Nor could Raphael run his course without setting the stamp of his mind on this sacred head. But this does not come within the category of conceptions of Christ as man; for his exquisite head in the Disputa embodies Christ, though seen with His wounds, as in glory.

As Art exulted more and more in her mechanical triumphs, the likelihood of a true homage to that head diminishes. The juicy and facile brush of the Venetian school scarcely rises above a courteous and well-liking benevolence of expression, and Christ in Titian's Tribute Money falls even below that standard. Albert Dürer, however grand in his Man of Sorrows, is most so when he hides the face. Flemish Art passes from the meanest and ugliest conceptions, in the engravings of the end of the 15th and beginning of the 16th century, to the handsome, florid, earthly head by Rubens, and that, more refined, but scarcely more spiritual, by Van Dyck; while the highest conception of latter days was reserved for that Dutchman who occasionally transfigures vulgar forms with a glory that hides every blemish; so that Christ, under the hand of Rembrandt, though not beautiful, and not dignified, has yet a holiness which scarcely any other master has attained.

The Fall of Lucifer and of the Rebel Angels.

Ital. La Caduta di Lucifero e de' suoi Seguaci. *Fr.* La Chute des Anges.
Germ. Der Sturz der Engel.

THE Fall of Lucifer and of the rebellious angels occupies the first place in the chronology of Sacred Art, as the Day of Judgment the last. The fact of angels who 'kept not their first estate' is alluded to, rather than expressly told, both in the Old and New Testament. In this manner it is employed by Isaiah (xiv. 12) as a metaphor of the prophesied fall of the kings of Babylon, 'How art thou fallen from heaven, O Lucifer, son of the morning!'— a fall from heaven being both a Hebrew and classic figure for expressing a great and sudden calamity. In this sense also, as an allusion, it is used by St. Peter (2 ii. 4), who says, 'For if God spared not the angels that sinned, but cast them down to hell, and delivered them into chains of darkness, to be reserved unto judgment,' so He 'knoweth how to reserve the unjust unto the day of judgment to be punished.' But, beyond these purposes of metaphor and illustration, no hint is afforded in the Scriptures of the mode and period of so stupendous an event, which thus, in the reticence of Revelation, is left to concern us no more than as a mysterious warning, and as a clue to the comprehension of the final judgments prophesied against the powers of Evil in the book of the Revelation. Whether, therefore, the rebellion in heaven was the beginning of evil, and the region to which the apostate angels fell the first institution of hell, are questions on which speculation is useless. Here, as throughout this work, we cannot too often recall the words of Bede, 'we cannot know that on which truth keeps silence.' The existence of evil, however, in the shape of the temptation which caused our first parents to err, has been accepted by early Theology in evidence that the fall of the angels preceded the creation of the world. St. Augustine (4th century), by a curious theory, founded on those strained typical comparisons so greatly in favour with both early and mediæval Fathers, goes so far as to opine that the creation of the angels took place on that first day, when God said, ' Let there be light,' and their fall on the second day, when He 'divided the waters which were under the firmament from the waters which were above the firmament'—on which subject we shall have more to say. Having thus supposed that the angels fell before man was made, Theology went further still, and a scheme was suggested which ingeniously connects the Creation of the World and the Fall of Man with the forfeited estate and ruined natures of Lucifer and his companions. With the true *naïveté* of fable, it is related by the writers of the 12th century, and doubtless by others of an earlier date, that Man was created by God to repair the breaches in heaven occasioned by the lapse of so many angelic spirits. That for this reason he became the object of Satan's especial malice, who saw in his ruin the means of revenging himself on the Almighty. Further, that having succeeded in tempting him to fall, the plan of man's recovery was devised by the Second Person of the Trinity, urged on to it by the remonstrances of the angels, who complain that the caves of Tartarus alone are replenished by the race of Man, but not, as had been intended, the thrones of heaven.[1] This was a scheme so generally accepted, that even a Life of Christ was considered legitimately to begin with the Fall of Lucifer. Here we find the scheme of our Milton's 'Paradise Lost;'—by Addison and other critics attributed to the unassisted inspiration of his genius, but which, imbued as he was with Italian literature and art, must have been so familiar to him, as a theological tradition, as to require no acknowledgment of its origin. The Archangel Raphael thus relates to Adam the announcement—on the return of the Son, victorious with His saints—of the divine intention to create a new race in place of those spirits whom Lucifer had drawn after him :—

> But lest his heart exalt him in the harm
> Already done to have dispeopled Heaven,
> My damage fondly deemed, I can repair
> That detriment, if such it be to lose
> Self-lost, and in a moment will create
> Another world, out of one man a race
> Of men innumerable, there to dwell,
> Not here, till by degrees of merit raised,
> They open to themselves at length the way

---

[1] St. Bonaventura. Vita Christi.

> Up hither, under long obedience try'd,
> And earth be changed to Heav'n, and Heav'n to Earth,
> One kingdom, joy and union without end.
>
> *Paradise Lost*, book viii.

That Art, as well as Poetry, should receive the impress of these theological ideas was rationally to be expected, and thus the fall of the Angels—and sometimes, as we shall see, their creation—is found consistently heading various series of the Creation of the World and the History of Adam and Eve.

The character and personality of Lucifer himself was a frequent subject with the fervid preachers of the 11th and the succeeding century. The great haughty spirit, who, in right of his rank as seraph, had stood above the throne of God—'Above it' (the throne) 'stood the seraphim' (Isa. vi. 2)—was held up like a hero of

14   Lucifer in rebellion. (MS. 13th century. Mr. Holford.)

wickedness in the ears of an imaginative race, invested with all those far-fetched analogies and comparisons which in those days doubtless formed the charm and strange moral of such tales. His crime, according to the curious interpretation of the 12th century, consisted in not being content to stand—there, where only the highest order of angelic beings were privileged to stand at all—but, in a blasphemous ambition, to assume a position in heaven proper only to the Holy Trinity. For Isaiah saith, 'How art thou fallen from heaven, O Lucifer, son of the morning! how art thou cut down to the ground, which didst weaken the nations! For thou hast said in thine heart, I will ascend into heaven, I will exalt my throne above the stars of God: I will *sit* also upon the mount of the congregation' (xiv. 12, 13). This presumptuous desire to sit—in opposition to his duty to stand—is the prominent figure under which St. Bernard presented the apostasy of Lucifer to his hearers. We meet with traces of this idea in Art, namely, in a Bible Historiée of the 13th century, belonging to Mr. Holford; where Lucifer, a grand and disdainful figure, is seated on a throne, while three angels, standing by, look on with gestures of surprise. We give a fac-simile of the figure of Lucifer (woodcut, No. 16). To this there followed an ingenious speculation on the symbolism of his wings, for, like all seraphs, as described by Isaiah, Lucifer had six wings; two with which to hide his face—or, as being one of God's counsellors, the purposes of Deity; two with which to hide his feet, or, in other words, the messages of the Most High; and two with which to fly. In these two last lay the respective causes for his power and for his fall. For by the two centre wings, according to St. Bernard, 'not affirming, but conjecturing and opining,' were represented—by the one the light of Nature, and by the other the ardour of Grace. By the one the seraphim shone with intellect, by the other they glowed with love. But Lucifer, inclining only to intellect—true light-bearer, as his name bespeaks—preferred, in his pride, to shine rather than to burn, to use one wing and not both; for the shining glorified himself, while the burning rendered homage to God. Thus disdaining to stand where it was forbidden him to sit, and unable to fly with only one wing on which to lean, there remained no other alternative, in this inexorable syllogism, than for the perverse seraph to fall—that fall from which, having been tempted by his own innate pride, and not, like his victim, man, by evil counsels from without, he forfeited all power of recovery.

The following is another version of the origin of that pride which came before the seraph's fall. It is related that when the angels were created, Lucifer was the first who broke out into a hymn to the thrice holy Creator, to which all the other angels immediately responded. For this God gave him praise, which so elated his proud spirit that he began to aspire to be equal with God, and to persuade his fellows to join him in rebellion. And here the angels are described as having thought and acted much as mortal men would have done; for some took his part at once, but others preferred to remain neutral, and await the event, with the intention of siding with the strongest in the end. These were called the Doubters, and they received justly the same punishment, being cast out of heaven with the rest.

Lucifer is also said to have been distinguished from the rest by a large crown, which seems to have belonged to him in the quality of light-bearer.[1] Of this idea we see traces in the crown sometimes worn by the serpent when tempting Eve.

The subject of the Fall of the Angels required too great a development of the mechanical powers of Art to be treated otherwise than rarely and meagrely by the early artists. Nevertheless, no contemptible example is found in a Bible of the 10th century, in the British Museum, where the subject occupies the whole of the first page. The scene is very dignified. The Deity—for there is no nimbus to indicate which Person of the Trinity—sits solemnly in an almond-shaped glory, upheld by two angels; while two more hide their hands, in token of respect, beneath their drapery. From the threshold of heaven the angels are seen falling in attitudes indicating no small knowledge on the part of the unknown artist of nine centuries ago. They are in human forms—denuded of wings and drapery—the angel stripped till nothing but the man is left. Their faces are caricatures—those lowest being the most hideous; Lucifer himself lies beneath, brutified already with a tail—his person enveloped, strange to say, in an almond-shaped glory, which a red dragon seizes in his jaws and encircles with his coils. This is a unique instance, it is believed, of Satan thus encircled with an attribute hardly seen even sur-

[1] Fabricius, vol. i. p. 37.

rounding the persons of angels. But here all its glory is dimmed. It is dull and dark, and was probably introduced to distinguish the arch-rebel from his followers.

On other occasions greater dramatic action is given to the powers above. Michael, as the captain of the armies of the Lord—or three archangels, as in Cimabue's ruined fresco in S. Francesco at Assisi, are made striking with their lances, from the semicircle of heaven, at two or three falling figures in strange postures of foreshortening. In an early example,[1] Michael stands alone, with a small falling figure on each side with flapping wings, like empty sails which have lost all buoyancy—and as if, according to the quaint moral, Nature and Grace alike failed to support them. Generally Lucifer, already transformed into a dragon-like form, lies below; sometimes he is undistinguishable in a flight of figures descending like wounded birds, and turned simply by change of colour into angels of darkness.[2]

In other examples, the presence of the Almighty under the form of Christ is introduced, presiding over the scene of discomfiture, as if the archangels acted under His immediate orders. The presence of Christ also is proper to the Greek Church, which places the fall of Lucifer immediately before the creation of Adam, and which, according to the 'Guide,' gives in greater detail the principle of gradual brutification. 'Le Christ assis comme un roi sur un trône, et tenant l'Évangile ouvert à ces mots: "J'ai vu Satan tombant du ciel comme un éclair." Tout autour, les chœurs des anges dans une crainte profonde. Michel se tient au milieu, disant sur un cartel : "Que notre maintien soit plein de crainte, adorons ici le roi notre Dieu." Au-dessous, des montagnes; au milieu d'elles, une grande ouverture, au-dessus de laquelle on lit cette inscription, "Le Tartare." Lucifer et toute son armée tombent du ciel. Tout en haut, ils paraissent très-beaux ; au-dessous, ils deviennent anges de ténèbres ; plus bas, ils paraissent plus ténébreux et plus noirs ; plus bas encore, ils sont à moitié anges et à moitié démons ; enfin ils deviennent entièrement démons noirs et hideux. Tout en bas, sous tous les autres, au milieu de l'abîme, le diable Lucifer, le plus noir et le plus affreux de tous, étendu sur le ventre, et regardant en haut.'

This dramatic metamorphosis, which in its gradual nature seems

---

[1] Denkmäler der Kunst des Mittelalters in Unter-Italien, von Schultz und Quast, xxxix.
[2] D'Agincourt. Pittura, pl. l.

to point to Milton's nine days' length of fall—probably also traditional in origin [1]—is seen curiously illustrated in a miniature of the 13th century,[2] which furnishes an exact illustration of the Greek text. Here, as the rebellious hosts fall over the precipice of heaven, they have still celestial forms and attributes—the glory, the wings, and the stole. A little lower down the change commences—the features become animal—glory and wings disappear; as they enter the fatal gulf a tail has sprouted—hands and feet are turned into paws—nails into claws—and by the time they reach the bottom the transformation from the angel to the monster is complete.

The fall of Lucifer is found in all forms of the 'Speculum Salvationis,' always commencing the History of the World. In an early German edition the homeliness of character, and the absence of all imagination, render this subject almost irrecognisable. Christ sits on a chair, holding the globe and cross in the right hand, and with an action of almost burlesque astonishment in the left. At His feet is a figure like an ourang-outang, with long arms, about to swing itself, apparently headforemost, into space, while two angels, scarcely less hideous, with long poles, poke at him from behind their singing-desks.

As Art gradually grew more equal to cope with so difficult a theme as the Fall of the Angels, the subject became, in great measure, confounded with scenes from the Apocalypse, or replaced by the Legend of Antichrist which prevailed in the 15th century. This last was embodied by Luca Signorelli at Orvieto. As a phase in Christian history, however, Michael Angelo, who, unspiritual as was his conception of all Christian subjects, adhered with a fidelity, obsolete in his time, to the traditionary schemes of Art—(witness the scheme, both as a whole and in detail, of the Sistine ceiling) —Michael Angelo intended to have executed the Fall of the Angels on the great wall facing that of the Last Judgment, thus making these two subjects, consistently with early usage, the beginning and the end of the History of the Creation. There is no doubt that the

---

[1] An apocryphal book of Genesis, of about the year 1458, appended to a German Bible, gives a more early version of this same idea, showing the multitudes that fell, rather than the time of falling: 'Da regnete es drei Tage und drei Nächte nichts als lauter Teuffeln herab.' Quoted in Fabricius, vol. i. p. 38.

[2] Psautier de St. Louis. Arsenal, Paris.

task would have afforded the most congenial exercise for his powers, and one in which a stern conception of God's anger towards angelic rebels would not have been so repugnant to the feelings as the character he has given to the Saviour in his Last Judgment.

By all painters since Michael Angelo's time, the Fall of the Angels, properly speaking, has been ignored; for Raphael's magnificent Michael combating Satan, in the Louvre—Guido's picture of the same, in the church of the Capucini at Rome—Franz Floris' well-known work at Antwerp—the Cavaliere d'Arpino's picture in Stafford House, and all that may be mentioned, showing angels fighting with demoniacal forms, are all various versions of that 'war in heaven, when Michael and his angels fought against Satan.' Nay, even to take an early example, the so-called fall of Lucifer, executed (1407) by Spinello Aretino in his ninety-third year, in S. Maria degli Angeli at Arezzo, is really the Fight of St. Michael with the Seven-headed Dragon of the Apocalypse. For the contest in heaven, which may be supposed to have preceded the fall of the apostate hosts, can only be conceived as Milton conceived it, as between angels and their rebellious fellows. Had Milton written, like Dante, at the dawn of a great period of Art, it may be presumed that the sublime images of his pen would have been turned to fertile account. As it is, no painter has risen to that grand conception of the great adversary, swelling with pride and wicked disdain, measuring himself in fight unspeakable with the prince of angels, till the angelic throng retired in speed from their vicinity

> Unsafe within the wind
> Of such commotion ; such as, to set forth
> Great things by small, if Nature's concord broke,
> Among the constellations war were sprung,
> Two planets rushing from aspect malign
> Of fiercest opposition in mid sky
> Should combat, and their jarring spheres confound.
> *Paradise Lost*, book vi.

As for Rubens' magnificent pictures—sometimes misnamed the Fall of the Angels—no traditions of Art or words of Scripture can be applied to them. Mere cataracts of figures are these, unparalleled in knowledge of drawing, and in the poetry of the horrible—men and demons, serpents and foul monsters, interlaced with those luminously coloured female figures, the introduction of which it was not in Rubens to resist, and which prove the subject to have been intended for the Fall of the Damned. Even the idea of the Last Judgment is incompatible with a Saviour who casts thunderbolts like Jove, and with a Michael whose shield, like the antique fable of the Gorgon's head, annihilates all on whom its baneful light is turned. Here, therefore, the mind must be content to look only for triumphs of human skill—for Art in its most gorgeous pride of the eye, but not for sacred history, or even for the traditions of what may be called sacred fable.

Thus far we have considered the Fall of Lucifer as a separate subject. It also takes its place as the terminating scene of a series rarely met with, illustrating the Creation of Angels. Such a series exists in a remarkable miniature at Brussels[1] of about the date 1475. Six small pictures are here grouped in one page (see etching).

1. First we see an abstract female figure of Wisdom, a type of Christ, seated on a throne, holding a scroll in her hand, on which is inscribed 'Ab initio et ante secula creata sum,' in allusion to the passage 'Ab æterno ordinata sum, et ex antiquis, antequam terra fieret'—'I was set up from everlasting, from the beginning, or ever the earth was' (Prov. viii. 23).

2. The next below shows the Three Persons of the Trinity, the Second Person with a cruciform glory in the centre, as the active agent of all creation. They are concerting together to make the angels.

3. The third subject represents three angels, habited like deacons, already created; each humbly kneeling before a Person of the Trinity and receiving their injunctions.

4. Here the Trinity are seated, pointing in gestures of sorrow to the scene of rebellion going on below.

5. This picture is very effective. Lucifer, the crowned seraph, is in the midst of a ferment of excited angels,—red-hot, not with love, but with rebellion, with rampant wings. He holds a scroll in his hands—'In coelum ascendam'—'I will ascend into heaven' (Isaiah xiv. 13). In the foreground are seated four angels in white, in attitudes of deep dejection; one looking over the edge of the picture into the gulf below, with hands expressive of astonished dismay.

[1] Library of the old Dukes of Burgundy. Bible, 2 vols. No. 9002.

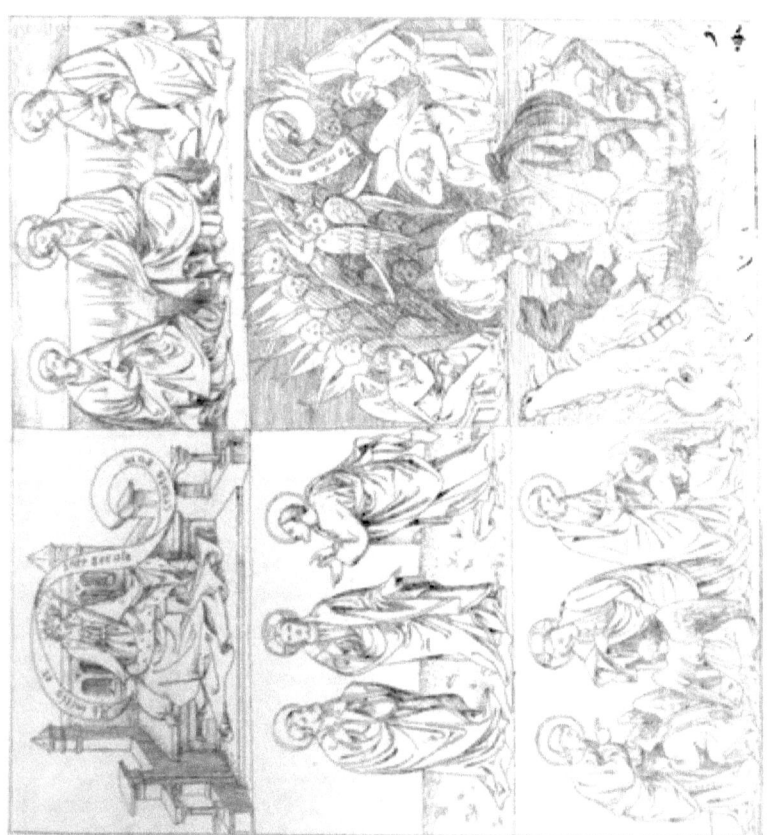

6. This lower scene is the moral of the tale. Lucifer, crown foremost, is falling with outstretched arms into the jaws of hell, represented literally, being like a great boat filled with fire, into which demons are hastening the fallen seraph's descent.

We return to the theory of St. Augustine,[1] by which he supposed the angels to have been called into being on that first day, when God said, 'Let there be light,' and to have fallen on the second day, in which, 'God made the firmament, and divided the waters which were under the firmament from the waters which were above the firmament,'—this last act being considered a type of the division of the good angels from the bad. This idea—in other words, the connection between Satan or Lucifer and the second day—was curiously enlarged upon by the early schoolmen,[2] who have preserved in their disquisitions traces of Jewish thought and usage. For why, they ask, does it happen that of the second day alone it is not recorded that 'God saw that it was good?' The answer is that the Jews believed that on that day the angel Lucifer became the devil Satan, and that therefore the second day was alone of the six days *not* good in God's sight. A curious representation of this simultaneous creation of light and of angels is seen in the series of wall-paintings, representing the Creation, in the choir of the cathedral at Monreale (woodcut No. 17, over leaf). Here the Almighty sits on a globe, not typifying our world, but rather in the sense of the heavens, which are His throne, and which rests on waters; for 'The Lord sitteth upon the flood; yea, the Lord sitteth King for ever' (Ps. xxix. 10). His right hand is extended, His left holds the volumen. Before Him, in adoring postures, stand the angels, with spikes of light projecting beyond them—a radiant company, who truly seem to have burst into light and existence at the same moment. But such ideas as these are rarely seen in monumental forms, being scattered here and there in miniatures and old engravings.[3]

On some occasions a slight change in the arbitrary type, which has been made significant of the fall of the angels, has been introduced—likening their rejection from heaven, by a rather more intelligible idea, to the division of the light from the darkness, and

---
[1] Confessions, l. xiii. c. 15. [2] Comestor, fol. 2.
[3] Zani, vol. ii. p. 173.

17   Creation of Angels and Light.   (Monreale.)

not to that of the waters which were under the firmament from the waters which were above the firmament, and thus placing it on the first day. A curious Bible of the end of the 13th century, in Paris,[1] furnishes full authority on this system of interpretation. Here fact and type in small pictures, and Scripture and gloss in text, are given side by side. Thus the Second Person of the Trinity is seen creating light on the one side, and angels on the other. Below the first is written : ' Et Dieu dit, Lumière sois faite, et Lumière fut faite;' below the other the following explanation : ' La création de lumière emporte [importe] la création des anges, car ils ont lumière d'entendement' (understanding). Again God is seen dividing light from darkness under the semblance of a half-eclipsed

[1] Bible Historiée. Bibliothèque Impériale. Français, No. 167.

sphere, and in the next picture the angels are falling, the text being, 'Et Dieu vit que la lumière était bonne, et divisa la lumière des ténèbres, et appela la lumière jour, et les ténèbres nuit;' and the gloss which here grasps at another moral analogy: 'La division de la lumière des ténèbres importe la division des bons anges des mauvais, et signifie la division des vertus et des vices.'

There is another way also in which Art has recorded the legendary connection between the angels and the creation of this world. It would appear that as the light was called day—as the word day, or *dies*, was derived from a Greek word meaning brightness—and as angels are in Scripture always invested with the quality of brightness—for example, when Cornelius saw a man stand before him in bright clothing—that by a too far-fetched logic, the angels were made typical of the days. This is a solution which is evident when we study the series of the creation—one of the most curious existing—in the mosaics of St. Mark's, where each day in succession is personified by an angel, a fuller description of which, with woodcuts, will be given in the account of the days of Creation.

The Creation of the World.

We have thus briefly considered those acts of Omnipotence connected with the creation and fall of angels which Theology has supposed to have happened before, or to have been coeval with, the creation of our world, and which have left their impress on Art. This department alone would furnish abundant and interesting matter for the iconographist. The limits of this work permit of little more than the indication of the existence of the subject.

That these scenes and those we are about to consider as illustrating the creation of the world and of our race, should, however, enter into the scheme of this work, will be obvious to all. The connection between the History of the Creation and the History of our Lord is immediate. In all religious Art, as in all sound theology, Christ is the Creator, in the active and visible sense, on the First Day, as truly as He will be Judge on the Last Day. This doctrine is frequently asserted in the Scriptures—indirectly in the Old Testament, directly in the New. God's declaration to Moses, 'For there shall no man see me and live' (Ex. xxxiii. 20), shows that His appearances to Adam and to the patriarchs were not in His own person. This declaration is repeated in the broadest terms in the New Testament, 'No man hath seen God at any time' (St. John i. 18). The direct assertion that the powers of creation were vested in the person of Christ is also contained in the words commencing the Gospel of St. John, 'In the beginning was the Word, and the Word was with God, and the Word was God. The same was in the beginning with God. All things were made by Him; and without Him was not any thing made that was made.' This all-embracing authority for the chief mysteries of our faith is again repeated by St. Paul as regards the creatorship of Christ, 'And to make all men see what is the fellowship of the mystery, which from the beginning of the world hath been hid in God, who created all things by Jesus Christ' (Eph. iii. 9). Finally, such being the warrant for this dogma, it takes its place among the articles of the Nicene Creed: 'Being of one substance with the Father; By whom all things were made.'[1] Here, therefore, we find full indication of the system of early Art, which, with reverent consistency, never represented the Person of the Father, except by the Hand from a cloud, or from a portion of the circle which typifies heaven; and which invariably shows us the Son, 'the express image of the Father,' as the outward and visible manifestation of God, whether in the creation of the world and of our race, or in the various other occasions, of which we shall speak, in the Old Testament, where the presence of the Almighty is made known to man.

To early theology the days of Creation were abundantly suggestive of those types in which contemplative minds found occupation and delight.

In a general way, the Scripture language, which typifies good by light, and evil by darkness, was amplified with equal whimsicality and ingenuity. Next, the six days were morally analysed; the history of the world being considered a sort of mirror of the history of the Creation, and therefore divided into six periods. The first, from Adam to Noah, the evening of which was the Deluge; the second, from Noah to Abraham, the evening of which was the confusion of tongues; the third, from Abraham to David, of which the evening was the wicked reign of Saul; the fourth, from David to the Babylonian Captivity, the evening of which was the sins of the Jews, which drew upon them this judgment; the fifth, from the Babylonian Captivity to the Coming of Christ, the evening of which was typified by the wickedness and blindness which hid the true Messiah from their sight; the sixth, from the first coming of Christ to His second coming to judge the world, the evening of which these ancient commentators express by the question, 'When the Son of Man cometh, shall He find faith upon the earth?' Finally, they considered the whole Creation a type of the eternal existence of God, who is from everlasting to everlasting, having neither beginning nor end; for on the first day they observed that no morning is mentioned, and on the seventh, in which the saints entered into rest, no evening.

Besides these types, a number of theories as regarded the Persons

[1] The belief that the world was created by the Word, and that it was the same mysterious manifestation of God which conversed with Adam and the patriarchs, appears in the earliest Jewish writings. See Cruden's Concordance: introduction to 'Word.'

and modes of Creation were propounded, the earliest based on reverential and literal examination of the words of Scripture, though diverging later into assumptions, and leading to deductions to us fanciful, and in the sense of edification unintelligible.

'In the beginning God created the heavens and the earth.' This was regarded as indicative of the agency of the Father summoning forth something where nothing before had been, and that at a period indefinite in time before the days of Creation began. But the first Person having thus furnished the materials, the task of further operation was delegated by Him to the Second Person, or the 'Word.' For here the inspired language is no longer 'God created,' but 'God *said*'—the same form of utterance being preserved throughout the six days of Creation. Later theologians departed from this child-like, however quaint, exposition of the great facts of the first page of Genesis. The presence of the Trinity—sufficiently clear in another sense to all commentators—and the exact part each took in the great work, were defined with that spirit of force and fanciful speculation which, in the 12th and 13th centuries, took the place of the former simplicity. According to them, three acts, each characteristic of one of the Three Persons, were necessary to the formation of the machine of the world—the act of creating, of distinguishing, and of ornamenting. The first, which called the heavens and the earth out of nothing, belonged to the Father. The second, which comprehended the three first days, and saw the division, or, as it was termed, the distinction, of light from darkness—of the waters under the firmament from the waters above the firmament, and of the gathering together of the waters, and the appearance of the dry land—was assigned to Christ. The third act, which comprehends the three last days, and in which the heavens were adorned with lights, the firmament with fowls, the waters with fish, and the earth with animals, and, finally, with man, were pronounced the work of the Holy Ghost. In this category of creative acts, not borne out in the first instance by Scripture, as reference will immediately show, were seen the great and separate attributes of the Trinity: by Creation, the Omnipotence; by Distinction, the Wisdom; by Adornment, the Goodness; or, as given in another of the numerous forms in which the changes are rung upon this theme, the Omnipotence of the

Father, by producing; the Omniscience of the Son, by distinguishing; and the Benevolence of the Holy Spirit, by influencing.

We give this as a specimen of the kind of rhetoric, mistaken for logic, which, as we shall have occasion to show, affected Art as much as it did Theology. In this instance, however, no impression has been left upon Art, which, up to the 14th century, exhibits the person of our Lord—or intends the person it represents to be interpreted as His—as engaged in every act of Creation. The fact that Art attempted to render these acts at all, is a no little curious phase in her history. That Poetry, with her powers over motion, space, and time, should aspire, and chiefly by a close but diffuse paraphrase, to give expression to the monumental utterances of Genesis, was natural, because possible; yet demanding such a combination of the highest qualities as only to have been worthily done once. But that Art should venture upon ground interdicted to her by the very conditions of her nature, speaks of times when Piety was more developed than the agents she employed. Milton, repeating the fiat of the Almighty, 'Let there be light,' adds:—

> And forthwith Light
> Ethereal, first of things, quintessence pure,
> Sprung from the deep; and from her native east
> To journey through the aery gloom began.

Thus conjuring up a mental image of which movement is the great feature.

And again, in the emerging of the dry land, and growth of herb and tree:—

> He scarce had said, when the bare earth, till then
> Desert and bare, unsightly, unadorned,
> Brought forth the tender grass, whose verdure clad
> Her universal face with pleasant green;
> Then herbs of every leaf, that sudden flowered,
> Opening their various colours, and made gay
> Her bosom swelling sweet: and these scarce blown,
> Forth flourished thick the clustering vine.
>
> *Paradise Lost*, book vii.

Here the sense of fragrance is added to that of movement and of continuous action, while chief and foremost in both quotations is the knowledge of that previous moment—indispensable for the expression of this subject. But Art has no previous moment, no power of expressing the Nothing that was, before the Something that is; therefore, strictly speaking, no power of exhibiting an act of Creation. For what she holds up to our view has neither Past nor Future—only one moment of the permanent Present, powerless even to say when itself began. If she gives us light, we have no means of ascertaining that darkness has been before; if she shows us herbs and trees, we know not but that they may have stood there for ages.

It is well such reasonings were postponed till Art, or rather its votaries, grew older, wiser, and prouder. For there are uses, as we shall see, in the mental growth of nations, even for the infancy of Art—that true infancy, we mean, when innocence goes hand in hand with ignorance. Mankind truly seem to have been like children in these matters, asking questions impossible of solution. And Art can only be compared to a good mother, doing her best to answer in some tangible analogous form; remote enough from the truth, yet supplying something intelligible to the eye, and with a certain *naiveté* that has a charm of its own. The farther back we trace these subjects, the more are we struck by that spirit, which disarms a too easy criticism by supposing a kindred child-likeness in the spectator.

But there are acts in this dim beginning of all things, in which Art and Poetry may be said to be equally helpless. For how should either treat that great assertion of almighty power: 'In the beginning God created the heavens and the earth?' accompanied as it is by a context which instantly places a veto on all modes of human conception—'And the earth was without form and void, and darkness was upon the face of the deep.' Before the might of this sentence, which to our infinite apprehension thus sternly dashes out what it has just imaged forth, every language of Art is silent. Formless! empty! dark! to God's eye alone this teemed with all things; to ours it offers nothing. Here Art and Poetry, as we shall see, were driven to much the same devices.

We will first consider those efforts of Art, more or less rude and reverent, which have grouped the earlier days of Creation into one picture, or rather diagram, of which there are various examples. These are chiefly found in early miniatures. The earliest we know is a large drawing of the 10th century in the 'Bible de Noailles' at Paris.¹ This presents a combination of maplike and caligraphic signs, with reminiscences of classic imagery of a rude but intelligent kind. Here we see the heavens, 'cœlum,' divided into four parts, each studded with stars. Below, on one side, showing the French origin of the work, is the word '*Abisme*,' written above a great head, with streams flowing from it, in and on which are already fish and fowl. On the other side is the earth, 'terra,' rude enough

18   Sol and Luna.   ('Bible de Noailles.'   Bibliothèque Impériale, Paris.)

in outline, but already bearing the plant that has seed within itself after its kind. Above, on each side of the heavens, are the full-length figures of Dies and Nox (woodcut, No. 18), supporting the bust-length effigies of Sol and Luna in circles, and holding them with an effort and submissiveness, showing the literal words of Scripture, which are generally the only clue to such representations —'The sun to *rule* the day, and the moon to *rule* the night.'

¹ Bibliothèque Impériale.

Another humble picture, still more diagrammatic in character, but of a higher class of thought, we take from a grand Anglo-Saxon miniature in the British Museum,[1] of about the year 1000. Here no classic imagery helps the artist in his tale, but such acts of the first days as were reducible to form are given, accompanied by those types and symbols relating to the mystery of Creation, and to the agency of the Second Person, which are found scattered in other parts of Scripture. This is a kind of problem, to be worked by the eye of Faith and Scriptural research. God is here in the person of Christ, holding the sphere of the world. His

1. Diagram of Creation. (Anglo-Saxon MS. British Museum.)

head encircled by a fillet, and His hands alone visible—the seats of wisdom and divine activity. The right hand, the source of all life, natural and spiritual, holds the compasses and the scales—both symbols of Almighty power, which aid the eloquence of the inspired writers in expressing acts beyond human description. The figure of the compasses is taken from that magnificent passage in Proverbs (chap. viii.) ending with these words : ' When

[1] Tiberius, C. IV.

He prepared the heavens, I was there: when He set a compass upon the face of the deep.'

The symbol of the scales is derived from Isaiah xl., where the prophet turns suddenly from the tenderness of the good shepherd carrying the lambs, to the omnipotence of Jehovah creating the world, 'who comprehended the earth in a measure, and weighed the mountains in scales, and the hills in a balance.'

Of one of these devices to image forth the mechanism of divine power Milton has also made use, where he describes 'the Omnific Word,' on the wings of cherubim uplifted, riding far into chaos:—

> Then stayed the fervid wheels, and in His hand
> He took the golden compasses, prepar'd
> In God's eternal store, to circumscribe
> This universe, and all created things:
> One foot He center'd, and the other turn'd
> Round through the vast profundity obscure;
> And said, 'Thus far extend, thus far thy bounds,
> This be thy just circumference, O World!'
>
> *Paradise Lost*, book vii.

But this device of the Compasses has not the same propriety in poetry. In the Scripture language it is a figure, in Art a symbol; but here it becomes an actual thing actually used, and, as such, an absurd human implement to place in the grasp of Omnipotence.

To return to the diagram.

The two trumpet-like forms proceeding from the mouth of the Creator are not easily interpreted, unless supposed to typify the double command, 'Let there be a firmament in the midst of the waters, and let it divide the waters from the waters:' at all events, this is the chief intention of this part of the subject; the segment of a circle in the centre being intended for the firmament, between waving lines of water above and below, while the dove, also with the cruciform nimbus, which is frequently seen, and part of the Vesica glory visible around it, standing with flapping wings, shows the Spirit of God which moved on the waters.

If there is much in this diagram which only the pious innocence of early Art could suggest, we see its ignorance, too, in the thumb on the wrong side of the right hand.

There is a representation of the early works of Creation among the ruined frescoes by Cimabue, in the Church of S. Francesco at Assisi. He, in the 13th century, also in part resorted to classic imagery to express the subject.[1]

By the 14th century, however, the literal translation into Art of the words of Scripture gave way, as regards the subject, to those theological speculations, the offspring of the schools, which mixed up astronomy and astrology in their conjectures on things beyond the reach of human reason. According to the schoolmen, the whole frame of Nature consisted of two parts—the one celestial, the other elementary. The celestial was divided into three principal heavens, the empyreal heaven, the crystalline heaven, and the firmament. In the firmament, again, were contained the seven orbits of the seven then known planets—Saturn, Jupiter, Mars, Sol, Venus, Mercury, and Luna. Next to these planets came the spheres, or the four elements—Fire, Air, Water, and Earth. Thus there were nine celestial circles, and four elementary spheres.[2] In these consisted the whole machine of the world, reaching, as St. Bonaventura terms it, 'from the hinge of the highest heaven to the centre of earth.'

Art has reproduced this with perfect fidelity, in what the Italians call 'Il mappamondo,' being a nest of concentric circles, the intention of each indicated by signs or words. Christ sits in the action of Creator, above the great disk, as seen in our etching. We take the illustration from a magnificent miniature of the 14th century in the British Museum,[3] which gives most of these divisions, ending with 'Infernus,' or the Jaws of Hell, in the centre.

A mappamondo, on a gigantic scale, was also seen on the walls of the Campo Santo, now nearly obliterated. This, which is of the 15th century, by Pietro d'Orvieto, shows a variety and extension of the idea, but far less thought and system. First in order in concentric circles are the nine angelic hierarchies. Then come the three heavens: the first, or empyreal, void of all sign; the second, or crystalline, containing the signs of the Zodiac, at that time popular arbiters of human destiny; the third, or firmament, with the indication of stars. Then ensue an arbitrary succession of diminishing circles, ending in the centre with a little landscape of Europe,

---

[1] See Piper. 2te Abtheilung, p. 20.
[2] These theories were familiar to Milton at an early age. See Hymn to the Nativity, stanza xiii.   [3] Arundel, 83.

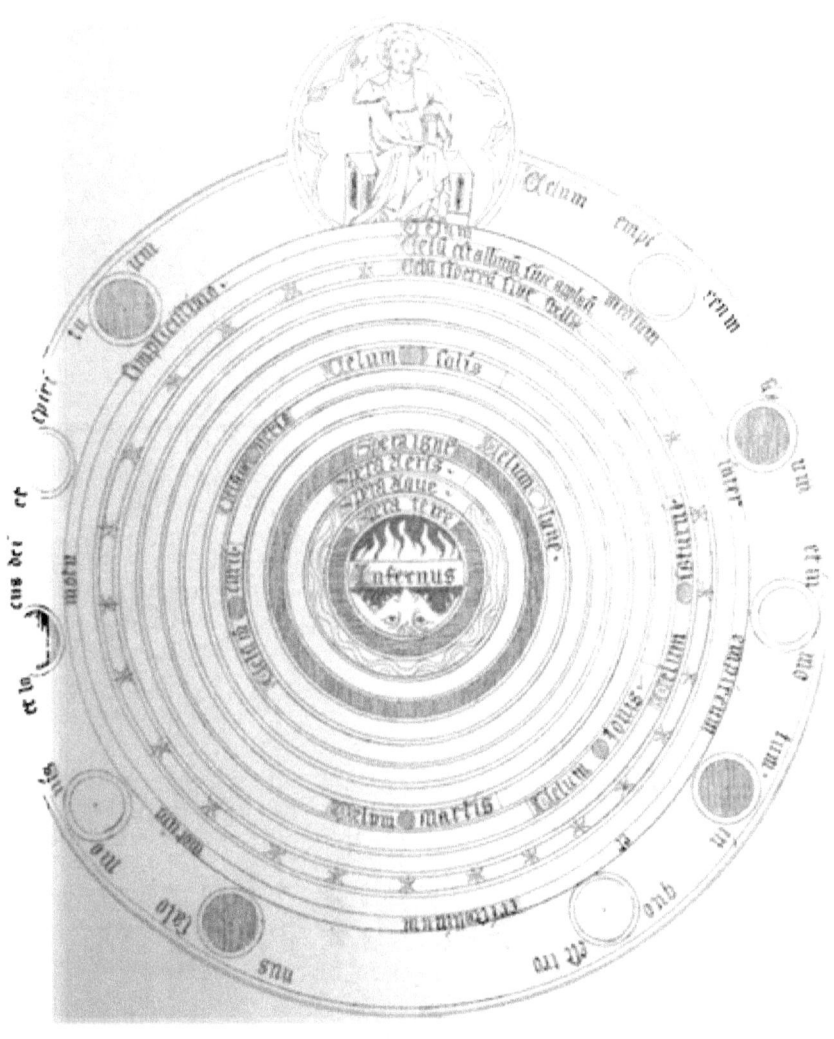

English MS. Early 14th century. B. Museum.

Asia, and Africa. The disk is upheld by a huge figure, from which all signs of the Second Person, or symbolism of Creation, have vanished. Vasari speaks of this as a grand invention—'Un Dio Padre, grande cinque braccia,' with the orbs of the celestial and natural world in His embrace; evidently unconscious how little novelty there was in the idea. To our view such a form is unspeakably inferior to those in which the piety of early Art endeavoured to convey the mysteries of Creation to our eyes.

DAYS OF CREATION.

FOR the representation of the Days of Creation in separate order, we have to look to the serial forms in which these subjects were given, and which, for the causes assigned, abounded only in early Art. One of the most important of these series is found in the mosaics of the small cupola in the right-hand vestibule of St. Mark's Cathedral, Venice, known to have been executed in the 11th century. We have alluded to them in connection with the angels, typified as days, p. 65. These give such quaint and naive forms of illustration, and so completely represent this class of subjects, that we describe them briefly in succession by way of example—the number of subjects in different circles increasing with the expansion of the cupola.

FIRST CIRCLE.

1. Spirit moving on the waters. Dove with glory over a vague space of dark waving lines.
2. The Creator, with cruciform nimbus. An angel with outstretched wings and arms above a red globe: a black globe on the right; each with rays of light from them; the angel being darker on the side next the dark globe. 'And God called the light Day, and the darkness He called Night. And the evening and the morning were the first day' (see woodcut No. 20, over leaf).
3. The Creator with a sceptre. The dark globe in midst of waters; two angels present.
4. The Creator separating waters. The black globe on one side, and on the other a space of waters, divided by a cross-shaped

20   First Day. Division of Light from Darkness. (Mosaics. St. Mark's, Venice.)

causeway of land. 'And God made the firmament, and divided the waters which were under the firmament from the waters which were above the firmament. . . . And the evening and the morning were the second day.'

5. Same figure creating trees and plants—the apple-tree conspicuous. Three angels present. 'And the earth brought forth grass, and herb yielding seed after his kind, and the tree yielding fruit. . . . And the evening and the morning were the third day.'

SECOND CIRCLE.

1. The Creator standing: before Him a globe studded with the sun, moon, and stars. Four angels present. 'And God made two great lights; the greater light to rule the day, and the lesser light to rule the night: He made the stars also. And God set them in the firmament of the heaven. . . . And the evening and the morning were the fourth day.'

2. The Creator with space of water before Him, in which are seen fishes, and birds flying above.

3. The Creator with five angels, each standing on a globe with stars

And God said, 'Let the waters bring forth abundantly the moving creature that hath life, and fowl that may fly above the earth. . . . And the evening and the morning were the fifth day.'

4. The Creator with animals in couples before Him.

5. The Creator with six angels, and a dark formless figure, which He is touching. 'And God made the beast of the earth after his kind. . . . And God said, Let us make man in our image. . . . And the evening and the morning were the sixth day.'

6. The Creator sitting on a throne, three angels on each side of Him, and blessing another angel (the seventh day), who bends

21   Christ blessing Seventh Day.   (Mosaics. St. Mark's, Venice.)

before Him. 'And on the seventh day God ended His work which He had made; and He rested on the seventh day from all His work which He had made. And God blessed the seventh day, and sanctified it.' Thus God is seen in our illustration (No. 21) literally blessing the seventh day under the form of an angel; in whom, it may be observed, the absence of wings—the others being all winged—ingeniously typifies the inactivity of the Sabbath. Thus we see that the nameless designer of these mosaics (11th century), however backward in technical knowledge, was on a par with any period in power of felicitous allusion.

There is another interesting series of the Days of Creation, painted on the walls of the choir of the Cathedral of Monreale, and alluded to p. 63. These belong, possibly, to the beginning of the 13th century. We give a woodcut (No. 22) of the first, which represents the Spirit of God moving on the face of the waters. Here a decided decline from that true simplicity of imagery which dictated the symbol of the balance and the compass is apparent. Christ is seen leaning forward from the circle of heaven, His arms extended. From beneath Him issues the divine ray, or afflatus, along which the Dove is seen descending. This afflatus rests on a great human head in the midst of the agitated waters, whence also they seem partially to proceed. This head, or rather face, may be considered at first sight a relic of that classic impersonation which clothed the elements of nature in human forms. But it is far more probably an attempt to literalise the very words of Genesis—the same in Hebrew, in Greek, and in Latin, as in English—'the *face* of the waters.'[1] This is an instance of an error which we shall see too frequently in mediæval Art, by which no distinction was made between the embodiment of a symbol addressed to the eye, and that of a mere figure of speech, or, as in this instance, of a word of double meaning. The compass and the balance may be considered as emblems of

22 Spirit moving on Face of Waters. (Monreale.)

[1] In the Hebrew Bible and in Symmachus (Greek Bible) the word used both for the 'face of the deep' and the 'face of the waters' is the same figurative term, put instead of surface. In the Septuagint, and in the Vulgate, the word face is applied to the deep, 'super faciem abyssi,' but not in the second passage, which is thus expressed, 'Spiritus Sanctus ferebatur super aquas.'

almighty power, and thus explain themselves; the face in the midst of the waters requires an explanation to put it back again into the words from which it had been falsely translated, and does not suggest an idea to sight even then. For 'the face,' as all know, is only another word for surface, and in no way is intended, even in language, to convey the idea of a human countenance. The fallacy is further seen by the fact and the type being here together, for we have the surface of the waters besides the great face.

23   God resting on the Seventh Day.   (Monreale.)

In this same Monreale series the seventh day is also represented, and with a simplicity and effect derived solely from the literal representation of the text, 'And God rested on the seventh day.' The Creator is seen seated on the globe of heaven, His hands resting on His knees, in the action of one reposing after labour. Around Him are signs of the natural world, plants and trees, while His upcast eyes remind us that it is the Son who has thus executed the will of the well-pleased Father.

As we advance in time, those single acts of Creation naturally became most prominent which were most amenable to direct illustration. In the 13th and 14th centuries the Dove moving over the waters became the sole type of the opening words of Genesis.

Another subject which also obtained the artist's preference was that of the Creation of the Sun and Moon. Classic impersonation, as we have before seen, lent its help here. An example from the 10th century is seen in a miniature in the British Museum,[1] where the Creator appears in the most animated action, as if dancing, while He extends His arms to call into being the two orbs, which are represented as bust-length figures with torches, and drawn, both exactly alike, by red oxen.

The action of the extended arms calling the sun and moon into existence on each hand, is a composition by no means unfrequent in miniatures,[2] and was thus handed down to Michael Angelo, who adopted it in the Sistine Chapel ceiling.[3]

In other acts of Creation the very improvement in Art was to their disadvantage. In the *naïveté* of early helplessness, the figure of Christ standing before, or pointing to a brown hillock, or a space of blue lines, supposed to represent water, had been readily admitted to typify rather than represent the Creator calling the dry land earth, and the gathering together of the waters sea. But when the same subjects are directly represented by a figure in perfect drawing, with a small plot of garden ground, or a little pond equally true to nature, before him—or when, by way of the creation of fishes, the Lord stands by a winding stream, admirably given, holding in His hand a salmon-trout, or pike, which He seems to have just caught rather than created—we feel the age of innocence and ignorance alike to be passed, and the imagination no longer consents to such delusion. One subject which frequently occurs in the 13th and 14th centuries, from the particular meaning given it by ancient commentators, was the work of the third day, when God said, 'Let the earth bring forth grass, the *herb* yielding seed,' &c. This herb was interpreted to

---

[1] Cotton. Claudius, B. IV.

[2] One may be observed in a Bible at Brussels, in the Library of the old Dukes of Burgundy, where almost the same animated action is preserved in the Creator.

[3] The same incident occurs in the mosaics of the cupola in the Baptistery at Florence.

mean exclusively *corn*, as in Genesis iii. 18, 'Thou shalt eat the herb of the field;' and in Psalm civ. 14, 'He causeth the herb to grow for the service of man.' Christ as Creator is therefore seen in these early works with a verdant world around, but especially with a small plot of ripe corn before Him, 'yielding seed' for another harvest, to which His act of benediction is directed.

And this observation applies the more to those earliest acts of Creation, necessarily typified by a repetition of the same forms, where a figure is seen touching, or holding, or pointing to a spherical form, either light or dark, according as it is meant to represent light, or the firmament, or the earth—or half eclipsed, as in the Division of Light from Darkness. That such hieroglyphics, set forth with all the maturer beauties of Art, should have existed late into the 14th century, was owing to no causes of ignorance or innocence in powers of conception, but to a stimulus given to them by the types and interpretations of the later schoolmen. To them the whole outward creation served but as a commentary on the one sole text, 'the Church.' In a French Bible to which we have often alluded, the distant tide of the Reformation is heard swelling in the very anxiety here shown to proclaim the stability of the Roman Church, and the excellence of the monastic orders. Carrying on the fanciful connection between light and darkness and good and bad angels, the monkish commentators drive their speculations beyond all limits of moral tension. The firmament in the midst of the waters is the Church firm among dangers; the division of the waters is 'la dissévrance des bons et des mauvais.' Again, the appearance of the dry ground is also the Church rejoicing in her stability. The creation of birds, by an extraordinary stretch of fancy, represents those who withdraw into a life of contemplation, and think 'aux biens du ciel;' that of trees, the Christians who bear fruit; while the sun, the moon, and the stars do duty as emblems, the first, of the great prelates, the second, of the monks, and the third, of the common people. It is incredible what immense labour and time have been bestowed in illustrating such ideas as these by innumerable finely-executed miniatures, and explaining them by a corresponding amount of most delicate caligraphy—incessant repetition being inseparable from both.

We now turn to Art proper, which presents but few instances of these subjects. As the development of its powers gradually outstripped the short-hand process of early efforts, the acts of the first days, except in such cases as we have just instanced, were gradually omitted. The curious sculpture on the west front of the cathedral at Orvieto, executed, it is supposed, by followers of the Pisani, is perhaps the most important series of the Days of Creation existing. Here, in some measure doubtless owing to the conditions of sculpture, which does not admit of subjects requiring colour, the series commences with the Creation of Fishes and Birds on the fifth day (see woodcut, No. 24).

24   Creation of Fishes and Birds.   (Orvieto.)

Here the Creator is seen attended by two angels, who accompany Him throughout, and seem, by their expression and actions, intended to suggest the emotions proper to the scene. Thus they hover behind Christ as He stands on the brink of a stream blessing the fish who are disporting in it, while the birds stand on the opposite cliff in a stiff row, as if awaiting the divine mandate. In this scene the eagle and the goose are easily recognisable; while some songster of the grove alights with outspread wings on a bush close by, and in the distance a hawk stands by itself.

Our next woodcut (No. 25) gives the sixth day. Here the same figure, attended by the two angels in gestures of admiration, is seen blessing the animals, who stand in two files before Him. In front are the smaller quadrupeds—the goat, the pig, and two species of long-haired sheep, which remind us of similar fancy animals, doubtless then cultivated in Italy, which appear in pictures by old masters.[1] Behind them are the ox, the horse, and, farther from us, the lion and the camel. A dog, that dumb friend of man, is seen beneath the ox, his well-known companion.

It would be difficult to point out another series of these subjects, of any importance, in the 15th century, and in the 16th, the connection between the days of Creation and the History of Christ, as

Creation of Animals. (Orvieto.)

seen in Art, vanishes altogether. In the Sistine ceiling the true theological idea is entirely repudiated. Though one of the last of painters in adhering to the schemes of traditional Art, as in the introduction of the Sibyls and Prophets in the Creation, and of the sun and the moon at the Crucifixion, yet from Michael Angelo we trace the great starting-point of departure in respect of Christian doctrine and feeling. The Creator is here the Author of Life, the Ancient of Days, the vague Jove-like impersonation of the First Cause—in short, that forbidden thing in Christian Art which

[1] One in Mantegna's Triumphs at Hampton Court; another in the Basaiti, No. 599, in the National Gallery.

Italians have since that time familiarly denominated the 'Padre Eterno.' Grandeur of forms and broadness of intention here take the place of those quaint literal renderings, which are inexplicable without the words of Scripture, but so fertile with them. In the proud majority of Art a point had been reached where the two were utterly incompatible. Whether Michael Angelo has been most right or most wrong in his conception will probably never be decided. A child, with the Bible in its hand, can read those early forms; rhapsodists have so widely differed as to the great Florentine's intentions as to bequeath to us the unsettled question whether one of the most remarkable figures in these acts of Creation is intended for the figure of the Deity or for that of Chaos.[1]

Raphael, in his Vatican Loggie, has followed the same taste, vitiated, whatever the Art, as regards religious truth. An old man with flowing beard and scarf, flying above the upper portion of a globe, on which great trees are growing, or holding a conventional sun and moon in each hand, suggests neither fact nor type, nor any other idea.

Yet the greatest of painters is vindicated in one of these series— the Creation of Light—where the powers of imagination and the ripe resources of Art leave the lisping literalities of early limners far behind. Here the Almighty is seen rending like a thunderbolt the thick shroud of fiery clouds (see woodcut, No. 26), letting in that light under which His works were to spring into life. Not that this really approaches a whit the nearer to the revealed fact. To the unassisted reading of the eye it tells no especial tale; it may just as well be interpreted as the Almighty amid clouds and fire and thick darkness on the top of Sinai, or as an episode in the Battle of the Giants. It leaves, however, a grand image in the sense of Art on the eye, and criticism on other points is silenced.

Not so with the Creation of the Animals, the fourth subject in the Loggie. Here we are reminded that the formality of the

---

[1] Some writers suppose that the back view of a figure in the same compartment of the Creation of Sun and Moon, speeding away with a magnificent velocity, is intended for the Almighty hurrying to create the dry land. Quatremère de Quincy calls it 'le Père éternel chassant le génie du Chaos.' We entirely agree with him, for the position and action, however grand, are strangely derogatory if applied to the Deity Himself.

Creation of Light. (Raphael.)

Orvieto sculpture, with the animals standing in a row, awaiting, as it were, the power of moving, is far more impressive than Raphael's conception of the horse and tiger with their heads just emerging from the ground, and the rest of their bodies still buried beneath the sod.

As single pictures, few subjects from the Days of Creation can be quoted, except in the case of those masters who selected the Creation of Animals as a scope for their particular excellence. Jean Breughel is conspicuous here, with his landscape teeming with animal life in every form. Little interest beyond the beauty of the execution is excited, however, by these large Happy Families, who eye each other with a suspicious blandness, not altogether unsuggestive of the approaching rupture.

The Creation of Adam.

Ital. La Creazione d' Adamo.   *Fr.* La Création d'Adam.
Germ. Die Erschaffung Adam's.

THE account of the creation of the world, and of its principal features and inhabitants, is given in the Book of Genesis with that brevity and strength which belongs to things at once true and incomprehensible. The narrative stalks on with a mighty tread, bearing down all cavil from religious minds. At every step new orders of creation appear; each verse unfolds a fresh kingdom of nature. Nevertheless, the crowning work, of which it most concerns us to know, receives the due preponderance of divine description. With instinctive propriety of design, the creation of mankind, and of their right of possession over all things hitherto made, is given as the last act of Omnipotence in the general relation of the six days' doings.

'And God said, Let us make man in our image, after our likeness: and let them have dominion over the fish of the sea, and over the fowl of the air, and over the cattle, and over all the earth, and over every creeping thing that creepeth upon the earth. So God created man in His own image, in the image of God created He him; male and female created He them.' Then, God having pronounced all 'very good,' and having rested and blessed the seventh day, the sacred narrative returns to a separate and fuller consideration of the mode in which this image of God was physically fashioned and spiritually vivified—'And the Lord God formed man of the dust of the ground, and breathed into his nostrils the breath of life; and man became a living soul.' After which it briefly mentions the garden to which he was taken, the instructions and warnings for his guidance which he received, and the first proof of intellectual endowment—viz., the naming of animals—which he exercised. Thus, in the first instance, we learn the mere fact of the creation of the race for which all previous acts had been preparatory, and in the second, the particular description of the formation of the man Adam—of his destiny, responsibility, and mental powers, while yet alone upon the earth.

The origin of Adam, and his history during the time preceding Eve's creation, have been the fertile source of Rabbinical fables. There is no need to wonder at the inventions concerning the cosmogony of the world handed down by other ancient nations, though believed to be all derived from the Hebrew Scriptures, when we see how the Jews themselves made the Word of God void through their traditions. Had the Old Testament been hidden from our knowledge, there is no account of the origin of our race which would have surpassed in wicked absurdities that invented by the chosen people. These were rendered the more profane by the texts of Scripture (as in later speculations) wrested to give them a false authority. We need give but a few specimens of the manner in which they sought to fill up the reticence of Scripture. Nothing being said in revelation of Adam's stature, this became the object of fabulous assertion. God is stated in their writings to have made Adam a rude mass of earth, so enormous that he touched the firmament, and reached from East to West; for the Psalmist says, 'The mighty God, even the Lord, hath spoken, and called the *earth* from the rising of the sun unto the going down thereof' (Ps. l. 1). Again, that this mass of earth was shapeless and unformed; for 'Thine eyes did see my substance, yet being unperfect' (Ps. cxxxix. 16). That being thus enormous and shapeless, he was propped up by God; for 'underneath are the everlasting arms' (Deut. xxxiii. 27). That Adam, thus formed, had, according to some, two bodies; for 'Thou hast beset me behind and before' (Ps. cxxxix. 5). Further, that the angels, taking fright at this colossus, exclaimed that God had made two powers in the world. Whereupon the Creator laid His hand on Adam's head, and diminished him by 1000 cubits: 'And laid Thine hand upon me.' The Jewish fabulists further curtailed the dimensions of Adam, though leaving him still a stature of ninety feet; for why else, they ask, should God have feared that he would put out his hand and take of the tree of life?[1]

[1] This idea of Adam's size was shared by the Mahometans, who have followed otherwise, in general outline, the Scripture account of the father of mankind, and regard Adam as a prophet. They describe him to have strided at one step from a reef of rock

To turn from these repugnant inventions to speculations of a more pardonable nature.

The name of Adam had various significations. According to the Arabians and Ethiopians, the name conveyed the meaning of perfection and beauty; in confirmation of which his face is supposed to have shone in Paradise with the same celestial light, derived from converse with God, which Moses veiled from the Jews on his descent from Mount Sinai. In Hebrew, however, the name Adam signifies 'taken out of red earth.' Hence in great measure, doubtless, the idea which generally prevailed, that Adam was created in the fields near Damascus, remarkable for the red colour and plastic nature of their clay soil.

To Adam, as in later times to Cadmus, was attributed the invention of letters, since the names of the animals, they argue, would have been lost to mankind without the proper signs by which to distinguish them. He is also supposed to have left to his offspring a book upon 'the Divinity,' containing all that God taught and said to him in the garden; and also, later, with sad propriety, as the fruit of his experience in the labours of husbandry, to have written a work on the tillage of the earth. The 92nd Psalm, or song for the Sabbath-day, 'It is a good thing to give thanks unto the Lord,' is also attributed to him, since Adam being created on the sixth day, kept the first Sabbath with his Maker. Further, he is stated to have instituted certain fasts and feasts in the Jewish calendar; for when, in the first year of his expulsion, he began to see the days shorten, he ordained a three days' fast, and put on sackcloth, attributing this sad change in nature to his sin; but when, after the winter solstice was past, he observed that the light was returning, he gave thanks to God by ordaining a feast of eight days in His praise.

The fact of Adam's repentance, though nowhere told, is everywhere implied in the scheme of our salvation, since it cannot be conceived that the promise should have been given to obdurate hearts, or that without repentance there should be any remission of sins. The Christian Church therefore admits it; the Church of

in the Pacific to the mountain called Adam's Peak, in Ceylon, where the print of his foot, varying according to different writers from a yard and a half to eight and a half spans long, is still a place of Singalese pilgrimage.

the East places the father of mankind in the calendar of the saints; and the Latin Church, without having canonised him, believes, as we shall have occasion to show, in the delivery of Adam and Eve, along with the other patriarchs and saints of God, from Limbus, by the descent of Christ into hell.

By the Rabbins the particular mode of Adam's repentance is described, namely, that he stood up to his neck in the Ganges—interpreted as the river Gihon of Paradise—like a modern Fakir, for the space of three weeks.

Later Art shows traces of a belief in Adam's immediate translation. In the Bedford Missal, 1430, there is a magnificent plate, an epitome of the life of Adam, where he is seen dead outside the gate of Eden, and borne upwards by Christ and angels.

The Creation of Adam supplied a more intelligible subject for Art than those of the previous acts. We trace the representation back to a period still influenced by classic feeling. At first the artist, piously anxious to follow step by step the words of Scripture, with no thought of his own claims, divided the Creation of Man into two scenes. First we see the inert clay, shaped but not animated, lying flat on the ground, with Christ seen in a glory above, as in an early Greek ivory.[1] Or it is standing, with the Creator in the act of touching it, as in the mosaics before mentioned in St. Mark's. Even in the 13th or beginning of the 14th century, the lifeless figure still heads the series of the Creation, lying gracefully on the ground, as in the Orvieto sculpture. Or the figure is placed upright, as in the same series (woodcut, No. 27), with the

27   Creation of Adam.

Creator manipulating it with sculptor-like energy; or, again, held like a doll, stiff and lifeless, in the arms of Christ, as in Mr. Holford's MS.

---

[1] D'Agincourt. Scultura, pl. xii.

In the second act the infusion of the living soul is seen. In the mosaics of St. Mark's this is curiously and beautifully given, with the help of classic reminiscence, by a little spirit with butterfly wings—the true Psyche — which flies up to Adam's face, while the Creator stands by (woodcut, No. 28). Or again, in the series at Monreale, the Lord sits on the heavens, with Adam before Him, while a long stream of breath from the Creator's lips— literally rendering the words of Scripture — breathes 'into his nostrils the breath of life' (woodcut, No. 29).

28   The Living Soul.
(Mosaics. St. Mark's, Venice.)

Soon these two separate acts were combined in one of more general character. In a French Bible the Trinity all appear assisting in the work of creation, and man rises from the ground uplifted by the hands of the Father and Son, while the Dove hovers above him. This design is one of those few instances in which an artist has ventured out of the beaten track, and grasped, however quaintly, the capacities of his subject.

29   The Breath of Life. (Monreale.)

In Ghiberti's celebrated bronze doors of the Baptistery at Florence, Adam is just about to rise from the ground (woodcut, No. 30). Animal and spiritual life are both there, for the Creator is touching him with one hand,

30. Creation of Adam. (Ghiberti. Bronze doors, Florence.)

and blessing him with the other. We see here whence Michael Angelo, with those gates constantly before him, took the figure of his Adam in the Sistine ceiling.

ADAM IN THE GARDEN OF EDEN.

THE next step is the removal to that paradise called in Latin *locus voluptatis* or *deliciarum;* in old French, *le lieu des délices:* 'And the Lord God planted a garden eastward in Eden; and there He put the man whom He had formed.' The mode of transition is not attempted in Art. Milton vindicates it in poetry, where Adam describes his first recollections to the seraph :—

> One came, methought, of shape divine,
> And said, 'Thy mansion wants thee, Adam; rise.'
> . . . .
> So saying, by the hand He took me rais'd,
> And over fields and water, as in air
> Smooth gliding without step, last led me up
> A woody mountain. *Paradise Lost*, book viii.

The early painter contents himself with indicating Paradise by giving such a landscape around the man as his primitive powers permitted. Here we see, in miniatures and mosaics, stiff sprigs of plants with star-shaped flowers, and formal trees, yet laden with fruit—the date-palm, recognised in Art of eastern origin—and an attempt, as in the mosaics of St. Mark's, at something which represents the fatal apple-tree. 'And the Lord God took the man, and put him into the Garden of Eden to dress it and to keep it.' In the overstrained types of the scholastic times, which alternately interpreted metaphorical things literally, and literal things metaphorically, a naïve embodiment is given by Art to the latter part of this sentence. We see here (woodcut, No. 31) Adam standing in Paradise, Christ before him, giving him a spade and keys; and only by returning to the literal text can we understand the meaning of these implements—the spade to dress the garden and the key to keep it.

31 Christ giving Adam Spade and Keys.
(Bibliothèque Impériale, Paris.)

'Of every tree of the garden thou mayest freely eat: But of the tree of the knowledge of good and evil, thou shalt not eat of it: for in the day that thou eatest thereof thou shalt surely die.' This injunction is seldom given in Art. The French Bible of the end of the 13th century, already mentioned, one in which the pictorial steps are unusually abundant and close, gives it. The Creator is pointing to the apple-tree, while Adam's action is peculiarly that of asseveration.

'And out of the ground the Lord God formed every beast of the field, and every fowl of the air; and brought them unto Adam to see what he would call them: and whatsoever Adam called every living creature, that was the name thereof.' This subject, Adam standing with the animals in couples before him, is scarcely seen but in very diffuse series in later illustrated Bibles. It is given also by Bloemart.

The Sleep of Adam and the Creation of Eve.

Ital. Il Sonno d'Adamo e la Creazione d'Eva. *Fr.* Le Sommeil d'Adam et la Création d'Ève.
Germ. Adam's Schlaf, und die Erschaffung Eva's.

BOTH these events, according to the patristic writers, were replete with typical meaning. 'And the Lord God caused a deep sleep to fall upon Adam, and he slept: and He took one of his ribs, and closed up the flesh instead thereof; And the rib, which the Lord God had taken from man, made He a woman, and brought her unto the man' (Gen. ii. 21, 22).

While Adam slept, his side was opened, and Eve was thence formed. This signified that, while the second Adam hung on the Cross, His side was pierced, and the sacraments flowed therefrom. Thus Eve became a sacred figure in Christian Art, as the type of the Church. The greater importance, however, of her creation, and the conspicuous and frequent place it finds in all cycles, is owing to her being, in the sense of Christ's deriving His human nature from woman only, the great progenitrix of the Messiah. It was *her* seed that was to bruise the serpent's head.

[A. J.—Hence it is that Michael Angelo made the Creation of Eve the central subject on the ceiling in the Sistine Chapel. He had the good taste to suggest, and yet avoid, that literal rendering of the biblical story which in the ruder representations borders on the grotesque, and which Milton, with all his pomp of words, could scarcely idealise:—

> The rib he formed and fashion'd with his hands:
> Under his forming hands a creature grew,
> Man-like, but different sex. *Paradise Lost*, book viii.

A. J.]   A typical and prophetic meaning is also applied to the words of Adam, on his waking from slumber: 'This is now bone of my bones, and flesh of my flesh; she shall be called Woman, because she was taken out of Man. Therefore shall a man leave his father and his mother, and shall cleave unto his wife' (Gen. ii. 23, 24).]

This last declaration being interpreted that Christ, the Man, should leave His Heavenly Father, abjure his Mother the Synagogue, and cleave to his Spouse the Church.[1] Further, to each—

52.   Extracting Adam's Rib.   (Orvieto.)

to Adam and to Christ—were applied the words of the Psalmist: 'I laid me down and slept; I awakened: for the Lord sustained me.' St. Jerome and others believed that the sleep of Adam was a state of ecstasy sent by God, during which he was insensible to pain.

Later writers on the Creation of Eve have been more personal and speculative in their disquisitions. Many have treated our first mother with a certain deference, dwelling on her supposed advantages over Adam. For Eve, it was remarked, was formed from nobler materials than the man; she being made from his flesh and blood, and he from the dust of the earth. In the locality of her

[1] Bede. Liber de sex dierum creatione, p. 101.

creation, too, greater honour was discerned; for she was made within the garden of Eden, he without it. Further, in the part of Adam's body whence she was derived, a favourable intention towards her was seen; for she was not taken from his foot, lest he should despise her—nor from his head, lest she should rule over him—but from his side, and level with his heart, bespeaking the social equality of the companion thus given to man.

The literal rendering of the extraction of the rib from the sleeping Adam was confined to an early period of Art. This subject appears in the 10th century. In the 'Bible de Noailles,' Adam is seen lying asleep, his hand upon his head, attired in a long blue embroidered robe. Christ bends over him, with the rib already in His hand. This act is seen but seldom, and appears probably for the last time in the Orvieto sculpture (woodcut, No. 32), where Adam lies in a favourite position, and the Creator is performing the operation with a kind of surgical intensity.

Quaint, however, as is this literal version of the text, it is ill replaced by a form of conception which became stereotyped in Art. It would seem that the anxiety to impress the creation of woman on the mind in some very conspicuous form, and especially in one totally distinct from the creation of man, had diverted attention—and for Art most unfortunately so—from the real text. The abstraction of a rib from Adam might be ill fitted for pictorial exhibition; but that of Eve herself rising, or rather—as Art has no power of expressing movement—protruding midway from Adam's side, is an unsightly and monstrous image, and one for which the text of Genesis gives no kind of authority. For 'the rib, which the Lord God had taken from man, made He a woman.' The creation of Eve, therefore, was as much the work of the hand of God, whether taken metaphorically or actually, as that of Adam himself. Nor is Adam's presence even implied; for God 'brought her' unto him. In a few instances, the early artist has reverently followed the words of Genesis. In the mosaics of the Creation in St. Mark's, Venice, Adam lies sleeping in one compartment, the Creator merely touching his side; in the next, Eve rises beneath her Maker's hand —Adam not present; in the third, she is brought unto him. These works are rude; but their truthful simplicity is at once more suggestive and more picturesque. But these exceptions are solitary.

33   Creation of Eve.   (Orvieto.)

In almost every series of the Creation, whatever the form of Art, the Creation of Eve is sure to be represented under the image of a fabulous animal, with double head, chest, and arms, and the rest of the person single. As taste and feeling in Art improved, the efforts of artists may be seen endeavouring to disguise this frightful convention, which none of them entirely broke through. Sometimes the arm of Adam is so placed as to hide the aperture in his side, leaving the spectator to imagine that Eve is kneeling or standing on lower ground beside him. Gradually, also, she appears more and more extricated from her uncomfortable abode. In the Orvieto sculpture (see woodcut, No. 33), nothing more than her feet and ancles still invade Adam's side. But for this relic of an unsightly convention, this gives a beautiful rendering of the creation of woman—as her figure, just wakening into life under the touch and benediction of the Lord, rests gracefully on an adjacent rock.

Ghiberti, in his bronze doors, so nearly discarded this false idea as to leave the fancy undisturbed, while he satisfied that mere conventional eye of the Church, which rested in some instances so heavily upon Art. For the figure of Eve (woodcut, No. 34) floating upwards, upborne and encircled by rapturous angels, and turning with blissful adoration to her Maker, may be conceived either to have just risen from Adam's side, or simply to have been here first called into being. Nor is the figure of Adam in any way wanted to tell

34   Creation of Eve. (Ghiberti. Bronze doors, Florence.)

the tale. This is no Pagan goddess or nymph—no Venus rising from the sea, supported by the Loves and Graces—but the creature given by God as meet for man, and hailed by angels as the last

VOL. I.   O

refinement of Omnipotence—fair, holy, happy woman, before that curse of which she bears so large a share. There were few creations of Eve executed between the date of Ghiberti's doors and that of the Sistine ceiling, but, beautiful as is Michael Angelo's Eve, he has returned to the old convention. She is stepping out of Adam with an expression like St. Margaret from the monster's jaws, and seems rather to be thanking the *Padre Eterno* for her deliverance than for her creation.

As a rule, it may be said that the attitude of adoration is the first act of consciousness which Art has rightfully bestowed on the mother of mankind. Like a flower turning to the sun, she rises from the ground turning to her Maker—life and adoration simultaneously awaking—and at once asserts the independent responsibility of her being. Here the painter is morally and theologically superior to the poet, who, in oft-quoted lines, lays down the somewhat Mahometan doctrine, that Eve had no God but through Adam:—

> He for God only, she for God in him.

And again, Eve to Adam:—

> My author and disposer . . . . .
> God is thy law, thou mine.

THE MARRIAGE OF ADAM AND EVE.

MANY and close are the steps of Art in this history of mankind.

The moment when the Creator brings the woman to the man—'And He brought her unto Adam'—is seen in St. Mark's mosaics and other early forms. But it is not till the 14th and 15th centuries, and chiefly in the various editions of the 'Speculum Salvationis,' that we find the subject rendered like the ceremony of marriage—Christ between the two, uniting their hands. We take our illustration from a Speculum Salvationis, reproduced by Mr. J. Ph. Berjeau. It is evident that the monastic poet, who supplied the quaint Latin rhymes of this Speculum, shut his eyes very determinately to the nature of this subject, under which is the title, 'Of every tree in the garden thou mayest freely eat,' &c.—a sentence which was addressed, literally taken, to man only, and before the creation of woman. It is curious to observe how the ruminations of the convent brought out the conviction of the wickedness of the fair sex. The early Fathers were mirrors

35   Marriage of Adam and Eve.

of chivalry compared to the monks, who, in their rancour against the sour grapes, seem to have considered the serpent a superfluous personage in the sad drama of man's fall. A long list of the sorrows and evils which would never have happened but for the female enemy of souls, winds up thus pathetically :—

>Your ears would never have become thick,
>Nor your eyes dim,
>Nor your feet lame,
>Nor your teeth loose.[1]

---

[1] Speculum Salvationis.

[*A. J.*—There is an extraordinary composition by Duvet, 1485–1550, a French artist, who worked at the same time with Michael Angelo and Raphael, and engraved his own designs. It represents the Marriage of Adam and Eve. In the midst stands the Creator as High Priest, and joins their hands. Each of them holds a branch of the tree of life, and the tree of knowledge bends over them, its boughs laden with fruit. The whole celestial hierarchy, standing and hovering round in countless numbers, witness the union, but behind Eve is seen the serpent, looking and watching.]

Eve Listening to the Serpent.

This is not frequent, though of early date, occurring in the mosaics of St. Mark's, and wherever the series assumes a more than usually diffuse form.

It has been conjectured that the serpent appeared in so beautiful a form that Eve took it for an angel, and listened to it as a heavenly messenger. This idea receives further colour from the fact that the name 'seraphim' is given to the serpents who tormented the Israelites in the desert (Num. xxi.) St. Paul also notes that 'Satan is transformed into an angel of light;' in the same chapter (2 Cor. xi. 3, 14) in which he says, 'The serpent beguiled Eve by his subtlety.'[1] Art, however, knew better than to adopt this version, her conditions allowing of no double sense or ambiguity to the eye. Nevertheless, the serpent sometimes assumes a different figure in this subject from that seen when the Fall has been accomplished, being as yet free from the sentence which, as the scholastic writers term it, prostrated it on the ground. To this may be ascribed the upright position and fabulous structure occasionally given to the animal, which unites to its own snakelike body the wings and legs of a bird and the head of a woman. For Lucifer, according to Bede, chose the species of a serpent which had a female head, because 'like are attracted to like.' Sometimes the head is crowned, in allusion to

---

[1] Scott's Bible. Notes to Genesis iii.

Lucifer having been the crowned seraph. We here see the conversation passing between woman and her tempter: 'Yea, hath God said, Ye shall not eat of every tree of the garden?' while the woman, as if defending her Maker, answers: 'We *may* eat of the fruit of the trees of the garden: But of the fruit of the tree which is in the midst of the garden, God hath said, Ye shall not eat of it, neither shall ye touch it, lest ye die.' The woman, it

36   Eve listening to Serpent.

may be observed, is made to recapitulate both the bounty that gave every gift but one and the command which related to that one; thus taking from herself, as Bede argues, all excuse of want of comprehension of God's will, and condemning herself in her own words.

The Fall.

Ital. Il Peccare d' Adamo e d' Eva.   *Fr.* La Désobéissance d'Adam et d'Ève.
Germ. Der Sündenfall.

THE colloquy between Eve and her tempter was not long. It is enough that woman first, and man second, listened, touched, and ate. We are spared as far as possible the misery of dwelling upon second causes. The sacred writer knew that all that concerned us to hear was that man fell by disobedience. There was no need to cucumber that fact with extraneous argument. 'She took of the fruit thereof and did eat; and gave also unto her husband with her, and he did eat' (Gen. iii. 6). Let us throw no stones at the guilty couple, henceforth seen in Art under such mournful aspect. We know all along what their eyes were then only first opened to know, viz., that any Adam or Eve, under whatever circumstances, real or metaphorical, the event may be viewed, would have done the same. Here, therefore, beneath that fatal tree, where both have the forbidden fruit in their grasp, our true relationship to the first man and woman begins. We have no part in them while in the garden of innocence and happiness.

Here, too, begins the personal relation of Christ to man. Hitherto He has been the Creator only; now the eye of Faith sees a nearer bond in that cruciform nimbus, or in the other signs which in Art distinguish the Redeemer. With the fault of Man, therefore, commences that Christian structure which terminates in the sacrifice of God. As poles of the same argument, the Fall and the Atonement stand, in Theology and Art, in the relation of cause and effect.

There is no mistaking this subject in early Art. It is as distinct to the eye as its great correlative the Crucifixion. The tree in the centre, the serpent twined round the stem, and the yet unclad figure on each side.

[*A. J.*—That this original type was borrowed from the antique, l.] cannot be doubted by those who have compared the subject of the tree of the Hesperides guarded by the dragon (which has always the form of the snake) with that of the Fall as it exists on the early Christian monuments; and if, as in some examples, one of the Hesperides gives the apple to Hercules, the resemblance is all but complete. This is only one of the instances in which the earliest Christians, who in general avoided all *direct* representation of sacred things, borrowed a classical and familiar image in which to clothe a religious idea.

The earliest known is on the tomb of Junius Bassus (A.D. 359), where the Fall and the punishment are figured together. We have the tree, the tortuous serpent. Adam and Eve on each side, with looks averted from each other, as conscious of sin, clothed with the fig-leaf, and condemned to labour as the condition of earthly life. Adam with the wheatsheaf, for he was to till the ground, and Eve with the lamb, whose fleece she was to spin (see etching, p. 13). This division and communion of labour, the constant tradition with regard to the primogenial pair is expressed differently in another sarcophagus (woodcut, No. 37). Our Lord stands in the midst, and with one hand presents the wheatsheaf to Adam, and with the other the lamb to Eve. Some-

37 Christ giving Adam Wheatsheaf and Eve Lamb. (Sarcophagus.)

times there is no serpent, and sometimes the serpent presents the apple to Eve, and in one or two instances a third figure is introduced, as uttering the primeval curse.]

But whether grouped or single, the same simplicity of composition is remarked in sculpture and miniatures for centuries—the woman generally taking the apple from the serpent, the man already lifting it to his lips. It would seem as if the early artists regarded our first mother with peculiar tenderness. It is the serpent on whom they make the first act of transgression to rest. He it is who has invariably plucked the fruit and is giving it to Eve, while Adam is often plucking it for himself, as in the group of sculpture at the corner of the Ducal Palace, Venice. In this respect they only supplied what they doubtless conceived to be understood in the narrative; for it is not said that Eve plucked, but that 'she took of the fruit.' On the bronze doors of S. Zeno at Verona, the serpent is even reaching out its head with an apple in its jaws to Adam, who seems to retreat before it.

In early times the form of the serpent in no way departs from its true zoological character. It is simply a slender snake twined in few and loose coils round the tree, and with its head bending gracefully over a branch. As Art matured, more dramatic variety was bestowed upon the figures of Adam and Eve, and less truth on that of the serpent. As early as the 13th century it is seen with a female head, according to the notion of Bede (see p. 101), then revived in scholastic theology, and which, protruded on a long neck, is a very repulsive figure. There are instances, also, where the serpent has two female heads and two necks, and presents an apple to Adam and Eve at the same time.[1] As early as this, too, we see it with a woman's arms and bust in addition, though, with the fine instinct that often presided over obscure miniatures, it retains even in these portions the flexible and insidious character of the animal.

In all important works from the 13th century the female head is adopted—in the sculpture at Orvieto, in Ghiberti's doors, and in the fresco of the Fall, by Pietro d'Orvieto, in the Campo Santo, Pisa. Michael Angelo, in the 16th century, always wedded to tradition in invention, has returned to the bust and arms of the woman on the serpent's body. He has sacrificed, however, the reptile character, and his serpent, thus transformed, looks more like a frantic sea-nymph, very much out of her element in an apple-tree. Raphael has two versions of the Fall—in the series of the Loggie and in Marc Antonio's engraving. In both, his instinctive feeling for beauty has hidden by a bough the connection between the serpent's body and the lovely sorceress-looking female head (woodcut, No. 38).

It is interesting, too, to trace the increasing expression and variety in the figures of Adam and Eve. In Ghiberti the woman

[1] Annales Archéologiques, vol. i. p. 74.

THE FALL.

28   The Fall.   (Raphael.)

is eagerly giving the apple to Adam, who, while he takes it in one hand, holds up the other as if in deprecation.

> Nor Eve to iterate
> Her former trespass feared.

For she is reaching up her arm to pluck more from the tree, while the woman-headed serpent, turned to her, seems to hiss, rather than speak, words of encouragement.

Michael Angelo throws no responsibility on Eve. She is reclining on the ground, and there receives negligently an apple from the outstretched arm of the woman-serpent. But Adam needs no persuasion. With both hands on a stout bough above his head, he seems to be in the act of climbing the tree itself.

In the engraving by Marc Antonio from Raphael, the figure of Eve is beautiful; but the story does not tell itself. The fruit should have been in her hand, not in Adam's, who has more the air of offering it to her than of having just taken it from her.

[*A. J.*—In the story of the temptation of our first parents, given in Genesis iii., it should be borne in mind that the relation between the man and the woman somewhat reverses the accepted conditions and characteristics of sex. Eve falls through ambition and the desire of knowledge—

> Knowledge of good, bought dear by knowing ill.

There is nothing in Scripture of that flattery and blandishment which Milton puts into the speech of the Tempter:—

> Empress of this fair world, resplendent Eve.

But Adam falls through weakness, through affection for his wife, or by persuasion, and therefore Eve is to be made as alluring as possible, as the best excuse for Adam.]

The subject was not omitted in Northern schools. The single figures of Adam and Eve[1] form appropriately the two extreme wings of the upper part of Jan van Eyck's picture of the Adoration of the Lamb.

Lucas Cranach was the Protestant painter who especially made our first parents his subject. The accompanying woodcut (No. 39) is from the picture in the Uffizj at Florence. There is something serio-comic in the way in which Adam scratches his head, while he views the fruit with looks in which the sin is already accomplished. Here and there a later painter has transformed the Fall from a type of human disobedience into a mere victory by persuasive woman over feeble man—as in Cignani's picture in the Dresden Gallery—but, upon the whole, painters have been too just to feign anything more than a very slight show of resistance on Adam's part.

In representations of the Fall we occasionally see the old symbol of the rivers of Paradise revived. In the Campo Santo, a fountain or cistern of waters with four streams from it, placed behind the tree, represents the river in the garden, which 'was parted,

---

[1] Now in the Museum at Brussels. No one who sees these figures will complain of the Canons of St. Bavon for having shut them up for centuries.

THE FALL.

59   The Temptation. (Lucas Cranach.)

and became into four heads.' The first river, called Pison, was believed by ancient writers to be the Ganges; the second, called *Gihon*, to be the Nile; the third, Hiddekel, to be the Tigris. The fourth was the Euphrates.

We must now pass over the tree itself. This, by general consent, has been called the apple-tree, though on no further authority from Scripture than the generic term for all fruit, the word 'pomum.' In the same sense the word 'apple' is used in various texts in the Song of Solomon; as, for instance, 'Comfort me with apples' (ii. 5). In the Latin schools of Art the apple, as the fruit producing the largest variety of the same species, was appropriately selected to represent the idea of fruit *par excellence*. In Greek Art, from its great abundance, or from the idea that Adam and Eve had plucked leaves from the same tree as that of which they ate, the fig is chosen. In Italy, too, the fig is occasionally seen, and the orange-tree is also exceptionally common to East and West. We must not forget, too, that the pomegranate, so often seen in the hand of the Infant Christ, is an allusion to the Fall. Where, however, He appears as the Infant Saviour with the Cross, the apple, with a piece bitten out of it, sometimes lies at His feet, as in our illustration from Luini, vol. ii. p. 379. It is the apple, too, in the mouth of the dragon, whom the Virgin treads under foot.[1]

A mystic and typical connection is sometimes seen in Art between the Tree of the knowledge of good and evil and the Cross. Abbé Crosnier[2] mentions an instance in Sculpture where the tree of the Fall has taken the form of a cross.

In an apocryphal MS. called 'The Book of the Prophet Moses,' in the possession of the Hon. Robert Curzon, the following conversation takes place between God and Adam after the Fall:—
'Then I called him, saying, O Adam! thou hast transgressed my command; lift up thine eyes. Then I said unto him, What seest thou? He said, I see a tree standing above my head.

'Then I answered him, and said to him, Thou hast spoken truth.
'He said, O Lord! this tree above my head is like a cross.'

[*A. J.*—In the old ecclesiastical edifices, especially in those dedicated to St. Mary, the Creation, with the Temptation and Fall of the Mother of Mankind, is conspicuously placed, so as to prepare us for the exaltation of her who was the Mother of the Saviour.]

---

[1] M. Didron remarks that each country seems to have chosen its favourite fruit (Guide de la Peinture, p. 80). In Burgundy and Champagne the vine is sometimes seen; in Picardy, he believes the cherry. One would think, by that rule, that the Italians would have preferred the fig to the apple. But the Abbé Zani (vol. ii. p. 245) reminds us that Eve judged by look, and not by taste, 'that it was pleasant to the eyes;' and he thanks Heaven that there is no one so mad as to affirm the fig to be more beautiful than the apple. [2] Iconographie Chrétienne, p. 147.

The story of Adam and Eve occurs in predella pictures under the Annunciation, as in the Lorenzo di Credi, of that subject, in the Uffizj. The Fall singly is seen under the Crucifixion.

Adam and Eve hiding in the Garden.

Art has not ignored this immediate consequence of their changed natures. The subject is seen early, and only as a link in a series. The Orvieto sculpture (woodcut, No. 40) shows a remarkable attempt to portray the cowardice of a bad conscience. 'And the

40   Adam and Eve hiding. (N. Pisano. Orvieto.)

Lord God called unto Adam, and said unto him, 'Where art thou?' The position of the guilty pair in this illustration degrades them to the semblance of animals. Yet there is something fine in so vivid a conception of abject terror.

The Lord accusing Adam and Eve.

This subject, portrayed in rude lines, and with the most naïve disregard for all probabilities in the accessories, yet with redeeming truth of intention, is fully given in a miniature of about the year

41 The Lord accusing Adam and Eve. ('Bible de Noailles.' A.D. 1000.)

1000, in the 'Bible de Noailles' (Bibliothèque Royale, Paris). The position of Christ as He sits against the table is as natural as that of a master arraigning guilty servants—the action of His hand to His mouth, an ancient gesture of anger: 'Who told thee that thou wast naked? Hast thou eaten of the tree, whereof I commanded thee that thou shouldest not eat?' And Adam hangs his head and points sulkily to Eve: 'The woman whom Thou gavest to be with me, she gave me of the tree, and I did eat.' And Eve, in return, with a deprecatory gesture of flippant humility, not destitute of grace, points to the serpent: 'The serpent beguiled me, and I did eat;' while the serpent justly stands at the bar too, still semi-upright, as not yet judged. Domenichino, in his small picture in the Louvre, more than six centuries later, has the same intention, but not so well expressed. His Adam is a low Italian, shrugging his shoulders, and voluble in accusation of his wife, a poor drudge, who has evidently never had a moment's happiness with him, even in Paradise.

In the mosaics of St. Mark's a higher conception is depicted. Adam and Eve kneel in penitence before the Lord, while He curses the serpent who has misled them.

The Coats of Skins.

It is conjectured by theologians that these coats were the skins of the first animals slain as expiatory sacrifices. The Scriptures mention no sacrifice before that of Cain and Abel, though that is not recorded as the first instance. But the promise which had been given that the seed of the woman was to bruise the serpent's head, leads to the inference of immediate sacrifices typical of that seed. By the same reasoning, the first sin of man may be supposed to have been followed by the first tokens of that special Providence which had been needless before to creatures in a state of innocence. Early artists were not ashamed to portray this act literally, though it hardly occurs after the 11th century. 'Unto Adam also, and to his wife, did the Lord God make coats of skins, and clothed them.' In the mosaics of St. Mark's, Adam is seen standing, already clothed in a garment, as if prepared for a journey and awkwardly hanging his head, like a culprit attired in some garment of disgrace; while the Creator is Himself helping the no less dismayed Eve on with hers. The unquestioning innocence of this representation strips it of all absurdity.

Giving Adam a Spade, and Eve a Spindle.

This, which is usually the act of an angel, is supposed to have occurred before the expulsion, and, taken in connection with the last scene, has a certain propriety. Adam and Eve had just been clothed by the Lord Himself, to meet the change in their estate; now they receive the implements which point to its chief conditions —Adam, the spade to till the earth; Eve, the spindle to continue the clothing now become necessary to them.[1] This illustration (woodcut, No. 42), which is from a miniature of the 12th century in the British Museum,[2] has a certain pathos.

[1] The same idea, on antique sarcophagi, is given at page 103, woodcut No. 37.
[2] Cotton. Nero, C. VI.

42   Angel giving Spade and Spludle.   (MS. Brit. Museum.   Nero, C. VI.   12th century.)

The Expulsion.

This is one of those distinct subjects which immediately explain themselves to the eye. We need but to see those two figures, naked and miserable, side by side, to know that the moment of exile has arrived.

'So he drove out the man; and he placed at the east of the garden of Eden cherubims, and a flaming sword which turned every way, to keep the way of the tree of life.'

In the earliest form in which this subject is known to have been represented—in the codex of Genesis at Vienna—the text has been literally adhered to. A figure between Adam and Eve leads them forth, while the angel stands behind at the gate of Paradise with a wheel of fire (by which the sword that turned every way, and even the cherubim itself, has been interpreted) at his side. After that early time, the whole text may be said to have been contracted into one act and moment. It is the cherubim with the sword, sometimes with flames of fire upon it, which drives them forth with gestures that, according to time and school, descend through every grade of expression, from angelic dignity to human vindictiveness. Adam and Eve themselves have been no less calumniated in this sad passage of their story. They are generally represented degradingly wretched, both bewailing their fate, or one of them, Adam as often as the weaker vessel, impotently and unbecomingly appealing in gesture against it; while the angel's insolence increases with the abjectness of their demeanour.

This is one of the many instances in which mature Art in great measure overlooks the capacities of a subject, and frequently

Expulsion of Adam and Eve. Raphael. Lggi.

employs its better technical skill to degrade rather than raise it. Early Art, however limited its conditions, has always the vindication of a close adherence to Scripture. It was the punishment it had to represent—all ideas except that were beyond its means. So literal were these simple limners that we have to keep in mind the very words of Scripture—'And he *drove* them forth'—to comprehend a feature which frequently occurs in early versions; namely, the action of the Lord or of the angel, whose hands, one or both, are upon Adam's shoulders, literally thrusting them forth. We see this in almost all early forms—in the 'Bible de Noailles,' and in S. Francesco at Assisi. Finally, it occurs in Raphael's series in the Loggie, from which we give this illustration (woodcut, No. 43). But it is the business of mature Art to develop a subject, to draw out its finer touches and tenderer moral colours. Had later painters as closely looked at Scripture as their humble predecessors did, they would not have so entirely lost sight of all that mitigates the sternness of this moment. They would have remembered that these were beings who took with them from Eden the promise and the powers for the recovery of the race—who went forth criminals, yet pardoned—who were driven out, yet with so many signs of God's love and providence as to be an object of peculiar respect to the angels. They would, in short, have felt that this was one of the most pathetic and capable subjects that human skill could treat, and would have added strength to the fact of the punishment by jealously preserving the real dignity and importance of the creatures punished. For

> Not in entire forgetfulness,
> Nor yet in utter nakedness,
> But trailing clouds of glory do we come
> From God, who is our home.

The forms of Art are a safe thermometer by which to judge of the respect for man entertained in different periods; and truly this only sure sign of civilisation is seen at a deplorably low ebb in what we have been taught to look upon as brilliant epochs of the world's history. Not in one instance that can be named have these accompanying facts been attempted. Adam's torso is more anatomical, Eve's hair more graceful; but in all that distinguishes Christian feeling this subject has lost instead of gained.

That Art should have made the place of our first parents' exit a gateway either of Italian or Gothic design is no feature for criticism. The idea of a boundary was what was needed, and the necessary solecisms thus bequeathed to us by the artists, who looked to the daily-seen forms around them for their modes of expression, are among the most fertile and interesting lessons we can receive.

Adam and Eve may be said, with the exception of the earliest forms of representation, to be always seen issuing from Paradise in an unclad state. The literal rendering of Scripture would have given them garments. A wall-painting in the church of St. Angelo in Formis, in the Benevento territory, shows Adam going forth with a pickaxe on his shoulder, and both fully dressed—Eve daintily holding up a long furred robe, as her poor feet step for the first time into the miry ways of this wicked world.

The adoption of the chief facts of Genesis in the Koran has made our first parents the objects of numerous Eastern legends. In one of these the Mahometans have added misery to misery—reporting the unhappy couple, after the expulsion, to have lost and perpetually sought each other in the wide world for forty years, after which they lived together in a cave, still shown, not far from Mecca.

ADAM AND EVE IN THEIR FALLEN CONDITION.

THE new life commenced by Adam and Eve has found such touching, though homely, expression in early Art, as to make one wonder that the subject has been not more dwelt upon by modern artists. It assumes one form, with a few variations. On one side sits Eve, spinning, or with one or two children on her lap; on the other side, Adam wields the spade or pickaxe. The expression of each, if not always dejected, is that of beings on whom life presses heavily. Eve sometimes looks sorrowfully at Adam—as a wife at a husband overstrained with toil. Early miniatures and woodcuts are, however, inadequate to do justice to the pathetic capabilities of a subject which is interwoven with the daily experience of so large a proportion of their descendants. Sometimes the two infants on Eve's lap are of equal age, and must be interpreted according to a tradition that Cain and Abel were each born with a twin sister, which sister they afterwards married; for only thus, it was argued, could the sons of Adam have been provided with wives. At other times, it is Cain and Abel who occupy Eve's

Adam and Eve. (Raphael. Loggia.)

knees. Raphael—the last, perhaps, who can be said to have treated this subject, prompted, doubtless, by early representations familiar to his eye—has added both a retrospective and prospective allusion. Cain and Abel, two little naked boys, are striving with each other; Cain, the elder and stronger, has obtained possession of the disputed prize, and holds up to Eve an object she knows too well—the fatal apple. Adam is here represented as a Sower casting forth his seed—a thought also seen in early forms—thus recalling the typical relation of the first Adam to the Second.

It is strange how little in other respects Art has recorded the changed estate of the fallen pair. In Adam, bent with toil or grey with care, his manly, thoughtful face telling the unspeakable sense of the past and future, Art might have found a fitting and legitimate comparison to that other great Type of Sorrow. A statue of the

17th century—one of the army of figures which peoples the exterior of Milan Cathedral—is almost a unique instance of the thought in Art, and shows how pathetic is every touch of this human chord (woodcut, No. 45).

Lucas van Leyden has a beautifully-executed etching of Adam and Eve, in their outcast state, walking along through a stony

45   Adam. (Statue on Milan Cathedral.)

landscape, the wind blowing the leafless trees, and carrying Eve's luxuriant hair and Adam's dishevelled beard horizontally on the blast. But Adam himself is a low conception of the great ship-wrecked father of mankind, and the two (Eve with a child in her arms) look rather like tramping beggars—by no means familiar with the taste of that bread which they were to earn by the sweat of the brow.

ABEL.

[*A. J.*—ABEL is an accepted type of our Lord, not only in his death, but in his personal character. He was the first of mankind who was perfectly chaste and perfectly righteous in the sight of God; he was the first priest, because he was the first who laid a sacrifice on an altar to God, and the first martyr, for he was the first who was put to death unjustly.

In general, the story of the Fall is continued to the death of Abel, for sin was to bring death into the world; but as Abel, the innocent and just man, is a type of Christ, and Cain of His murderers, we often find the story of Cain and Abel treated apart as symbolic of the death of our Lord, who, like Abel, was sacrificed by hate and envy.

The first example of the story of Cain and Abel treated in Art is on a sarcophagus in the Catacombs.[1] A figure—intended, I suppose, for the Creator—is seated on a throne. Cain approaches with his offering of the fruits of the earth, apparently grapes. Abel brings his lamb in his arms.

But in later times the two sacrifices are represented in a less ideal form. There are two altars, built up of turf or stones—the fruits of the earth on one, the 'slain lamb' on the other; rays of peace from high descend on that of Abel, clouds and lightning overwhelm that of Cain.

But, generally, we have the same subject perpetually repeated—the great typical sacrifice of the just Man: either Cain is in the act of killing his brother, or Abel is lying dead and lamented by his parents, while Cain, cursed from heaven, is flying in the distance into exile and despair.]

In the oldest forms Cain is represented with a spade—the appropriate implement of a tiller of the earth. [*A. J.*—In later Art, Cain is usually armed with a club; but in the Greek Church he stabs his brother with a poniard, which has been as much criticised and ridiculed as the similar anachronism of giving Adam an iron spade

---

[1] Bottari, ii.

J.] or hoe. Where it was the sole aim of the artist to convey the idea, not to delineate the event, such criticism is wasted: in these days the mistake would be simply ridiculous.] He is also sometimes represented as killing his brother with a stone, or with stones. D'Agincourt gives an illustration from a bas-relief, where Cain is literally stoning Abel (Scultura, pl. xii.) Cowley, in his sacred poem of 'Davideis,' says, with poetic licence:—

> I saw him fling the stone, as if he meant
> At once his murder and his monument.

[*A. J.*—On the gates of Ghiberti, the highest compartment on the right contains the whole story of Abel, thus arranged:—

1. A rude hut. Adam and Eve with their children.
2. Abel keeping sheep.
3. Cain ploughing the ground with oxen.
4. Cain and Abel offer their sacrifice on an eminence.
5. Cain slays Abel.
6. 'And the Lord said unto Cain, Where is Abel thy brother?' (Gen. iv. 9.)

The death of Abel has been treated by most of the great painters, and very finely; but the conception varies but little. Abel lies prostrate on the ground; Cain strikes him with his club. In Titian's picture, he sets his foot on his brother—a superfluous barbarity. There is a fine woodcut by Albert Dürer (1511), and by Rubens a single figure of Abel lying dead and lamented by his dog—very real and pathetic.]

There was a tradition, perhaps known to Rubens through early forms of Art, of Abel's dog who kept his sheep, and who, seeing his master dead, defended the body against the beasts of the field and the fowls of the air.[1]

In mediæval commentaries it is stated that Adam, while they were both children, preferred Abel to Cain. According to Eastern legends, also, Adam assigned Abel's twin sister to Cain, as wife, and Cain's to Abel. But Cain's sister was the more beautiful, and he desired her for himself. On this account, after his sacrifice had been refused by the Almighty, and Cain's mind was embittered, 'he talked with Abel his brother: and it came to pass, when they were in the field, that Cain rose up against Abel

---
[1] Fabricius, vol. ii. p. 47.

his brother, and slew him' (Gen. iv. 8). This being 'in the field' is interpreted, even by modern commentators, as Cain's having drawn Abel cunningly forth, and was strained into a type of Judas betraying the Lord. It was further assumed, that being 'in the field' implied having left a more populous place. Thus the two brothers are represented as having just passed through the town gates.

46 Cain and Abel. (Bible Historiée, Bibl. Imp., Paris.) 47 The Lord accusing Cain. (Bible Historiée, Bibl. Imp., Paris.)

Our next illustration shows the Creator inquiring of Cain, 'Where is Abel thy brother?' while the fratricide, still with the murderous weapon on his shoulder, turns with anger and rudeness: 'Am I my brother's keeper?' Between them is a reft in the ground, whence blood is bursting forth. This is another instance of the matter-of-fact literality of these early limners. 'And now art thou cursed from the earth, which hath opened her mouth to receive thy brother's blood' (Gen. iv. 11). Our two woodcuts, Nos. 46 and 47, are both taken from the same often-quoted French Bible of the end of the 13th century.

In another instance Cain is insolently keeping on his hat in the presence of God. In early Art his face is always as rude as his manner. Later Art has more politely, but less truly, made the murderer listening with deference to the voice of the Judge.

[A. J.—In the best pictures the brothers have been carefully discriminated. Abel is in general a slender youth, quite or almost beardless, with a mild beautiful face, and fair curling hair—the antique shepherd type; and Cain is a muscular figure, swarthy with toil, with black hair and beard, and scowling features, in accordance with the character of each. When Abel appears in a procession of the patriarchs, as a single figure, with his sheepskin tunic, and the lamb in his arms, it is difficult to distinguish him from John the Baptist, except by his place next to Adam.]

ADAM AND EVE LAMENTING OVER THE BODY OF ABEL.

THIS is one of those pathetic subjects which have been bequeathed by early Art. Our illustration (woodcut, No. 48, over leaf) is from an Italian Speculum of the 14th century. The whole conception —the elegant Italian Loggie—the youthful parents—the almost infantine Abel—is a fiction, but one which the intense pathos converts into a truth. That sorrow is there, over the first stiffened form of death, of which Scripture did not need to say one word. The lamentation of Adam and Eve for the death of Abel was a favourite theme of Eastern tradition. It was said, that on first perceiving that Death had entered the world, Adam and Eve sat down by the body, weeping and bewailing, and not knowing what to do with it, for they were ignorant of the usages of sepulture. Then there came a raven, dragging a dead raven, and dug a hole in the ground, and buried it before their eyes. Then Adam said, 'As the raven has done, so will I do;' and they took up the body of Abel, and covered it with earth.[1] Tradition adds, that they sorrowed for Abel one hundred years, thirty years after which they were com-

[1] Cain is seen in Queen Mary's Prayer Book (14th century), in British Museum, trying to cover up the body with leaves.

forted by the birth of Seth, whose name signifies the Resurrection. He was a godly man; his progeny being called the sons of God, in opposition to those of Cain, who were called the daughters of men. Seth retired with his family to a very high mountain, where Adam was buried.

Tradition continues the history of Adam after his death. For

48   Adam and Eve lamenting over the dead Body of Abel. (Mr Roxall's Speculum.)

Noah, it is said, took his bones into the Ark,[1] and when he first descended again upon the earth, he offered up a prayer that God would not again send the curse of waters; for the sake of the bones—others say the sorrows—of Adam, the blood of Abel, and the righteousness of Seth.[2] After which he distributed the bones of Adam to his three sons, Shem, Japhet, and Ham. Shem, as the

[1] Fabricius, vol. i. p. 61.   [2] Idem, p. 74.

eldest, obtained the head for his share, finally brought it with him to the land of Judæa, and buried it on Mount Calvary. Here we take leave of our first father for the present. Further legendary fables will be found in the 'History of the True Cross,' in the second volume. Eve, not able to survive him, is said to have died seven days after him. Peace be to them!

Lamech kills Cain.

[*A. J.*—This is a very uncommon subject, and not strictly Scriptural, but I have met with it.

49   Lamech and Cain.   (Lucas van Leyden.)

A. J.] According to a Jewish tradition, Lamech, growing blind, when hunting in a forest where the unhappy fugitive had taken refuge, killed Cain, ignorantly, with an arrow, mistaking him for a wild beast; and afterwards slew his son Tubal Cain, the 'young man' who had been the cause of this murder, by pointing to a certain thicket where he heard something stir,[1] and this event, they say, is alluded to in Genesis iv. 23. It is represented in sculpture on the stalls of the Cathedral of Amiens, and also in the Campo Santo, at Pisa, and on the north side of the Cathedral at Modena. Also there is a fine engraving by Lucas van Leyden, in which Lamech is seen in front, in the act of bending his bow, while a boy near him, with an arrow in his hand, points to an eminence in the distance, where Cain is seated under a tree, with a jaw-bone of an ass by his side.[2]]

It may be observed that Lamech is *always* represented blind, as in the woodcut (No. 49) just given. The origin of this idea we have not discovered. It is told as an accepted fact in Bibles of the 13th century. Of Lamech, it is said that he was the first to introduce bigamy, for he had two wives. In the 'Speculum Salvationis' he is related to have been tormented by them—' Lamech constringitur a malis suis uxoribus '—as Job is falsely represented in Art to have been by his wife. Lamech always, in these mediæval series, forms the companion to the man of Uz—both being types of the Flagellation of our Lord.

ENOS.

[*A. J.*—ENOS, the son of Seth. He holds a branch of olive. His wife has a child in her arms. Two boys follow with a lamb.

ENOCH.

ENOCH, the father of Methuselah, was the just man who, according to an obscure passage in Genesis, did not die, as all men, but

---

[1] This Rabbinical legend is mentioned by St. Jerome, and is related in 'La Mer des Hystoires,' where it is 'un jeune enfant qui conduisait Lamech ' who commits the fatal mistake. (Chap. xx. fol. xxviii.)

[2] Bartsch, vol. vii. p. 345.

J.] was taken up into heaven. St. Paul alludes to this text, and cites Enoch as one of the types of faith: 'By faith Enoch was translated that he should not see death' (Heb. xi. 5); and his ascension into heaven is, in the 'Biblia Pauperum,' one of the types of the Ascension of our Lord. Separately, and in later times, it is very rarely met with.]

54   Translation of Enoch.   (Bible Historiée.   Bibl. Imp., Paris.)

We give an illustration from a Bible of the end of the 13th century.

[A. J.—There is an engraving by Sadeler, after Mostaert.

It must be observed that, in the much more common representations of Elijah taken up to heaven, he always drops his cloak, which distinguishes the translation of Elijah from that of Enoch.

NOAH.

A. J.] NOAH is the third patriarchal type of our Lord; and it is easy to understand how, when every part of the Old Testament was considered only as a foreshadowing of the New Testament, the character and story of Noah came to be thus interpreted. First, there was his expressive name, which, in Hebrew, signifies 'rest' or 'comfort.' 'He called his name Noah, saying, This same shall comfort us concerning our work and toil of our hands' (Gen. v. 29). Through him came the covenant of mercy: he built the Ark, wherein the remnant of mankind were saved, which is the Church built up by Christ for His redeemed. The Deluge signifies baptism, the waters through which the old world was cleansed and purified from sin: and that this comparison was as old as the time of St. Peter, we know from the passage in his First Epistle: 'Once the long-suffering of God waited in the days of Noah, while the ark was a preparing, wherein few, that is, eight souls, were saved by water. The like figure whereunto even baptism doth also now save us' (1 Peter iii. 20, 21). And the same image was used by Tertullian and other Fathers of the Church. So then we cannot be surprised to find on the very oldest monuments which Christian Art has bequeathed to us, Noah represented as a type of the Redeemer, and the Deluge as a type of Redemption through baptism. He appears frequently on the sarcophagi and on the mural paintings in the Catacombs, a purely ideal symbol. He is always young and beardless (as the typical figure usually is), and is sitting or standing in a kind of chest or square box representing the Ark, and small out of all proportion; and he stretches out his hand, or both arms, to a dove which hovers near with the branch of olive (see woodcut, No. 3, p. 16)—in some instances there are two doves. There are only two instances known in which this simple and purely ideal image assumes some features of reality. On one sarcophagus preserved at Trèves, Noah is seen with all his family, and several animals, as well as the Ark; also on a gem (an onyx), wherein the Ark, the eight human beings, and several

] beasts and birds, are clearly depicted. In these early times, in
the abodes of the dead, the image of Noah and his dove signified
merely redemption and eternal peace; but in after times the more
recondite meaning was given to the Ark—it was the Church of
Christ floating safely while all around perished—and the whole story
of the Patriarch, without losing its sacred significance, came to be
considered as a part of biblical history, and to be historically and
popularly represented as such in several different scenes.

Noah receives from God the command to build the Ark (wood-

51   God appearing to Noah.   (Raphael. Loggie, Vatican.)

cut, No. 51); and, at the same time, the promise of safety for himself
and his family. Noah kneels on the right hand in an attitude of the
most profound reverence, holding in his arms his son Shem, the
future patriarch of the Jewish race. Behind, at the door of a hut,
stands the wife of Noah, leading Japhet, and carrying her youngest
son, Ham. On the left above, floating in the air, is seen the form
which represents the visible apparition of Jehovah: 'The end of all
flesh is come before me. But with thee will I establish my covenant.'
It is the most sublime figure ever drawn by Raphael—so mighty and
so tranquil—we cannot but trace in it the influence of Michael
Angelo. Here it is not the type of the Second Person of the Trinity,
but the Paternal Godhead, 'the Ancient of Days,' whom Daniel
beheld in his vision. This representation is from one of the four

A. J.] frescoes on the ceiling of the 'Chamber of Heliodorus,' which illustrates the four great promises of covenants of divine mercy and protection—to Noah, to Abraham, to Jacob, and to Moses.

2. Noah, according to the commandment of God, builds the Ark. In the Campo Santo at Pisa, we have the building of the Ark, by Pietro d'Orvieto, or by Buffalmaco. Noah as an aged man (he was then 600 years old) directs his sons, who are busied in bringing and preparing the gopher wood, while several graceful female figures, leaning against the open timbers, are watching the progress of the work. Another early master, Paolo Uccello, painted the same subject in the cloisters of S. Maria Novella at Florence. In Raphael's composition, in his series of the Loggie, Noah, a most majestic patriarchal figure, stands in an attitude of command; his three sons are employed with saw and axe fashioning the timbers, and the scaffolding of the Ark rises behind.

The animals entering the Ark with Noah and his family is not a religious subject, but has been chosen by artists who excelled in animal painting, as a *tour de force* to exhibit their skill; for instance, by Bassano (several times), Castiglione, Sneyders, and others.

3. The third subject, the Deluge, is of course the most important of all, the climax of the religious significance of the story. Often and variously as it has been treated, the general conception is nearly the same: an atmosphere surcharged with clouds portentously dark and lurid; the floods rising and descending; the struggles of a crowd of hapless human beings, sometimes mingled with animals in the foreground; and in the distance, floating above the wild waste of waters, the consecrated Ark of salvation.

In Raphael's composition we have a few expressive groups. A man, holding his child in one arm, is trying with the other to rescue his wife; a miserable wretch with a dead woman in his arms gazes on her with horror; a man tries to save himself on a horse. The Ark far in the distance.

Michael Angelo's great fresco is with reason celebrated; it contains many more figures and incidents than Raphael's, and I may observe that, though the pathos of a single group, or a single figure— one dead woman floating past with golden hair outspread upon the wave—may strike us more, yet as the idea to be conveyed was the destruction of a whole sinful world, the more crowded pictures, when well managed, are, or should be here, the most effective as a whole. There is a fine large print of the Italian school, in which the crowds of actions and actors are wonderfully varied. Men and women are clinging desperately to the outside of the Ark, some try to climb trees and rocks, to save themselves in boats, rafts, tubs; a man repels with blows another man who is trying to save himself on the same raft—a horrible and significant expression of selfishness which I have seen repeated in other examples—but in this fine print the effect is missed, because of the want of that horror of overwhelming gloom, which such an artist as Rembrandt would have given it, had he treated the subject, which I believe he never did.

One of the finest attempts to realise the horror of the scene is a picture in the Louvre (No. 156) by Antonio Carracci. The works of Antonio are extremely rare; he painted more as an assistant to his uncle Annibale than on his own account, and died young. This shows what an artist he might have become, or rather, must have been. Here the gloom and the terror, the man climbing the rock, the woman kneeling on its summit, the bark going down in the midst with its freight of despairing wretches, and the sacred Ark floating in safety, are conceived and rendered in a truly poetical spirit. A similar picture, also very fine, is in the Berlin Gallery, there attributed to Domenichino.

Excellent also, and in a sublimely poetical spirit, is the picture by Niccolo Poussin. The sun is blotted out; one tint of uniform darkness envelops earth, sea, and sky, and is broken only by flashes of lightning, through which the Ark is just visible. A woman tries to save her infant by holding it out to a man who has reached the summit of a cliff. Here also a bark is going down in the surging waters, and struggling wretches make a last effort for life, or a last appeal to Heaven for mercy. A very fine effect is produced by the presence of a huge half-dead serpent (the old origin of evil), which hangs distended, bloated, upon a shelving rock in the foreground.[1]

4. The Sacrifice and Thanksgiving of Noah. It is expressly said in Genesis viii. 20, that after leaving the Ark 'Noah builded an

---

[1] Louvre. One of a series.

A. J.] altar unto the Lord,' and that on this occasion the Lord made a covenant with Noah that He would not again curse the ground for any man's sake, nor again bring a flood to destroy the earth; and this sacrifice and this covenant of mercy I believe to be the subject of Michael Angelo's grand fresco in the Sistine, and of all the representations styled 'The Sacrifice of Noah.' It is not said in Genesis that Noah offered a sacrifice *before* he entered the Ark.

5. The Vineyard of Noah. His intoxication and its consequences, and the curse uttered against Ham, are very disagreeable and painful subjects, not often treated. In the Campo Santo at Pisa, where this part of the story was painted by Benozzo Gozzoli, one half of the picture—the vineyard, the graceful girls gathering and carrying baskets of grapes, the man treading the wine-press, and the old bearded patriarch with his grandchildren at his feet—is most beautiful, the other part of the picture hateful, not the less from being made the vehicle of a famous but most vulgar satire. Michael Angelo has also treated it; but the only endurable instance I have ever seen is by Luini. Having to be treated as a point of biblical history, it could not be better done than he has done it.

The story of Noah occurs as a series in ecclesiastical sculpture, painted glass, and in the old biblical prints.

We find it painted on one of the windows at Chartres in great detail.

1. The Lord commands Noah to build the Ark.
2. Noah builds the Ark, aided by his sons.
3. The Animals enter the Ark.
4. The Deluge. In the centre medallion the Ark is on the waters; and in the medallions on each side men and animals perish together.
5. The Dove returns to Noah.
6. Noah and his Sons, with their Families, leave the Ark.
7. The Sacrifice of Noah and the Covenant of Peace, surmounted by the rainbow.
8. Noah plants his Vineyard.
9. The Vintage.
10. He is seated with a cup of wine, and becomes intoxicated.
11. He curses Ham, and blesses Shem and Japhet.

.J.] On the gates of Ghiberti the story is thus arranged. On the left, in the background—

1. The Ark, which, curiously enough, has the form of a huge pyramid. All the animals enter—the group of Noah and his family being in front.	2. The thanksgiving and the sacrifice of Noah, and the covenant made with God, who appears above. 3. The vineyard and intoxication of Noah.]

The representation of the Ark itself, as the principal object, is only seen in early Art. When artists advanced beyond that state of innocence which invests their simplest efforts with a charm and an excuse, no one seems to have referred to Genesis, and painted what he read there described. That the early limners did so there is no doubt, when we look at their three-storied erections, 'with lower, second, and third stories shalt thou make it,' which generally stand like a doll's house in a little boat. In the driving the animals into the Ark, these ancient limners have often some homely and humorous trait. On the bronze gates at Verona (11th century), a restive pig is likely to cause Noah some trouble in getting him up the plank which leads into a machine something like an old sedan chair. On coming out, too, the delight of the animals (a cow, for instance, dashing off at a clumsy gallop, with her tail straight up in the air) is full of drollery and character. In later Art, the coming in and going out is conducted with a most uninteresting decorum, the animals marching docilely in pairs on both occasions. In a miniature of the early 14th century, in the so-called Queen Mary's Book, in the British Museum, Noah is ascending the ladder to the Ark with one of his children on his head, which is hidden beneath the child's clothes.

Where the Ark is seen floating in the waste of waters—generally one scene in a series—an incident is frequently observed which may be traced from the 11th century. This is the figure of a bird of prey feeding on the carcase of a dead horse which floats on the surface. This is also taken from Genesis, as a little reflection will show. When Noah sent forth the dove, she returned again to him, for 'she found no rest for the sole of her foot.' But Noah had previously sent forth another bird, which did not return, but 'went forth to and fro, until the waters were dried up from off the earth.' There can be no doubt that the bird thus often represented upon the dead horse was meant for the raven—to the shape and colour of which it is always true—which did find both food and rest upon the floating objects. In later miniatures, this idea has not been improved upon by representing the raven as preying upon the body of a human being.

In the Bedford Missal (1430) the Ark is made all gilt and glorious-looking, as a type of the Church or of Christ.

ABRAHAM AND ISAAC.

[*A. J.*—Isaac is the fourth patriarchal type of our Lord, and one of the most important of all. He has been from the earliest times the scriptural symbol of the Great Sacrifice. As *he*, the child of promise, the well-beloved son of his father, yielded himself unresistingly to death, in accordance with the Divine will, so did our Lord. As he carried the faggot for sacrifice up Mount Moriah, so up the selfsame path did Jesus carry His Cross. And as Isaac meekly knelt to receive death, and, brought as a lamb to the slaughter, he opened not his mouth, even so did our Saviour. And Abraham, the greatest of the patriarchs, and the father of nations, is not only the accepted type of a perfect and unshaken faith, but also an earthly symbol of that Divine Paternity which refused not to give His beloved Son to die for the redemption of mankind (Heb. xi. 17). Such, even from the days of St. Paul, was the importance given to the story of Abraham and Isaac; and that it was used in the very earliest ages of Christian Art, as a symbol to express the Christian's faith, we have testimony in the writings of St. Gregory of Nyssa (born about 331), who alludes to the frequency of such representations, and tells us that he often could not refrain from tears, 'beholding Isaac, with his hands bound behind his back, and Abraham, with one hand grasping the hair of his son, while looking down on him with sorrow, and in the other hand holding the weapon raised to strike.' This is just the group which appears on the sarcophagus of Junius Bassus (see etching, p. 13), who died A.D. 359, and which we find perpetually repeated on the sarcophagi and mural paintings with slight variations. Sometimes Isaac kneels before the altar, on which fire is burning; sometimes he kneels upon the altar, sometimes on a faggot—'he laid him upon the wood' (Gen. xxii. 9). The Divine command is invariably figured by the hand appearing from heaven; and the ram which was caught by the horns in the thicket is, I believe, as invariably without horns, and figured as a lamb, or rather *the Lamb*. We have also, in *one*

A. J.] instance, a third person standing near, which some suppose to be the angel of the Lord, and others, with more reason, the servant of Abraham. The previous moment of the story, Isaac bearing the faggot to the altar, and Abraham walking beside him with the sword unsheathed, is only once represented, and in *one* instance only we find the third scene of the story. Abraham himself stands on the altar with his arms extended to heaven in thanksgiving: on one side is Isaac, and on the other the ram (or *Lamb*).

Such are the antique representations which have come down to us, and this simple ideal group of the Father and the Son has the advantage of being so dramatic and so pathetic in itself, so intelligible as regards the action, and so awful in its more profound significance, that those who have treated the same subject in later times, with all the appliances of modern Art, all the charm of colour and expression, and all the beautiful accessories of scenery, have scarcely rendered it more effective. In our National Gallery, for instance, the magnificent landscape of Gaspar Poussin is contemplated and admired, while scarcely a thought is given to the significance of the figures of Abraham and Isaac, who are ascending the Mount of Sacrifice under the shade of melancholy boughs, one bearing the fire, the other the faggot. Another instance of the Sacrifice of Abraham, treated merely as a group in a landscape, occurs in a fine Tintoretto at Castle Howard, and another in a landscape by Annibale Carracci; but this is in fact a desecration of the awful significance attached to the incident, and contrary to all the principles and rules of religious treatment, to which I now return. In this sense it forms either the central group in a history of Abraham, or it is represented as a separate subject, as the type of the Great Sacrifice. The design by Raphael has only the two figures and the angel.

The small fresco in the Loggie of the Vatican is nearly destroyed; the original drawing is in the Queen's Library.

An important instance of the introduction of this subject into ecclesiastical decoration, and its application in the most awful sense, occurs on the pavement of the Cathedral of Siena (16th century). Here the Sacrifice of Abraham fills up the space in front of the high altar: the composition, as usual, contains several groups, and several different actions at different times.

On the right hand, Abraham is seated with Isaac, a beautiful boy, [A. J. near him, and four attendants. He receives from an angel, hovering above, the command to sacrifice his son. In the centre, on a rocky eminence, stands the altar. Isaac, kneeling, is 'laid on the altar upon the wood.' On the left stands Abraham with his sword raised in his right hand, and the other in a very awkward attitude, as if he had just removed it from grasping his son. Above hovers the angel, with wide outspread wings and warning hand, the action of flight being finely conceived; near the altar, the *lamb* caught in a thicket, and drinking from a little spring. On the right hand, as if below the eminence, is seen the usual group of 'the two young men' and the loaded ass, and two others conversing with them. In the background, on the left hand, Abraham, sitting among his flocks and herds, receives the promise of a son by Sarah (Gen. xvii. 16). He points to the right hand, where Hagar is seen playing with Ishmael, and seems to say, ' Oh, that Ishmael might live before thee!'

A very poetical version of this subject is the picture by Andrea del Sarto in the Dresden Gallery, in which the resigned expression in the features of Isaac, and the fine drawing of his undraped youthful figure, life size, are deservedly admired. Titian's picture is also celebrated (Venice, Santa Maria della Salute), and a fine large woodcut after his design, in which we have the whole story (as in Beccafumi's composition) is also famous. The two attendants waiting, with the saddled ass, the return of Abraham and Isaac, are very frequently introduced.

I remember a miniature in an illuminated MS., in which Abraham, about to offer up his son, appears in a full suit of armour, probably because of the story of his warlike prowess; but this is a mistake in regard to sentiment and character. Abraham is in this scene the venerable priest and father—not the warrior.

Rembrandt has treated the subject with a terrible *realism*—quite the reverse of the antique symbolic group. Isaac is crouching on the altar, on which there is a dish to catch the blood, while Abraham holds down his son's head, covering the face and eyes with his hand, and grasps the knife as if about to cut his throat. An angel from behind seizes both his arms with a most energetic

A. J.] action. This etching (of which there is a superb impression in the British Museum) is deservedly famous, but it has a horrible prosaic truth, which makes one shudder.]

In the mediæval series of Christian Art, Isaac bearing the wood is the type of Christ carrying His Cross. On this account the wood is generally placed crosswise on Isaac's shoulders. The analogy of this incident gains force from the prevalent belief that Mount Moriah and Calvary are the same locality, and that the type of the sacrifice was acted at the same place where the sacrifice itself was consummated. We borrow this illustration (No. 52) from Miss Twining's 'Types and Figures' of the Bible.

52 Isaac carrying Wood.
(Bible, 13th century. British Museum).

[*A. J.*—The sacrifice, or intended sacrifice, of Isaac is of course the most important event in the history of Abraham, whether we consider it historically or take it in its typical sense. There are two other incidents of his history to which a profound mystical significance is given, and which are for that reason very important as artistic representations.

The first is the meeting of Abraham and Melchisedec. This mysterious personage of the Old Testament is not only accepted as an important type of our Saviour, but has been by some commentators considered as a vision of the Saviour Himself. St. Paul first made the comparison, applying the well-known text in Psalm cx. 4 directly to the person and character of Christ, 'Thou art a priest for ever after the order of Melchisedec.' The name Melchisedec signifies king of peace and king of justice. Unlike the other personages in the Book of Genesis, he has no genealogy mentioned, and no posterity. It is an Oriental tradition that he had the sun for his father, and the moon for his mother; that is, that he

J.] descended direct from heaven. He was at once High Priest and King; he brought forth to Abraham bread and wine, and Abraham gave him 'tithes of all.' From these striking analogies,

53   Abraham and Melchisedec. (Memling. Munich Gallery.)

Melchisedec is the accepted type of Christ, and the meeting is the type of the sacrament of the Lord's Supper; and in this mystical sense we find the subject continually represented in the old Gothic sculpture, the stained glass, and the early biblical prints and pictures. The conception of course varies as to the style of treatment, but very little in the general arrangement. Abraham,

A. J.] who has just returned from his victory over the five kings, is dressed in armour, as in our illustration from Memling (woodcut, No. 53). Sometimes in a plumed helmet, shield, and spear, like a knight of romance; or an attendant bears his helmet and shield, while others of his train bring forward the spoil of the enemy, gold and silver, captives, &c. He bends low before Melchisedec, who, king and priest, wears a rich tiara, and often the same dress that is given to Aaron.

The next incident is the Visit of the Three Angels, or, as it is often styled, the Hospitality of Abraham. In this subject the three angels (whom Abraham addresses in the singular—'my lord') are a type of the Three Persons of the Trinity. They are either carefully portrayed as all alike, having the same nimbus, or *one* has the cruciform nimbus given to Christ; they are all winged, as angels, or unwinged, as spirits. In the gates of Ghiberti they are all alike robed and winged, and floating on the air. In Raphael's most beautiful composition they are unwinged, but so full of dignity, and with such a light ideal grace in their figures and movements, that they do not require the superhuman appendage of wings to prove them angelic—they approach as if they did not need the earth to sustain them. Abraham, when he receives them, is always prostrate before them, and Sarah is just seen hiding within the door of the tent or hut. In some instances the three celestial visitants are seated at a table which Abraham has spread before his tent under the shade of a tree, and he waits upon them reverently, while Sarah is seen within, kneading the three measures of meal, and preparing the three cakes. In the statues in the choir of the Cathedral at Ulm, Sarah is distinguished among the famous Jewish women by the attribute of these three cakes, which express her hospitality to her three angelic guests. In other cases (as, for instance, in the Campo Santo) Abraham is seated at the table, listening to the promise of the angels, and Sarah, within the door of the tent, is laughing to herself (see woodcut, No. 54).

In Murillo's picture, in the Sutherland Gallery, the three angels are three young travellers, in no way distinguished from mortal men, and in a picture by Eli Mudo the three celestial strangers have beards.

In Rembrandt's etching it is clear that he intended to represent

54 Abraham entertaining Angels. (Benozzo Gozzoli. Campo Santo.)

J.] the mystical idea of the Trinity. According to the theological interpretation, one of the strangers is a venerable man with a long beard; another, younger, is winged as the Holy Spirit. The eager adoration in the face of Abraham, who is serving them, and holds a pitcher in his hand, is quite wonderful.

In neither of these subjects, we need hardly say, does Isaac appear; and we must observe that, though so prominent a person as the type of our Lord, he is, as a subject of Art, quite secondary to his father Abraham.

Lot.

Another important episode in the history of Abraham is the story of Lot, to which a doctrinal significance has been given from the

A. J.] earliest times; yet it is not frequently met with in early Art, though very common in the later Italian and German schools.

The principal event in the history of Lot—the destruction of Sodom and Gomorrah, and his escape under the protection of the good angels—is understood as a type of the condemnation of the wicked in the last day, and the place they are to go to.

In this sense the story is represented separately, besides forming a scene in the pictured history of Abraham.

1. The two angels sent to warn Lot, and his hospitality to them, has been painted by Poussin.

2. Lot and his family escape from Sodom. The figure of the wife standing as petrified behind them, and in the distance the burning city. Sometimes (as in the Campo Santo) destroying angels fling fire from heaven on the doomed city. Sometimes two angels lead the family, sometimes only one—the daughters generally, but not always, precede the father. 'And while he lingered, the men laid hold upon his hand, and upon the hand of his wife, and upon the hand of his two daughters; the Lord being merciful unto him: and they brought him forth, and set him without the city' (Gen. xix. 16).

The daughters frequently carry bundles of raiment or baskets. The only scene of the history of Lot which has been represented by Raphael in the series of the Loggie is the Flight from Sodom.

In a beautiful composition, by Paul Veronese, one of the daughters stoops down to fasten her sandal.

The picture by Guido in our National Gallery represents Lot escaping with his daughters, the three figures rather more than half-length. One daughter carries a rich golden vase, and the other a bundle of raiment; the faces are very handsome, but in the first there is a tinge of coarseness, and in the second a tinge of cunning. Lot, between them, seems to consult them as to the road they should take.

Rubens has represented the scene of the escape with all that vigour of colour and animated dramatic vivacity of conception which belong to him, and with much more refinement, both of form and feeling, than is usually met with in his best pictures. This is in the Louvre.

The subsequent scene, Lot intoxicated by his two daughters in the cavern above Zoar, is so inexpressibly painful and disgusting, that we are astonished to find it so often repeated. It does not occur in any very early picture that I know of. In the Campo Santo, where the story of Abraham and Lot is told with great detail, it is, I think, omitted: it seems to have been avoided in ecclesiastical decoration, in the old illuminations of the Bible (not always remarkable for decorous feeling), and in Byzantine Art. There is no example by Raphael, nor by Albert Dürer, nor by Martin Schön, nor by Titian, nor by any of the religious painters of the 15th century. The early German artists of the 16th century afford the first instances I can remember—that by Lucas van Leyden being, perhaps, the finest. These early Germans were famous for treating the scenes of the Old Testament with great talent and fancy, but seldom with much regard for the typical significance in the choice of the subject, or with refined taste in the treatment of the character.

The later Italian and Flemish schools, the Carracci, Guercino, Schalken, Rubens, Rembrandt, Van der Werff, &c., seem to have had a predilection for it, because of the picturesque accompaniments; but, however finely executed, it remains, as a subject of Art, inexcusable and intolerable.!!(²)

HAGAR.

The history of Hagar is another episode in that of Abraham. When treated separately it is with reference to the application and interpretation as made by St. Paul. In a striking passage of his Epistle to the Galatians, he draws a distinction between the children of the bondwoman (Hagar) and the children of the freewoman (Sarah). The dismissal of Hagar signifies the division between those who are heirs to the Church of Christ and those who have been rejected from it; hence it has a sort of religious popularity as a separate group. It is the freewoman, the Church, who repels from her house and precincts the bondwoman and her child, though he be the eldest born. In this special form, however, I find the dismissal of Hagar has been rare in the earlier schools, but it became a favourite subject in the later Italian and German schools, perhaps from its pathetic and dramatic sentiment, when the mystical significance was unthought of, at least by the painters.

Sarah presenting her maid to Abraham to be his second *wife*

A. J.] (Gen. xvi. 3) has been painted by Philip Vandyck (Louvre, 156), by Dietrich, by Van der Werff, and others.

I do not recollect any example by an Italian painter, except the group in the Campo Santo.

Hagar, presuming on her maternal privileges, treats her mistress with disrespect, and, being 'afflicted' or chastened by her, flees to the desert, but is commanded by an angel to return. This is the subject of the picture by Rubens, in the Grosvenor Gallery, where the imperious and threatening gestures of Sarah, and the humiliation of the weeping Hagar, are as fine as possible, in his way; and when Hagar is seen lamenting *alone* in the wilderness, it is this part of her story which is represented. Her return to Abraham by command of the angel has been painted by Pietro da Cortona. Hagar and Ishmael dismissed at the request, or rather the demand, of Sarah, has been, of course, very frequently painted—'Cast out the *bondwoman* and her son'—and I believe the most celebrated example is the picture by Guercino, in the Brera; but I do not think it deserves its celebrity—the pathetic is there alloyed with vulgarity of character. I remember that when I first saw this picture, I could only think of the praises lavished on it by Byron and others, as the finest expression of deep, natural pathos to be found in the whole range of Art : I fancied, as many do, that I could see in it the beauties so poetically described. Some years later, when I saw it again, with a more cultivated eye and taste, my disappointment was great. In fact, Abraham is much more like an unfeeling old beggar than a majestic patriarch resigned to the Divine will, yet struck to the heart by the cruel necessity under which he was acting. Hagar cries like a housemaid turned off without wages or warning, and Ishmael is merely a blubbering boy. For expression, the picture by Govaert Flinck (Berlin Gallery, 815) seems to me much superior; the look of appealing anguish in the face of Hagar as she turns to Abraham, and points to her weeping boy, reaches to the tragic in point of conception, but Ishmael, if very natural, with his fist in his eye, is also rather vulgar. Rembrandt's composition is quite dramatic, and, in his manner, as fine as possible. Hagar, lingering on the step of the dwelling whence she is rejected, weeps reproachfully; Ishmael, in a rich Oriental costume, steps on before, with the boyish courage *l.*] of one destined to become an archer and a hunter in the wilderness, and the father of a great and even yet unconquered nation; in the background Sarah is seen looking out of the window at her departing rival, with exultation in her face.

But the most beautiful scene of all, at once pathetic and picturesque, and the most frequently treated because of its scenic capabilities, is Hagar in the wilderness of Beersheba, when the water is spent, when her son faints for thirst, and she flings herself on the earth at a distance—' Let me not see the death of the child.' And as she weeps in her desolation, the angel of the Lord descends to comfort her, and guide her to the hidden spring. We must observe, that to make Ishmael an infant, as some painters have done, is a mistake, for he was at this time about thirteen years old. The incident has been frequently treated in a rich and luxuriant landscape, verdant with grass and foliage; the proper locality, the Arabian or Syrian Desert, being quite overlooked. The 'shrubs' under which Hagar laid her fainting boy, 'that she might not see him die,' were probably those stunted prickly bushes which are found in that arid, inhospitable wilderness—not the wooded heights and green tangled glades, such as Claude and Gasper drew.

There is a picture by Rembrandt of this subject in the gallery of Count Shönborn, which I cannot recall without emotion; so intense is the pathos. Hagar sits under the withered stump of a tree, in the foreground, her hands clasped, her swollen and tearful eyes raised to heaven and averted from the boy, who lies on the barren earth at some distance behind her.

REBEKAH.

The meeting of Eleazar, the messenger of Abraham, and Rebekah, commonly called 'Rebekah at the Well,' is a popular and beautiful subject, full of picturesque circumstances. Our illustration (woodcut No. 55, over leaf) is from Benozzo Gozzoli's fresco in Campo Santo. Sometimes Rebekah is giving drink to Eleazar, and sometimes he is exhibiting the earrings and bracelets of gold which he has brought for her. The two most beautiful examples I know of are, first, the picture by Paul Veronese, in

55   Rebekah and Eleazar.   (Benozzo Gozzoli.   Campo Santo.)

A. J.] Lord Yarborough's collection, glowing with colour and sentiment, and full of strange but picturesque anachronisms; and that by Poussin, in the Louvre—studied, elegant, correct, and graceful. Rebekah, while Eleazar displays the jewels, seems to hesitate whether she shall accept them. Of the other twelve or thirteen female figures round—the maidens who have come to draw water—one is so intent on the scene between Eleazar and Rebekah that she forgets her task, and the water runs over the edge of her vase. This picture, which Poussin painted for his friend the banker Pointel, 'qui lui avait demandé un tableau de plusieurs jeunes filles dans lesquelles on pût remarquer différentes beautés,' is certainly one of his finest.

The journey of Rebekah (*Il viaggio di Rebecca*) is the title given to a fine drawing by Baldassare Peruzzi, in the Florentine Gallery. It is in the form of a long frieze, seven feet in length by twelve or fourteen inches high. The bride is seen bearing a lily, and with a luminous glory round her head, mounted on an ass, and with a numerous train of attendants, and she is journeying to her new home and her unknown bridegroom. Further on, a number

I.] of men—Abraham and others—are seated in a semicircular sort of amphitheatre, cut in the side of a hill, *à l'antique*, while a number of youths and maidens are dancing in a circle. It is difficult to make out the meaning of other episodes in this luxuriant invention, or to reconcile them with the Scriptural story; but in this respect Peruzzi and other artists of his time were not particularly accurate; and I imagine that this drawing was prepared for the two sides of a *cassone*, a large chest in which the bridal *trousseau* was generally packed, to accompany the bride to her home.

On the sculptured stalls of the Cathedral of Amiens, no less than eight subjects are consecrated to Rebekah.
1. The Oath of Eleazar (Gen. xxiv. 2–9).
2. The Journey of Eleazar (Gen. xxiv. 10).
3. Rebekah by the well, holding a pitcher, and in a rich dress. Eleazar craves a drink.
4. Rebekah gives him drink from her Pitcher (Gen. xxiv. 18).
5. And, 'she said, I will draw water for thy camels also.' Eleazar meanwhile takes the jewels from his casket (Gen. xxiv. 22).
6. Rebekah receives the Presents.
7. Eleazar is feasted in the House of Bethuel and Laban (v. 32).
8. Rebekah bids adieu to the House of her Father (v. 61).

The beautiful scene of Isaac receiving his bride is, however, omitted, and instead of it we have—9. Rebekah about to become the mother of twins, and receiving on her knees the mysterious promise. 'And she went to inquire of the Lord. And the Lord said unto her, Two nations are in thy womb . . . and the elder shall serve the younger' (Gen. xxv. 22, 23).

ISAAC RECEIVES HIS BRIDE REBEKAH.

'And Isaac went out to meditate in the field at the eventide: and he lifted up his eyes, and saw, and behold, the camels were coming. And Rebekah lifted up her eyes, and when she saw Isaac, she lighted off the camel' (Gen. xxiv. 63, 64). With the early painters, to whom camels were not familiar things, the Eastern camel becomes a horse or an ass. It is surprising that this most

A. J.] beautiful subject has not been oftener treated; it is rich in sentiment and in all the elements of the picturesque. I remember only one example, and that by an unknown painter, of the Paul Veronese school, ignorant of the character of the locality, and, like all the Venetians, perfectly indifferent as to propriety of costume. Isaac is dressed like a Venetian cavalier, and gallantly assists Rekekah to alight, receiving her in his arms: in colour and execution beautiful.

Rebekah is a beautiful subject for Art, both as a single figure for sculpture and in painting, because of the picturesque accompaniments of her story: in the pastoral scene at the well, where she shows to such advantage, through her beauty and her graceful courtesy—on the journey—and in the meeting with Isaac. She has also a mystical importance, for she is considered by the early Fathers as a type of the Church (the SPOUSE), and consequently of the Virgin Mary, near whom she is placed by Dante in Paradise.[1]

Of the History of Abraham as a series, the most interesting and complete example is that in the Campo Santo of Pisa. It begins with the seventh compartment of the North wall, with a Rabbinical and Oriental legend concerning the early life of Abraham, which is not to be found in the book of Genesis, but appears in Josephus. It is related that while Abraham still dwelt in the land of the Chaldees, where the people and even his own relations were infected by idolatry, he was cast into the fire because he refused to worship in the temple of Belus, whence he escaped miraculously, while his accuser, Nacor, was consumed. In the earliest translation of the Bible, called the Vulgate, a passage in Esdras (ix. 7) is so translated as to lend some authority to this tradition. With this legend, Benozzo Gozzoli begins his story of Abraham; the first compartment above represents in the centre the temple of Belus, with Ninus sitting in judgment on one side, and Nacor perishing in the flames on the other.

(We must read the story as *related* in these compartments as we would read a printed book, from left to right, each compartment being like a chapter.)

---

[1] Rebecca est le type de l'Église, choisie parmi les Gentils pour devenir l'Épouse de Christ. Abraham représente Dieu le Père; Isaac, Jésus-Christ; Rebecca, l'Église, ou l'âme fidèle; Éliézer, les apôtres et tous les ouvriers évangéliques.—*Cathédrale d'Amiens*, p. 109.

J.] In the second compartment (Gen. xii. 5), Abraham and Lot with their families, mounted and with many attendants, and flocks and herds, issue from Haran, and prepare to go into the land of Canaan. Then God appears to Abraham, who kneels before Him (verse 7). Then the strife between the herdsmen, and next, a little above, the compact between Abraham and Lot (xiii. 8). In the third compartment, the five confederate kings attack Lot and take him prisoner; then Abraham, in a full suit of armour, and wearing a helmet, attacks the enemy and rescues Lot. On the right hand, Melchisedec meets Abraham, and offers him bread and wine (Gen. xiv. 9, 14, 19). In the fourth compartment we have, first, the story of Hagar. There are tents on the left hand. Sarah speaks to Abraham, then she presents Hagar to him; then she chastises Hagar, who flees from the face of her mistress to the desert, whence the angel commands her to return. In the centre the angels are seen coming down the hill to visit Abraham. He spreads a banquet for them; the attendants approach with dishes of meat. Sarah is seen laughing in the tent behind. Above, on the extreme right, the angels part from Abraham; two go to warn Lot, and one goes to destroy Sodom (see woodcut, No. 56).

56 Angels taking leave of Abraham. (Ben Gozzoli. Campo Santo.)

In the fifth compartment is the destruction of Sodom, on which destroying angels rain down fire; and, on the extreme right, Lot and his daughters escape; but they are not here accompanied by angels, as is usual, and according to the text (xix. 16).

In the sixth compartment is the story of Isaac. Sarah expostulates; Abraham is seated in front; the two boys, Ishmael and Isaac, are seen contending, and Ishmael, the stronger, seizes Isaac by the hair. Hagar looks on smiling; then she is dismissed with her son, and is seen far in the distance comforted by the angel.

A. J.] Then Abraham receives the command to offer up his son. They ascend the mountain (xxii. 5); then the sacrifice, as usual; and next, on the extreme right hand, Abraham, his son, and the attendants are refreshing themselves at the foot of the mountain.

In the last, Abraham, seated under a splendid portico, sends his steward, Eleazar, to the land of his fathers, to take a wife for his son Isaac—the departure of Eleazar, the beautiful pastoral scene of Rebekah at the well. The reception of Rebekah in the house of Abraham, who unites her to Isaac, and then the wedding banquet, within a palace of splendid fanciful architecture, which concludes this series.

I must again observe, that in the chapter of Genesis which contains the story of Rebekah, it is expressly said that she journeyed from Padan-aram on a camel—a circumstance of Eastern life which is almost always neglected in early Art.

In the story of Abraham and Isaac on the gates of Ghiberti, we have only two scenes, which are strictly typical, and refer chiefly to Isaac. On the right hand, his birth is promised by the three angels, who are here hovering winged spirits, wonderful for ethereal grace and beauty. On the left hand is the sacrifice of Isaac on Mount Moriah, with the attendants, as usual, waiting at the foot of the mountain; the first scene prefigures the Annunciation, and prophesies the birth of our Lord, and the second prefigures the Great Sacrifice.

SERIES BY G. PENCZ.[1]

1. Sarah presents Hagar to Abraham.
2. Abraham entertaining the three Angels, who are seated at a table.
3. Abraham dismisses Hagar and her Son.
4. Abraham and Isaac ascend Mount Moriah, the latter carrying the wood and the fire for the sacrifice.
5. Abraham, about to slay his Son, is stayed by the Angel.

[1] Bartsch, vol. viii. p. 321.

JACOB.

] JACOB is the fifth patriarchal type of our Lord. 'Was not Esau Jacob's brother? saith the Lord. Yet I loved Jacob, and I hated Esau.' But Jacob is not one of the most important of these patriarchal types, and though his history is full of interesting episodes, there is something cowardly, servile, dissembling, and selfish in his nature, which renders him personally unattractive, and hardly a good example of morality; and this, I suppose, is the reason that there are not many more works of Art in which he figures. Some events of his life have, however, a very profound mystical signification. There is, first, the allusion made by St. Paul to the selection of Jacob in preference to his brother Esau; and the struggle between the two brothers, both before and after they were born, is assumed to be the symbol of the struggle between the Church of Christ and the Synagogue, the new and the old Law.

Then there is the mysterious vision of the ladder let down from heaven to earth, and the angels of the Lord ascending and descending on it. To which our Lord Himself makes allusion: 'Verily, verily, I say unto you, hereafter ye shall see heaven open, and the angels of heaven ascending and descending upon the Son of Man.' Also in the Roman Catholic Church, 'Jacob's Ladder,' as it is usually styled, has many interpretations, besides being regarded as a type of the Virgin-mother through whom was the Incarnation, which, indeed, united earth and heaven, the human with the divine.

Therefore, as a strictly devotional subject, I shall first dwell on this sublime and prophetic vision, for when represented apart as a single subject, it is not an event in the history of Jacob, but a religious symbol. It is, however, a very uncommon subject.

There is an example in early Byzantine Art as early as the 9th century, which is one of the most beautiful I have ever met with. It occurs in that fine Greek MS. painted for the Emperor Basil.

Here the attitude of the sleeping patriarch is quite remarkable for grace and *abandon*—finer even than Raphael's; and the angels

A. J.] who are passing up and down the radiant ladder are themselves all glorious in kingly robes of blue and crimson and gold.

Raphael has twice painted this: first, on the ceiling of the Chamber of Heliodorus, as a separate and symbolical subject; and the second time in the Loggie, as one of the series of the Life of Jacob.]

57   Jacob's Dream.   (Raphael. Loggie.)

We give the above-mentioned illustration from Raphael (woodcut, No. 57). Nothing can be more beautiful than the figure of Jacob; while the angels, two and two, carefully illustrate the words 'ascending and descending.' In early illustrated Bibles this expression is curiously rendered, for the descending angels will be generally found gliding down the ladder head foremost.

[*A. J.*—Rembrandt has in this instance, as in others, converted light and shade into poetry. Jacob, whose figure is that of a common peasant, and scarce distinguishable amid the palpable obscure, *l.*] lies asleep on the left beneath some bushes. The ladder has no steps, but descends like a stream of light from above, while from its summit a strange winged shape, 'not human, not angelical, but bird-like, dream-like,' comes floating downwards, and beyond it another figure just emerging from a fount of splendour, in which its ethereal essence was confounded, seems about to take some definite form, and glide after its companion. In all the realm of creative Art, I know nothing more unearthly and visionary than this little picture.[1]

Another Dutchman, Ferdinand Bol, one of Rembrandt's scholars, has treated the same subject (Dresden, No. 1201) in quite a different manner, and yet with a certain originality. Jacob, a mere rustic figure, sleeps, leaning on a rock, and behind him the angels, as seen at a distance, ascend and descend the visionary ladder; but one bright-haired, white-robed, and majestic, though not ethereal, Being stands at the head of the sleeper, and seems to pronounce the blessing.

Ribera has a fine picture of Jacob's vision in the Gallery at Madrid.

Jacob wrestling with the angel has received from St. Augustine an elaborate mystical interpretation, but hardly calculated for popular intelligence, so that we find it seldom treated except when it is merely an incident in the life of Jacob, or, in spite of its sublime character, merely a group in landscape (as Claude has *twice* so introduced it, also Salvator Rosa and Mola).]

We give an illustration (from the French Bible of the end of the 13th century, so often quoted) which is remarkable for the easy dignity with which the angel does his part.

In the 'Biblia Pauperum,' Jacob wrestling with the Angel is a regular subject. It forms a type to the Incredulity of St. Thomas.

68 Jacob wrestling. (Bible Historiée. Bibl. Impériale, Paris.)

[1] In Dulwich Gallery.

[A. J.—Of the other incidents in Jacob's life, several are disagreeable; for instance, the scene in which he takes advantage of his brother's hunger, and where the unsuspecting Esau sells his birthright for a mess of pottage; and again, the scene in which, prompted and aided by his mother, Rebekah, he deceives his father; and a third, in which he contrives to overreach Laban. All these incidents enter into a complete series of the History of Jacob, but have not often been treated separately except by the Dutch masters. The scene with Esau has been painted by Honthorst (Berlin, 434), who has introduced Rebekah prompting her son Jacob (which is not scriptural, though perhaps probable), and has made the whole group an effect of artificial light; and Carravaggio (Cobham Hall —Lord Darnley) has given to the two patriarchs the same look and almost the same costume as to his oft-repeated gamblers. I think a picture I saw in Count Harrach's collection at Vienna was the truest in character and expression—two boys: the one, open, eager; the other, smooth and sly. The scene in which Jacob steals his father's blessing is recommended by his picturesque capabilities, and as being at once domestic and dramatic. The *motif* does not vary: the aged Isaac, half blind, with white hair and flowing beard, reclines on his couch, and stretches forth his shrivelled hands to feel the hands of Jacob, who kneels before him; Rebekah, standing near, watches the result of the stratagem. There is here sufficient variety of character, suspense in the action, and contrast of expression, for great dramatic effect; and abundant material in the rich draperies of the couch and the costumes for accessories of colour, light and shadow; hence, though not a favourite subject in the Italian schools, it has been often and beautifully treated by the Flemish and Dutch painters.

I must speak first of Raphael's composition. It is the first of six subjects which he has dedicated to the story of Jacob in the Loggie, but it is not one of the best, nor is the story nor the intention of the artist clearly made out—faults most unusual with Raphael. Besides Jacob, there are three other figures kneeling by the bed, witnesses to the fraud, which I do not understand; and Jacob is not disguised—his hands and arms are bare. Esau is seen entering the door behind with a dead fawn on his shoulder. In the next compartment, which is better, but not among the best, Esau is imploring

J.] the blessing: 'Hast thou but one blessing, my father? bless me, even me also, O my father.' But the dead fawn lies at his feet, so that the previous request, 'Let my father arise, and eat of his son's venison' (Gen. xxvii. 31), has not been forgotten. These are obvious inadvertencies, not admissible in an historical series.

Among the Flemish painters, Rubens, Van Dyck, Rembrandt, Govaert Flinck, and Jan Victor have painted the same subject.

Jacob then flies from his brother's fury to Padan-aram, and on his journey is favoured with the mysterious vision of the angels, already described. It is a symbolical subject, but it also forms a scene in the life of Jacob. The meeting between Jacob and Rachel by the well is one of the most beautiful of all the scenes in his life, and for sentiment has been best treated by the Italian painters—first by Raphael, where Jacob has just removed the stone; the finest of all being that by Giorgione (Dresden), inimitable for that tenderness of expression and pastoral simplicity of treatment in which the Venetians excelled—'And Jacob kissed Rachel, and lifted up his voice and wept'—and by Murillo, in the Dulwich Gallery.

It forms a fine group in a landscape, and has been so introduced by Claude and by Francesco Mola.

Jacob consents to serve Laban for the love of Rachel another seven years; Rachel stands by her father, while poor Leah stands behind Jacob with downcast eyes. The scene is evidently from Gen. xxix.

Jacob fleeing with his wives and little ones.

The first incident in the journey is where Laban overtakes the fugitives, and accuses Jacob of having not only stolen his daughters, but stolen his gods.

The picture by Murillo is celebrated, but there is no attempt either to render the truth of the locality, or the Scriptural dignity of the personages.

The journey of Jacob when he returned to his own land with his wives, his handmaids, his children, his herdsmen, his camels, and his flocks of cattle and sheep, and all the riches which God had given him, has been a fine subject for the artists who excelled in animal painting, such as Bassano, Castiglione, and Vandervelde; but here again, though, from the style of subject, one

A. J.] would not have expected it, Raphael has excelled them all. First, the great flock of sheep disappearing over the winding road; then two herdsmen; then the graceful women and children seated on the camels, and in front Jacob himself on his ass indicating the road, and with a sort of inward satisfaction in his vast possessions visible in his countenance, render this composition a masterpiece of skill in the arrangement, as well as elegant drawing. It is the last of the six compartments which include the history of Jacob.] The return of Jacob to his own country is given in the series of the 'Biblia Pauperum' as a type of the return of the Holy Family from Egypt.

[*A. J.*—Next to Raphael's, and in its way very fine, is the composition by Vandervelde.

The meeting and reconciliation of Jacob and Esau is a fine subject, seldom treated, and not by any first-rate Italian master. There is a small but very beautiful picture by Rubens, in which the brothers meet, Jacob bending lowly before the generous Esau; behind Jacob, a crowd of women, children, herds, &c., and behind Esau a troop of warriors.]

This subject occurs in the series of mosaics in the Basilica of S. Maria Maggiore at Rome, and also in the Campo Santo, by Benozzo Gozzoli. In each instance Jacob is on his knees before Esau, who bends over him. This is in strict illustration of Scripture, which says that Jacob bowed himself to the ground seven times, and that Esau ran to meet him, and fell on his neck. Behind Esau in each case are soldiers with lances. Behind Jacob are Leah and Rachel with their children, so disposed that Esau lifting up his eyes from his brother's neck would see them.

[*A. J.*—It must be remembered that a mystical significance has been given to the two wives of Jacob. Rachel, the most beloved, signifies contemplative or holy life—and Leah active life. Rachel is also a type of the Virgin Mary, and Dante has placed her at the feet of the Virgin in Paradise, next after Eve, and before Rebekah.

Of the whole story of Jacob represented in a series of groups or scenes, there are several instances. In the Campo Santo, it fills three compartments. We begin with the birth of the twin brothers (Gen. xxv.), Rebekah sitting up in bed, surrounded by a number of attendants; in front, several others are occupied [*A. J.* with the new-born children—the astonishment of one of them at the unusual appearance of Esau (verse 25) is expressed with great *naïveté*. I must observe, that, in the scenes with Isaac he is neither blind nor decrepit, and is usually standing; and the marriage scene, in which Jacob is sitting with his wives Leah and Rachel on each side, while youths and maidens dance before them, is eminently beautiful. The last groups of this series represent a dreadful episode in the history, and one seldom treated—the story of his daughter Dinah, and the barbarous and treacherous revenge taken by her brothers. The same story concludes the series of the Life of Jacob in Santa Maria Novella, but I do not know that it has ever been treated separately.

The History of Jacob is seen on the gates of Ghiberti. Also on the carved stalls at Amiens, in twenty different groups. By Murillo it has been treated in five large landscapes.]

JOSEPH.

JOSEPH is the sixth patriarchal type of our Lord, and, both in his personal character and in his history, the favourite, and, it may be said, the closest type that the Old Testament supplies. For he was gentle and faithful, wise and virtuous, full of love and pity even for his enemies, and no trait of violence or cunning, as with the other patriarchs, enters into a story the most romantic and touching that has ever been recorded. So far his personal similitude. His history further supplies general analogies obvious to every reader. For Joseph was the beloved son of his father; he was hated by his brethren, sold by them for a few pieces of silver, and cast into prison, between two malefactors. That he there underwent great sufferings, mental as well as bodily, on which Genesis is silent, is told by a passage in the 105th Psalm: 'Whose feet they hurt in the stocks: the iron entered into his soul; Until the time came that his cause was known; the word of the Lord tried him.' Thence he was raised to great honours, and became the saviour, temporally speaking, of his brethren, whom he saved from destruction, and finally planted in the land of Goshen, the received type of a state of rest.

Nor were the early Fathers slow in tracing endless and more particular analogies between Joseph and Christ. For the coat of many colours given him by his father Jacob signified, according to St. Jerome, all the nations of the earth united in the body of our Lord. His dreams that his brothers' sheaves bowed themselves before his, and that the sun, moon, and stars did him homage, were interpreted as fulfilled in the person of Christ, of whom it is said, in the 72nd Psalm: 'All kings shall fall down before Him, all nations shall do Him service;' and in the 148th Psalm: 'Praise Him, sun and moon; praise Him, all ye stars and light.'

Again, his brothers, on seeing Joseph come to them in Dothan, exclaimed, 'Come now, therefore, let us slay him.' So the Jews, when our Lord stood before them, cried, 'Away with Him, crucify Him!'

Further, Joseph's coat was stained with the blood of a kid, and our Lord's body was stained with the blood of the very Lamb of God. Joseph was cast into a pit; Christ descended into Limbus. He resisted the wickedness of Potiphar's wife; Christ, that of the Synagogue. Potiphar's wife caught Joseph by his garment, who left it in her grasp and fled; the Synagogue took Christ captive in the body, who left it torn on the Cross, and escaped by death.[1]

Later analogies by the schoolmen, which are seen in the form of Art in the 'Biblia Pauperum' and the 'Speculum Salvationis,' are far more strained. The sorrow of Jacob at the sight of Joseph's blood-stained coat finds its type in the sorrow of the Virgin at the descent from the Cross. The event of his brethren putting him into the pit becomes the prefiguration of the entombment of Christ by His Mother and disciples; while Reuben's return to the pit, and dismay at not finding Joseph there, is equally strangely represented by the Maries coming to the tomb, and finding it empty.

On the other hand, the history of Joseph was also the favourite theme of Oriental and Jewish fables. That the Egyptians, in the course of years, forgot their debt of gratitude to the Hebrew stranger, is shown by that other Pharaoh who arose, 'who knew not Joseph.' Nevertheless, there are believed to be traces in Oriental history of honours paid to the wise and good patriarch, under the titles of Phœnix, Serapis, Adonis, Osiris, as the Hermes of the Egyptians, as the angel of God, and even, in unconscious fulfilment of his typical relation, as the Saviour of the People and the Son of God.

The apocryphal fables include a series of letters between Pharaoh and Joseph. The correspondence commences between Pharaoh and the Egyptian magicians; he demanding an interpretation of his dream, they excusing their inability. Then the chief butler takes the pen, protesting his sorrow not to have sooner remembered an excellent interpreter, 'young in age, but old in wisdom,' whom he recommends to the king's divine magnificence. Whereupon Pharaoh enters into direct communication with Joseph, whom he addresses as 'the only sage, the incomparable interpreter, the man strong in deeds and in discourse, the most desired friend, Joseph the Hebrew.[2]

---

[1] Bede, vol. viii. p. 182. Quæstiones super Genesim.
[2] Fabricius. Codex Pseudepigraphus, V. T., cxxxiv. p. 441. Morale Somnium Pharaonis.

There is also preserved in the Talmud an address of an educational character on the part of Joseph to Potiphar's wife, the virtuous prosiness of which is admirably calculated to check any feminine predilection for the writer. Fragments, too, of a reputed prayer by Joseph exist, and two discourses on the subjects which his life principally illustrates, viz., one on chastity, and the other on brotherly affection.

But the most interesting apocryphal relic is the story of Joseph's first meeting and marriage with Asenath, the daughter of Potipherah, the priest of On (Gen. xli. 45), in which Joseph's typical relation to Christ is throughout discerned. Here, also, we see indications of the persecutions which the comely Hebrew met with from the ladies of Egypt, and the unalterable propriety which he opposed to them.

This Asenath was proud and elated, and greatly despised all men, though she had been seen of no man but of her father. She dwelt in a tower, next her father's house, ten stories high, which contained everything that the eye could desire; and also Egyptian idols in gold and silver, to whom she daily immolated sacrifices. 'Asenath was as tall as Sarah, as comely as Rebekah, and as beautiful as Rachel.'

Now Joseph being on his way through Egypt, sent word to the great satrap and priest Potipherah that he should pay him a visit. Whereupon Potipherah was glad, and told his daughter that Joseph of the Strength of God was coming, and that she should become his wife. At this Asenath was very indignant, and spoke angry words of Joseph, declaring she would be wife to no man, unless to the king's son. And, while they spoke together, came Joseph, seated on the chariot of Pharaoh, which was all of gold, drawn by four horses white as snow, with gilt reins. And Joseph was dressed in a radiant tunic, with a robe of crimson woven with gold, and with a crown upon his head; and round the crown were twelve stones, and over each stone a golden star, and he held a royal sceptre in his hand and a branch of olive with the fullest fruit.

Then Potipherah and his wife came and did him homage, and Joseph entered the hall, and the doors were closed. And Asenath beheld Joseph, and she was troubled at what she had said of him, and said to herself, 'Behold the sun has come to us from heaven in his chariot. I knew not before that Joseph was the son of

God. What father could have begotten so much beauty, and what mother born so much light?' And Joseph entered into the house, and they washed his feet.

Then Joseph said, 'Who is the woman who stood in the hall?' And Asenath went to her chamber; for she feared to molest him, as other women did, who vied with each other in sending him messengers with various presents, all of which Joseph refused with indignation and contempt. And Potipherah said, 'My Lord, my daughter is a maiden, and holds every man in hatred, and no man has seen her except myself, and you this day. If thou wilt, she shall come and salute thee.' Joseph therefore, thinking that, if she hated all men, she would never be importunate to him, said to the father, 'If your daughter be a maiden, I will regard her as my sister.' And they brought her unto him, and she stood in the sight of Joseph.

And her father said, 'Salute thy brother, who hateth all foreign women as thou hatest all men.' And Asenath said, 'Hail! thou that art blessed by the Supreme God.' And Joseph said, 'Be thou blessed by God, who gives life to all things.' Then Potipherah told his daughter to kiss Joseph. But when she approached to kiss him, he stretched out his hand against her, saying, 'It becomes not the man worshipping the living God, eating the bread of life, and drinking the cup of purity, to kiss an outlandish woman whose lips kiss deaf and dumb idols, who eats unsanctified bread from their table, and drinks the cup of deceit from their cistern, and anoints herself with unholy oil.'

Asenath, hearing these words from Joseph, fell into great grief, and wept. Then Joseph took compassion on her, and laid his hand on her head, and blessed her. And Asenath was glad because of his benediction, and went to her couch, and was ill with fear and with joy. And she turned with penitence from the gods whom she served, and renounced them. And Joseph ate and drank, and went away, promising to return in eight days.

Then Asenath put on a black tunic, and, the door being closed, she prayed. And she threw all her idols out of the window, and cast her supper to the dogs, and put ashes on her head, and on the pavement; and she prayed fervently for seven days.

Here we must cut the story short. An angel visits her from

heaven, bids her put aside her black tunic, and the ashes from her head, for that her prayers are heard, and she shall eat from that day of the bread of life, and drink of the cup of purity, and become the wife of Joseph. And at that moment one of the attendants of Potipherah entered, saying, 'Behold, Joseph of the Strength of God approaches; already his outrider is at your door.' And when Joseph entered the hall, Asenath met him, and said to him the words that were spoken to her of the angel. And she washed his feet. And the following day Joseph asked Pharaoh to give him Asenath to wife; and Pharaoh gave her, and placed on their heads crowns of the purest gold. And he bade them kiss one another, and made a great supper which lasted for more than seven days, and commanded that no man should work on the days of the marriage of Joseph. And he called Joseph the son of God, and Asenath the daughter of the Most High.[1]

But to return to the simplicity of the Scriptures. That a history so abounding with dramatic and pathetic scenes as that of Joseph, and so imbued with Oriental feeling, should have found favour with the early Byzantine artists was justly to be expected. The fulness and continuity of the narrative, also, sustained from the early youth to the old age of the patriarch, fitted it especially for a series of representations. And it is in this form that it is first found, and also in that part of Italy most accessible, in the 6th century, to Oriental ideas. The ancient chair of St. Maximian, in the Cathedral of Ravenna, is covered with ivory slabs, with reliefs of Scripture history; those occupying the two outer sides representing the Story of Joseph. This is given in nine compartments, containing the following subjects:—

1. Joseph is being put by his Brothers into a Well, in form like an antique tomb. At his side is a lamb being slaughtered to stain his garment.

2. The bloody garment is brought to Jacob, whose hands are raised above his head in the antique action of sorrow.

3. The Brothers are taking the Money.

[1] Fabricius. Codex Pseudepigraphus, V. Testamenti, Vol. I. chap. cxxxix. p. 774. Historia Asseneth Uxoris Josephi.

4. Potiphar's Wife catching Joseph by the Garment. At the side is Joseph being led away a prisoner—his hands bound—and pulled along by his hair. Before him is the prison—a tower—out of which the chief butler and baker are looking.

5. Pharaoh's Dream, with the fat and the lean kine.

6. Joseph interpreting Pharaoh's Dream.

7. Joseph enthroned; his brothers pouring corn into their sacks. The corn is represented by heads of Indian wheat.

8. Benjamin being given up by Jacob.

9. The meeting of Jacob and Joseph. The sentiment is here very beautiful, and the animals and cattle good.

It is believed that the slab of ivory containing the first of this series—the Dream of Joseph—is lost. For, as a rule, the Dream of Joseph forms the first subject of a series, since, on that, by his arousing the jealousy of his brothers, depends all his subsequent life. St. Jerome, further carrying on the types, says: 'Had not the patriarchs sold Joseph, the inhabitants of Egypt would have perished; and had not Christ been betrayed, the world would have been lost.'

In the prescribed routine of the Greek Church, the history of Joseph takes a conspicuous place. These are the subjects, and their description :—

1. The Dream of Joseph. Joseph asleep; above him the sun, moon, and stars, before him the twelve sheaves.

2. Joseph sold to the Ishmaelites. Two of his brothers are lifting him out of the pit—in form of a well—while the other brothers receive the money, which an Ishmaelite counts out upon a stone.

3. Joseph and Potiphar's Wife. Joseph, abandoning his mantle, avoids sin.

4. Joseph in Prison, explaining the dreams of the chief butler and baker.

5. The Dream of Pharaoh. Here the king is seen asleep on a golden bed. Behind is a stream with seven fat and white kine, and seven lean and black kine; near them are the seven good and the seven bad ears of corn. Farther still is the king upon a throne, and Joseph standing before him, holding a scroll inscribed, 'The seven fat kine are seven years of plenty, and the seven lean kine are seven years of famine.'

VOL. L.   Y

6. Joseph established by Pharaoh as master of the land of Egypt.

7. Joseph enthroned—his ten brothers kneeling before him. Behind are camels laden with sacks.

8. Joseph embracing his Brothers.

9. Joseph embracing his Father Jacob.

This selection of subjects is not so good as that on St. Maximian's chair, and points to an Art which helps itself out by the aid of scrolls with explanatory sentences.

The beautiful story of Joseph is nowhere given with such cir-

59 Joseph dropping Wheat in River. (Biblia Regia, 2 B. VII. Brit. Museum. A.D. 1320.)

cumstance and pathos as in the illustrated Bibles of French or English origin of the 13th and 14th centuries. In these the closely following events of the patriarch's life are dwelt upon with particular interest by the unknown limners. Such an instance is seen in the MS. called Queen Mary's Prayer Book, in the British Museum. Here both text and miniatures show the infusion of legend. Potiphar is turned into the King of Egypt, who goes to the chase and leaves Joseph with the queen 'in the *hostel*.' Also 'the famine over all the face of the earth' gives occasion to a pretty tale, too poetic and picturesque to be strictly censured. According to this, when the famine was at its height, Joseph, who never forgot his father, took straw, and threw it into the river, that it might convey the tidings to the country of his father that wheat was to be had. Whereupon Jacob, being in his '*castel*,' saw the straw and corn floating on the water, and said to his children, Go saddle your asses, and take money, and inquire everywhere whence the straw comes—'car là est blé.' We give an illustration of this picturesque legend (woodcut, No. 59), which took its origin probably from the mere words in Gen. xlii. 1 : 'Now when Jacob *saw* that there was corn in Egypt.' Joseph on one side is seen here dropping, not straw, but wheat, into the river. Jacob in the centre sits in his '*castel*,' seeing it float by, while the brothers on the other side are seen starting on their journey to Egypt.

In other series of the 14th and 15th centuries the story of Joseph is generally confined to the particular subjects which illustrate the types; sometimes he is being lowered into the pit—the pit being always represented as an elegant well or cistern—the type of Christ's descent into Limbus.

Or Jacob is receiving the blood-stained garment, as a type of the Virgin's sorrow at the descent from the Cross. We give an illustration, of great simplicity and pathos, from an Italian Speculum belonging to Mr. Boxall (see woodcut, No. 60, over leaf.) In other instances, a more cruel scene appears. Joseph, as a mere child, is seen dragged away by the bound wrists by an Ishmaelite on horseback; the horse showing the Western as opposed to the Eastern forms of Art, where the camel is introduced. The antitype to this is our Lord being mocked.

A series of the Life of Joseph in two long compartments, with numerous figures, is given by Benozzo Gozzoli in the Campo Santo. It contains no very striking conceptions.

Maturer Italian Art also recognised the picturesqueness of this narrative, and Raphael, Andrea del Sarto, and Pontormo have each illustrated it. From Raphael's hand it came in the form of designs for the Loggie, which are four in number.

1. Joseph's Dream.
2. Selling him to the Ishmaelites.
3. Joseph and Potiphar's Wife.

Jacob receiving Joseph's Garment. (Mr. Boxall's Speculum.)

4. Joseph interpreting Pharaoh's Dream.

Here the first subject (woodcut, No. 61) is very properly not given as the dream of Joseph, but as his narration of it to his brothers—thus giving occasion for figures of the utmost grace and variety. The introduction of the subjects of the dream in two circles in the sky is a remnant of a traditional and hieroglyphical form, hardly worthy of the 16th century.

The pictures by Andrea del Sarto, and Pontormo, his pupil, each two in number, are now placed in different public galleries in Florence—those by Andrea in the Uffizj, those by Pontormo in the Pitti—but they were originally painted for the same room. An interesting story is told regarding them by Vasari. It appears that Pier Francesco Borgherini, a gentleman of Florence, on the occasion of his son's marriage with Margherita Accaioli, decorated, in their

61 Joseph's Dream. (Raphael.)

honour, a room in his house, with bed, *cassoni*, and other furniture carved by the hand of Bagno d'Agnolo. To these decorations he added pictures which, from a passage in Vasari, and from their form, size, and highly finished character, were evidently let into the carved framework of *cassoni*, or of other objects destined to be near the eye. The painters selected were Andrea del Sarto, Pontormo, Granacci, and Il Bachiacca, and each chose, or had assigned to him, the life of Joseph for his subject. These pictures were all completed before the period of the siege of Florence (1529), when many homes were despoiled of their precious contents by the instrumentality of the magistrates, who sent them to France, hoping thereby to propitiate Francis I. The carvings and pictures in the Casa Borgherini were destined to the same fate, and Giovanni Batista della Palla, a low kind of furniture-dealer, and a creature of the magistrates, appeared with his men for the purpose of carrying them off. But he had not calculated on the spirit of Margherita. Knowing his errand, she met him with such abuse as, according to Vasari, was never poured on the head of man before. 'You!' she exclaimed, 'you! Giovan Battista, vile lumberer, petty twopenny shopkeeper! you have the audacity to come and confiscate the ornaments of gentlemen's apartments, as you have done of other rich and noble things in this city, and all to embellish with them foreign countries, and to favour the enemies of our own! I am not so much surprised at you—plebeian creature as you are, and enemy of your country—but I am surprised at the magistrates of this city, who favour your abominable scoundrelism. This very bed which you greedily covet, however you may mask your designs, was the bed given to me at my marriage, on which occasion my father-in-law fitted up these apartments with these magnificent objects, which I honour for his memory, and for the love of my husband; and which, let me tell you, I intend to defend with my life's blood. Get out of this house, Giovan Battista, you and all your troop, and go and tell those who sent you on this pretty errand, that I am not one to allow a thing to be moved hence; and if those who employ you— contemptible wretch—wish to send such presents to the King of France, let them despoil their own homes, and the ornaments and beds from their own apartments. And if you ever venture to show your face again in this house, I'll let you know, to your cost, the respect that is due from you and your like to the houses of your superiors.'[1]

It is to be hoped that this spirited Italian lady retained her well-defended property as long as she lived, and bequeathed it to her descendants. No record remains of when these pictures were ultimately dispersed, or how those by Andrea and Portormo found their way into the galleries of the State. The companion pictures by Granacci and Il Bachiacca have disappeared. Thus only four of the original number are left: and these are of such beauty as to augur a high standard of excellence in all. Without sacrificing the individuality of either artist, these pictures agree so remarkably in size of figures, and general mode of composition, as to show the contiguity for which they were intended. The introduction of several events of Joseph's life into each, has rendered the figures

---

[1] Vasari, vol. ii. p. 281. Vita di Pontormo.

small, and given, as in the series of the Life of Joseph in the Campo Santo, by Benozzo Gozzoli, which it is evident they had before their eyes, a large space to landscape and architecture. It would seem, too, that both had been enjoined to preserve that decorum in the treatment of the subject desirable for the private apartment of a young married pair; for Andrea altogether omits the episode of Potiphar's wife, and Pontormo only gives Joseph at a distance, escaping from the house, and pursued by the lady, as if he had been surprised in a robbery.

Yet it must be avowed that both these masters, though seen to the highest advantage in point of beauty and technical skill, have, as is also the case with Raphael, entirely failed to render the deeper pathos which marks the tale.[1] In this respect a picture by an early Flemish painter, by name of Steuerbout, at S. Donato, the villa of M. Demidoff, near Florence, is far more impressive. Here the young Joseph, going down unresistingly into the pit, with his hands clasped in prayer, has a solemnity and pathos of expression which tells that 'the Lord was with him.'

As a single subject, Murillo is one of the few later painters who has chosen the story of Joseph sold by his brethren. A picture of this composition is in the collection of the Marquis of Hertford, at Manchester House, but, though pleasing in tone, it entirely ignores the capabilities of the moment.

This chapter is not complete without the episode of Potiphar's wife. No more beautiful version, in point of grace and propriety, exists than in Raphael's designs for the Loggie, to which it belongs as a part of a series. Later painters, such as Parmigianino, Palma Giovane, Carlo Maratti, Cignani, Luca Giordano, and others, have selected this subject alone from Joseph's history. In a print by Aldegrever, in the British Museum, the subject is curiously rendered: Joseph is stalking off with an air of offended dignity, whilst the lady pulls him back by the hood of his mantle.

The pathetic scene of Joseph making himself known to his brethren has, wisely, been seldom attempted, for Art has few means of representation proportioned to the force and pathos of

---

[1] Andrea's pictures do not even contain an allusion to the advent of Joseph's brothers in Egypt. He seems to have made this good by a later predella picture—'Joseph making himself known to his Brethren'—now at Panshanger.

these words. Nevertheless, the ineffable grace of Ghiberti here triumphs, by very simple means, over every difficulty. This composition is seen in very low relief, and on a small scale, on an

62   Joseph recognised by his Brethren. (Ghiberti. Bronze doors, Florence.)

entablature of the architecture above the larger central forms of the compartment of the Story of Joseph on the Baptistery gates. Here Benjamin is on his brother's neck, and, it may be, Reuben at his feet, while Joseph's extended hand to the group before him, 'who could not speak, for they were troubled at his presence,' seems to say, 'Come near to me, I pray you, . . . I am Joseph, your brother, whom ye sold into Egypt' (Gen. xlv.), (woodcut, No. 62).

Joseph's meeting with his father is also seen in early Art. We take our illustration from a circular casket of the Byzantine school of very early date, preserved in the Cathedral of Sens,[1] which is ornamented with the histories of Joseph and David—the former twenty-four in number. This illustration (woodcut, No. 63) is

[1] A fac-simile exists in the Arundel Society.

taken literally from the text (Gen. xlvi. 29), 'And Joseph made ready his chariot and went up to meet Israel his father, to Goshen; .... and he fell on his neck, and wept on his neck a good while.' Joseph is here supposed to be in Egyptian costume.

Jacob's reception by Pharaoh also appears in miniatures. The old man approaches bareheaded. Pharaoh advances from his throne, and they shake hands cordially. A picture of this subject by Ferd. Bol, is in the Dresden Gallery. But the later painter has much

Meeting of Jacob and Joseph.
(Ancient ivory. Arundel Society.)

lowered the sentiment between the Egyptian monarch and the Hebrew patriarch. Pharaoh sits on his throne, swelling with pride, and looking with a suspicious and contemptuous air at old Jacob, who, with his hands crossed on his breast, approaches like a menial about to beg or flatter.

A more frequent subject connected with the sojourn of Jacob in Egypt is the blessing bestowed by him upon Ephraim and Manasseh, the two sons of Joseph.

There are few more touching narratives in the Bible than this, when Joseph brings the two boys to the venerable Israel, who said to his son, 'I had not thought to see thy face, and lo, God hath showed me also thy seed.' The meeting of the three generations, the contrast between dying old age and childhood—for Joseph brought his sons 'from between his knees'—is sufficient to furnish a beautiful subject. It had, however, a typical meaning; for Manasseh, the elder, was considered to set forth the Jewish nation; Ephraim, the younger, the Christian—'So the first shall be last, and the last shall be first;' while the position of the crossed hands—the right hand on Ephraim's head, the left on Manasseh's—denoted, according to Bede, the mystery of the Cross.

We see this subject from the earliest time of miniature-painting. We give a quaint illustration (No. 64) from the often-mentioned Bible of the end of the 13th century.

68   Jacob blessing Joseph's Children.
(Bible Historiée. Bibl. Imp., Paris.)

The finest modern example of this subject, treated singly, is by Rembrandt, in the Louvre, where Israel, a magnificent old man, places his crossed hands on the children's heads.

The last appearance of Jacob, in Art, is his burial by Joseph. This is seen in early miniatures, simply a swathed figure borne along on a vehicle, followed by a great multitude; for with Joseph 'went up all the servants of Pharaoh, the elders of his house, and all the elders of the land of Egypt, . . . a very great company' (Gen. l. 7, 9).

Overbeck, Cornelius, and others painted the history of Joseph in fresco in the Casa Bartholdy, at Rome.

Moses.

Moses is the seventh patriarch who prefigures our Lord, of whom he may be considered a type in a larger sense than any of the preceding. He was the head of the Old Covenant, as Christ is that of the New. By the ordinances of the Temple, revealed through him, the sacrificial idea of a Redeemer was developed to the Jewish people; while, by his constant intercession for them, he represented in his own person the mediatorial idea. Accordingly, in subjects which represent the interior of the Temple, the figure of Moses, with the two Tables, is seen seated on the altar on the same place occupied in a Christian church by the cross or crucifix. Further, besides the type presented by his own person, the whole history of Moses is marked by events directly interpreted in Scripture as prefigurations of the Christian dispensation. We need only allude to the blood of the Passover—to 'the baptism unto Moses in the sea and in the cloud'—to the waters from the spiritual rock, 'which rock was Christ'—to the lifting up of the brazen serpent in the wilderness—as some of the types familiar to every Christian. With these examples, it is no wonder that commentators should have evolved figures and signs of minuter character and subordinate details—from the ark of bulrushes in which the child was exposed, to the similarity between the Latin words for rod and virgin (*virga* and *virgo*) which occupied the speculations of a later period.[1] In addition to this, Art has preserved to us traces of Egyptian and Hebrew legend, which assist to fill up, however arbitrarily, a history of the first forty years, on which Scripture is almost silent.

In studying the impersonations of Moses, we are at once struck with that convention in Art which embodies the idea of the glory that shone from his face, under the form of horns. In sculpture, these are absolute excrescences growing on the forehead of the patriarch—as in Michael Angelo's statue, which has the budding strong horns of a young ox; in painting, they are frequently the

[1] Visions of St. Brigitta.

same, or at all events rays of light streaming horn-like from his brows. The origin for this lies in the fact that the Hebrew words for radiant and for horned are synonyms. The Vulgate adopted the latter reading, 'videntes autem Aaron et filii Israel cornutam Moysi faciem;' whence, as Fabricius says, the 'preposterous industry' of artists in affixing horns to the effigies of Moses.

None of the patriarchs have supplied Art with so many subjects of typical and picturesque import: some of them coeval with the earliest Christian forms. Our business is now to trace the chief characteristics of these events in their historical and apocryphal succession.

Regular series of the Life of Moses are not frequent. The most important as a monument of Art, and in a typical sense, is that which formerly extended over the space above the altar where Michael Angelo's Last Judgment now is, and which still remains on the side walls of the Sistine Chapel. We give them in order, type and antitype together:—

Over the altar—now destroyed :—

1. Moses in the Bulrushes. *Perugino.* | 1. Christ in the Manger. *Perugino.*

On left wall—still existing :— | *On right wall—still existing :—*

2. Moses and Zipporah on their way to Egypt, and the Circumcision of their Son. *Luca Signorelli.*
3. Moses overcoming the Egyptian, and driving away the Shepherds. *Sandro Botticelli.*
4. Moses and the Israelites after Passage of Red Sea. *Cosimo Rosselli.*
5. Moses giving the Commandments from the Mount. *Cosimo Rosselli.*
6. The Punishment of Korah, Dathan, and Abiram. *Sandro Botticelli.*
7. Moses giving his last Orders to Joshua. *Luca Signorelli.*

2. Baptism of Christ. *Perugino.*
3. The Temptation, or Christ overcoming the Power of Satan. *Sandro Botticelli.*
4. The Calling of the Apostles from the Lake of Gennesareth. *Domenico Ghirlandajo.*
5. Christ preaching on the Mount. *Cosimo Rosselli.*
6. The Sacrament of Holy Orders, or Christ giving the Keys to Peter. *Perugino.*
7. The Last Supper. *Cosimo Rosselli.*

On entrance-wall :—

8. Michael victorious over Satan, and bearing away the body of Moses. *Cecchino Salviati.* | 8. The Resurrection. *Domenico Ghirlandajo.*

Beccafumi, in his designs for the pavement in the Siena Cathedral, has six scenes from the history of this prophet, as well as from that of Abraham. These, however, refer only to his receiving the tables of the Law and to the worship of the golden Calf.

Raphael has ten designs, embracing the chief points of the history, in his Loggie series.

Poussin has also treated the history of Moses frequently, and has repeated some of the incidents several times.

In closely-illustrated Bibles, the entire history may be traced, beginning even with subjects before his birth, which was accounted a type of the Nativity. In the Bible in the Bibliothèque Impériale, at Paris, we see Pharaoh speaking to the two midwives mentioned in Exodus. In the next picture, his command that every son that is born of the Hebrews shall be thrown into the river, is being executed. The artist here gives the architectural forms most likely to be understood by French eyes, while Pharaoh's throne stands on the old-fashioned *parà*.

In the same quaint Bible, the exposure of the child is given with peculiar simplicity; the swaddled babe in its cradle floating on a retired piece of water, and the princess, richly attired, standing by (woodcut, No. 65). This first scene in Moses' life occupied no part in early Christian types; and even when Art was able to cope with its manifold beauties, they were seldom done justice to.

65   Finding of Moses.
(Bible Historiée. Bibl. Imp., Paris.)

A child in a cradle on a river's brink, with nymphs or fine ladies leaning over it, is, however beautiful the composition, the limit of the subject in Raphael, Poussin, and others. Or, as if impatient of this meagre idea, it takes gorgeous forms unconnected with the story, as in Bonifazio's magnificent picture in the Brera, all redolent of pic-nicking and love-making, in full Venetian costume, which exemplifies the very opposite extreme of treatment to that seen in the French Bible.

Another picture by Bonifazio, of similar treatment, is in the Pitti. It needed, indeed, that fresh and literal searching of the Scriptures of which we see no trace in the palmy times of Italian Art, to draw out the pathetic beauty of this episode. The finding of the child by the princess was, it is true, the needful moment to indicate his adoption by the Egyptians, and even the meaning of his name, for 'she called his name Moses: and she said, Because I drew him out of the water.' But this in no way precluded the expression of the mother's love, which makes this simply-told tale one of the most touching that Scripture bestows on the artist. A limner of the 13th century has not lost sight of this incident. In a Bible in the British Museum there is this semi-ludicrous, semi-pathetic drawing, which we have traced line for line (woodcut, No. 66), which thus gives the little sister—so officious afterwards to call 'a nurse of the Hebrew women'—who 'stood afar off, to wit what would be done to him.' No great master seems to have perceived the beauty of this moment, which lay in the Scriptures unseen and uncared for from the 13th century till the 19th, when it inspired Paul de la Roche's exquisite picture in the hôtel of Baron Rothschild at Paris. Here the 'goodly child' lies in his magnificence, full front to the spectator, deserted by all except by that young eye which watches him furtively through the flags.[1]

66   Sister watching Infant Moses.
(Bible 13th century. British Museum.)

Jewish tradition gives an immediate reward to the humanity of the princess, and a sign of the predestined greatness of the babe;

---

[1] A picture by Mr. Lauder, of the Scotch Academy, gives another and later moment, when the mother has clasped the child to her breast, and, with her back turned to the princess, is pressing its little hand to her lips.

for Josephus says, that, being troubled with a disorder, she had sought the waters of the Nile to assuage it, when, having touched the weeping babe, she was immediately healed. This decided her to bring him up as her own son, for which, the story adds, she obtained divine favour. Another account, compiled by Mr. Robert Curzon from Coptic legends, increases the number of Pharaoh's daughters to seven—all lepers, and all healed by the touch of the infant Moses, by which their beauty was so much increased that the king their father, Pharaoh Valid by name, allowed them to bring him up in the palace. Art, however, has adhered to the Scripture account of the one daughter, to whom tradition gives the name of Thermutis. The story continues to say that she, having no children, and becoming exceedingly attached to the gracious child, contemplated his succeeding to the throne of Egypt.

Therefore, when he was three years of age, she brought him to Pharaoh, who caressed him, and, in sport, put the crown on his head, when the child eagerly pulled it off, and dashed it on the ground: for it is said that the crown was engraved within with figures of idols, which Moses instinctively abominated. Mr. Curzon's account says that it was the covering of the king's beard —of black linen, set with jewels—which Moses in play pulled off. Another version is, that the crown falling off, the child accidentally trampled it under foot. At all events, those around Pharaoh looked upon it as a bad omen. 'And they counselled the king that he should be slain; but another counsellor said that he should be pardoned, because he was too young to know right from wrong; and a third counsellor said, "There is in this child something miraculous and uncommon. Cause, therefore, a burning coal and a ruby ring to be set before him; and if he take the ring it will show that he knows right from wrong, and then let him be destroyed, lest he should spoil the kingdom of Egypt. But if he take up the burning coal, it will show that he is too young to know right from wrong, and then let his life be spared." Then the king said, "Let the hot burning coal and the king's signet ring" (which was a large shining ruby) "be placed side by side, and we shall see what the child will do." And immediately the child stretched out his hand to take the signet ring; but the angel Gabriel (who instantaneously took the form of one of the attendants) turned his hand aside, and the child Moses took up the burning coal, and put it to his mouth, and his tongue was burned therewith, so that he was unable afterwards to speak distinctly, even to the end of his days.'[1]

This story is seen in Art as early as the 14th century in an Italian Speculum belonging to Mr. Boxall, and it is evident that it must have been familiar to painters in the 16th and 17th cen-

67. Moses' Choice. (Giorgione. Uffizj.)

turies. One of the two pictures by Giorgione, in the Uffizj, represents it. Here the figure who holds the brazier may well be the archangel in disguise. Instead of the signet ring a plate of fruit is offered.

Poussin has two pictures of the first part of the incident—the trampling on the crown. One was in the Orleans Gallery.

The next that we see of Moses in Art is his appearance after

[1] History of the Prophet Moses. Compiled by Hon. Robert Curzon.

slaying the Egyptian in the land of Midian, where he sat down by a well. 'Now the priest of Midian had seven daughters; and they came and drew water, and filled the troughs to water their father's flock. And the shepherds came and drove them away: but Moses stood up and helped them, and watered their flock' (Ex. ii. 16, 17). This only appears in mature Art. It is the principal incident of one of the magnificent frescoes already alluded to in the Sistine Chapel, by Sandro Botticelli, which is generally overlooked by those who think themselves bound to admire only Michael Angelo there. Those who appreciate the other great Titan in Art, will find much to admire in the grand conception of Jethro's daughters, and the pastoral beauty of the scene.

Poussin has also two pictures of this subject, less romantic, but with all his beauty of lines.

The subject of Moses and the Burning Bush is early seen in Christian Art. It appears on the walls of the Catacomb of St. Calixtus, and also on an ancient sarcophagus,—in both stripped, as is usual in the economy of classic forms, of all incident but that which suffices to convey the main idea. This main idea was the presence of the Lord, indicated by the passage in Scripture, 'Draw not nigh hither: put thy shoes from off thy feet, for the place whereon thou standest is holy ground.' The whole story, therefore, is told, as we see (woodcut, No. 68) through the single figure of Moses,

68 Moses untying Sandal.
(Wall-painting, Catacomb.)

who, with one foot raised, is untying his sandal.[1] This act was the more readily adopted as an expression of the subject, from the classic usage of taking off shoe or sandal preparatory to sacrifice, and also in presence of superiors. The same conception appears in the mosaics of St. Vitale at Ravenna—executed about 547—only that the hand of the Almighty is added above.

The subject soon expanded in the Art of the miniaturist, with such variations as time and schools supplied; but one feature, owing

[1] This figure is strikingly like the antique statue of Jason tying on a Sandal, now in the Louvre.

doubtless to the unchanging nature of ecclesiastical Art, held its place for ages—Moses is always untying his sandal. In due time the figure of Christ (for so 'the angel of the Lord who appeared in a flame of fire out of the midst of the bush' was, and is interpreted) was substituted for the typical hand of the Father. We take our illustration (No. 69) from a miniature of the 12th century, in the old Burgundian Library at Liège (Evangelia, No. 8 of catalogue), where the formal glory of flames encompassing the head of Christ, and the attempt to imagine an Oriental bush, have resulted in something grand though fantastic. Here Moses is occupied in his usual way, further explained by the scroll in our Lord's hand, 'Solve calceamentum de pedibus tuis,' while the rod anticipates a subsequent incident by its transformation into the form of a serpent. The sheep here have a reality which shows the aptitude of almost all early schools —like that of many boys—for the delineation of animals.

69 Moses and Burning Bush. (MS., Liège Library.)

The 5th and the 12th centuries are more nearly allied in this conception of the subject than are the 12th and beginning of the 16th in Raphael's conception of the same. Here reverence is at once belied by the figure of the First Person, so sternly kept from mortal sight in the story itself, which appears in the flames; while the figure of Moses exemplifies the reading of the Vulgate. 'And Moses hid his face,' as distinguished from that of the Septuagint, where it is given, 'and Moses turned away his head.' The Vulgate version required Moses' hands to hide his face, and was, therefore, incompatible with the old action of untying the sandal, which is, however, retained even so late as by Parmigianino. It was also detrimental to Art, where the hiding the human face is a cowardly way of untying the Gordian knot.

According to early commentators, the types derived from this subject were all of a moral kind. The bush was the Church, burnt, but not consumed, in the flames of persecution; while the shoes of Moses were the worldly ties to be cast off before the soul could have communion with God. This supplies an additional key to the prominence of this action in early Art. But by the 15th century the bush that was burnt, but not consumed, had become a type of the Virgin, and Art, faithfully reflecting modes of thought, has seated her, with the Infant in her lap, in the bush. This is seen in a picture falsely attributed to the troubadour king René, in one of the principal churches at Aix, in Provence, where Moses sits taking off his shoes, with the angel of the Lord, no longer interpreted as Christ, standing by his side. This is also the form of the burning bush in the Greek Church to the present day.

The history of Moses now continues for some space without leaving any deep traces in Art, obviously for the reason that it suggested no types for early forms, and no picturesque materials for later. It is interesting to observe how Music here asserts her powers, and takes up those subjects inapplicable to the use of the sister art. Who will not think of Handel's sublime 'Israel in Egypt,' with its moving panorama of audible images? No Finding of the Infant Moses, no Burning Bush here: but we hear the people 'sigh, by reason of the bondage;' the Plagues pass before us, until the tremendous Hailstone Chorus seems to move and fill every sense; and even in the Passage of the Red Sea, and Overthrow of Pharaoh, the imagination is more vividly stirred than by the positive images of pictorial Art. Thus it is only in some quaint 'Bible Historiée' that we find Moses, and Aaron, who was to him 'instead of a mouth,' standing before Pharaoh performing miracles and bringing down plagues. But swarms of frogs, flies, and locusts were no subject for Art, and a thick darkness over the land, and fire mingled with the hail, which ran along the ground, required a development of landscape skill only known to modern days, and a Turner to exercise it.

The ordinance of the Passover forms one of the types in the 'Biblia Pauperum;' otherwise it is seldom seen unless in pictures of comparatively modern date, and then as a Jewish institution rather than an historical event in Moses' life. But there is one incident of which we give a naïve illustration, namely, the striking on the two sideposts and upper doorposts of the houses. That artist is always to be respected who expresses a scene in the forms most familiar to his eye. This has been done by the French or Flemish limner in this illustration (No. 70) from the Bible, before quoted, in Paris. He evidently did not go beyond his own old-fashioned street for his mode of conception.

70 Israelites striking the Doorposts.
(Bible Historiée. Bibl. Imp., Paris.)

We pass on to the Passage of the Red Sea, which, as a Scriptural type of Baptism, was a subject to be expected in early Christian Art. It is grandly rendered on a sarcophagus in the Vatican in a few figures—the idea given rather than the scene. Here Pharaoh is seen aloft on a quadriga—the sinking action of the nearest horse being of the greatest beauty; his 'host' are seen in three figures sunk to their heads in the flood. Moses stands on dry ground, with his rod, directing the waters (woodcut, No. 71).

The same classic convention is kept up for centuries whenever the overthrow of Pharaoh's host is attempted. The real scene it was impossible to give, and Art availed herself of a kind of pantomime by means of abstract impersonations of natural objects. It is thus that, in a magnificent psalter in the Bibliothèque Impériale, of the 10th century, the intention is assisted and dramatised. Moses stands on the shore—a fine youthful figure with a glory—extending his rod. Around him are a few figures of men, women, and children, typifying the mingled nature of the multitude. Above is a figure with circular veil dotted with stars, with the Greek word **NTΞ**, or Night. A little farther is another female figure, seated, and turning her face away. She is **EPEMOC**, or the Wilderness, to which their steps were tending. Before Moses are Pharaoh and his host, partly immersed in the huge wave. Pharaoh, in armour, is contending in vain against a grand male figure, BTΘOC, or the Deep, which is pulling him down, and in front is a female with green drapery round her hips, and in her hand the form of an antique rudder, who is EPTΘPA ΘΑΛΑCCH, or the Red Sea: thus the tale is told with a vividness which no mere realistic conception could convey. The scene is bounded on the side of the Israelites by a lofty column of flame, representing the pillar of fire.

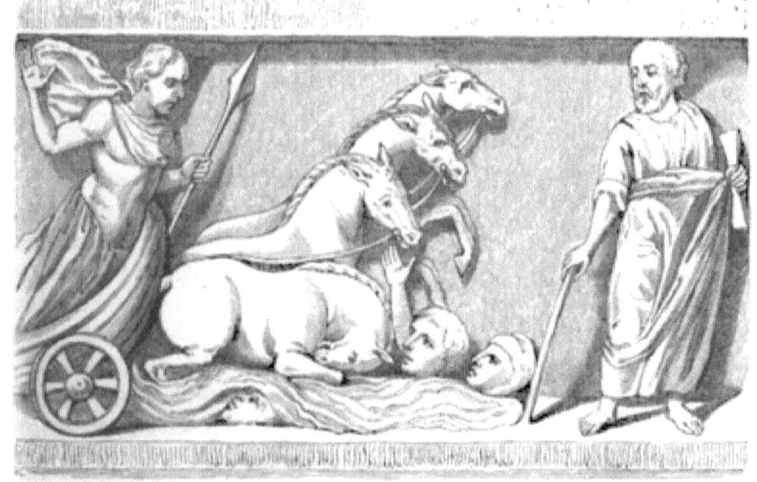

71   Overthrow of Pharaoh.   (Ancient Sarcophagus.)

The overthrow of Pharaoh, in its natural forms, was too vast a task to be often attempted, even in mature Art. Titian is known as the designer of a large woodcut of the subject, and an oil study by him for it exists in Paris. Raphael also has more than one version of the subject; and, more finely than by either, it is given in the little Cappella Medici in the Palazzo Vecchio, seldom seen by the traveller, by Angelo Bronzino. Modern Art, too, by the hand of Martin, has lavished on the subject all the appliances of space, multitude, and scenic effect; but, for power over the imagination, nothing approaches the conception of that supernatural figure clutching Pharaoh by the hair and dragging him down to his doom, as in the old Byzantine miniature.

The gathering of the manna is sometimes seen in mature Art. It gave occasion to graceful figures and postures of men and women bending to collect it. In the series of Old Testament subjects by Ercole Grandi, in the Costabile Gallery at Ferrara, the gathering of the manna is conceived as taking place in an Italian court, with wooden booths, intended for tents.

Another picture in the same series shows the Israelites dancing after the passage; for 'Miriam the prophetess, the sister of Aaron, took a timbrel in her hand, and all the women went out after her with timbrels and with dances.' Here Moses is seen with his rod still in his hand, and Aaron stands by, beating a drum.

72   Moses striking Rock.   (Ceiling in Catacomb.)

The subject of Moses striking the Rock is again one of those types seldom absent from early Christian cycles. This rock was Christ; these waters were living waters for the perishing soul. Moses, therefore, strikes with his rod, the stream gushes forth, one or more figures receive it eagerly on their knees; or as often he stands alone, as in our illustration from the Catacombs (No. 72), where nothing more is wanted to give an idea altogether typical.

Later Art treated this as a real event, sometimes with an admixture of the supernatural, which by no means assists the effect. Thus Raphael, in the Loggie, gives the figure of Moses striking with one hand, and with the other gathering up his robe, apparently lest it should be wetted by the puny stream which issues from the rock; above which is the apparition of the Almighty, borne on cherubs, which completely neutralises the effect of the miracle as far as Moses is concerned.

With Poussin this is a favourite subject. He treated it four times, with that grandeur of drawing and idyllic feeling which idealised all he touched. Otherwise the scene—little as verdant pastures and umbrageous trees are consistent with a parched desert —is realistic. We give an etching, from a picture formerly in the collection of M. Dufourny. Moses stands in the act of striking a mass of rock. Old men are about him, for he did it 'in sight of the elders.' Aaron is behind him, as if addressing the people, who throng in every picturesque antique *pose* around. The stream rushes down into the foreground, where grand male figures stoop to drink, or scoop up the water in their hands, or fill beautiful vases which are passed on to eager groups of women with full forms, and round babies, looking, properly, none the worse for their sufferings. Age and infancy are first thought of in the struggle for water; but there is one thirsty soul who thinks only of himself, while his furious wife grasps at the jar with a vehemence explained by a wailing child behind. The same idea occurs in another picture, as if Poussin had no great hopes of a French husband's generosity in such a strait. On the other hand, a young man (see etching) stands in consternation over a broken pitcher, with its precious contents spilt on the ground. An old man points to the copious stream still descending from the rock. The reader will see the spiritual image thus conveyed. These pictures are full of stirring and beautiful episodes.

The fight between Amalek and Israel in Rephidim is rarely rendered, though accompanied by a highly pictorial incident, namely, the figure of Moses on the hill, with Aaron and Hur holding up his hands. This position was considered by early commentators (such as Bede) as a type of the Cross, and of its conquest over evil.

The perpetual obligation of the Moral Law contained in the Ten Commandments rendered the subject of Moses receiving the tables of the Law of indispensable adoption in early Christian Art. It therefore appears with the earliest cycles on the walls of the Catacombs, and on the sarcophagi found in these subterranean chambers. In accordance with the other classic delineations, the fact alone is given. There is no indication of the Mount, or of the smoke, or of thunder and lightning, but a single figure stands receiving a tablet or book, which a hand projecting from the clouds reaches to him. The only idea needful to be conveyed was that the Moral Law came direct from God (woodcut, No. 73).

73 Moses receiving the Law.
(Ancient sarcophagus.)

Here, again, as in the other subjects we have considered, the imagery of the real scene was reserved for riper Art. Raphael gives Moses on the Mount, with thick clouds and lightnings, and full-cheeked cherubs blowing trumpets, and the figure of the Almighty (differing no more from the prophet than one bearded old man from another) delivering the two tables. Aaron, Nadab, and Abihu, representing the seventy elders, are seen half-way up, with gestures of awe, and the people and their tents are below on the plain.

This subject stamps Moses with that especial character of lawgiver which belongs to most abstract representations of him. Henceforth that effulgence from his face, for which Art, for the reason mentioned (p. 171), adopted the arbitrary signs of horns, belongs properly to him. And it is thus that Parmigianino has conceived his fine figure of Moses (a fresco in the Church of the Steccata at Parma) as breaking the two tables at sight of the people worshipping the golden calf. Though, in the mechanical and unreasoning character of much so-called Christian Art, he is often seen with it in earlier incidents.

As a subject, these two incidents—the Receiving the Law, and the Breaking the Tables—are sometimes united in one picture. This was the case with Poussin and Claude and others, who combined the power for figures and landscape, or who wanted a biblical foreground for a glowing Italian scene; as, for instance, the magnificent Claude in the Grosvenor Gallery. Moses is seen in the middle distance, generally attended by Joshua, dashing the tables to the ground.

The story of the Brazen Serpent is one of those Scriptural types given in Art for the ends of doctrine: 'And as Moses lifted up the serpent in the wilderness, even so must the Son of man be

lifted up' (John iii. 14). This type, so expressly exemplified by
the lips of Christ Himself, does not appear in early cycles at all.
This would seem strange till we consider that the subject involved
the figure of an animal representing one of the oldest forms of
idolatry. The very shape of a cross, too, needful to illustrate
the spiritual meaning, was, as we shall see further, kept out of
sight for the first four centuries and a half. It is no wonder,
then, that the Catacombs show no instance of this doubly-shunned

74   Burial of Moses.   ('Bible de Noailles,' A.D. 1000.)

symbol of salvation. It takes its place among the mediæval types
as a symbol of the Crucifixion (see woodcut, No. 4, p. 28, from the
'Biblia Pauperum'). Maturer Art seems to have felt other
objections: the painful nature of the subject would interdict it
to all who sought chiefly for scenes of beauty in Art, while its
adequate representation involved difficulties not to be undertaken
by many. In due time the painter was born into the world whose
spirit and hand shrank neither from the horrible nor its diffi-

culties, and of whom it might be predicated that a spectacle of struggling women and agonised men, tormented by fierce fabulous animals, would offer especial attractions. Thus Rubens fills up the gap, and has left us a picture of the Brazen Serpent, now in our National Gallery, which, with every quality peculiar to himself, has not one which can lead the mind to the intention of this type.

'So Moses the servant of the Lord died there in the land of Moab, according to the word of the Lord. And He buried him in a valley in the land of Moab, over against Beth-peor: but no man knoweth of his sepulchre unto this day.' Our rude little illustration (woodcut, No. 74, last page), one of the very few we have seen of this mysterious subject, is taken from a Bible of the 10th century. It tells the tale, and is not without beauty, nor without its type. 'For when Moses died, the Lord buried him, but when Christ died, He was raised from the dead; thus the Mosaic dispensation was superseded by the Christian, but Christianity shall endure till the end of time.'[1]

[1] Scott's Bible, Deut xxxiv. 5, 6. *Note.*

Joshua.

Joshua is the eighth type of our Lord; each in turn representing a distinct portion of the Divine character, person, or history. Here his very name—Joshua, or Jesus, a Saviour—is in accordance with the acts by which he prefigures Christ; for as Moses represents the Old Law, so Joshua represents the New. Thus the word of the Lord did not come unto Joshua until the death of Moses, when the first behest was to lead the people, after their weary wanderings, over the river Jordan into the promised land. Here, therefore, Christ's mission towards the human race is plainly foreshadowed; for as the wanderings in the wilderness are interpreted as a type of this life, so are the crossing the Jordan and entrance into Canaan, under the conduct of Joshua, looked upon as that of the believer's passage through death and translation into heaven through the merits of Christ. In every way does this view hold good, for Christ himself, as the Ark of the Covenant, passed through the waters before the Israelites, and only by His intervention were the floods stayed from overwhelming them.

The history of Joshua appears early in Christian Art, and under peculiar circumstances, being the subject of one of the most remarkable works of the 7th or 8th century that has been preserved to us. It consists of fifteen pieces of parchment, gummed together, forming a running story, above thirty-two feet long, by eleven inches wide. This is a true specimen of the antique 'volumen,' or roll. It is preserved in the Vatican. Here classic forms still maintain their supremacy. It would be difficult to conceive the miraculous and warlike incidents of this ancient book better given. The story of Joshua is here divided into twenty-one subjects, which we give in order.

1. The two spies whom Joshua sent out escaping to the mountains, while two soldiers on horseback, sent by the King of Jericho, go out in a different direction to seek for them : 'And they went, and came unto the mountain, and abode there three days, until the pursuers were returned' (Josh. ii. 22). Above the two Israelites is a figure seated upon a hill, personifying the mountain.

2. The priests bearing the Ark of the Covenant, followed by Joshua, preceding the Israelites. 'When ye see the ark of the covenant of the Lord your God, and the priests the Levites bearing it, then ye shall remove from your place, and go after it (Josh. iii. 3). Joshua here is seen in armour—a commanding figure, with a glory round his head.

3. The Levites standing with the Ark of the Covenant in the midst; the people following, some of them taking up stones. 'And the priests that bare the ark of the covenant of the Lord stood firm on dry ground in the midst of Jordan, and all the Israelites passed over' (iii. 17). 'And Joshua said . . . take you up every man of you a stone upon his shoulder, according unto the number of the tribes' (iv. 5). The waters of the Jordan are not given, but, according to antique usage, the figure of a river god, with his arm on his urn, is seen seated above.

4. The Israelites, some of them bearing stones, preceded by Joshua. 'And the people carried the stones over with them unto the place where they lodged' (iv. 8).

5. Joshua piling the stones; the Israelites behind him. 'And those twelve stones, which they took out of Jordan, did Joshua pitch in Gilgal' (iv. 20).

75   Joshua's Vision.
(MS., Vatican. D'Agincourt.)

6. The circumcision of the Israelites at Gilgal by the command of the Lord (chap. v.).

7. The vision of Joshua. This is curiously represented (woodcut, No. 75). On one side stands an angel with a drawn sword—a noble figure; opposite to him that of Joshua, addressing him; between the two, another figure of Joshua, prostrate before the angel, and stripped of his glory, as proper before a superior being. This illustrates the two parts of this vision. 'And, behold, there stood a man over against him with his sword drawn in his hand: and Joshua went unto him, and said unto him, Art thou for us, or for our adversaries? And he said, Nay; but as captain of the host of the Lord am I now come. And Joshua fell on his face to the earth, and did worship' (v. 13, 14).

8. The priests carrying the Ark of the Covenant, and preceded by seven figures blowing trumpets, round the walls of Jericho, which are personified by a female figure of great beauty sitting within the ramparts. Farther on, the walls falling, and the people rushing in, some with torches to fire the place, preceded by Joshua. And again the same grand female figure seated outside in a disconsolate attitude. 'And seven priests bearing seven trumpets . . . went on continually. . . . And it came to pass, . . . that the wall fell down flat, so that the people went up into the city. . . . And they burnt the city with fire' (vi. 13, 20, 24).

9. Joshua seated, sending off two men to explore the city of Ai: the same two farther on. Above the first two is a female figure with mural crown, representing Ai; above the second, the city itself, with walls and towers. 'And Joshua sent men from Jericho to Ai, . . . and the men went up and viewed Ai' (vii. 2).

10. The two men returned, reporting to Joshua the results of their journey.

11. The Israelites marching up against Ai, and, farther on, repulsed before the city; some on the ground, intended for the wounded. Above, an abstract figure, seated, very different from the preceding, with a glory round its head, and pointing to the host of the men of Ai. It may be interpreted as the same angel favouring the enemies of Israel. 'And they fled before the men of Ai. And the men of Ai smote of them about thirty and six men' (vii. 4, 5).

12. Joshua kneeling, with figures in the same posture behind him, and, above, the hand of the Lord blessing. 'And Joshua rent his clothes, and fell to the earth upon his face before the ark of the Lord, . . . he and the elders of Israel' (vii. 6).

13. Achan taken, and brought before Joshua, confessing his guilt; farther on, the Israelites stoning him in the valley of Achor—represented by an abstract male figure above.

14. The hand of the Lord appearing to Joshua, bidding him go up to Ai. Men entering the city on one side with torches; a band coming out of it on the other; another band fleeing before them. The same figure with a glory, seated above, favouring the retreating body. In this manner, with a few figures, and in a small space, is the history of the stratagem given, by which the men of Ai were drawn out of the city, whilst the Israelites pretended to

retreat before them, and the bands who were in ambush entered the city and set fire to it.

15. In the distance the King of Ai, with hands tied behind him, dragged along by the hair; in the foreground the same brought before Joshua; farther on, the same hanging dead.

16. Joshua worshipping at an altar, with the people behind him.

17. In the distance, two men with knapsacks; in the foreground, the same two men bowing before Joshua, with their hands under their garments—an Oriental token of respect. Joshua, a grand figure, seated on a throne, with spear in hand. These are the Gibeonites, who acted wilily, and pretended to come as ambassadors from a far country.

76   Joshua arresting Sun and Moon. (MS., Vatican. D'Agincourt.)

18. The same two men on their knees before Joshua, confessing their stratagem.

19. The Israelites fighting the five kings; in the midst Joshua, arresting the course of the sun and moon. 'Then spake Joshua to the Lord, in the day when the Lord delivered up the Amorites before the children of Israel, and he said in the sight of Israel, Sun, stand thou still upon Gibeon, and thou, Moon, in the valley of Ajalon' (x. 12). The conception of Joshua's figure and those of the combatants about him is full of animation. We give this subject (woodcut, No. 76), which comprises, from the position of the moon, the preceding subject, with the Gibeonites kneeling before Joshua. The fine figure with a mural crown is probably that of the city of Gibeon.

20. Joshua seated on his throne, with the people behind him; two men eagerly addressing him. In the distance, five figures

retreating on horseback. 'But these five kings fled. . . . And it was told Joshua, saying, 'The five kings are found hid in a cave at Makkedah' (x. 16, 17).

21. Joshua enthroned. At a distance the five kings, with their hands bound, dragged along by the hair; nearer to Joshua, the same on the ground before him, and the captains of Israel putting their feet on their necks. Farther on are the five kings, hanging.

Since the period of this remarkable work, the subjects contained in the Book of Joshua have been of rare occurrence in Art.

Raphael gives the passage of the Jordan, with the ark standing in the centre; but, as with Moses striking the Rock, he neutralises the effect of the miracle by a double agency, for here, more prominent than the ark, sits the figure of a river god (if it be not intended for that of the Almighty Himself), upholding the walls of waves on one side.

The Fall of the Walls of Jericho, by Raphael, is also singularly devoid of its usual miraculous characteristics. No signs of trumpets or shouting are here, but a body of armed men, in the foreground, are going against the city, which is already in flames, most of it upright, and one tower falling, apparently, by the ordinary means of assault.

Where Joshua is represented singly, he generally appears as a warrior. In a Bible at Brussels (about 1470), Joshua, kneeling, is receiving a lance and pennon from Christ, out of a starred nimbus, as a sort of investiture.

JUDGES.

THE Book of Judges is a continuous history of the sins, and consequent punishment, of the Israelites, and of the individuals raised up from time to time—considered as types of Christ, or of the Church—to deliver them out of the hand of their enemies. The first of whom Art takes notice is Shamgar, son of Anath, 'which slew of the Philistines six hundred men with an ox goad: and he also delivered Israel' (Judges iii. 31). He is adopted in the 'Speculum Salvationis' as one of the types of Christ's power, which levelled the guards to the ground who came to capture Him.

Jael, the wife of Heber the Kenite, who invited Sisera into her tent and slew him with a nail, is next the subject of illustration. She not being an Israelite, but one of the people of the land, is looked upon as a type of the Gentile Church. This is a subject scarcely seen till the 16th and 17th centuries. Altdorfer, Goltzius, and Lucas van Leyden have all treated it. Sisera, a large man in armour, lies asleep on the floor, and Jael, usually seen with a turban, as a type of her foreign descent, is in the act of fixing a tent-nail into his ear, having the hammer in her other hand.

GIDEON.

'AND the children of Israel did evil again in the sight of the Lord.' Gideon was now chosen to rescue them. To him appeared the angel of the Lord, 'as he threshed wheat by the wine-press, to hide it from the Midianites. He entreats the angel to stay, and prepares an offering, which is miraculously consumed. Rembrandt, in one of his etchings, has treated the subject of the angel with his rod, striking the rock, whence issues fire.

The sign requested by Gideon, and vouchsafed by the Lord, that his fleece should be dry when all around was wet, and *vice versâ*, is seen in Bibles and Speculums as a sign of the Incarnation (see woodcut, No. 77). The older commentators interpret the fleece of

77   Gideon. ('Speculum Salvationis.' M. Berjeau.)

Gideon as the Hebrew nation, who were first moistened with the dew of God's grace when all other nations were dry, and then in their turn were left unrefreshed when it fell on the Gentiles.

The conquest of Gideon, at the head of 300 men, over the camp of the Midianites, is seen occasionally in illustrated Bibles of a late time.

JEPHTHAH.

JEPHTHAH, the Gileadite, is interpreted as one of the minor types of Christ. Like Joseph, he was persecuted by his brethren, and fled from before them. Afterwards he delivered them from their enemies, the Ammonites, and finally sacrificed his daughter, or, as the early commentators interpret it, his own flesh, in a vow to God for their salvation. Later theologians considered Jephthah's daughter as a type of the Virgin—making a somewhat forced analogy between the sacrifice of the maiden to God and the Virgin's dedication in the Temple. In this sense the incident appears in the 'Speculum Salvationis.' The daughter kneels before a little wayside shrine, and Jephthah, with an immense sword, is about to strike off her head. Later French painters, Coypel and Vouet, have treated the subject with the feeling it may permit, but which it does not strictly dictate, for Coypel makes her taking leave of her mother.

SAMSON.

We now come to a name in Israel which Christian genius has invested with the loftiest thoughts in verse, and the grandest strains in music. Milton and Handel, those names so often twin, here also go hand in hand. The art of the painter can hardly be said to stand on the same level, for no great master has made the history of Samson his subject, though portions of it have been finely rendered.

Samson is an important type of Christ; his birth, like that of our Lord, having been announced to his mother by an angel, who further declared that the child should be a Nazarite, or dedicated to the Lord from his birth, and that he should deliver Israel out of the hand of the Philistines. We are not aware that this act of annunciation was ever attempted in Art—probably from its too close resemblance, in general features, to the Annunciation to the Virgin Mary. It is rather implied by the next following scene, as given by Rembrandt, who represents Manoah and his wife kneeling before the altar, with the angel ascending in the flame of the burnt-offering.

The life of Samson furnishes various other types. The first of which Art takes cognisance is the occasion of his going to Timnath, when, 'behold, a young lion roared against him, . . . and he rent him as he would have rent a kid.' This is taken as a type of the Temptation, when Christ overcame Satan, who is described in the New Testament as a roaring lion. This incident was adopted by early designers. It is seen in an Anglo-Saxon MS. of the year 1000 (British Museum, Tiberius, C. VI.) Samson kneels with one knee on the lion, and tears him by the jaws. The same form, which admitted of great elegance of action, continues for centuries. We take an illustration (No. 78, over leaf) from Mr. Boxall's Italian Speculum of the 14th century. Albert Dürer and Israel van Mechenen have treated the subject.

The subject of Samson's destroying a thousand Philistines with the jaw-bone of an ass is treated as one of the types of the guards

78   Samson overcoming Lion.   (Mr. Boxall's Speculum.   14th century.)

falling backwards to the ground at the sound of Christ's voice. It thus appears in the 'Speculum Salvationis,' which abounds in illustrations from the Book of Judges. But in the desire to magnify Samson, the early artist has diminished the miracle, for the Nazarite is made a giant in size, and wields so tremendous an implement that his victory over his Lilliputian assailants seems no way surprising.

Guido Reni has chosen a subsequent moment, when, being sore athirst with his exertions, his prayer is answered by a miraculous flow of water from the hollow place in the jaw-bone, whence he drank and was refreshed (woodcut, No. 79).

Another subject is supplied by Samson's carrying off the gates of Gaza. This is the type of our Lord's Resurrection, who burst the gates of the tomb. This is too peculiar in character to have

79   Samson drinking from Jaw-bone.   (Guido Gallery, Bologna.)

been treated by any great master; though a design by Albert Dürer is in the Pourtalés Collection at Paris; but it occurs in enamels and miniatures, as well as in the 'Speculum Salvationis,' where Samson, with a gate under each arm, and in the costume of a German burgher, is seen issuing from the city, leaving an open portal behind him.

The far more picturesque subject of Delilah betraying her lover has been treated by masters of the maturest times of Art, and scarcely seems to have been attempted till its beauties and difficulties were appreciated. Those masters who treated it earliest, such as Lucas van Leyden, Burckmair, &c., chose the quieter moment, when Samson lies in deep slumber upon the knees of the enchantress, whilst she cuts off his luxuriant locks. The Philistines are approaching in the distance. In some of these representations a vessel of wine stands near, implying that he had been overcome with the juice of the grape; but this is contrary to the sense of Scripture, which nowhere gives us to believe that Samson broke his vow of abstinence as a Nazarite. Here Milton is more correct:—

> Desire of wine, and all delicious drinks,
> Which many a famous warrior overturns,
> Thou could'st repress.

Painters of more advanced anatomical knowledge chose a later moment, when the Philistines are upon him, and Samson is vainly struggling to set himself free. Van Dyck has a splendid conception of the scene, in which brawny Philistines, not inconsistently, are putting forth all their strength to overcome the dreaded but now feeble foe.

Rembrandt has a tremendous conception of this struggle, where four soldiers assault their victim, and one of them proceeds to deprive him of sight. Delilah is seen escaping behind, carrying off her money.

Jan Steen, with all his coarseness, has conceived this scene with a touch of pathetic satire unseen in other pictures. Delilah is counting the money received for his capture, while the blind warrior, loaded with chains, is led by a cord held by a beautiful little child. Probably this great painter and vulgar man intended this as an allusion to the God of Love; but the pathos lies in the literal meaning. This picture belonged, or belongs to Mr. Nieuwenhuys, at Brussels.

In the manuscript of the 14th century, in the British Museum, often quoted as Queen Mary's Prayer-book, an incident is given scarcely seen elsewhere. This is Samson, blind, bent, and dressed in menial attire, turning a wheel; an overseer close by is striking the unhappy prisoner on the head, the hair of which is still short. This is a touching picture, and not without grace.

The last act of Samson's life, which caused and which revenged his death, is also given, under the title of Samson mocked by the Philistines, as a type of Christ mocked by the Jews. He is seen in the Speculum, within a temple, with figures around him, pulling a column greatly out of the perpendicular; or again, as standing between two columns, with a guard on each side in the act of tying one hand to each.

Samuel.

Samuel, the priest and prophet, though no direct type of our Lord, must not be passed over in a pictorial history of Christ. His birth of one childless before, his dedication to the Lord, and the preference of him before the sons of Eli, the High Priest and Judge of Israel, have been interpreted as signifying the adoption of the Gentiles and the rejection of the Jews. A close analogy also is found between the song of his mother Hannah and that of the Virgin. Each is a 'Magnificat' of the Most High; each celebrates the discomfiture of the Proud and the exaltation of the Humble. The direct illustrations of Samuel's history are chiefly confined to his dedication in the Temple, which is the type of the Presentation. This subject is capable of much beauty, but has hardly found its way into the category of Art proper. We take an illustration of charming character from Mr. Boxall's Speculum (woodcut, No. 80, over leaf). Here the pious obedience which marked the life of Samuel is beautifully indicated in the action of the child; while his shyness of the strange priest, and his natural turning to his mother, are worthy of a more advanced period. Nor is the little coat forgotten.

Rembrandt has the subject of Samuel and his mother, now in the Stafford Gallery. It is not very intelligibly told. Hannah is here represented as an aged woman, musing upon the sacred volume, with spectacles in hand, and her stick at her side—indications incompatible with her having borne three sons and two daughters after the birth of Samuel. The scene is in the Temple, for in the background are the Brazen Serpent and the tables of the Law. Beneath these is the High Priest, receiving a child from its parents, doubtless intended for the Presentation in the Temple. Samuel kneels at his mother's side.

Sir Joshua Reynolds, by the addition of a ray of light, has turned another common figure of a child saying its prayers into an infant Samuel hearing the voice of the Lord.

But a living painter, Mr. Sant, has, in the sense of conception,

80   Presentation of Infant Samuel.   (Mr. Boxall's peculum. 14th century.)

given us a more faithful view of this touching scene, where the young boy, obedient to the letter of Eli's instruction, answers, 'Speak, Lord, for thy servant heareth.' Here the child is sitting up with dilated eye and upraised hands—a sweet type of infant piety and awe.

Otherwise, the history of Samuel becomes merged in that of Saul and David, both anointed by him.

DAVID.

DAVID is in a closer sense the type of Christ than any other that the Scriptures afford. His name and the Idea of Christ have a mysterious and an actual identity throughout the sacred text. Through David's mouth, and in David's person, Christ soliloquises of Himself, 'Thou shalt not leave my soul in hell.' In an earthly sense, David is the only progenitor of our Lord. Christ is appealed to by the blind man as the 'Son of David;' He is mentioned as 'the seed of David,' 'the root of David,' the 'offspring of David;' while His salvation is designated as 'the sure mercies of David.' It is needless to multiply instances, familiar to all, of this intimate relationship of the flesh and of the Spirit. Commentators have extended this affinity throughout the chief acts of David's life; while even the music of the sweet singer in Israel was interpreted as prefiguring the gracious harmony of the New Testament.

No history has suggested more analogies for the cycles of Mediæval Art than that of David. The 'Biblia Pauperum' and 'Speculum Salvationis' abound with them, and no history also more clearly proves how little mere motives of feeling—the highest which Art intrinsically possesses—entered then into her choice of subjects. The sudden and faithful love, for example, of Jonathan for David, whom he loved as his own soul, is one of those tender episodes which rise here and there from the time-hardened soil of the Old Testament, as if to show that men of all periods are kin. Nevertheless, Art has taken so little cognisance of this beautiful story, that no conception of Jonathan's person can be said to exist. On the other hand, incidents are, as we shall see, stereotyped in Art, from reasons of supposed analogy, which the reader of Scripture would probably overlook.

The representations of David may be divided into three classes: the first, personal and abstract; the second, typical and historical; the third suggested by the language of the Psalms.

Those of an abstract character begin on a ceiling in the Catacombs. Here the sling, as the instrument by which he overcame

81 David with Sling
(Ceiling, Catacombs.)

the giant, is his distinction. This characterises him as the shepherd. The same idea is intended in Michael Angelo's statue before the Palazzo Vecchio at Florence, which, without this attribute, would be scarcely interpreted as a youthful David.

A series of the life of David, in which the abstract element and grand beauty of antique Art is equally and remarkably retained, exists in a psalter of the 9th or 10th century in the Bibliothèque Impériale at Paris.[1] It consists of many magnificent pictures of a quarto size, the finest of which are:—1. The Anointing of David; 2. David overcoming the Lion; 3. Nathan before David; 4. David playing the Harp; and 5. David between Wisdom and Prophecy.

Both the last subjects may be considered to belong to the abstract class. We give a woodcut of each. David playing the harp while keeping his sheep embodies both the musical and pastoral idea (woodcut, No. 82). He is here accompanied by a grand female figure, who sits gracefully with her hand on his shoulder: at her side, in perpendicular letters, according to Greek fashion, is the word *Melodia*. Before him, in one corner, is a hill, expressed by a male figure, with an inscription signifying the hilly country of Bethlehem; in the distance is Bethlehem itself. The dog and the sheep are well rendered.

Our next woodcut (No. 83, over leaf) shows David between Wisdom and Prophecy, whose names in Greek are inscribed above their heads. David is here seen with the Holy Ghost, or the gift of inspiration, above the glory that surrounds him. He holds the Book of the Psalms open, to which the hand of Prophecy is pointing. Both the allegorical figures are raised above David—the one holding a scroll, the other a book. David is in the attire of the emperors of Byzantium. He is of middle age, according to the time when his Psalms were penned. The same idea partially pervades a grand miniature in an Anglo-Saxon MS. of the year 1000 (British Museum, Tiberius, C. VI.), where David is seen seated,

[1] Described in Dr. Waagen's *Kunstwerke und Künstler in Paris*, p. 217.

82   David with Harp (Greek MS. Bibl. Imp., Paris. 9th century.)

with a sceptre in his hand, and a dove perched upon it. Above is the hand of the Almighty, holding a horn, betokening the horn of oil with which Samuel anointed him. But here the beauty of the antique has yielded to the grand and weird character of Anglo-Saxon Art.

In later times, the accessories by which David is known became more fixed. When he is seen among the prophets, he is recognised by his crown, as in the Tree of the Cross; when among the kings of Israel, all playing on musical instruments, as in the Root of Jesse, he is known by his harp. In the series of the 14th and 15th centuries, we frequently see David as a youth attacking the

83. David between Knowledge and Prophecy. (Greek MS., 9th century. Bibl. Imp., Paris.)

Philistine, and yet already crowned. This is a combination of the real event with the fact of his being already the anointed of the Lord.

In later times, pictures containing a series of the life of David were often given in the form of a *cassone*. Two of this class, by the rare master Pesellino, are in the collection of the elder Marchese Torrigiano at Florence. The subjects they contain are the following:—

1. David on the left sitting and tending cows and sheep; killing a lion with stones; brought to Saul, who is on horseback; and slinging the stone at Goliath, who is about to fall. Israelites fighting with Philistines.

Byzantine MS. 9th century. Bibl. Imp. Paris.

2. The Triumph of David. We shall describe this further in its historical place.

The Anointing of David—the first incident of his life in an historical sense—is very grandly rendered in the series of the 9th century enumerated in page 202. Samuel the Priest of the Lord, with a glory round his head, stands with a twisted horn in his hand, from which he is shedding the divine consecration on the head of the youthful form bending reverently before him. Behind David is his father Jesse, a grand figure, looking on with much awe, and behind Jesse are the six brethren, with their names in Greek above them; the eldest, Eliab, being bearded, the others smooth-cheeked youths. Above David stands a female allegorical figure, intended for Mildness, with a nimbus and bare arms and chest, pointing to him.

In later Art the subject is seldom seen. Raphael has it in his Loggie series. The youthful shepherd, with his staff, stands in the midst, while Samuel pours the oil from the horn upon his head. The seven other sons of Jesse stand around; Jesse himself is busy with the sacrifice.

The next incident is one which appears early and frequently in Mediæval Art. This is his victory over the lion and the bear, which David relates to Saul as a plea for his going out against the Philistine: 'Thy servant kept his father's sheep, and there came a lion and a bear, and took a lamb out of the flock; . . . thy servant slew both the lion and the bear.' This was considered by Bede as an important type of our Lord's victory, first over Satan, and then over Antichrist. Under this view, in the earlier representations, the conquest over the lion is alone given; according to David's words, 'I went out after him and smote him, and delivered it [the lamb] out of his mouth; and when he arose against me, I caught him by his beard, and smote him, and slew him.' Nothing can be grander than the way in which this is given in the series of the ancient Psalter. We give an etching which, however inadequate in means, conveys a true idea of the character of the original. David's figure is the grandest conception of youthful strength and courage. The figure of Ischus, or Force, behind him, partakes of the same rapid action, as if suddenly flown to his assistance. The harp of the shepherd lies on one side on his cast-off mantle. The lion and sheep have much truth of rendering, while the bear in the foreground, already dead, shows less familiarity with this class of animal. Behind a rock is a figure in terror, which may possibly represent some attendant shepherd.

In a miniature of the 12th century (British Museum, Nero, C. VI.), all power over vehement action has departed. David walks by the side of the lion with his arm over his neck, taking the lamb from his mouth, with much the same action that a boy walks beside a favourite Newfoundland dog, and extricates a stick from his jaws.

By the 14th century the conquest over the lion and the bear was fused into one incident, having become meanwhile a more particular type of the Temptation—in allusion to its two parts, Greediness and Avarice, or, as here interpreted, Rapacity. In Mr. Boxall's Speculum, David is quaintly slaying both at once. In a later Speculum, a great economy of labour is observable—David is killing the bear, and the bear is killing the lion.

The encounter between David and Goliath comes next in history. Here the size of the Philistine, increased by his armour, offers the strongest contrast to that of the youthful David, who stands before him in his shepherd's tunic in the act of slinging the stone. This is another type of the Temptation—of that first part where our Lord is tempted by Pride; Goliath is also considered as the type of Lucifer, who fell by pride, and by measuring himself against God. This is given in many quaint ways in early miniatures, where the contrast between the swelling giant and the puny David is rendered with intentional exaggeration. In a Bible belonging to Mr. Holford, the giant even advances on horseback, while David awaits the charge on foot. But in mature Art this part of the subject is seldom treated, the colossal figure of the giant being a sufficient objection. The next moment was therefore chosen, which represents the victory over, and the slim youth kneeling or standing —which is truer to the text, 'Therefore David ran, and stood upon the Philistine'—upon the prostrate body, preparing to cut off the head with Goliath's own sword. Michael Angelo has the subject in one of the angles of the Sistine ceiling, as the type of the victory over Evil. David is most energetically astride the foreshortened figure, and is wielding the tremendous sword with one hand, while he presses down the giant's head with the other.

Here Goliath is evidently still alive—a fact adhered to by most painters, and authorised by the text; for David first smote Goliath with the stone, so that 'he fell upon his face to the earth,' and then 'took his sword, and drew it out of the sheath thereof, and slew him, and cut off his head therewith' (1 Sam. xvii. 49-51).

David and Head of Goliath. (Guido.)

Raphael has a fine design, engraved by Marc Antonio, where the giant lies prone, with David kneeling with one knee upon him. The result of the victory is seen in the immediate terror of the Philistines and onslaught of the Israelites.

A second design of the subject, very like this, is in the Loggie of the Vatican.

35 Triumph of David. (Pesellino. Collection of Marchese Torrigiano, Florence.)

Daniel da Volterra has also the subject twice over, with slight variety of composition, back and front of a standing picture in the Louvre.

The next moment of this history in Art is rather of an abstract kind. It is David victorious—the young conqueror contemplating his spoil. He is generally with the head near him, or in his hand; the sword or the sling in the other. Giorgione, Pordenone, Guido Reni, and several German painters of the 16th century, have rendered this a very picturesque subject. David is here no longer the shepherd, but he is a noble youth with jewelled cap and plume and flowing mantle. We give an illustration from Guido (No. 84, last page). Pordenone, however, and others, have committed the mistake of dressing David in full armour, in defiance of Scripture, which relates that David put off the armour wherewith Saul had armed him: 'And David said unto Saul, I cannot go with these; for I have not proved them. And David put them off him.'

David's Triumph. (Matteo Rosselli. Pitti.)

The Triumph of David. 'And it came to pass, . . . when David was returning from the slaughter of the Philistine, that the women came out of all cities of Israel, singing and dancing, to meet King Saul, with tabrets, with joy, and with instruments of musick. And the women answered one another as they played, and said, Saul hath slain his thousands, and David his ten thousands' (1 Sam.

xviii. 6, 7). This is seen in the form of a magnificent equestrian procession in the *cassone* picture by Pesellino, mentioned p. 204. Here the young hero stands aloft in a car, the head of Goliath, held by the hair, in his hand, and the body of the giant most dexterously disposed in the space behind him. Before him is the chariot of Saul, with Philistines—grand figures in black armour —attached to it. An immense procession of horsemen, eighty-one in number, precede and follow, with trumpeters, heralds, spearmen, and all the array of old Florentine pomp. A number of animals—a bear, panthers, and hunting-dogs—add great picturesqueness, while graceful female figures, with instruments of music, advance dancing from the gates of Jerusalem. A splendid landscape crowns the whole length. We give the figure of David from this gorgeous picture, as he stands upon his chariot (woodcut, No. 85, page 208).

This subject has a different class of beauty when given more simply. Matteo Rosselli has a charming picture in the Pitti— David here, though heavily laden with the head and sword, stalks along with the double buoyancy of youth and success. Three beautiful female figures dance and sing as they precede or accompany him (woodcut, No. 86, last page). The triumph of David is a type of the Entry into Jerusalem.

The jealousy and treachery of Saul in due order follow. The sacred narrative has told us that David's harp had refreshed Saul, so that the evil spirit departed from him. But on the morrow after the triumph, as 'David played with his hand, as at other times,' the king cast his javelin at him. This is called in the Speculum, 'King Saul returning to David evil for good,' and is given as a type of Christ betrayed by Judas. Saul sits with crown and sceptre, and a lance horizontally aimed in his right hand. David stands before him, playing on the harp. Holbein and Rembrandt have both treated this subject, and also Lucas van Leyden. The latter in a magnificently executed engraving.

Here follow various subjects in historical order, used as types in Bibles and Speculums, but which have scarcely made their way into more refined forms of Art. We give them briefly.

Michal letting David down through a window. Type of Flight into Egypt.

The Amalekite who slew Saul killed by order of David. Type of last Judgment.

David inquiring of the Lord whether he might go up into any of the cities of Judah. Type of Return from Egypt.

Abner visiting David at Hebron. Type of Adoration of Magi.

A number of shields upon the Tower of David. This subject may possibly allude to the shields of gold which David took from the servants of Hadadezer and brought to Jerusalem (2 Sam. viii. 7). This typifies the Marriage of the Virgin, who, among other titles, has that of 'Turris Davidica.'

The King of Ammon disfiguring the messengers of David. Type of Christ crowned with Thorns.

There is also a stereotyped subject, 'David slaying eight hundred Men at one time,' which, as a companion to Samson slaying the Philistines, typifies the guards who fell prostrate at the voice of Jesus. This would appear to be a false reading of 2 Sam. xxiii. 8: 'The Tachmonite that sat in the seat, chief among the captains; the same was Adino the Eznite: he lift up his spear against eight hundred, whom he slew at one time.'

On the other hand, the subject of Bathsheba has no place among types, though too picturesque in its capacities to be overlooked by Art proper. Raphael has the subject in his Loggie subjects. The lady sits combing her hair on a balcony, while the king observes her from an opposite window. The painter has anticipated the fatal result by showing the armed men already going out against the children of Ammon.

Rembrandt has an exquisite picture of this subject in the gallery at Brunswick, which is the *ne plus ultra* of the picturesque in colour and effect. Bathsheba is seated on a rich carpet: a black woman with a gay turban is combing her hair; an old duenna is wiping her feet. Two peacocks and two marble lions complete the glowing contrasts and rich harmony. It may be remarked that in most pictures Bathsheba is washing her feet, which seem to have typified the larger measure of ablution. In a German picture in the Dresden Gallery she is receiving a *billet doux*, which David sends her by a messenger. Another German painter, Johann Grosamer, shows his idea of a lady's weak side by the plate of sweetmeats which she is accepting.

Ferdinand Bol has a picture of David sending the letter to Joab which contained the order for Uriah's death.

We have now entered that phase in David's life so fertile in warning and consolation for the human race. There is no mysterious and puzzling turning away to idolatry, like the son that was to follow him; but sin having entered, repentance follows, and every form of punishment, showing how heavy was the hand of the Lord in retribution upon the servant who was yet after His own heart :—

> Sad success, parental tears,
> And a dreary gift of years.

Nathan before David, telling the parable of the rich man with his many flocks and herds, and the poor man with his one ewe lamb,

87 Nathan before David.
(Italian Speculum. 14th century.)

is the form in which Repentance is set forth in the Old Testament. In the ancient psalter before alluded to, and which is believed by some to be of Sicilian origin, the allegorical figure of Repentance is introduced to assist the tale. The accompanying etching shows the treatment, the pathos of which it would be difficult to exceed. Here are two moments : first, Nathan charging the guilty monarch, who is in the act of taking off his crown ; and, secondly, David crouching on his knees in self-abasement, whilst above him is seen the sorrowful figure of Metanoia, or Repentance. Nathan before David afterwards became the type of the parable of the Prodigal Son, and of the Magdalene washing the feet of Christ. It is curious to see how one part of the treatment is preserved through centuries. We give a quaint and simple illustration from Mr. Boxall's Speculum

Byzantine MS. 2th century. Bibl imp Paris

(woodcut, No. 87). Nathan has just uttered the words, 'Thou art the man,' and David, in self-abasement, takes off his crown. In other later forms David retains his crown, but wrings his hands in unmistakeable anguish.

After this form of reproof comes that of insult. Shimei, 'a man of the family of the house of Saul,' meets David whilst flying from Absalom, accosts him with opprobrious language, and throws stones at him. This incident is called 'Shimei cursing David,' and is chosen to typify our Lord crowned with Thorns. Shimei, generally with stones in his hand, sometimes with a club, is seen menacing David, who casts up his hands in sorrow and shame.

The Death of Absalom is seen in biblical series, but it was too strange a subject (a man hanging by the hair of his head) to recommend itself to mature Art. As a type, it is one of the many proofs that might be given of the curious irrelevancy, morally speaking, of these mediæval analogies, for it is chosen to represent Christ's Crucifixion. Absalom is generally seen just caught by the bough, his horse dashing from below him, while two or three horsemen are tilting at the pendant figure with fixed spears, one of which has gone straight through him. In a Bible of the 13th century in the British Museum, Joab, at full gallop, is driving three spears at once through the body of Absalom, literally illustrating the text, 'And he took three darts, . . . and thrust them through the heart of Absalom.'

The incident of the seven sons of Saul who were sacrificed to appease the Lord in the matter of the Gibeonites, and whose bodies were watched over by Rizpah, the daughter of Aiah, was a type of the Descent from the Cross. It scarcely inspired the hand of any real artist until its picturesqueness was discerned by the eye of our great Turner. If he had left no other proof of his historical powers, this would have sufficed. Nothing more solemn can be conceived than the figure of Rizpah, the mother of two of the sons of Saul; her face covered with one hand, a lighted torch, to scare the wild beasts, in the other, and the dimly outlined bodies of the dead, lying under the sackcloth she had spread upon the rock. The bird of prey flits in front—the lion prowls on an eminence behind—a crown fallen from one of the heads, betokening their royal lineage, lies on the ground—the waning moon and shooting stars have a sinister effect, and the dawn streaks the sky behind the monumental trees. Here intense feeling supplies all the requirements of Christian Art.

We now come in the course of chronology to the subject of 'the three mighty men of David,' who have furnished picturesque materials, but rather an arbitrary type in a Christian sense. 'And David was then in an hold, and the garrison of the Philistines was then in Bethlehem. And David longed, and said, Oh that one would give me drink of the water of the well of Bethlehem, which is by the gate.

'And the three mighty men brake through the host of the Philistines, and drew water out of the well of Bethlehem, that was by the gate, and took it, and brought it to David: nevertheless he would not drink thereof, but poured it out unto the Lord.

'And he said, Be it far from me, O Lord, that I should do this: is not this the blood of the men that went in jeopardy of their lives? therefore he would not drink it. These things did these three mighty men' (2 Sam. xxiii. 14, 15, 16).

This beautiful incident is interpreted by the early commentators in a mystical sense, namely, that David thirsted not for the natural waters of the well, but for the living waters that were to proceed out of Bethlehem, and that he poured out the water unto the Lord to prefigure the blood that was to be shed. Art, however, did not adopt this subject till the time when interpretations had become more strained, and thus the three mighty men of David are given as the type of the three kings bringing presents to the Infant Christ. David is seen upon his throne with crown and sceptre, with three men in armour before him, each holding forth a vessel of water. Claude has the subject in the foreground of one of his pictures in the National Gallery (No. 6).

The consequences of David's last fault—the numbering of the people—is occasionally rendered in Art by his prostration before the Lord, in order to avert the divine anger. Lucas van Leyden has the subject. David is seen kneeling, his crown and sceptre on the ground. Above is an angel with two arrows in one hand and one in the other.

The closing scene of David's life (Bathsheba presenting Abishag the Shunammite to him) is not known in early Art, but has been chosen by modern painters—Guercino and Van der Werff—for its picturesqueness.

The representations of David which particularly illustrate the Psalms are peculiar and various. One that often recurs is that of David playing on the bells, a hammer in each hand (woodcut, No. 88). This especially accompanies the 81st Psalm, where he directs the instruments of psalmody to be brought to him. He is also as often seen with the harp, and other musical instruments suggested by the period, lying around him.

Another passage, generally illustrated, is that in the 53d Psalm, 'The fool hath said in his heart, There is no God.' David is playing with all his might, but a fool with cap and bells stands by.

In the British Museum there is a monument of human vanity—the Psalter of Henry VIII. of England, where the king himself, with his bloated cruel face, is represented as David. The fool here is a portrait of Somers, the Court jester.

88 David playing on the Bells. MS. A.D. 1310. Mr. Holford ?

In a Flemish Bible of the 15th century, in the Burgundian Library at Brussels, the opening passage of the 69th Psalm, 'Save me, O God; for the waters are come in unto my soul,' is very literally translated. David is seen floating on the water, with nothing on him except his crown. The shore, with comfortable Flemish houses, is close by, and the Almighty is seen in the sky. This is an instance rather of poverty than simplicity of conception, since the execution far outstrips the power of invention.

SOLOMON.

SOLOMON is looked upon as a type of Christ, first in his name, which means 'peaceable,' and next, as being the most beloved son of his father. In his wisdom and knowledge, too, there is manifest analogy; and in his building and consecrating the Temple, as Christ raised up and sanctified the Church. 'Yet in many things,' as an old commentator says, 'Solomon was no type of Christ at all.'[1]

The subject which inaugurates Solomon's character for wisdom is his judgment regarding the two mothers—placed in the 'Biblia Pauperum' as a type of the Last Judgment. This is a subject in Art which should immediately interpret itself by features very distinct from another incident, in which a king on a throne, with executioners and mothers before him, and sometimes only one dead and one living child, is introduced—namely, the Murder of the Innocents. Here the king on the throne is a youth, for Solomon is believed to have been not above twenty years of age. Before him stand two women with eager gestures. A dead child usually lies on the ground, and a living one is generally held by one leg, head downwards, by an executioner, or by both legs between two executioners, sword in hand. A very early version of this subject is seen in an ivory of the 9th century, of which there is a cast in the Arundel Society, and which is far more expressive than many of a higher class of Art. Here the conditions of space—the frequent dictator to many an ancient artist, and which has divided the scene into an upper and lower half—have been turned to good account in the action of the real mother. With all faults of drawing, there are few versions of this incident which are so pathetic. It also shows how early the action of the child held by the legs between two executioners, evidently to facilitate the order for the division, was known.

The same occurs in Mantegna's drawing in the Louvre. Solomon sits on the throne in profile to the spectator, with an expression of

[1] Keoch's 'Key to open Scripture Metaphors.'

sympathy not quite legitimate, while the child is held head downwards between two men. The real mother seizes the one who holds the sword by the shoulder and arm.

Giorgione has left an unfinished picture, now at Kingston Lacy, formerly in the Marescalchi collection at Bologna.[1] He has treated the incident in a Roman sense. Solomon is the Prætor, and next him is an elderly Assessor, which somewhat diminishes the force of the story. The two women are grand and beautiful alike, with too little difference in their action, as each points to the same object—one to save, the other to destroy. In another picture by him of the same subject, in the Uffizj—the companion to that of Moses choosing between the fruit and the coals—he has had more regard to humanity in the treatment of the children. The dead one lies peacefully on a cushion, and the living child is held by both its hands. Here, as generally, the true mother is on her knees, and the false one standing urging the execution of the sentence.

Poussin has the subject. The two women kneel opposite one another with furious Italian gestures. The false mother, rather infelicitously, with her dead child hanging over her arm.

A German painter, George Pencz, has given a touch of the burlesque to the scene, for the false mother is holding out her robe to catch her half of the suspended child.

On the other hand, Coypel, the French painter, with a tender but incorrect sentiment, has made the child the real betrayer of the truth, for he is stretching out his little arms to his terrified mother. The veracity of the story is only maintained by making the children mere babes, as they doubtless were, so that no evidence of this kind was possible. But often a great blubbering boy is given, quite old enough to have told his own name.

The next chronological incident is Solomon placing his mother, Bathsheba, on his right hand when she came to him in the matter of Adonijah and Abishag the Shunammite (1 Kings ii.) This is converted into a type of the Coronation of the Virgin, though for no other apparent reason than the similitude of form.

Solomon building the Temple has been treated by Raphael in his Bible. The king stands on an elevated terrace, looking at

[1] Waagen, Treasures of Art. Supplement, p. 377.

plans which an officer holds before him. Below are workmen sawing wood, and oxen drawing slabs of stone.

The Visit of the Queen of Sheba to Solomon is the established type in Art of the visit of the Three Kings to the Infant Christ, both being the prefiguration of the Calling of the Gentiles. Painters, therefore, have kept up the analogy, by giving a conspicuous place to the presents she brought. Her attendants carry vessels heaped with gold and precious stones. Raphael shows a man pouring out gold coins at the foot of Solomon's throne; camels are usually seen in the distance. There is no mention of Solomon's having caused the Queen of the East to sit in his presence, which may account for the ungallant form usually given, the king being seated on his throne, while the beautiful woman stands before him. It may also have been adopted to distinguish this incident from that of Bathsheba's visit. At most, he slightly rises and bends forward as she advances. A beautiful design by Baldini is a refreshing exception to this arrangement. Here Solomon advances, like a gentleman, from without his grand Italian palace, to meet the queen, and takes her by the hand. On the other side are graceful figures, with animals and dogs, and men with hawks on wrist, by way of the most acceptable present in the artist's eyes at that time.

Art has not scrupled to show the idolatry that mysteriously overtook Solomon in his later days. This was no rare subject in the 15th or 16th centuries, when it was treated chiefly by artists north of the Alps. Lucas van Leyden represents Solomon under the garb of a burgomaster, with a gold chain round his neck, kneeling before an altar, on which is a hideous figure seated on a globe, holding a sheep's head, and with ass's ears. Next him stands a tremendous Dutchwoman, with seven high feathers in her cap, pointing to the idol, and evidently using intimidation. This master has left three designs of this subject.

The throne of Solomon, with its twelve lions personifying the twelve patriarchs, is a never-failing subject in the types of mediæval Art. It sets forth, also, the Adoration of the Kings. Sometimes a figure of the Almighty stands behind the throne, with a hand supporting each side of it—illustrating, possibly, 'the everlasting arms.'

The Temple of Solomon is a direct prefiguration of the Virgin

Mary, in whom Christ dwelt, as the glory of the Lord did in the Temple.

Even the figurative language of the Bible finds its literal antitype in the ever ingenious series of the 'Speculum.' 'The stone which the builders rejected has become the head of the corner;'—this verse is translated from a figure back to a reality. The temple is that of Solomon, and workmen are laying a head corner-stone on one of the towers. In this form it constitutes a type of the Ascension.

There are two fables in connection with Solomon, which have found their way into Christian Art. The one is a paraphrase of the judgment between the two mothers. It is as follows. A question was brought before Solomon as to who was the real son of a certain dead man. Three young men presented themselves as claimants of the inheritance. Solomon decreed that the body should be raised before them, and that whoever should hit the head with his arrow should be the heir. Two of them tried their skill in vain, but when it came to the turn of the third, he fell before Solomon's feet, and protested that he would rather forego the inheritance than thus insult his father's body. Then Solomon recognised him in whom the voice of nature spoke, and made him the heir accordingly. This subject is often seen in miniatures, and early German pictures also give it.

The other legend is given in a rare edition of the 'Speculum,' and offers a type of the delivery of the souls from Limbus. It represents a high glass vessel, with a young bird imprisoned by Solomon in it. The mother-bird flies off into the wilderness, and brings a particular worm whose blood has the power to break glass. She kills it, and sprinkles the glass with the blood, which immediately breaks, and the young bird is delivered. Thus Hell, or Limbus, was burst open by the blood of Christ.

Solomon, when seen among the prophets, is represented young, crowned, and with a scroll in his hand, inscribed, 'Morte turpissima condemnamus eum,' from the Wisdom of Solomon (xi. 20). Or, he appears holding a temple and the scroll from the passage in Proverbs : 'Wisdom hath builded her house' (ix. 1).

A Byzantine miniature of the 13th century shows Solomon crowned, and in the costume of a Byzantine emperor, with a book in his hand, and a grand angel seated by his side, assisting him with his counsels.[1]

See illustration. Annales Archéologiques, vol. i. p. 160.

Elijah and Elisha.

ELIJAH THE TISHBITE is one of those names in the Old Testament which suggest ideas of the most wild and picturesque nature. His life is a series of pathetic, sublime, and miraculous events. Elijah is sometimes considered a type of Christ, and his very name is interpreted 'God our Lord.' But he is declared in Scripture to be especially the type of John the Baptist, of whom Malachi prophesies in the last verse but one of the Old Testament: 'Behold, I will send you Elijah the prophet before the coming of the great and dreadful day of the Lord.' The angel, also, who announced the birth of the Baptist to Zacharias, says: 'And he shall go before him (Christ) in the spirit and power of Elias.' Thus, both Elijah and John the Baptist may be said to have been voices in the wilderness, crying to a wicked generation; each came neither eating nor drinking, nor living with men, and both were clad in garments of camel's hair.

There is much analogy, also, between the life of Moses and of Elijah. Like Moses, he defies an iniquitous ruler, performs miracles, and converses with God on Mount Horeb itself. Both were strong to perform the Divine will, both weak in their human despondence; the end of each was marked with supernatural circumstances, and, finally, they appeared together at the side of Christ in the glory of the Transfiguration. Yet, in one chief characteristic, they were opposite; for Moses was the meekest of men, and Elijah one of the most courageous.

Art proper has not much availed herself of these materials, though in the sense of Christian illustration they appear early on the scene.

We now take the incidents of Elijah's life chronologically. In the unpremeditated character of the Scriptures, Elijah starts suddenly into notice. 'And Elijah the Tishbite, who was of the inhabitants of Gilead, said unto Ahab, As the Lord God of Israel liveth, before whom I stand, there shall not be dew nor rain these years, but according to my word' (1 Kings xvii. 1). Then Elijah goes by the word of the Lord, and hides himself by the brook

Cherith, 'that is before Jordan,' and is fed by ravens. This is a subject found in closely illustrated Bibles, but it has not been treated by any well-known master.

Elijah's meeting with the widow of Sarepta has, from the time of Bede, borne a curious interpretation. 'And, behold, the widow woman was there gathering of sticks.' The passage is given in the Vulgate as gathering *two sticks*, which were interpreted as a sign of the Cross, which she was going to seek for herself and her son, and then die. Accordingly, in ancient illustrations, the woman is seen holding these sticks in the form of a cross. In the 'Biblia Pauperum' the same subject is given as a type of Christ carrying His Cross.

The next incident is the restoration to life of the widow's son, who was the first person raised from the dead recorded in Scripture. This occurs in the 'Biblia Pauperum' as a type of the raising of Lazarus.

The rival sacrifices of Elijah and the priests of Baal, on Mount Carmel, is a subject seen in illustrated Bibles. In a French Bible of the 15th century, in the Burgundian Library at Brussels, the lamb lies on the altar in flames, and Elijah himself is hewing at the priests of Baal with a large sword. In the 'Biblia Pauperum,' this event is a type of the descent of the Holy Ghost, and is treated as a mere fact: Elijah kneels on one side of the altar, while flames consume the offering.

Elijah comforted by the angel, as he lay and slept under a juniper tree. This is also occasionally seen in Bibles. It has been painted as a foreground to a landscape by Paul Potter. Rubens has treated the subject as symbolical of the Sacrament of the Eucharist. The two figures are seen under a grand proscenium, and the angel is presenting to him bread and the chalice.

Elijah, on Mount Horeb, listening to the still small voice. Elijah is seen at the entrance to the cave, covering his face with his mantle.

Elijah taken up into heaven, or 'Il Ratto d' Elia,' as it is called in Italian, was viewed from the earliest times as a type of the Resurrection. It is one of the most striking groups that the sculpture of the Catacombs has preserved. The ancient quadriga, the Jordan river-god lying beneath, leaning on his urn, Elijah himself, already transfigured with immortal youth, like an Apollo guiding the chariot of the sun, are all features which bespeak a classic origin (woodcut, No. 89). Below stands Elisha, receiving the mantle and the spirit of his master, and already divided from him in his humanity, for he is mature in age, and bearded. This is seen also on the walls of the Catacombs, where, in one instance,

Translation of Elijah. (Ancient sarcophagus.)

there is no chariot at all, the idea being only given by the action of the horses. This subject lost in later times its larger meaning of the Resurrection, and became, in the 'Biblia Pauperum,' a particular type of the Ascension of our Lord. It is curious to mark the complete change of feeling within a possible lapse of ten centuries. Elijah, in the 'Biblia Pauperum,' being given as an old man, seated in a clumsy cart, while, instead of horses without a chariot, a vehicle without horses sometimes appears.

ELISHA.

ELISHA also serves with theologians as a minor type of Christ. His name signifies 'the Health of God,' and he succeeds Elijah as Christ succeeds to the Baptist. The analogy is even carried to his servant, the covetous Gehazi, who is compared to Judas.

The sons of the prophets coming to meet him at Bethel, before the translation of Elijah, is a subject which figures in the 'Biblia Pauperum' as a type of Christ's entry into Jerusalem. Also the little children mocking him, as that of our Lord crowned with thorns.

The raising of the Shunammite's son forms a companion type with that of the widow of Sarepta to the resurrection of Lazarus. A picture of the subject, by Benjamin West, is in the Grosvenor Gallery, and another in the National Gallery.

Two other incidents also occur in the history of Elisha, which find their way into the Speculum. The first is the immolation of the son of the King of Moab (2 Kings iii. 26, 27): 'And when the King of Moab saw that the battle was too sore for him, . . . then he took his eldest son that should have reigned in his stead, and offered him for a burnt-offering upon the wall.' This is a type of Christ being fastened to the Cross. A king is seen upon a city wall smiting a young man, who is also crowned.

The next and great incident in the life of Elisha, rendered by Art, is the washing of Naaman the Syrian in the Jordan. This is treated as a type of the Baptism of Christ. In one Speculum, Naaman is seen standing in a pond, his hands folded in prayer, and with a glory round his head. This is explained in the text. For the seven dippings in Jordan figured the cleansing from the seven mortal sins in baptism. Also that his flesh came again as a little child, was considered a type of the regeneration of his soul. Thus Naaman was considered at that moment free from all sin, and therefore entitled to be invested with the bright circle of sanctity.

90. Elisha. (Painted window. Lincoln College, Oxford.)

Elisha is seen represented with a double-headed dove seated on his shoulder. This is the peculiar attribute of the prophet Elisha, and it becomes intelligible on referring to his petition to Elijah, when he entreated that a 'double portion' of his spirit might rest upon him [1] (woodcut, No. 90).

[1] Miss Twining's Symbols, p. 64, plate xxxi., from a window in antechapel of Lincoln College, Oxford.

JOB.

THE history of Job is isolated and distinct in Scripture. The man of Uz—'Vir orientalis timens Deum'—was a Gentile, and, though traditions of Abraham's religion may have lingered in that land, he shows no sign of knowing God's dispensation towards the Israelites. He thus bears witness to an independent revelation from above, and declares the great doctrine of the Resurrection, nowhere else so clearly given in the Old Testament, and which our Saviour found the Jews disputing. Patience is the great quality attributed to Job: we say attributed, for few can read his book without wondering at the origin of a proverb so much at variance with the recorded facts. It doubtless arose from the simple misconception of the word 'patience,' which belongs to the patriarch in the sense of suffering rather than of uncomplaining endurance. For, however briefly his sufferings may be narrated in the sacred text, they are believed to have lasted more than a twelvemonth. In this sense, evidently, St. James compares him to our Lord: 'Ye have heard of the patience of Job, and have seen the end of the Lord.' It was natural, therefore, that the early Church should choose him for a type of those sufferings which their Art only expressed by a proxy from the Old Testament. St. Jerome pronounced Job to be a figure of Christ, and his friends that of the unbelievers. Accordingly, the suffering figure of Job is among the earliest representations in the Catacombs, while, as if to illustrate the words of St. Jerome, it is given at first with all the circumstance of reality. We see it thus on the tomb of Junius Bassus (see etching, p. 13), where he sits on an eminence intended for a heap of ashes. His right shoulder is bare, as a sign of his degradation and humility, for thus slaves were attired in order to have the right arm free for the purposes of labour, while the position of his hands is singularly indicative of suffering. At his side is his wife; she covers her nose with her robe, and holds a cake of bread in a kind of long-handled spoon, as if to extend food to him without approaching him. The other figure represents the friends. It would be difficult to tell the mere story better. In other representations on the walls of the Catacombs, the mere idea of the fact is given. Job sits alone, in the same closely observed attitude of endurance.

The position and action of Job's wife are retained in Byzantine Art. D'Agincourt gives an example of the 12th century, where Job sits on the ground, and his wife stands afar off, covering her nose, and holding out the same instrument with bread.

A series of small subjects of the 13th century, from the Book of Job, also given by D'Agincourt (tab. lx.), are very remarkable. Here the sons are calling, according to the letter of Scripture, for their sisters—the hindermost of the three men leading the foremost of the three women by the hand. Then they feast together, side by side, at a semicircular table. Then Satan, a black figure with wings, is seen with two angels opposite to him, and with the Almighty in the sky. The same figure, with a hook in his hand, next drives away the sheep and asses; thus showing that it was Satan who instigated the Sabæans. Then a human figure, representing Eolus as 'a mighty wind,' with distended cheeks, is seen blowing through a tube, while figures lie prostrate beneath him, and a house is seen falling in the distance. The other trials of Job, from the Chaldæans and the fire, are omitted, but four messengers stand before Job, who is in the act of taking off his garment: 'Naked came I out of my mother's womb.' Satan then appears again, and gives Job a letter, signifying the fresh edict of God, by which he was smitten from the crown of his head to the sole of his foot. Job here sits on a dunghill, naked, and covered with spots. In the next scene his wife stands before him, as usual, covering her nose. Job holds in his hand, and seems to show her, the letter or edict of God: 'What! shall we receive good at the hand of God, and shall we not receive evil?' Then his three friends, all crowned (for the Septuagint declared them to be kings) are seen travelling on horseback. In the next picture they are seated on the ground, one before the other, afar off, sprinkling dust on their heads. Finally, Job sits with upraised hands praising God, who appears in a glory in the sky.

Giotto has a series of these frescoes in the Campo Santo, beginning with the finely-treated subject of Satan presenting himself before God, of which Mrs. Jameson has given a description and illustration. The rest refers to the raids of the Sabæans and Chaldæans, with Satan flying above, directing their movements. These frescoes are miserably injured.

But to return to the usual version of the subject in later times, Job's wife, like a dog with a bad name, found no mercy at the hands of the mediæval theologians. Her impatience, on the nature of which commentators widely disagree—her words, 'Curse God and die,' being interpreted by some as 'Bless God and die'—was magnified, beyond all warrant of Scripture, into Job's chief trial. At first, as we have seen, she was represented ministering to his wants, though in a mode intended to set forth the loathsomeness of his disease. But in the cycles of the 14th and 15th century, she is made second only to Satan in acts of torment. Job appears invariably seated on the ground, in the deepest dejection, with Satan scourging him on one side, and his wife scolding him on the other, and looking as if he relished the one as little as the other. It is probable that this very unamiable conception took its origin, like other corruptions in Art, from a mere play of words. The old rhymed Latin text of the Speculum, the author of which is unknown, gives a clue to this:—

> Beatus Job fuit flagellatus duobus modis,
> Quia Sathan flagellavit eum verberibus et uxor verbis.

The picture was therefore accommodated to the text, and Job's wife's character sacrificed for generations to point, not a moral, but a pun. This is one of the regular types of the Flagellation. So common was this view, that the Italian title for Job's trials is '*Giobbe tentato dalla Moglie!*' The good Abbé Zani, *à propos* of this subject, gives a very impertinent quotation, to the effect that God

> Gli lasciò la moglie sola,
> Perchè Femmina in essenza
> Ha dal Diavol miglior scuola
> Per far perdere la Pazienza.

Guido is the only painter who restored Job to his former estate. St. Job is seen in kingly dignity, with a glory round his head, receiving gifts from his friends. It is called 'Il Trionfo di Giobbe.'

Job is the patron saint of a church at Venice—this being one of the few places under the sway of the Latin Church where religious edifices are dedicated to personages from the Old Testament. There is also in Venice a church dedicated to S. Moisè, founded in the 8th century. The Orientalised character of Venice explains this, for in the Eastern Church the saints from the Old Testament are preferred as patrons, and St. Abraham, St. Isaac, and St. David are usual names for churches. In the case of S. Giobbe at Venice, the dedication to him is explained by the church being, or having been, attached to an hospital. It was built in the 15th century.

91   Job. (Fra Bartolomeo. Uffizj, Florence.)

Fra Bartolomeo has a fine picture in the Uffizj of Job seated as a prophet, holding a scroll 'Ipse erit Salvator meus' (woodcut, No. 91).

Job also is the only saint from the Old Testament who appears in pictures before the throne of the Madonna, and this also only in the Venetian school. Bellini has introduced him twice. He here presents rather an unhappy figure—the story of his sufferings being simply told by the absence of his clothes. He stands, a very uncomfortable-looking old man, for he is represented with a white beard. He is thus given in a picture by Bellini in the Venice Academy (woodcut, No. 92), where John the Baptist, St. James Major, St. Rosa of Lima, and Job form the group round the Virgin and Child.

The sons and daughters of Job feasting at a table are a frequent type of the Last Supper.

In Greek Art Job is represented as a prince or king in royal habiliments.

A fine picture of the Crucifixion, with the Virgin and St. John, by Francia, formerly in the Church of S. Giobbe at Bologna, represents Job lying at the foot of the Cross. He is crowned, and holds in his hand a scroll, with the words, 'Majora ipse sustinuit.'

We should ill do justice to the history of this patriarch in Art, did we not advert to 'The Book of Job, invented and engraved, by William Blake. 1825.' This English artist, with his eccentric but deeply religious pencil, was peculiarly adapted to conceive the mysterious facts and lofty images of this, as some believe, most ancient work extant in the world. These illustrations are twenty-one in number, and each surrounded with a framework of fantastic but typical forms, intermingled with portions of the text. Some of them, in pathos, poetry, and sublimity, yield to no pictorial conceptions of the Old Testament of any time or school. We instance the most striking.

92 Job. (Bellini. Belle Arti, Venice.)

No. 4. The first messenger of evil tidings, breathless with haste, appears before the patriarch—the second is seen fast approaching in the background. Job and his wife sit together; monumental forms of architecture, Stonehenge-like, are near them; sheep are feeding at their side. The wife throws up her arms in anguish. Job lifts his eyes and hands in resignation.

6. Satan standing in exultation with both feet on the prostrate Job, emptying upon him a vial of plagues. The wife kneels at his feet. The sun is setting with a lurid glare.

7. The three friends scattering dust on their heads. Job seated on straw with intense pathos of suffering. His wife supports his body behind, with gestures of deepest compassion.

8. Job, with upstretched arms and rivulets of tears, cursing the day on which he was born. His friends keep silence before him.

10. Job appealing to Heaven; the three friends pointing at him

93   Almighty appearing to Job in Whirlwind. (Blake.)

with ominous arms, like the witches in Macbeth. 'The just upright man is laughed to scorn' (Job. xii.) His wife is close at his side.

13. 'Then the Lord answered Job out of the whirlwind.' The

fancy and majesty of the figure of the Almighty distinguish it from every other conception of the First Person. Job and his wife kneel upright before the vision. The friends are bent to the ground. We give an illustration (woodcut, No. 93).

14. 'When the morning stars sung together, and all the sons of God shouted for joy.' The figures of the angels are unique in character. Mrs. Jameson gives them in 'Sacred and Legendary Art,' vol. i. p. 85.

18. 'Also the Lord accepted Job.' The Patriarch stands in attitude of praise before an altar, the flame of which ascends spirally into the opened heavens.

21. Job, with wife and numerous sons and daughters playing on musical instruments, and singing to the Lord. 'So the Lord blessed the latter end of Job more than the beginning.'

It would seem as if the English painter knew and resented the calumnious treatment of Job's wife by older Art, and had devoted these most remarkable illustrations in some degree to her vindication. Throughout the series she appears tenderly compassionating the afflicted partner of her life—sunk at his feet in grief, or kneeling in prayer by his side. The painter also adds a trait omitted by Scripture, for the same gentle sympathising woman figures in the last plate as the mother of the second fair family that was given to Job.

Daniel and the Three Children.

The history of Daniel, including that of the Three Children, as given in Scripture, is full of miraculous and picturesque events, setting forth principally the direct interposition of God, in favour of His faithful servants, living in a land of idolatry. Nevertheless, Art has borrowed so largely from the extravagant and far less picturesque fables of Apocrypha, in the illustration of Daniel's life, that we depart from our usual chronological arrangement here, and commence with two subjects—Daniel in the Lions' Den, and the Children in the Furnace—which, having been adopted in the early ages of Christianity, are both of strictly Scriptural treatment. These two subjects show themselves early and very frequently in the Catacombs. That of Daniel is seen on the tomb of Junius Bassus in our etching (see p. 13). This composition is preserved throughout the Art of the Catacombs. He stands with uplifted arms—denoting the action of prayer and praise—between the two animals, safe, apparently, so long as he thus invokes the heavenly aid. He is thus seen on sarcophagi, side by side with the miracle of the loaves, or with the Fall of Adam and Eve; always distinct to the eye, because, after the manner of classic Art, never varying from the appointed motive. The subject is hardly seen between the period of the Catacombs and that of the 16th century, when the difference in the conception sufficiently points to the lapse of time. From the nature of the subject, it could only be undertaken by painters capable of rendering animals. Rubens' great picture at Hamilton Palace is one of the grandest efforts of the master. The lions are hungry, impatient, savage creatures, prowling restlessly about the prey thus miraculously preserved from their jaws. Breughel, too, has the subject in an exquisitely-painted picture in the Ambrosian Gallery at Milan. Here the prophet kneels, but it is in terror more than faith, while lions and tigers, in every attitude of ferocity and evil intention, skulk and growl around him. King Darius and a company are looking on from not very high banks round the pit.

The Three Children in the Furnace is a subject which depicts the same miraculous aid, and is equally seen on sarcophagi and on the walls of the Catacombs—in some instances, as in our illustration (No. 94), opposite to Daniel in the Lions' Den—with the

94 The Three Children in the Furnace. (Catacombs.)

Good Shepherd, who cared for these persecuted sheep, forming the subject between them. They are always treated in the same way —standing side by side in the flames, their hands upraised in prayer. No attempt is made to give the real scene—the furnace, &c.—it is sufficient that they stand there alive in the flames, expressing the miracle. Sometimes a man is feeding the flames under them, and in one example the fourth figure stands unmistakeably by the side, with the volumen in his hand. In most instances they are given fully dressed; sometimes with the Phrygian cap, the usual attribute of a race not Roman.

This subject also appears in the mediæval series as a type of the Last Judgment, in allusion to being saved by Christ from the fire. Mr. Boxall's Speculum has a very quaint and beautiful conception. The scene is a kind of domed oven, with fire issuing from port-holes. Within are the three children, kneeling upon a large veil, which an angel interposes between them and the fire. That they are called children is in reference to the age at which they were taken by Nebuchadnezzar from Jerusalem. Thus the familiar name was retained in the apocryphal writings. Scripture, however, speaks of 'three men,' as being bound in their coats, their hosen, and their hats; also the king's words are, 'Lo! I see four men loose, walking in the midst of the fire.' It was in

95   The Three Children in the Furnace.   (Italian Speculum. 14th century.)

the furnace that the Song of the Three Children, retained in the Prayer Book, is recorded, in Apocrypha, to have been uttered. This beautiful hymn is accompanied in the original by much irrelevant matter, which mars its simplicity. Thus the oven is described to have been fed 'with rosin, pitch, tow, and small wood, so that the fire streamed forth above the furnace forty and nine cubits.' This is seen in a picture by Aldegrever in the Landauer Brüder Haus, at Nuremberg, where a tremendous fire occupies the chief place in the picture, and in itself constitutes a subject to the detriment of the figures; thus intruding an attempt at a vulgar reality in place of the important lesson intended to be conveyed.

To return to the Scriptural history of Daniel, as given in the mediæval series. The Dream of Nebuchadnezzar is one of the regular subjects of the Speculum; by an analogy between the apocryphal idea of the images which fell before the Infant Christ and the stone of Nebuchadnezzar's dream, it is converted into a type of the Flight into Egypt.

96   Nebuchadnezzar's Dream. (Speculum. 15th century).

The Second Dream of Nebuchadnezzar is also given, in which he saw the tree under which the beasts of the earth had shadow, and in the boughs of which the fowls of heaven dwelt. By a curious disregard of the text, where the person figured is interpreted by the Prophet of the Lord as Nebuchadnezzar himself, this tree is declared to be Christ, and, accordingly, this second vision is given as a type of the Crucifixion. The subject is naïvely rendered (woodcut, No. 96). Nebuchadnezzar lies asleep on his bed—always with his crown on—and by his side is the tree, with the stag, the unicorn, the lion, the boar, &c., gathered under it, and its boughs full of birds, while a man with a hatchet strikes at its root. These two visions are only seen in typical Art, not being adapted for historical or picturesque treatment.

Last in the Speculum is the Handwriting on the Wall, as a figure of the Last Judgment. Our eyes, in this subject, are so accustomed to the crowded gorgeousness of a late painter, that we can hardly conceive it without the Feast of Belshazzar, the vessels of the Temple, the terrified women around, and the perspective lines of palaces in the distance. Here there are none but the figures necessary to tell the story—a king on his knees, a prophet before him, and a hand above, holding a pen and tracing characters on the wall. And yet the idea of one of the most startling apparitions that Scripture has recorded, is perhaps thus most intensely given.

We now turn to the apocryphal history of Daniel, given under the name of Bel and the Dragon, and adopted in scholastic history. The story was this. There was an idol in Babylon by the name of Bel, and every day he received many measures of fine flour, forty sheep, and six jars of wine. And the King of Babylon adored the idol, and said to Daniel, 'Why do you not worship him?' And Daniel answered, 'Because I worship not a thing made with hands, but the living God.' Then the king said, 'See you not that Bel is also a living god, since he eats and drinks every day?' Then Daniel smiled, and replied, that an image of clay within and brass without could never eat. So the king called the priests, and said, 'If ye tell me not who eateth all these provisions, ye shall die; and if you prove that Bel eats them, then Daniel shall die.' And the priests of Bel were threescore and ten, besides their wives and children. And the king went with Daniel to the temple. And the priests said, 'Lo! we will go out; but thou, O king, set on the wine and make ready the meat, and shut the door, and seal it with your signet ring.' And the king put the food before Bel, and Daniel strewed ashes on the pavement in the sight of the king, and they went out and shut the door, and sealed it with his signet ring. And when the night was come, the priests and their wives and their children entered through a private passage under the table, known to them only, and ate and drank all, as it was their custom to do. Early in the morning came the king to the temple, and Daniel with him, and they found the seals unbroken. And when they opened the door, and the king perceived that the table was empty, he cried out, 'Great is Bel!' But Daniel held the king, that he should not enter, and pointed out the prints of the footsteps in the ashes on the pavement. And the king was wroth, and called the priests, and made them show him the private door, by which they came in and went out. And the king killed them all, and delivered Bel to be destroyed by Daniel.

And in the same place there was a great dragon in a pit, and the Babylonians worshipped him. And the priests gave him plenty to eat, and had instruments made of calf's skin, which they struck, so that they made a great noise, and thus excited the dragon, till he vomited fire and smoke. And the king said to Daniel, 'You cannot say now that this is not a living god.' And Daniel answered, 'Give me power over him, and I will kill him without sword or staff.' And Daniel took pitch and fat and hair, and mixed them in a lump together, and thrust it into the dragon's mouth, and he was suffocated and died. And the Babylonians were indignant, and said, 'The king has become a Jew.' And they said, 'Deliver Daniel to us, or we will destroy thee and all thy house.' And they took Daniel, and cast him into a lions' den, where there were seven lions, to whom they daily gave two carcases, and now they gave them none. Now there was in Judæa Habacuc the prophet, and he prepared pottage for the reapers. And the angel of the Lord said to him, 'Take the pottage to Babylon unto Daniel, who is in the lions' den.' And Habacuc replied, 'I never saw Babylon, neither know I the place of the den.' And the angel took him by the hair of his head, and held him over the den; and Habacuc cried out, 'O Daniel! servant of God, take the pottage which I have brought.' And Daniel ate, giving thanks. Then the angel took Habacuc back to his home. And the king came on the seventh day, and mourned for Daniel; and seeing him seated in the midst of the lions, he exclaimed, 'Great is the God of Daniel!' and he took him out from the den of lions.

In the Speculum these two stories are given as a type to that part of our Lord's Temptation which represents gluttony. Here Daniel is about to thrust something into the dragon's mouth, while Bel sits aloft, the amphora of wine stands below, and on the step is seen the print of two feet in the ashes. The subject of Habacuc has been treated by Northern artists. There is also a design believed to be by Raphael, and painted by Maestro Giorgio on majolica. Hemskirk has a series of ten designs, comprising the whole apocryphal narrative.

Daniel appears as one of the Prophets in all series where the canonical Prophets are given. He is fantastically represented by Baldini.

JONAH.

THE miraculous incident which marks the history of the Prophet Jonah has received its interpretation from the lips of our Lord Himself: 'An evil and adulterous generation seeketh after a sign; and there shall no sign be given to it, but the sign of the prophet Jonas: For as Jonas was three days and three nights in the whale's belly; so shall the Son of man be three days and three nights in the heart of the earth' (Matt. xii. 39, 40).

Thus Jonah became the most direct figure of the Burial and Resurrection of Christ, the chief events of whose Death and Passion thus find symbolic narration in cycles of early Christian Art. It may be said that no subject is so frequent in the Catacombs as the two great facts of Jonah swallowed and disgorged by the whale. These are always placed in juxtaposition, and sometimes the same scene holds both. We give an illustration (woodcut, No. 97) from a sarcophagus, which is full of meaning. Here classic feeling reigns supreme, for on one side is the figure of Eolus, personifying the tempest. The ancient artist has not lost sight of the fact that the mariners of Tarshish did all they could to avert the Prophet's fate, 'and rowed hard to bring the ship to land.' The feeling is perceptible in the boatman, who covers up his eyes, not to see the sacrifice. Nay, the economy of space in classic Art goes farther, for before the legs of Jonah are free from the monster's jaws, we see him reposing—the hand above the head being the attitude of sleep—beneath the gourd.

Frequently, also, the story is given in three compartments. He is swallowed in the one; he is flying with outstretched arms from the fish's mouth on to a high cliff in the next, and above or between

97   The History of Jonah. (Ancient sarcophagus.)

he lies reposing under the thick bower of the gourd. Occasionally the lesson intended here by the withering of the gourd is represented. The leaves are gone, the fruit is shrunk, and Jonah sits with his hand to his mouth—an action which is generally found in early Art to denote anger. In one instance the subject departs from its usual convention. Jonah is standing on dry land, his arms raised in prayer and praise—the fish's head seen in the water at his feet. The whale is here always a marine kind of horse, with long neck, fore-feet, and a dolphin's tail.

One of the statues believed to have been modelled by Raphael is that of Jonah. Here the whale serves as a kind of attribute, for Jonah is seated upon it, holding the jaw open with one hand, as if pointing to the means of his escape. The composition is not very impressive.

The subject of Jonah, from its peculiar conditions, is rare. Poussin treats it as the foreground of a marine landscape.

Rubens designed it, and, in order to obtain opportunity for his power of representing violent action, sacrificed the truth of the story, for he makes the mariners overpowering Jonah by force— one of them with his foot on the Prophet's head.

Jonah as a Prophet is seen holding a fish, as in Balaini's series of etchings.

The Prophets.

The Prophets are necessarily important and conspicuous figures in the scheme of Christian Art. To the pious Israelites under the Old Covenant, many of the passages scattered through the prophetic writings, which are now known to refer to our Lord, could only present images more or less obscure, as seen through the veil which they were not intended to pierce. To them the promises, however, seen afar off, were the legitimate objects of study. And these were clear and unambiguous—' In thy seed shall all the nations of the earth be blessed.' But it cannot be supposed that the Hebrew reader dwelt upon sentences of little intrinsic meaning, and which could only derive force from their fulfilment. To us, however, no word can be unimportant which has had accomplishments in any detail of Christ's course on earth. The more apparently insignificant the allusion, the more wonderful its coming to pass. We have, beside, the testimony of our Lord Himself to the importance of the fulfilment of the smallest fact in the Old Testament referring to Him, who entered Jerusalem upon an ass, and who drank the vinegar, ' that the Scripture might be fulfilled.' Separately, therefore, these passages, preserved in the ancient books, stand forth now to our sight with a clearness proportioned to their former obscurity; while, collectively, they furnish a connected view of our Lord's birth, mission, time of appearance, and sufferings.

Thus the Prophets are no longer looked upon as the positive and active impersonations of promises and denunciations to the Hebrew nation, but are become the exponents of a new set of declarations, unheeded and obscure once, but now irresistible in the strength of a complete accomplishment. They are therefore, in most instances, in the economy of Christian Art, to be considered as neutral characters, whose part is that of bearers, each of one jet of that great light of fulfilled prophecy which burst forth at the call of the Gospel. This is the principle on which we are to view the figures of the Prophets in Art; though, in application, their meaning is often confused and vague, and the text proper to one frequently given to another.

Properly speaking, the Prophets are sixteen in number; the four greater—Isaiah, Jeremiah, Ezekiel, and Daniel, and the twelve lesser—Hosea, Joel, Amos, Obadiah, Jonah, Micah, Nahum, Habakkuk, Zephaniah, Haggai, Zechariah, and Malachi. These are the canonical prophets, as distinct from certain of the patriarchs, judges, and kings of Israel, who also prophesied regarding our Lord. They generally hold a scroll, on which some particular passage from their writings is inscribed. These are varied, some of them, in the Latin and the Greek Churches, or according to the particular occasion to which the prophecy is intended to refer. Thus, in the instance of Isaiah (who, of the canonical Prophets, most abundantly furnishes these predictions), if the Flagellation be the subject, he holds the scroll, 'I gave my back to the smiters' (Isa. l. 6). If the Entombment, his words are, 'Surely He hath borne our griefs' (see etching from Taddeo Gaddi, vol. ii.). Generally, however, the texts which allude to the usual scheme of Christ's life and death are the following:—

Isaiah: 'Behold, a virgin shall conceive, and bear a son' (vii. 14); or, He hath poured out His soul unto death' (liii. 12). This last is seen in our illustration (woodcut, No. 98, over leaf) by Gaudenzio Ferrari, in the Church of the Franciscans at Varallo: on the scroll is the contraction of the words, 'Tradidit in mortem animam suam.' 'Esaia 53.'

Jeremiah: 'The breath of our nostrils, the anointed of the Lord was taken in their pits' (Lam. iv. 20).

Ezekiel: 'A new heart also will I give you, and a new spirit will I put within you' (xxxvi. 26).

Daniel: 'And after threescore and two weeks shall Messiah be be cut off' (ix. 26).

Hosea: 'O Death, I will be thy plagues' (or 'death') (xiii. 14); or, 'I called my son out of Egypt' (xi. 1); or, 'After two days will He revive us: in the third day He will raise us up' (vi. 2).

Joel: 'The Lord also shall roar out of Zion, and utter His voice from Jerusalem' (iii. 16).

Amos: 'It is he that buildeth his stories in the heaven' (ix. 6).

33   Prophet Isaiah. (Gaudenzio Ferrari.)

Obadiah : ' And the house of Jacob shall be a fire ' (i. 18).

Jonah : ' I cried unto the Lord, and He heard me out of the belly of hell ' (ii. 2).

Micah : ' But thou, Bethlehem Ephratah, though thou be little ' (v. 2).

Nahum : ' Behold upon the mountains the feet of Him that bringeth good tidings ' (i. 15).

Habakkuk : ' He had horns coming out of His hand ' (iii. 4).

Zephaniah : ' The great day of the Lord is near ' (i. 14).

Haggai : ' And the desire of all nations shall come ' (ii. 7).

Zechariah : ' Behold thy King cometh, riding upon an ass ' (ix. 9) ; or, ' So they weighed for my price thirty pieces of silver ' (xi. 12) ; or, ' They shall look upon me whom they have pierced ' (xii. 10) ; or, ' They shall mourn for Him, as one mourneth for his only son ' (xii. 10).

Malachi : ' The Sun of righteousness shall arise with healing in His wings ' (iv. 2).

But the canonical Prophets are seldom given unmixed with other personages from the Old Testament. For where prophecy of our Lord was concerned, David could not be left out, whose psalms supply some of the minutest as well as the largest circumstances of His Nature and Passion ; nor Jacob, who said that a star should arise; nor Moses, who spoke of the seed of the woman. In this way, as the original intention of the figures was more and more lost sight of, the number increased, till, by the 16th century, we find their number swelled, in series of engravings, &c., to more than thirty. Thus they included Noah, Jacob, Moses, Aaron, Job, Joshua, Samuel, David, Solomon, Elijah, Elisha, Baruch, &c.; while the Latin Church admitted Dionysius the Areopagite; and the Greek Church, at a later date, Solon, Thucydides, Plutarch, Plato, Aristotle, Sophocles, &c.

The Prophets are not seen collectively until the 13th century, when the four greater Prophets appear at the great west door of cathedrals—as at Cremona—holding their long upright scrolls, which almost cover their persons. These set forth the main characteristics of Him whose temple we are about to enter—that He was born of a virgin, that He was cut off at a certain time, &c. The Prophets people also the arch of the same door in Gothic cathedrals, with angels and apostles in the courses next to them, environing the Last Judgment; or sometimes with the Coronation of the Virgin, as a type of the Rest of the Church, in the centre. Their place is also upon the screen, between the nave and the choir, or along the nave, which represents the Old Testament, as the choir, or place of the sacrifice, represents the New. Thus, in the Church of the Frari at Venice, there are sixteen bust-length figures of Prophets upon the screen, projecting out of brackets of foliage. These are very miscellaneous in choice: on one side, Moses, Elijah, Isaiah, Zechariah, Jeremiah, Ezekiel, David, Daniel; on the other, Samuel, Habakkuk, Enoch, Jonah, Jacob, Elisha, Abraham, and John the Baptist.

At the time when so much importance was attached to the mystic meaning of numbers and multiples of numbers, the Prophets appear in what St. Augustine calls the sacred 'combination of twelve.' They were thus collated with the Apostles; and in MSS. of the 13th and 14th centuries we frequently see a Prophet and an Apostle coupled together—the scrolls of the Prophets being made to correspond with the twelve sentences of the Creed, supposed each to have been composed by an Apostle. Thus Zechariah's scroll contains the words, 'They shall look upon me whom they have pierced;' and St. John's, 'He suffered under Pontius Pilate.'

Hosea holds forth the words, 'Death, I will be thy death;' and St. Thomas, 'He descended into hell.'

Often, in the absence of scrolls, the name of the Prophet is inscribed upon the pedestal on which he stands, as if in recognition of the neutrality of the figure itself.

To some, however, a certain individuality, Scriptural or traditional, belongs. Thus in the same Greek psalter of the 9th or 10th century —whence we have taken some of the most remarkable illustrations of the history of David[1]—the prophet Isaiah, a grand figure with a nimbus, his name inscribed in Greek above him, appears. His hands are raised in adoration to the hand of the Almighty, whence emanate rays of light, or inspiration, upon him. On one side is a female figure with a reversed torch; above her written, ΝΤΞ, or Night. On the other side is a beautiful boy with a burning torch, who impersonates the Morning Star. This representation, which occurs more than once in Art of that early time (see D'Agincourt, t. xlvi.), refers to chap. xxvi. v. 9 of the book of Isaiah: 'With my soul have I desired thee in the night; yea, with my spirit within me will I seek thee early.' Isaiah is also seen barefooted, having received the Divine order to traverse the streets of Jerusalem barefooted. Also occasionally holding the burning coal with the tongs (vi. 6). More often and later, however, he appears with a saw, the tradition being that this was the instrument of his martyrdom, in allusion to the text in the 11th chapter of Hebrews, relating the persecutions of the Prophets—'They were stoned; they were sawn asunder.' This is given as an event in the Speculum, where it serves as a type of the nailing of the Lord to the Cross. Isaiah is also seen holding the Infant Christ, whose nativity he prophesied.

Zechariah appears with the seven-branched candlestick (iv. 2); or is himself seen riding upon an ass. Hosea, who predicts the Lord's triumph over death, has a skull at his feet. Jonah holds a fish. The regular attribute of a prophet, however, is a book, generally open, as showing the obvious fulfilment of their predictions.

We reserve the application of the figures of Prophets in various pictorial cycles for a subsequent page, where they will be considered together with the Sibyls.

---

[1] Described in Dr. Waagen's Kunstwerke und Künstler in Paris, p. 224.

The Sibyls.

The Sibyls are heathen prophetesses, who figure in the scheme of Christian iconography as having predicted the coming of Christ to the Gentiles, as the Prophets did to the Jews. We have seen that in the Greek Church the sages of antiquity were, on the strength of real or supposed allusions to the nature of God and the mission of Christ, admitted in Art among the ranks of the Prophets. The Latin Church acted in a similar way by the adoption of the Sibyls as witnesses of the great facts of Christianity. These mysterious personages, whose historical origin is wrapt in obscurity, were regarded by the ancients as holy women, devoted to a life of virginity and solitude, who lived in caves and grottoes, were endowed with the power of seeing into futurity, and returned oracular answers to the interrogations of their votaries. Varro, the historian, who lived above a century before Christ, mentions their number as ten, and their names as derived from the locality of their habitations. They are as follows:—

The Sibylla Persica	. . .	from Persia.
,,	Libyca . . .	Libya.
,,	Delphica . .	Delphi.
,,	Erythræa . .	Erythræ, a Greek city of Asia Minor.
,,	Cumana . .	Cumæ.
,,	Samia . . .	Samos.
,,	Cimmeria . .	The Black Sea.
,,	Tiburtina . .	Tivoli.
,,	Hellespontina .	The Hellespont.
,,	Phrygia . .	Phrygia.

Two other Sibyls were, in later times, added to this number, generally called the Agrippa, or the Hebraica, and the Europa— besides others more seldom referred to, whose names are various; and, lastly, the Queen of Sheba is sometimes introduced as one of the mysterious sisterhood.

The story of the Sibyl who presented herself to Tarquin is supposed to relate to the Cumæan Sibyl. She offered him nine books of Sibylline oracles at a certain price. Tarquin refused to purchase them. She went away, burnt three, returned with six, and demanded the same price. Again her offer was refused, and again she left, burnt three more, returned with the last three, and still demanded the same price. Astonished at her pertinacity, Tarquin now consulted the soothsayers, who advised him to secure the remaining volumes, telling him that the destinies of the world depended on their preservation. The books were therefore purchased, for centuries preserved in the Capitol under the guardianship of an order of priests, and consulted on all national emergencies. At the destruction of the Capitol, during the wars of Marius and Scylla, these volumes perished. To repair the loss, messengers were sent over all the provinces of the empire to collect the scattered Sibylline leaves, and these, in turn, were guarded in the same way. The fate of this second edition it would be impossible to tell; but, at all events, the idea entertained by the Roman people, and quoted by Tacitus and Suetonius, that out of Judæa should come those who would be rulers of the world, is believed to have proceeded from the Sibylline remains.

The Christian community early concerned itself with speculations regarding the predictions of the Sibyls and their claims to respect. Some of the early Fathers believed them to have been prompted by diabolical agency; others, including St. Jerome, Eusebius, St. Clement of Alexandria, and St. Augustine, pronounced them to have been inspired by divine grace. Lactantius, who lived in the 4th century, was especially the champion of these Pagan women as prophetesses of the New Religion. By certain passages of their supposed writings, relating to the nature of the Divinity, the Creation of the World, and the Incarnation of the Son, he shows the conformity between the Sibylline leaves and the doctrines of Scripture. But it is chiefly by a passage in the fourth eclogue of Virgil (lived forty years before Christ), believed to have been suggested by a Sibylline tradition, that their power of foreseeing the Advent of Christ is sought to be established:—

>Ultima Cumæi venit jam carminis ætas;
>Magnus ab integro sæclorum nascitur ordo:
>Jam redit et virgo, redeunt Saturnia regna;

Jam nova progenies cœlo dimittitur alto.
Tu modò nascenti puero, quo ferrea primùm
Desinet, ac toto surget gens aurea mundo,
Casta, fave, Lucina.

Which is thus translated: 'The last age of the Cumæan song now approaches; the great series of ages begins again: now returns the Virgin (Astræa), now return the Saturnian kingdoms; now a new progeny is sent from high heaven. Be but propitious, chaste Lucina, to the boy at his birth, through whom the iron age will first cease, and the golden age dawn on the whole world.'

How far the believer may admit this and other more remote and less trustworthy sayings as witnesses from Heathendom, permitted in the designs of Providence, it is not the part of this work to inquire. At all events, it was not in the early ages of Christianity that the belief in the authority of the Sibyls was enlisted into the service of Art. There is no Sibylline figure in the Catacombs, nor in the earlier mosaics. Nor is it believed that the story of the Sibyl and the Emperor Augustus, by some called Octavius, was current before the 12th century. It is as follows.

The Roman Senate having decreed divine honours to the Emperor Augustus, he sought the Tiburtine Sibyl, and consulted her whether he should accept them. She replied that it behoved him rather to depart in silence from her, whose power was coming to an end, for that a Hebrew child should be born who would be ruler over the immortal gods themselves; or, according to another version, that a king should come from heaven who should be king for evermore. On which the heavens were opened, and a vision of the Virgin, standing on an altar, with the Infant Christ in her arms, appeared in a glory; and a voice was heard, saying, 'Hæc ara filii Dei'—'This is the altar of the Son of God.' The emperor adored the vision, reported it to the Senate, and erected upon the Capitol an altar, with the words, 'Ara primogeniti Dei.' On this spot was afterwards founded the Church of S. Maria in Capitolio, called from the tradition, the 'Ara cœli.'

This incident was adopted in the 14th century as a type of the appearance of the star to the Wise Men, or the manifestation of Christ to the Gentiles. Thus we see in the one the Annunciation of Christ's coming to the East; in the other, the same to the West. In this sense, a picture of the Sibyl and the Emperor takes its place in the 'Speculum humanæ Salvationis,' where they are both seen kneeling, while she points to the vision of the Virgin and Child in the clouds. The emperor's sceptre, or his crown, lies on the ground, in sign of his adoration. Sometimes the sun and the moon are on each side, as witnesses on the part of the powers of Heaven.

A triptych by Rogier van der Weyden, in the Berlin Gallery (No. 535), illustrates this story. In the centre is the Nativity; on the right wing, the three Kings adoring the Vision of the Child in the Star; on the left, the Vision appearing to the Emperor and Sibyl. He is swinging a censer, to show his devotion.

Garofalo especially treated this as a separate subject. In a picture by him in the Gallery of the Vatican, the emperor is in the act of taking his crown from his head, and bending his knee (woodcut, No. 99). Another picture by him is in the Pitti.

Whatever the nature of this story, the belief of the Roman Catholic Church in the testimony of the Sibyl is shown by the well-known hymn, said to have been composed by Pope Innocent III. at the close of the 13th century, beginning with the verse:—

> Dies iræ, dies illa,
> Solvet sæclum in favilla,
> Teste David cum Sibylla.

Which is thus translated in the English version of the Missal:—

> The dreadful day, the day of ire,
> Shall kindle the avenging fire
>   Around the expiring world.
> And earth, as Sibyl said of old,
> And as the prophet-king foretold,
>   Shall be in ruin hurled.

It may be inferred that this hymn, admitted into the liturgy of the Roman Church, gave sanction to the adoption of the Sibyls into Christian Art. They are seen from this time accompanying the Prophets and Apostles in the cyclical decorations of the Church—either environing the arch of the principal portal, or ornamenting the stalls in the choir, or imaged forth in the painted glass. Giotto's Campanile at Florence shows the Sibyls

Sibyl and Emperor. (Garofalo. Vatican.)

with Prophets and Patriarchs on its third tier; Ghiberti's bronze doors contain their graceful figures in the framework of the subjects; on the Holy House at Loretto, they stand in couples; and in some churches they have separate chapels to their honour. Such is the case, for instance, in St. Jacques at Dieppe, where twelve niches are reserved for the twelve figures of these Pagan witnesses to Christianity. But the chapel is immediately at the entrance of the church, which is their typical place as forerunners of the Lord. Thus they occupy the frontispiece in sacred manuscripts, and the framework in pictures; in all cases being supposed, like the Prophets, to stand on the threshold which leads to more holy ground. Their number in such representations varies much, either for reasons of space or of analogy. Thus they are frequently four, as the Evangelists are four and the Fathers of the Church are four. But their proper number in Christian cycles is twelve. Sometimes but one appears as the representative of all, as in Fra Angelico's picture of the Adoration of the Cross, where she forms the *pendant* to Dionysius the Areopagite. She is there, *par excellence, the* Sibyl—an idea derived probably from the Eastern Church, where only one, '*la sage Sibylle*,' is admitted.

Properly speaking, the Sibyls, like the Prophets, should be chiefly recognisable by the predictions contained upon their scrolls. But these have been in comparatively modern times so amplified in amount as to make these witnesses from Heathendom far more communicative and explicit than the Prophets themselves. And further, they have been so indiscriminately applied, that, in the absence of all canon to which to refer, it is impossible to class them with any consistency. Nor in their juxtaposition with the Prophets is there any rule of analogy followed between their respective predictions. Thus the attribute, dress, or age—and even these are too capricious to be adopted as archæological rules—become the only distinctive sign. We give them as far as they are deducible from various examples:—

1. The Sibylla Persica, generally an old woman, holds a lantern in her hand, and has sometimes a serpent under her feet. She predicts the coming of the Messiah, and was supposed to be a daughter-in-law of Moses.

2. The Sibylla Libyca—aged twenty-four years. She holds a lighted torch, as having prophesied the manifestation of Christ to the Gentiles.

3. The Sibylla Erythræa—an aged woman dressed in black like a nun. She is supposed to have lived at the time of the Trojan war, and to have predicted it. She is the prophetess of Divine vengeance, and holds in her hand a naked sword. According to other representations, she holds a white rose, and predicted the Annunciation.

4. The Sibylla Delphica has a horn in her hands, or the crown of thorns.

5. The Sibylla Samia—supposed to have lived at the time of Isaiah. Holds a reed, or a cradle.

6. The Sibylla Cimmeria—aged eighteen years. Holds a Cross of the Passion, as having foreseen the Crucifixion.

7. The Sibylla Cumana—aged fifteen years. Holds a manger, as having predicted the Nativity in a stable.

8. The Sibylla Hellespontina. Prophesied the Incarnation and the Crucifixion, and holds a flowering rod, or the Cross of the Passion.

9. The Sibylla Phrygia, with a processional cross and banner, as having predicted the Resurrection.

10. The Sibylla Tiburtina, dressed in a tiger's skin or goat's skin. Holds a hand, or a rod, in allusion to the Mocking or the Flagellation.

11. The Sibylla Agrippa—aged fifteen years—with a scourge.

12. The Sibylla Europa, also aged fifteen, with a sword. Foretold the Murder of the Innocents.

All the Attributes referring to the Birth and Passion of our Lord are of late introduction; viz., the 16th century. Often the Sibyls have no attributes but their books, in which, like the Prophets, they are reading or pointing to a passage. They are sometimes seen bearing torches or lanterns. Some of them with a sun on their head, their position in the Church being defined as 'a Light shining in darkness.' Often the inscriptions convey the words from Virgil; and an early picture is described of the Nativity in which David and the Prophets are singing and dancing around, and Virgil leads the concert with a fiddle.[1]

In the great system of Christian Art the Sibyls may be said to go hand in hand with the Prophets, and there can be no doubt that grand and picturesque female figures, of inspired action and countenance, were exceedingly welcome to painters and sculptors in this juxtaposition, either in series, or in composite representations. Baldini in his etchings has two sets of the Prophets, and one of the Sibyls, twelve in number. These are women in grandly fantastic costume. Cimmeria with wings on head, like Mercury. Erythræa, like an abbess, seated within a magic circle of stars, with sword in hand. The Cumana is especially beautiful, her head showing all the grace of Raphael (woodcut, No. 100, over leaf). She is seated on formally shaped clouds. The Delphica, also, is

---

[1] Piper. Christliche Mythologie und Symbolik. 1ter Band, 1te Abth., p. 499.

100   Sibylla Cumana   (Baldini.)

a remarkable conception, with a horn in her hand; she is on a rock surrounded with water. The celebrated St. Bavon picture, by Hubert and Jan van Eyck, so often described and illustrated, has two Sibyls, the Erythræa and Cumana, flanked by two Prophets, Micah and Zechariah, on the outside of the wings over the Annunciation.

But the highest honour that Art has rendered to the Sibyls has been by the hand of Michael Angelo, on the ceiling of the Sistine Chapel. Here, in the conception of a mysterious order of women, placed above and without all considerations of the graceful or the individual, the great master was peculiarly in his element. They exactly fitted his standard of Art, not always sympathetic, nor comprehensible to the average human mind, of which the grand in form, and the abstract in expression, were the first and last conditions. In this respect, the Sibyls on the Sistine Chapel ceiling are more Michael Angelesque than their companions the Prophets. For these, while types of the highest monumental treatment, are yet men, while the Sibyls belong to a distinct class of beings, who convey the impression of the very obscurity in which their history is wrapt—creatures who have lived far from the abodes of men; who are alike devoid of the expression of feminine sweetness, human sympathy, or sacramental beauty; who are neither Christians nor Jewesses, Witches nor Graces, yet living, grand, beautiful, and true, according to laws revealed to the great Florentine genius only. Thus their figures may be said to be unique, as the offspring of a peculiar sympathy between the master's mind and his subject. To this sympathy may be ascribed the prominence and size given them—both Prophets and Sibyls—as compared to their usual relation to the subjects they environ. They sit here in twelve throne-like niches, more like presiding deities, each wrapt in self-contemplation, than as tributary witnesses to the truth and omnipotence of Him they are intended to announce. Thus they form a gigantic framework round the subjects of the Creation, of which the Birth of Eve, as the type of the Nativity, is the intentional centre. For some reason, the twelve figures are not Prophets and Sibyls alternately; there being only five Sibyls— Persica, Erythræa, Delphica, Cumana, and Libyca, to seven Prophets—Jeremiah, Ezekiel, Joel, Zechariah, Isaiah, Daniel, and Jonah; so that the Prophets come together at one angle. Books and scrolls are given indiscriminately to them.

The Sibylla Persica, supposed to be the oldest of the sisterhood, holds the book close to her eyes, as if from dimness of sight, which fact, contradicted as it is by a frame of obviously Herculæan strength, gives a mysterious intentness to the action.

The Sibylla Libyca, of equally powerful proportions, but less closely draped, is grandly wringing herself to lift a massive volume from a height above her head on to her knee (woodcut No. 101, over leaf).

101   Sibylla Libyca.   (Michael Angelo.   Sistine Chapel.)

The Sibylla Cumana, also aged, and with her head covered, is reading with her volume at a distance from her eyes.

The Sibylla Delphica, with waving hair escaping from her turban, is a beautiful young being—the most human of all—gazing into vacancy or futurity. She holds a scroll.

The Sibylla Erythræa, a grand bareheaded creature, sits reading intently with crossed legs, about to turn over her book.

The Prophets are equally grand in structure, and though, as we have said, not more than men, yet they are the only men that could well bear the juxtaposition with their stupendous female colleagues. Ezekiel, between Erythræa and Persica, has a scroll in his hand that hangs by his side, just cast down, as he turns eagerly to listen to some voice.

Jeremiah, a magnificent figure, sits with elbow on knee, and

102   Jeremiah. (Sistine Ceiling.)

head on hand, wrapt in the meditation appropriate to one called to utter lamentations and woe. He has neither book nor scroll (woodcut, No. 102).

Jonah is also without either. His position is strained and ungraceful—looking upwards, and apparently remonstrating with the Almighty on the destruction of the gourd, a few leaves of which are seen above him. His hands are placed together with a strange and trivial action, supposed to denote the counting on his fingers the number of days he was in the fish's belly. A formless marine monster is seen at his side.

Daniel has a book on his lap, with one hand on it. He is young, and a piece of lion's skin seems to allude to his history.

Isaiah, young, grand, and absorbed, leans upon his book.

Zechariah sits, like the Sibylla Persica, with his head close to his book.

Joel is reading a scroll, which he holds up in both hands.

In all these figures, in the absence, in every instance, of all individuality and attribute by which to identify them, the names of each are written on a slab beneath their feet. Each, it may be observed, is attended by genii, too undefined in character or purpose for their intention to be understood, but which are supposed to be the bearers of divine inspiration.

Raphael has also left us conceptions of the Sibyls and Prophets, and in no respect more strongly asserts the difference between his mind and that of Michael Angelo. These are seen over and around the arch of the first chapel on the right in S. Maria della Pace at Rome. Both series are known to have been executed by him. They are simply beautiful women of antique form, to whom, with the aid of books, scrolls, and inscriptions, the Sibyllic idea has been given, but who would equally pass for the abstract personifications of virtues, or cities. They are four in number—the Cumana, Phrygia, Persica, and Tiburtina; all, with the exception of the last, in the fulness of youth and beauty, and occupied, apparently, with no higher aim than that of displaying both. Indeed, the Tiburtina matches ill with the rest, either in character or action. She is aged, has an open book on her lap, but turns with a strange and rigid action as if suddenly called. The very comparison with her tends to divest the others of the Sibylline character. In this, the angels who float above, and obviously inspire them, also help, for while adding to the charm of the composition, which is one of the most exquisite as to mere Art, they interfere with that inwardly inspired expression which all other Art has given to these women.

We give an illustration of the Cumæan Sibyl and her attendant angel (woodcut, No. 103). The description on her scroll gives in Greek the words, 'The Resurrection of the Dead.' The Persica is writing on the scroll held by the angel. 'He will have the lot of Death.' The beautiful Phrygia is presented with a scroll, 'The heavens surround the sphere of the earth;' and the Tiburtina has near her the inscription, 'I will open and arise.' The

103 Sibylla Cumana. (Raphael. Church of La Pace, Rome.)

fourth angel floats above, holding the seventh line of Virgil's Eclogue, 'Jam nova progenies.'

Andrea del Castagno, in the figures painted by him in the Villa Pandolfini, at Legnaja, has introduced the Cumæan Sibyl, possibly for the pictorial inducement of varying the male element. These are single full-length figures surrounding a room, and now placed in a chamber at the Uffizj. We give an illustration of the Sibyl (woodcut, No. 104, over leaf). Her companions are Queen Esther (a half-figure, on account of a door) and Queen Tomiris.

In later times the Sibyls lost their significance, and only

furnished appropriate names for single pictures of beautiful women, with inspired looks and Oriental turbans. Guido, Domenichino, and Guercino, have all left such representations.

104   Sibylla Cumana.   (Andrea del Castagno.   Uffizi.)

The Murder of the Innocents.

Ital. Lo Strage degli Innocenti. *Fr.* Le Massacre des Innocents.
Germ. Der Kindermord.

[*A. J.*—The artistic treatment of all the Scriptural and legendary incidents connected with the early years of our Lord, from the apparition of the angel (*i.e.*, the promise of the Incarnation) down to the return of the Holy Family from Egypt, have been fully described in a former volume of 'Legendary Art,' and 'Legends of the Madonna,' second edition, pp. 166-245. Those scenes in which the Redeemer appears as an Infant, and the Virgin Mary as a principal personage, belonged properly to the historical subjects relating to the life and character of the Madonna. There is, however, one important event, in which neither our Lord nor His Mother are in any way actors, which yet remains to be treated more at large, namely, the *Massacre of the Innocents*.

This painfully tragic incident is recorded by one Evangelist only—St. Matthew. The silence of the others, of all contemporary historians, and especially of Josephus, who has written in full detail the life and actions of Herod the Great, has thrown some doubt upon the fact, and there are writers who have gone so far as to consider the brief notice in St. Matthew as an interpolation. Such objections, I think, have been fairly met and answered. Among other arguments, it has been well observed that amid all the atrocities which darkened the reign of Herod, and all the splendour of the era in which he lived, the slaughter of a few children in a remote village of Judæa might easily pass unnoticed, and that, setting aside the authority of the Evangelist, in itself conclusive, this terrible incident derives probability from the personal character of Herod, and from some peculiar circumstances of his life. The man who put to death his wife, his wife's mother, his sister's husband, his three sons, and who had never been known to spare from torture or from death, man, woman, or child who stood in his way, or excited, for a moment, his jealousy

A. J.] or his displeasure, was not likely to hesitate in a case in which his suspicions had been so strongly awakened. Herod, we must remember, was by birth an Edomite. He was so far from being allied to the royal race of Judah, that he was not even an Israelite. He had been placed on the throne by the power of the Romans, especially by the influence of Antony and Cleopatra, and the Jews regarded him as a stranger and usurper. He knew this, and his whole reign was passed in terror of a Jewish competitor, in terror of that *King* whose reign had been the theme of the prophets of old, and whose coming was near at hand. When, therefore, he found himself mocked by the Wise Men of the East, who had returned to their own land without even pointing out to him the new-born Messiah, he commanded all the male infants under two years old, in and round Bethlehem, to be destroyed, hoping with them to kill the Christ. But it was otherwise ordained; for 'Joseph arose and took the young child and his mother by night, and departed into Egypt.' There is a very old tradition, as old at least as the 2nd century, that Herod also sought to destroy at the same time the son of Zacharias and Elizabeth—the young St. John, whose greatness had been foretold to him; that Elizabeth escaped with her son from amid the slaughter, and was afterwards miraculously preserved, and that Herod, in his rage at being thus baffled, sent and slew Zacharias between the altar and the Temple.[1]

To return, however, to the massacre at Bethlehem. Bishop Taylor, in describing this event, amplifies the brief and simple Gospel notice—*paints* it, in short, with all the colours of his picturesque and exuberant style. 'This execution,' he says, 'was sad, cruel, universal: no abatement made for the dire shriekings of the mothers; no tender-hearted soldier was employed; no hard-hearted person was softened by the weeping eyes and pity-begging looks of those mothers that wondered how it was possible any person should hurt their pretty sucklings.' 'The sword being

[1] In a Greek MS. in the Bibliothèque Impériale at Paris, with Byzantine miniatures of the 9th century, these events are simultaneously given. Here Herod and two counsellors are present, while one executioner and one child represent the massacre. In the same picture we see Zacharias being pierced with a lance, and Elizabeth and the young St. John enclosed in a rock, and seen only to the shoulders. The subject is taken from the Protevangelion, chap. xvi.

J.] thus made sharp by Herod's commission, killed fourteen thousand pretty babes, as the Greeks in their calendar and the Abyssines of Ethiopia do commemorate in their books of Liturgy. The mourning was great, like the mourning in the valley of Hinnom, and there was no comforter. The sorrow was too big to be cured till it should lie down and rest with its own weariness.'[1]

With regard to the date of these events, it appears certain that Herod died a few weeks after the birth of our Lord—that is, in the beginning of the following March. It must have been, then, in February, when he was on his deathbed, dying of a lingering and horrible disease, that the cruel decree went forth for the murder of the Bethlehemite children : he could not, therefore, have been present. Five days before his death, he ordered the execution of his son Antipater, which probably gave rise to the tradition that one of Herod's own children perished with the victims at Bethlehem ; but Antipater was then forty years of age, and hardly less hateful, treacherous, and cruel than his father Herod.

The Innocents, though unconscious for whose sake they died, have always been considered as martyrs in the cause of Christ— 'martyrs in deed, though not in will'—and in His Church at once glorified and compassionated. Irenæus, writing within a hundred years after the death of our Saviour, speaks of the Innocents as already sanctified to the tender veneration of all good Christians. They keep their places in our English calendar, and we have in England four churches dedicated to their honour.]

105   Innocents as Martyrs.
(Choral Book. S. Ambrogio. Milan.)

The Innocents, as martyrs, are found rather in miniatures than pictures. This illustration (No. 105) is taken from an initial letter in a choral book of the 15th century in the Church of S. Ambrogio at Milan. They are all singing and praising God in this little picture,

[1] Life of Christ.

which shows the idea of the martyrdom, not the event. For they have each alike a wound in the throat and a palm-branch in the hand.

[*A. J.*—But notwithstanding their rank as saints and martyrs, pictures of them in this character have always been rare in churches. There were reasons why a group of bleeding children, as objects of public devotion, should be avoided, and I can remember no instance of such effigies previous to the latter half of the 15th century, except the very early mosaic group in San Paolo at Rome. While the massacre, as an event, necessarily entered into every complete series of the History of our Lord, as a separate or devotional subject it involved no point of doctrine—it was not profitable either as lesson or example; hence, I suppose, its comparative rarity in early Art.

All at once, however, in the latter half of the 15th century—that is, after 1450—we find the subject of the Holy Innocents assuming an extraordinary degree of popularity and importance. Then, for the first time, we find chapels dedicated to them, and groups of martyred children in altar pieces round the throne of Christ or the Virgin. From this period we have innumerable examples of the terrible scene of the massacre at Bethlehem, treated as a separate subject in pictures and prints, while the best artists vied with each other in varying and elaborating the details of circumstantial cruelty and frantic despair.

For a long time I could not comprehend how this came about, nor how it happened that through all Italy, especially in the Tuscan schools, a subject so ghastly and so painful should have assumed this sort of prominence. The cause, as it gradually revealed itself, rendered every picture more and more interesting; connecting them with each other, and showing how intimately the history of Art is mixed up with the life of a people.

There had existed at Florence from the 13th century an hospital for foundlings, the first institution of the kind in Europe. It was attached to the Benedictine monastery of San Gallo, near one of the gates of the city still bearing the name. In the 15th century, when the population and extent of the city had greatly increased, it was found that this hospital was too small, and the funds of the monastery quite inadequate to the purpose. Then Lionardo Bruni of Arezzo, who was twice Chancellor of Florence—the same

A. J.] Lionardo who gave to Ghiberti the subjects of his famous gates—filled with compassion for the orphans and neglected children, addressed the senate on the subject, and made such an affecting appeal in their behalf, that not the senate only, but the whole people of Florence responded with enthusiasm, frequently interrupting him with cries of 'Viva Messer Lionardo d'Arezzo!' 'And,' adds the historian, 'never was a question of importance carried with such quickness and unanimity' ('mai con maggior celerità e pienezza de' voti fu vinto partito di cosa grave come questa'). Large sums were voted, offerings flowed in, a superb hospital was founded, and Brunelleschi was appointed architect. When finished, which was not till 1444, it was solemnly dedicated to the '*Holy Innocents.*' The first child consigned to the new institution was a poor little female infant, on whose breast was pinned the name 'Agata,' in remembrance of which an altar in the chapel was dedicated to St. Agatha. We have proof that the foundation, progress, and consecration of this refuge for destitute children excited the greatest interest and sympathy, not only in Florence but in the neighbouring states, and that it was intimated in Pisa, Arezzo, and Siena. The union of the two hospitals of San Gallo and the 'Innocenti' took place in 1463. Churches and chapels were appended to the hospitals, and, as a matter of course, the painters and sculptors were called upon to decorate them. Such are the circumstances which explain, as I think, the popularity of the story of the Innocents in the 15th century, and the manner in which it occupied the minds of the great contemporary artists of the Tuscan school and others after them.

In speaking of the series of the Life of the Virgin, painted by Ghirlandajo in the choir of S. Maria Novella, at Florence, I have remarked on the fresco of the Massacre of the Innocents as being most unusual in such a series.[1] Half a century earlier, a selection of subjects, with reference to the Virgin *only*, would not have included such a representation, or it would have taken a secondary position in the background. The difficulty vanishes, however, on a comparison of dates. At the very time that Ghirlandajo was employed on the frescoes in the S. Maria Novella, he was painting the altarpiece for the Church of the Innocents attached to the

[1] Legends of the Madonna.

A. J.] hospital.[1] His mind must therefore have been full of the subject, and this grand altarpiece is the earliest example I can remember of the Innocents, as saints, martyrs, and patrons, introduced into a strictly devotional picture. Nothing can be conceived more poetical in conception, more beautiful in sentiment, more significant and suggestive in treatment, than this wonderful production, considering the purpose for which it was painted. In the centre the Virgin is seated on her throne; the Infant Saviour on her knee looks benignly down on the Wise Men of the East—magnificent venerable figures, bearded, and robed in jewels, who cast their crowns and gifts at His feet. On the right of the throne, and more in front, kneels St. John the Baptist, the protector of Florence, who presents a little martyred Innocent; on the left, St. Gallo, the patron of the former original foundation-hospital, kneeling, presents another. Both children are of exquisite beauty, habited in semi-transparent drapery, and they clasp their little hands and look up, appealing, to the Infant Saviour. In the background is seen the city and the slaughter of the Innocents, sufficiently distinct, but not too prominent. Angels above sing the 'gloria' from a scroll, on which the musical notes as well as the words are clearly written. Thus we find expressed at once, as in a poem, first, the reverence paid by age and wisdom to holy womanhood and childhood; secondly, the dreadful cruelty inflicted on helpless children; and, thirdly, the intercession of the infant martyrs, now saints in heaven, for the poor little martyrs on earth. I must add, that in this picture the finished beauty of the execution is equal to the sublime pathos of the conception; nor has it ever been touched by a restorer, nor removed from its place.]

This picture has never been engraved, nor could it be copied entire in its present position. We give an etching of the foremost figures only—St. John Baptist and St. Gallo, with the two Innocents—taken from the picture.

[*A. J.*—In another picture I have seen (attributed to Cosimo Rosselli), the Virgin and Child are enthroned, with saints and angels, attendant in the usual manner; while lower down, in front, are seen the children of Bethlehem, eighteen in number, in very curious and various dresses, who present themselves before

---

[1] The date of the frescoes is 1485–1490, and the date on the picture 1483.

Constantine Church of the Innocents Florence

A. J.] Christ, showing the wounds received for His sake, while He extends His hand in benediction.[1] In style this picture is more like Piero di Cosimo than Cosimo Rosselli.

As I have already observed, the presence of Herod was, at the supposed date, quite impossible, and the number of victims has been portentously exaggerated: instead of 14,000, it did not probably amount to forty. But the old painters and sculptors did not trouble themselves with minor dates and details; their object was to render the scene as frightful and pathetic as possible, and to represent Herod (whose very name has descended to us rather as that of a goblin to scare mothers and children than as that of an historical personage) as ugly and as horrible as possible.

It is an historical fact that King Herod had in his service, as body-guard, a legion of 1500 barbarian soldiers—Gauls and Germans—apparently because he could not trust his own people; and it is a tradition that he employed these strangers to execute his savage decree. Hence, in some of the pictures—for instance, in that by Rubens—the soldiers are habited as we see the Gauls and Dacians in the ancient bas-reliefs.

I have already observed that the Massacre of the Innocents as an *event* is included in every complete series of the history of our Saviour, and that the general character of the representation has scarcely varied from the earliest times. The locality is usually the court of Herod's palace, where, according to one version of the legend, he had assembled the victims. Herod, wearing that type of heathendom, the turban, is seated on his throne, or from a balcony commands the butchery; frantic mothers strive against the barbarous soldiery, their children are torn from them, or slain in their arms, the ground is strewn with dead and bleeding infants. In most instances, it will be remarked that amid the groups of despairing mothers two figures are conspicuous. One is a mother, who, concealing her child in her arms, or in her drapery, is escaping with headlong speed, or looking back in terror. This is obviously intended for Elizabeth, fleeing with her son, the young St. John. Another mother, seated on the ground, is contemplating

[1] Berlin Gallery, No. 1075.

A. J.] her dead child in mute despair, or wringing her hands. This is the painter's realisation of the woman in the prophecy, 'Rachel weeping for her children, and refusing to be comforted.'

In sculpture, and in architectural decoration, the action is expressed by as few figures as possible. In the mosaic in S. Maria Maggiore, probably the oldest existing example, on the one side is seen Herod seated on his throne, giving the order to his soldiers, and near him three other figures, perhaps the Three Wise Men; on the other side, several women stand with their children in their arms, and three soldiers opposite. Here the action is not expressed, only indicated. In the sculpture over the porch of the Lorenz-Kirche at Nuremberg, Herod is seated on his throne, and one soldier, holding up a child, is in the act of piercing it with his sword.]

Fra Angelico, whose gentle nature would seem to have least fitted him for scenes of such horror, has, nevertheless, treated the Massacre of the Innocents more than once, and with the utmost pathos of intention. One example forms part of the series of the Life of Christ in the Accademia at Florence. Another, of which we give an illustration (woodcut, No. 106), is in the form of a miniature in the choral books at S. Marco. Here Herod presides, like a bloated giant, over the slaughter, while some of the figures have a rapidity as well as grace of action, surpassing the master's usual standard of power. The mother in front, bending over her dead child, represents probably 'Rachel weeping for her children,' and is repeated in the picture in the Accademia.

I will now give a few examples of the Massacre of the Innocents treated dramatically as a separate subject.

[*A. J.*—Matteo di Giovanni di Siena, one of the most original painters of that original school, was living and working at Siena just at the time when the story of the Innocents was so popular at Florence: he appears to have adopted the subject and treated it in his own way, and to have rather liked it, for I remember three of his compositions, all remarkable, and all quite different.

The first is one of the compartments of the wonderful pavement of the Duomo at Siena; it is in the transept, to the left, near the chapel of St. John the Baptist. The scene is a splendid court

THE MURDER OF THE INNOCENTS.

106   Massacre of the Innocents.   (Fra Angelico. Choral Book. S. Marco.)

A. J.] surrounded by a frieze of heathen subjects—satyrs, centaurs, and arabesques—in a very good style; beneath are balconies and windows. Herod, on the left, gives the command to slay the

A. J.] children. Then we have the *mêlée* of desperate mothers and executioners; behind, looking out of a window of the palace, are frightened children.

The second is a fresco in the Church of Sant' Agostino at Siena. The scene is the court of a palace. On one side Herod is on his throne, looking horribly fierce, like an ogre. Executioners, ferocious and ugly as possible, pursue distracted mothers trying to defend their children; on the right sits Rachel, 'refusing to be comforted' by a man who bends over her compassionately. This is a touch of the pathetic I have never seen but in the Siena school. In the background frightened people and children look through the arcades—a very curious picture, a little exaggerated in expression, but full of movement and tragic horror.

The third is different, and the finest of all. It is in the Church of the Servi, forming the altarpiece of a chapel dedicated to the Innocents. Herod, seated on his throne, is in the centre facing the spectator, horribly fierce as usual; a counsellor stands on each side; in front seven mothers are contending with four executioners; dead children strew the ground; and from the windows behind, two children look on in terror. (This incident of the children as spectators being repeated in all this artist's pictures, has probably some significance—perhaps an ignorant allusion to the children of Herod. It increases, however, the horror of the scene.) These compositions date from 1482 to 1491.

The Padre della Valle, in the 'Lettere Sienese,' mentions a fourth example in the Church of S. Caterina in Formello at Naples, with the date 1418, which he thinks, and I have no doubt, should be 1468.

By Raphael we have two famous compositions. The first is, or rather *was*, a cartoon for the series of tapestries from the Life of Christ. Part of this cartoon is in our National Gallery, and there is a small and beautiful drawing in chiaroscuro in the

1. J.] British Museum. It is full of movement and horror—the usual ferocity on the part of the soldiers, and resistance of the hapless mothers; a man stooping down in front seizes a child by the leg with one hand, brandishing his sword in the other. This *idea* has been often repeated. In front a woman seated on the ground, her dead infant lying across her lap, contemplates it with a mute despair.

The second composition is the well-known admirable engraving by Marc Antonio, in which the classical elegance of the arrangement, the perfection of the drawing, and the pathos of the sentiment, almost redeem the horror of the subject, so that, as in everything by Raphael, the sense of beauty triumphs over all. The scene is a paved court with buildings in the background; there are eight women and five executioners; the principal group on the left is a soldier, who, having just drawn his sword, is rushing forward and has seized a child by the leg, while the mother, clasping it to her bosom, turns to fly, looking back in horror. In another group, more to the left, a dead child, of pathetic beauty, lies on the ground, and a mother, kneeling, holds back her terrified infant with one arm, while, with the other extended, she tries to defend him from a furious soldier.

This drawing and the engraving must have been executed about 1512 or 1513; and it is remarkable that Piero Soderini Gonfaloniere of Florence, who had been a friend of Raphael in his younger years, was a munificent patron of the 'Innocenti,' which in 1511 he endowed with large revenues, on condition of having a mass said for his soul yearly, on the day of his birth and the day of his death.

Baccio Bandinelli. This grand composition is also best known through the medium of the fine engraving by Marco di Ravenna —the drawing is at Chatsworth. Bandinelli was a sculptor and an architect, not a painter, and the whole is treated like a theatrical scene. The background is a splendid palace, with a flight of marble steps rising to a platform, on which stand five military officers round a column, and with their truncheons command the slaughter. One woman on the left bites the arm of a man about to seize her child; another, with dishevelled hair, in

A. J.] front, contemplates the severed head of her infant—a touch at once of the burlesque and the barbarous. There are about sixty figures in all, drawn with sculptural vigour and precision; but the conception is in the highest degree extravagant, unfeeling, and in the worst taste of the mannered school.

The picture by Daniel di Volterra, in the Tribune at Florence, is also crowded with figures (about seventy), and the scene takes place in the portico of a palace and on a flight of marble steps, which gives occasion to vary the attitudes. On the left hand Herod sits on a lofty throne, and two trumpeters stand before as proclaiming his savage decree. Here we have again repeated the Raphaelesque *motif*, the mother contemplating her dead infant.

Guido's picture is also famous in the history of Art; no picture has perhaps been more copied. Compared with those I have described, there are few figures. For grace and expression it is the finest of all his productions, and it gives the impression of having been most carefully studied. There are two executioners and five mothers. The *motifs* are similar to those in Raphael's composition; an executioner seizes a woman by the hair, two attempt to escape, and one seated in the foreground, her dead child beside her, looks up with tearless eyes and clasped hands: the whole is pathetic rather than horrible. This picture was painted for Count Bero Ghislieri, for his family chapel, at the time when Marini's poem, 'Lo Strage degli Innocenti,' was at the height of its popularity; and the poet addressed to the painter a much-admired madrigal, quite in the affected taste of that age —but the last four lines are certainly graceful, and contain a well-deserved, not less than a well-turned, compliment.

Rubens. His picture, almost contemporary with that of Guido, is in a very different style: a crowded dramatic composition conceived with more than his usual coarse power and vivid realism. The soldiers slay like butchers; the women fight like furies; the children bleed like pigs in a slaughter-house. One mother attempts to do what I suppose in such an extremity a mother might do— to tear out the eyes of the soldier who is about to transfix her infant with his sword; and, as a climax of horror, a dog is seen lapping up the blood of the murdered babies. I once saw this picture—'look on't again I dare not.'

I. *J.*] Andrea Celesti, in a grand mannered picture, with life-size pictures, and in the style of his school and time, has placed the action near a seaport—I suppose from a mistaken interpretation of the text, 'Bethlehem and all the *coasts* thereof.'

The picture by Nicolas Poussin contains only four figures. On the left an executioner has set his foot on an infant; the mother sinking on her knees attempts to ward off the blow. On the right hand, another woman with her dead child in her arms rushes forth, and, with raised head and open mouth, seems to shriek aloud in her despair.

Breughel (Höllen Breughel). A winter scene: the executioners, dressed like Dutch boors, and over their shoe-tops in snow, pursue the mothers and children. Horribly absurd. (Hampton Court.) This picture belonged to Charles I.

Jan Steen has treated the subject in the same style, with a coarseness equally tasteless and revolting.

I remember a picture in the Lichtenstein Gallery, by some late painter, in which, in the midst of a dark desolate landscape, two mothers sit on the ground bewailing their dead children. There is also a modern picture by a French painter, in which one solitary Bethlehemite mother, crouching down behind a wall, and clasping her poor doomed baby to her bosom, listens trembling to the sounds of fury, and agony, and strife which rise in the background. These simple episodes are infinitely more effective in realising the scene than the theatrical artifices of Bandinelli, the classical grouping of Guido, or the atrocious butchery of Rubens: and with these remarks I quit the subject, not without a sense of relief.]

The slaughtered children lying by the roadside, as the Holy Family pass in their flight into Egypt, are frequently seen in miniatures of the 15th century. A picture with this incident is in the Dresden Gallery.

In the Church of S. Giovanni Evangelista at Brescia is a picture of the Murder of Innocents, by Moretto. Herod sits on his throne in an open loggia at a distance; a struggle is going on in front, but scarcely a child seen. In the sky above is a glory, with the

Infant Christ holding cross and tablet, inscribed, 'Innocentes et recti adheruut mihi.'

The 'Spedale degli Innocenti' forms one side of the square of the Annunziata—that side being supported on open arcades. In the spandrel of each arch is the effigy of an Innocent, by Luca della Robbia—one of the countless beautiful decorations of Florence. Every little figure is half enveloped in swaddling clothes, and each differs from the other (there are twelve of them) in position and expression. The accompanying woodcut (No. 107) is taken from one almost in the centre.

107   Innocent.   (Luca della Robbia.   Florence.)

JOSEPH, THE HUSBAND OF THE VIRGIN.

[*A. J.*—THERE are few scenes in the childhood of Christ in which He appears without the presence and companionship of His Mother. Those pictures which place Him in particular relation with Joseph alone as His protector and foster-father, belong to the later schools of Art, and the most beautiful may be found in the Spanish and Bologna schools, in pictures by the Carracci, Guido, and Murillo. Joseph holding the Infant Saviour in his arms, caressing Him tenderly—our illustration (No. 108) is by Guido—or leading Him by the hand, became common and favourite subjects in the monasteries about the beginning of the 17th century, just as St. Catherine espousing the Infant Christ, or folding Him in her arms, became a favourite subject in nunneries; and for the same reason, viz., that blending of the devotional with the natural and affectionate instincts, which

108 Joseph and Infant Christ.
(Guido.)

has been in some cases so elevating, and in others so dangerous, to our humanity. St. Joseph almost always bears the lily as the emblem of chastity, or the rod which burst into blossom on his marriage-day, to mark his true relation to the Mother of his supposed Son. By Murillo, who excelled in this subject, we have a charming picture of St. Joseph leading the Child Jesus, who carries the basket of carpenter's tools, and looks up in his face with filial confidence. In another he holds the Child reverently and tenderly in his arms. In a picture by Elzheimer, Joseph is teaching his foster-son to walk. I remember a picture by a Spanish painter, A. de Tobar, who successfully imitated Murillo, in which the tenderly paternal look of Joseph as he bends over the Child, and the responsive expression in the face of the Infant Christ, are almost pathetic. In the Bolognese school the examples are

A. J.] numerous, and we have beautiful variations of the idea by Guido, by Guercino, Domenichino, Sasso Ferrato, Carlo Dolce, and Carlo Marratto; but the sentiment and intention are in all the same. St. Joseph, as patron saint of the Carmelites, and especially of St. Theresa, shared her popularity; and as patron of the Augustin Canons regular, he was also a frequent subject in churches from the end of the 16th century.

At this time the classical taste was in the ascendant, and in some pictures the attitude and reciprocal feeling in the Infant Saviour and Joseph are obviously taken from the famous group in the Vatican—Silenus embracing the Infant Bacchus.

The pictures which represent our Saviour, after the return from Egypt, in domestic life, and especially in relation to His Mother, the infant St. John, and others, and as associated with St. Joseph in daily labour, I have already treated at length. There remains, however, one incident of a purely legendary character, so seldom represented, that I can only remember to have seen a single instance, and to have heard of another.

The legend relates that when the Holy Family had returned from Egypt, our Lord being then about seven or eight years old, Mary was exhorted to send her Son to school; and although she knew perfectly that He required no human teaching, she complied. She brought him to a certain schoolmaster whose name was Zaccheus, and the schoolmaster wrote out the alphabet for Him, and began with the first letter, saying, '*Aleph;*' and Jesus pronounced after Him '*Aleph.*' Then the master went on to the second letter, saying, '*Beth;*' but Jesus said, 'Tell me first what means this letter *aleph*, and then afterwards I will say *beth.*' But the schoolmaster could not tell him. And Jesus began to teach him, and to explain the meaning and the use of all the letters—how they were distinguished, why some were crooked and some straight—until Zaccheus the schoolmaster stood in astonishment, and exclaimed, 'Was this child born before Noah? for behold He is wiser than the wisest man, and needs no teaching!' ('Gospel of Infancy,' chap. xx.)

This legend I have seen represented on one of the windows in St. Ouen. The scene is the interior of a schoolroom, with arches behind, and landscape background; a schoolmaster seated on

l. J.] high, with a rod in his hand, points to a book held by Jesus, who wears the dress of a student, with a glory round His head, and the Holy Spirit in form of a dove hovering over Him.[1]

I find also a description of an antique Christian bas-relief, once in the famous collection of the Borgia family at Velletri, which Münter in his 'Sinnbilder,' p. 80, supposes to represent this subject, or, at least, Jesus as learning or studying in a school. He is seated as a boy about twelve years old, in a short tunic on a low stool, with a roll of MS. held open in both hands, wherein He appears to be reading intently, or rather reflecting on what He had read there. 'Without doubt,' adds Dr Münter, ' it is a part of the Holy Scriptures which refers to Himself;' but I do not feel sure of the subject, not having seen the original. I have seen also similar groups on the bas-reliefs of Gothic cathedrals.][2]

Joseph warned by an angel in a dream to take the young Child and His Mother, and flee into Egypt, is frequently seen in early series. It served to set forth the other fact of the Flight into Egypt, for which early Art had hardly means of expression. It is generally naively given.[3] We add an illustration of the 14th century (No. 109), from the Italian Speculum belonging to Mr. Boxall. Here the angel bears a scroll as a message from on high.

109   Joseph's Dream.
(Italian Speculum. 14th century.)

In later Art the Dream of Joseph was never more finely rendered than by Mengs, in a picture in the Belvedere Gallery.

---

[1] See also 'A Ramble through Normandy,' by G. Musgrove, p. 75, where a similar subject is described at Pont Andemeer, near Caen.

[2] The subject is supposed to refer to the text in Luke ii. 52: 'And Jesus increased in wisdom and stature.'

[3] See work by Quast and Schultz, on Italian Antiquities, pl. 39.

THE APOCRYPHAL GOSPEL, CALLED THE INFANCY OF JESUS CHRIST.

It may be mentioned in this part of the work, that Mrs. Jameson's slightly indicated scheme, to which we have referred in the Preface, included a separate account of the so-called 'Gospel of the Infancy.' With unquestioning respect for Mrs. Jameson's judgment, we are inclined to think that, however interesting to the antiquary, this spurious history is not fitted to be analysed in a work intended for general readers. It is not only that the miracles ascribed to our Lord's childhood are of a puerile or vindictive nature, which do violence to the feelings of a Christian, but that the Art derived from this source is insignificant in amount, and generally inferior in quality. Mrs. Jameson has also forestalled one of the principal incidents—our Lord learning His alphabet—in the foregoing notice of Joseph, the husband of the Virgin (p. 274). We have also referred both to the Gospel of Infancy and to the Gospel of Nicodemus in various parts of this work. These reasons for the omission of a separate chapter on this head may be therefore deemed sufficient. For those who are curious on the subject, it may be added that traces of these spurious writings may occasionally be found in rude German pictures of the 15th century. A frame containing many small subjects, very rudely treated, is in the Berlin Museum. One complete series of pen drawings, of some beauty, of the 14th century, entirely dedicated to the Apocryphal Gospels, is in the Ambrogian Library at Milan.[1]

Pictures by known masters are few. Annibale Carracci has the subject of the young Jesus at the carpenter's board, in allusion to the miracles by which He rectified any mistake in Joseph's work. This picture is in the Louvre.

Albano also shows Jesus as a young child, helping Joseph to hang out the linen which the Virgin had washed.

---

[1] Histoire de la Nativité de Marie et de l'Enfance du Sauveur, attribuée à St. Jacques, fils de Joseph.

Christ disputing with the Doctors.

Ital. Nostro Signore che disputa coi Dottori. *Fr.* Jésus au milieu des Docteurs.
Germ. Christus lehrt als Knabe im Tempel.

[*A. J.*—The first event which occurred after the return of the Holy Family from Egypt was the appearance of our Lord in the Temple, when He was only twelve years old, generally, but improperly, styled the 'Dispute in the Temple.' When this incident occurs in a series of the Life of the Virgin, it is in reference chiefly to her, and in reference to her I have described it. The Mother seeks her Son 'sorrowing,' and finds Him in the Temple; but when the subject has a direct reference to the personal history of Christ—when it is the manifestation of His early wisdom and divine inspiration which is to be expressed—the whole scene assumes a different aspect and interest; and it is this which we are now to consider. The locality is the interior of a temple. Christ as a boy twelve years old, wearing the nimbus, and usually as beautiful as the Art of the painter could represent Him, is seated, or more seldom standing, and conspicuous above the other figures; then, below, are several doctors, or Jewish Rabbi, some turning over their books, others looking up to Him with amazement and admiration. The number of these, and of the spectators, varies in each composition. The Virgin and Joseph are seen entering behind, or at the side. Such is the usual representation: in a few instances only are the Virgin Mother and Joseph omitted.

There is no very antique example. It does not appear on the sarcophagi nor in the Catacombs. A group in one of the Catacombs, supposed to have this meaning, and engraved in Bosio (pl. 221), represents, I think, Christ teaching the Twelve Apostles. The very juvenile figure of Christ is in accordance with the usual representation at that time.

In the mosaics on the arch over the choir of S. Maria Maggiore at Rome, there is a group on the right in which Christ stands as a child, with hand upraised; a number of men in antique classical drapery, some in short tunics, are on either side. I cannot

A. J.] doubt that this is intended for the scene in the Temple, and that the two figures on the right are Joseph and Mary. This is the oldest extant representation.

I will now give some examples, which may be considered as particularly significant and characteristic:—

Pinturicchio. One of three large and fine frescoes, painted on the walls of the Baglioni Chapel at Spello.

1. The Annunciation; expressing the Incarnation.
2. The Nativity; the appearance of Christ on earth.
3. The Dispute in the Temple; the first manifestation of His divine character. It is a large composition of thirty-three figures.

Luini. A beautiful long-shaped fresco. In the centre, on a kind of raised pulpit, the youthful Saviour stands with the right hand uplifted and pointing to heaven, and the left extended. The attitude and figure are extremely majestic, simple, and graceful. On the right, fifteen doctors are seated, and in various ways expressing their wonder. On the left, the Virgin entering, addresses her Son. Joseph is behind. Seven other figures of Rabbi and spectators are present; among them a man whose head is seen from behind the pulpit, and who is staring at our Lord with an expression of curiosity and amazement; and conspicuous, seated and looking round out of the picture, with a book in his right hand, is a venerable bearded doctor, the portrait, it is said, of Luini himself. I believe the moment chosen is not that in which our Saviour is occupied with the doctors, hearing them and asking them questions, but that in which He replies to His Mother: 'Wist ye not that I must be about my Father's business?' The appealing expression in the face of the Virgin, who is a most majestic figure, is wonderfully beautiful.

Mazzolino da Ferrara. An altarpiece, once in the Church of S. Francesco at Bologna, now at Berlin. Christ is seated on a sort of throne, with a great number of scribes and doctors around, whose faces express an extreme of wonder and perplexity bordering on the grotesque. Joseph and Mary enter on the left. The heads of the three principal personages are of a superior type, and in fine contrast with those of the old doctors. On a gallery or balcony are other groups looking on and listening. On this

4. *J.*] building and on the balustrade of the gallery are four bas-reliefs in Mazzolino's usual manner. The first two represent Moses holding the tables of the Law, and again, with outstretched arms, imploring victory for Israel; the others are Judith with the head of Holofernes, and David with the head of Goliath. This is a very remarkable picture. Mazzolino seldom painted on a large scale, and, with all its animation and vivid colour, this composition suggests the idea of a little picture magnified. There was a small and elegant *replica* in the collection of Mr. Rogers.

Ribera has also painted the subject. We take this illustration (No. 110) from his picture in the Belvedere at Vienna.

110   Christ disputing with the Doctors.   (Spagnoletto.   Vienna Gallery.)

Garofalo. Another altarpiece on a large scale. In the centre, elevated above the others, Christ is standing with one hand raised. There are five doctors in front, and seventeen more behind. On the right the Virgin stands listening.

Rembrandt. A composition of about twenty figures. The young Saviour stands on the right, with both hands raised, as one speaking

A. J.] earnestly. There are twelve old scribes and doctors searching their books, and six spectators looking over a partition behind.]

The young Christ disputing with the Doctors occurs among the Seven Sorrows and among the Seven Joys of the Virgin; in the first case intended as 'Christ lost by His Mother,' in the second as 'Christ found by His Mother,' but in each usually under precisely the same form of composition, as may be seen in the Speculums and other illustrated books of devotion of the 15th century.

This poverty of idea is of course avoided by Modern Art. In the painted glass in the chapel in the garden of the convent at Namur, the subject given in the Seven Sorrows of the Virgin is rightly the Seeking of Christ; in the Seven Joys, the Finding Him. The Seeking is given with great power of expression in so confined a space, the Virgin and Joseph being seen back to back, as if each going different ways in their distress.

In miniature forms, the next moment to the Finding Him is sometimes given. The Child is no longer in the Temple, but standing between Joseph and Mary. A miniature of the 13th century, at Bologna, in the choral books of the 'Lyceo Musicale,' gives only their three figures—the young Child all in gilt garments, to show His divinity. The expression of the Virgin's reproof, and of His answer, is admirably given.

John the Baptist.

Ital. S. Giovanni Battista.   *Fr.* St. Jean Baptiste.   *Germ.* Johann der Taüfer.

[*A. J.*—The relation in which the young St. John, the son of Elizabeth, and afterwards the Preacher, Prophet, and Baptist, stood to the youthful Saviour, and the beautiful manner in which this relationship has been treated in Art, must now introduce us to the consideration of this great saint, as the principal incidents of his life preceded the ministry of our Lord.

The whole history of John the Baptist is related briefly, yet clearly, in various parts of the four Gospels, and must be so familiar to every reader of the Scriptures, that I do not give it here. The Gospel of St. Luke begins with the story of Zacharias and Elizabeth, the parents of the Baptist. The apparition of the angel to Zacharias, the visit of the Virgin Mary to Elizabeth, the birth and naming of John, are given in Luke i. 5-56, and these particulars are not mentioned in the other Evangelists. The sojourn of St. John in the wilderness, and his exhortation to the people, are related in Matthew iii. 1-12. St. Mark opens his Gospel with 'the voice of one crying in the wilderness;' and the hermit life of St. John in the desert, and his preaching to the people, are related in the most picturesque and striking manner in Matthew iii. 1-12, and Luke iii. 1-17. The baptism of Christ is described in Matthew iii. 13-17, in Mark i. 9-11, and in Luke iii. 21-23. The testimony of John the Baptist to the dignity of Jesus as Messiah is given in John iii. 22-26. The story of Herod and Herodias is given in Mark vi. 14-18, and in Matthew xiv. 3-5, and the death of St. John is related only by Matthew, xiv. 6-12, and by Mark, vi. 21-29.

Legend and tradition have added very little to these particulars. They relate the miraculous escape of Elizabeth and her son from the massacre at Bethlehem; they tell us that John retired to the desert while yet a child; that his death took place at Macheronta,

A. J.] a royal palace and fortress on the river Jordan, near the Dead Sea; that he was buried at Sebaster, and that the severed head was discovered and brought to Europe about the year 453. All these incidents have been, in the historical representation, combined with the Scriptural record of the life and death of St. John.

From the earliest time the Eastern and Western Churches have vied with each other in the veneration paid to this great and interesting saint, the near relation and precursor of the Saviour. Temples were dedicated to him in the first ages of Christianity, the earliest and most celebrated being that which was erected by Constantine at Rome, now known as St. John Lateran, which, as the episcopal church of Rome, is regarded by the Catholics as the first episcopal church in the world (*omnium urbis et orbis ecclesiarum mater et caput*). In all the ancient Christian edifices, even in the Catacombs, there was set apart a baptistery with a font for the baptizing of children and converts, always dedicated to St. John, and in the baptistery of the Lateran, Constantine, according to the old tradition, was himself baptized after the victory over Maxentius. Superior in beauty and next in celebrity is the baptistery at Florence, dedicated by that wise and good princess, Theodolinda, on the site of a subverted heathen temple, about 589. In this baptistery every child born in Florence of the Roman Catholic faith must be by law baptized. Very often, when at Florence, I used to go early in the morning, and seat myself where I could see the picturesque groups of every rank and degree gather round the font, sometimes five or six in the course of the morning. The munificence and piety of the Florentines have decorated this renowned and beautiful edifice, inside and out, with miracles of Art. You enter through the gates of Ghiberti (those 'gates of Paradise'), you sit under a dome resplendent and historied with mosaics, and you think of Dante, lamenting his exile from these beautiful precincts with such a tender feeling :—

Il mio bel San Giovanni !

As no saint has been more universally honoured, so there is not one of whom we have so many and such various effigies, in every different character, as the lovely devout child, the inspired youth, the haggard prophet of the desert. He is considered as

J.] the last of the prophets of the *Old*, and the first of the saints of the *New* Testament, thus forming the connecting link between the two dispensations.

In speaking of these multifarious representations of St. John, which date from the earliest ages of Art, I shall begin, as usual, with the strictly devotional and ideal subjects. These represent St. John principally in three characters :—

1. As Messenger or Precursor: 'Behold I will send my messenger, and he shall prepare the way before me.'

2. As Prophet and Witness : ' What went ye out for to see? A prophet? yea, and much more than a prophet.' Among those that are born of woman, there is not a greater prophet than John the Baptist, as bearing testimony to the superior and divine nature of Christ: ' Behold the Lamb of God, that taketh away the sins of the world.' ' He that cometh after me is mightier than I, the latchet of whose shoe I am not worthy to unloose.'

3. As Baptist and Patron Saint chiefly of all edifices consecrated to the purposes of baptism, of all those who seek salvation through that holy rite, and of several famous cities, especially of Florence.

In all early devotional effigies, and in all these characters, the personal appearance of St. John varies little. He is a tall meagre figure, sunburnt and haggard, as one wasted with vigils and fasting, and with the desert life, his hair and beard dishevelled : in the Greek pictures with black elf locks that literally stand on end ; covered only with a garment of camel's hair bound with a leathern girdle ; the limbs and chest exposed, the hand uplifted to warn or testify. Such is the most ancient and by far the most characteristic representation ; but in the modern schools of Art the sense of beauty was too strong to be sacrificed to the fitness and the truth of things. St. John is often a beautiful youth, with the form of a young Apollo, or a man in the prime of life, dignified and benign, and often, particularly when standing as Patron and Prophet by the throne of the Virgin, he wears over his scanty camel's hair shirt a mantle of red or green, flowing to the ground in rich ample folds.

St. John Baptist as Messenger and Precursor.

A. J.] He is generally standing, wearing the camel's hair garment, with the baptismal cup or the reed cross ('a reed shaken by the wind'), the mouth half open, the eyes dilated and inspired. He has a scroll, on which is written, *vox clamantis in deserto*, which is the proper inscription, but more generally it is 'Ecce Agnus Dei!' ('Behold the Lamb of God!')

In his character of *Messenger* (the Greek synonym for *angel*) the Greeks represented him with large wings, of which there are many examples in genuine Byzantine Art; for instance, in a Greek ivory diptych, in which he stands thus winged, with his head in a dish (charger) at his feet. In another instance, a picture half-length, he has large wings, and holds his own head in his hand. The wings and the head are merely the attributes of the Messenger and Martyr.

There is a beautiful figure of St. John standing with open mouth as crying aloud in the wilderness, and in his right hand the cup, by Campagnolo. Another by Parmigianino, as a youth holding the reed cross, and lifting his hand to warn or denounce. By Raphael, the well-known seated figure; but instead of the camel's hair, the leopard's skin, and, but for the cross to which he points, recalling in the pose, and in the full youthful forms, the idea of a young Bacchus. Another by Guido, also seated, more manly, with the lips unclosed and the hand raised—'Prepare ye the way of the Lord.'

St. John as Witness.

Effigies of St. John in this character are the most common of all, and often include the two others—as bearing testimony to the divine mission and character of Christ. We see him of all ages; sometimes introduced as a child into the Holy Families, with his little camel's hair shirt and cross and scroll, kissing the feet or the hand of the Infant Saviour, or kneeling or standing before Him—as in our illustration (No. 111), taken from Luini's fresco in the church at Lugano—and in pictures of the enthroned Madonna, standing at the foot of the throne, and pointing upwards to the Saviour

111   Virgin with Christ and Baptist. (Luini. Lugano.)

with hand outstretched and the forefinger extended: 'Behold!'
It is as Witness and Prophet that in representations of the Last
Judgment, Paradise, or the celestial Hierarchy, he is seated (or
more seldom *kneels*) on the left hand of the Saviour. There is a
signal example in the celebrated altarpiece by Van Eyck. On the
left hand of Christ, who is enthroned as Saviour, High Priest,
and Judge, St. John is seated, wearing over his hair garment a
magnificent green mantle, bordered with gold and jewels; his
features thoughtful and powerful, but rather coarse; his hair and
beard long and dishevelled; the forefinger raised in the usual
attitude. He has a book open on his knee, as if he had been
meditating on the prophets. The figures of St. John in the Last
Judgment are less richly dressed, but the pose and character
much the same. When represented as a single figure, he holds
the lamb in his arms, with the finger pointing. In a picture by
Memling (woodcut, No. 112, over leaf), the lamb rests on a book.
This was the general form of representation in early miniatures,
or the lamb in a glory, without the book.]

[*A. J.*—Murillo. St. John as a child embraces the lamb, and
at the same time points to heaven.

112   John the Baptist. (Memling. Munich.)

A. J.]   Leonardo da Vinci. The half-length figure in the Louvre, holding the reed cross and pointing upwards. The beauty of the face, the smiling lips, and the curled hair, give to the figure the look of a young Apollo.

St. John as Patron Saint and Baptist.

In this character St. John is seen in baptisteries, often as a statue in bronze or marble, with the usual attributes, standing upon the font or over the altar; sometimes in pictures as meditating in the desert, with the cup in his hand and a stream gushing from a rock, or the river Jordan flowing near him.

He also figures in many works of Art as the Patron Saint of Florence. There are two statues of St. John at the end of the North corridor in the Gallery at Florence, which are examples of two different styles of treatment. The first, by Donatello, represents the young patron saint as the dweller in the desert, meagre and wasted—too picturesque for sculpture; the second, by Benedetto da Majano, as a beautiful youth, too graceful for religious and historical truth. In the pictures in the churches and other sacred edifices of Florence, St. John, as the protector of the city, is constantly introduced; sometimes taking the chief place, as in a picture by Fra Filippo Lippi, where he is seated on a semicircular marble throne with the two chief patrons of the Medici family, St. Cosimo and St. Damian, on either side, and four other saints—St. Lawrence, St. Francis, St. Romualdo, and St. Peter—all patrons of members of the Medici family living at that time. This work is now in the National Gallery.

It is very interesting in these enthroned Madonnas and votive pictures to find St. John the Baptist grouped with the other saintly protectors of Florence—with the holy Bishops St. Zenobio or St. Antonino, in their rich episcopal robes—as in our illustration (No. 113, over leaf), after a drawing by Bellini; or with St. Verdiana, with her basket and her two tame snakes; or with St. Julian, who, as the patron of Giuliano de' Medici, became at one time very popular; or with St. Gualberto of Vallombrosa—combinations which will in most cases help us to the meaning and destination of the picture. For example, in a splendid picture by Filippo Lippi, painted for the chapel of San Bernardo in the Palazzo Publico, we have the Madonna and Child enthroned: he turns over the leaves of a large red book. On her right, the Baptist and St Antonino; on the left, St. Zenobio and St. Bernard, as patrons and protectors (the last, because the chapel was especially dedicated to him).

When St. John the Baptist is seen in companionship with St. Sebastian, it is a Florentine votive picture against the plague.

A beautiful devotional group, not unfrequent, exhibits the Infant

113   Baptist and Bishop.   (Drawing by Bellini.   British Museum.)

A. J.] Christ and the infant St. John playing together—caressing a lamb between them. There is a charming picture by Leonardo (or Luini) of this group; another by Rubens, where the little St. John presents a lamb to the Saviour—very beautiful; another by Van Dyck; another by Guido; another in which the young St. John, as he clasps his hands with a sort of timid childish devotion, is caressed and encouraged by Joseph. Such representations of the two holy children, sublime in their innocence—the one predestined to die for mankind, the other to prepare the way before him—have, as church pictures, an inexpressible beauty and

J.] significance, and might, I think, be multiplied among us with advantage to the young and the old. We need sometimes to be reminded of the sacredness of childhood.

There are other celebrated pictures in which St. John the Baptist appears either as patron of some votary named after him, or as patron of all who seek redemption through baptism. He is conspicuous in two celebrated pictures by Raphael—in the Madonna di Foligno, where he stands as patron and witness, pointing up to the Saviour, with a sort of wild, haggard, yet inspired look; and in the Madonna della Famiglia Ansidei, where he stands on the right of the throne, wearing a rich robe over his hair shirt, and with St. Nicholas on the left, as patrons of the family chapel.

In the old German and Flemish pictures, St. John appears with a characteristic sternness, and yet often with a simple dignity. There is a votive picture by Memling of great beauty, in which St. John points out to the devout votary kneeling at his side in a rich Flemish costume, and cap in hand, the figure of our Saviour, walking on the opposite bank of a river, in a meditative attitude with clasped hands—' Behold the Lamb of God!'

HISTORICAL SUBJECTS.

The history of John the Baptist abounds in picturesque scenes— striking, pathetic, and terrible. Both as a series and in separate subjects, we find most of them constantly recurring; some, however, are rare and mystical, and require explanation. A complete series, rarely met with, should comprise the following subjects :—

1. The Apparition of the Angel to Zacharias. The interior of a temple, with steps leading up to an altar, on one side of which is Zacharias offering incense; on the other, the angel pointing upwards. Sometimes spectators appear in the foreground.

2. Zacharias appears dumb before his Family. These two subjects, separate in series by Andrea Pisano, are generally combined, or the last omitted.

3. The Meeting of the Virgin Mary and St. Elizabeth. This important incident in the history of the Madonna is also included

A. J.] in a life of St. John the Baptist, because even before his birth he bore testimony to the divine nature of Christ (Luke i. 41). This is distinctly the purport of the Visitation by Raphael, in which the baptism in the Jordan appears in the background.

4. The Birth of St. John the Baptist. The day of his birth, Midsummer Day, has always been kept as a great festival in the Christian Church, especially at Florence. As a scene, however, it has not been often treated separately, like the Nativity of our Lord, or that of the Virgin Mother. We have the interior of a chamber; Elizabeth, as an aged woman, extended on her couch—attendants who bring her refreshments, and visitors who enter to congratulate], according to St. Luke, 'And her neighbours and her cousins heard how the Lord had showed great mercy upon her: and they rejoiced with her' (i. 58). [*A. J.*—One or two women are busied with the new-born child. There is a legend (noticed in the 'Legends of the Madonna') that the Virgin Mary prolonged her visit to her cousin Elizabeth till after the birth of St. John, received the child in her arms, and presented him to his father.[1] This legend has been so seldom adopted by the painters, that I know but two instances. In a little picture in the Liverpool Museum the female figure holding the little St. John is, I am now convinced, intended for the Virgin; and in the beautiful triptych, by Rogier van der Weyden, dedicated to John the Baptist (Berlin Gallery, 534*b*), the same personage is without doubt the Virgin Mary, and I think also in the exquisite little picture by Angelico, in the Florence Gallery.] The Virgin appears at the birth of the Baptist in numerous examples of early Art. We give an illustration from the Brentano miniatures (No. 114). In a picture by so late a master as Tintoretto, engraved in the Crozat Gallery, vol. i., the child is also received by a woman with a glory. An account of this is given in S. Bonaventura's 'Life of Christ,' whence the painters probably took the idea.[2]

[1] Legends of the Madonna, 2nd edition, p. 193.

[2] 'When Elizabeth's full time was come, she was happily delivered of a son, which our Lady received in her arms, and swaddled with becoming care. The infant, as if conscious of the majesty of its nurse, fixed his eye steadfastly upon her, so taken with her beauty, that when she delivered him again to his mother, he still looked towards her, as if he could take delight in none but her.'—*Life of Christ*, by S. Bonaventura. (English version, p. 17.)

114   Infant Baptist on the Lap of the Virgin Mary.   (Brentano miniature.)

[*A. J.*—5. The Naming of John the Baptist. In a chamber, or under a portico, Zacharias is seated, surrounded by his friends. He holds a tablet in his hand, on which he is in the act of writing, 'His name is John' (Luke i. 63). A female attendant presents the child.

In the series by Carlo Dolce, 'Il Sonno di San Giovanino,' the little St. John lies asleep, with a reed cross near him. Elizabeth, as a very aged, wrinkled woman, raises her eyes to heaven in a transport of gratitude. Zacharias is behind. One of the best pictures of the master.

Again, in the series by Andrea Pisano and that by Ghirlandajo, these two last scenes are separate; in that by Andrea del Sarto they form one picture, of exceeding beauty.

In the Florence Gallery is a curious and interesting example of the manner in which the Florentines mixed up their great protecting saint with their domestic life. It is a large, round, deep wooden dish, such as was used to present sweetmeats or presents to a lady in her confinement. In the centre Pontormo has painted very beautifully the Birth of St. John the

A. J.] Baptist, with all the usual accompaniments—Elizabeth reclining on her couch, attendants washing the new-born child, &c.

6. Elizabeth escapes with her son John from the Massacre at Bethlehem: in an attitude of fright, and clasping the child in her arms, she stands before a rock, which opens to receive her (see p. 260). This incident, which is seldom omitted in Byzantine Art, is as seldom included in the more modern series. It occurs on the magnificent ivory triptych in the Louvre, and I have seen it in the background of a Flight into Egypt. It is also, I think, on the silver *dossale* which belongs to the Baptistery at Florence.

7. John takes Leave of his Parents and prepares to retire to the Wilderness. According to the legend, John was a child of about seven years old when he became a dweller in the desert; this receives some colour from the expression in Luke i. 80. The scene in which he receives the farewell and benediction of his parents occurs frequently. There is a beautiful example by Fra Filippo in the series at Prato, of which we shall speak further. In several pictures of the 'Holy Family,' where the little St. John is represented as kissing the feet of Jesus, or the latter stoops from His mother's arms to embrace him, I imagine that the departure for the desert is implied—for instance, in a lovely group by Botticelli.

8. St. John the Baptist in the Wilderness—sometimes as a child, sometimes as a youth, praying or meditating, or attended by angels: often treated as a separate subject, as leading to meditation and religious retirement, and susceptible of the most beautiful treatment in the landscape accessories. In the Prato series by Fra Filippo, the lonely beautiful boy is praying devoutly, with upraised eyes, in the midst of a rocky solitude; or, seated as a child, he plucks a root from the ground, which expresses his abstinence, as by Giulio Romano; or, as a youth, he sits with his mystical cup by a stream gushing from the rock, as in our illustration from Bugiardini's picture (No. 115) in the gallery at Bologna; or, kneeling by the Jordan in a spiritual ecstasy, he sees a vision of the Messiah in the opening heavens above.

There are some beautiful instances, by Murillo, of the 'San Juanito' thus treated as a child in the wilderness. We have one in our National Gallery, where he stands with the lamb near him.

119   Baptist in the Wilderness.   (Bugiardini.   Bologna Gallery.

[J.] There are also representations of exquisite beauty, which place him at this period of his life in personal companionship with his divine relative, the Son of Mary. He takes leave of Jesus, who tenderly embraces him, or places in his hand the reed cross, as symbol of his mission. The young Christ and the young precursor meet together in the wilderness, near a gushing spring, and John acknowledges Christ as Lord, bending reverently.] This legend is related by S. Bonaventura, who says, that on the Virgin and Joseph leaving Egypt with the Child, they met the young Baptist on the skirts of the wilderness. There is a beautiful little picture in the Berlin Gallery (No. 94) of this subject, represented under pine trees, with a stag drinking from a rivulet.

[*A. J.*—The child John asleep in the wilderness, on the camel's hair garment, with his reed cross near him—a beautiful picture, by Murillo; and by the same we have Christ and John together as boys, in a fine landscape.

The meeting of the two children in the wilderness has again been beautifully treated by Murillo, and in a mystic sense Jesus gives the little St. John drink from a shell: 'I am the living water.' I have seen a print by Albert Dürer, in which St. John the Baptist, holding a book (the Prophecies), and St. John the Evangelist, holding his gospel, meet in the wilderness. A lamb lies between them.

9. John preaches Repentance to the Scribes and Pharisees.
10. John preaches to the People.

These two scenes, as separate subjects, are in the series by Andrea Pisano. Between denouncing hardened sinners and exhorting the people to amend their lives, there should be a difference of feeling; and both should be distinguished from the Prophet—'the voice crying in the wilderness.' The preaching of St. John has often been treated in single pictures and prints; especially by the Carracci and their school.

11. The Baptism of our Lord by John the Baptist. This is a most important subject as an incident in the history of our Lord, as well as in that of John, and occurs in both; the arrangement when thus treated is very little varied from the most ancient type. Christ stands in the river Jordan, with folded hands, and an expression of meek devotion. John pours the water on his head from a cup, and on the bank one or two angels, kneeling, hold with reverence the garments of our Lord. Above, the heavens are open, and the dove descends or hovers over Him; and often the figure of the Almighty is seen in the opening heavens, with the hand extended in benediction, as uttering the words, 'This is my beloved son,' &c.

When treated as a separate subject, expressing not merely an historical incident but a religious rite, the scene is varied by a sort of ideal treatment, and the painters have not kept quite so strictly to the Scriptural words.

Ravenna. Mosaic in the baptistery. In the centre of the roof is a circular picture. Christ standing with the water nearly up to

His waist, the lower part of His figure seen through the water.
.1. J.] The Jordan, represented in the antique manner, under the form of
a river god, rises up from his urn, and presents a cloth or napkin.
This was before the introduction of angels as assistants.

In the Catacomb of San Ponziano the antique representation is
slightly varied by a kneeling angel.]

A representation of the Baptism, almost invariably met with
during the early mediæval times of Art, shows the water standing

116   Baptism.   (MS., 13th century.   Lyceo Musicale, Bologna.

in a heap and covering Christ up to the shoulders, though His feet
are on a level with those of the Baptist. This was partly from a
devotional intention to show the Jordan rising to meet and cover
the divine Neophyte, and partly from the conditions of space, which
did not permit the figure to be placed lower. We give an illustration (No. 116), from the MS. 'Die Sanctæ Paschæ,' in the
library at Bologna.

[A. J.—As it was said that the Baptism of Christ took place at

A. J.] the confluence of two rivers, these have been personified by two little river gods, or genii, holding urns.] There is a tradition that the baptism took place at the junction of the rivers Dan and Jordan. In early Christian Art it is sometimes thus represented: the stream divided into two branches, which are labelled 'Fons Dan' and 'Fons Jordan' (see Paccianda de Ritu, p. 69). [*A. J.*— Two angels, however, kneel with the garments, the dove descends —sent forth by the celestial hands which just appear through the opening heavens.

When dedicated as a devotional picture, expressing salvation through baptism in a general sense, either the principal group and attendant angels are alone, or the witnesses are idealised: for example, in a beautiful picture by Cima da Conegliano (Brera), where the Baptism takes place in presence of St. Paul and St. Antony on the left hand, and St. Jerome and St. Augustine on the right hand.

Another, a most curious woodcut, is probably by Lucas Cranach, in which the Elector of Saxony stands on one side and Martin Luther on the other: and there are many others. Such representations are strictly devotional.

The historical representations are innumerable. I will mention only a few, which are remarkable or celebrated.

Raphael. Our Lord stands looking down meekly, with folded hands, as in prayer. There are four angels: the two kneeling, with a beautiful reverence, hold the garments over their arms, as if with a sort of respect for them; two other angels hover behind, and in the distance are five persons preparing for baptism.

The Baptism by Verrocchio, in the Belli Arti, at Florence (woodcut, No. 117), is celebrated, because one of the angels kneeling on the left hand is known to have been painted by Leonardo da Vinci when he was a pupil in the school of Verrocchio.

By another pupil of Verrocchio, Lorenzo di Credi, there is a beautiful Baptism—like that of his master in regard to composition, but far more graceful and tender.

Poussin has painted the Baptism as one of the seven sacraments —nearly twenty figures. John pours the water not out of a cup or a shell, as is usual, but from a pitcher with a lid, of the old Flemish form.

117   Baptism.   (Verrocchio.   Accademia, Florence.)

l. J.] Rubens has made it the subject of one of his exuberant compositions—about thirty figures and a magnificent landscape; but there is no divinity in Christ—though the rough manliness of John is well given.

For a subject of such deep religious import, it has too often been treated as a group merely accessory in a fine landscape. There is such a picture by Mola, in which an angel is disrobing our Saviour.

12. The Priests and Levites send Messengers to question John (John i. 19): 'Who art thou?'

Murillo. John stands, with a red mantle over his camel's hair tunic, holding his reed cross; three men before him, one of whom

VOL. L.   Q Q

A. J.] wears spectacles; a lamb lies in the foreground; above are angels, two scrolls and the emblem of St. Mark, from whom are taken the texts inscribed on the scrolls: *Inter natos non surrexit major;* and *Vox clamantis in deserto, parate viam Domini.*

13. John sends two of his Disciples to inquire of Jesus: 'Art thou He?' &c. (Matt. xi. 2–19; Luke vii. 18–35). I do not remember this subject as occurring even in a complete series as a separate picture. There is an example by Bernardo Strozzi (Vienna Gallery)—five figures, life-size, fine in colour and vulgar in expression, as is usual with this vulgar but powerful painter—a Genoese friar (1581–1644).

14. John reproves Herod. In the beginning of his reign Herod Antipas put away his wife, an Arabian princess, and took Herodias, the wife of his brother Philip. 'And John said unto him, It is not lawful for thee to have thy brother's wife.' She was also his niece.

The scene is in the interior of a splendid palace. Herod and Herodias are seated together on a throne, and near Herodias her daughter Salome. John stands before them, with his arm extended, as denouncing their sin. Herod looks down, and Herodias averts her head with a sullen defiant air. This striking scene has been seldom treated as a separate subject. There is, however, a picture by Domenichino, full of dramatic power and dignity. In a series it is scarcely ever omitted, and is particularly fine in the series by Andrea del Sarto.

15. John is imprisoned. He was imprisoned at Macheronta, a fortress on the Jordan, not very far from where the river discharges itself into the Dead Sea. He is seated as if seen in a dungeon above, while the iron gate and the guard are below. As a separate subject I have not met with it.

16. The Banquet of Herod. He is seen feasting: in some instances alone, or with Herodias only, but more frequently with numerous guests, as the feast was in celebration of his birthday. Salome dances before the guests, or she is kneeling and asking the fatal boon, or, which is more usual, she is seen entering with the severed head in a large dish or basin.

In Italian I believe they do not usually call Salome 'la dansatrice,' but 'la saltatrice'—a contemptuous appellation. But the daughter

1. J.] of Herodias was certainly a princess, and it seems hardly consonant with our ideas of Eastern manners, that such a person should dance before Herod and his guests. It may be for this reason that in some pictures only Herod and Herodias are at table, and Salome seems to dance only to please her mother and stepfather.[1]

In the ancient Gothic sculpture Salome has been represented as a tumbler, standing upon her head for the amusement of Herod (there is an instance over one of the doors of the cathedral at Rouen); and in the old German school she is often terribly coarse when not absolutely grotesque. On the contrary, in Italian Art she is often most elegant and graceful. I remember a beautiful and quaint little picture, once in the possession of Mr. Rogers, in which she appears as moving slowly and gracefully to the sound of the tambourine. It was evidently part of an ancient predella.

'The Dance of the Daughter of Herodias,' called 'La Danse d'Hérodiade.' In front, a long procession of men and women, hand in hand, dance along as if advancing to the banquet; three musicians are elevated on a pedestal in the centre. In the background, on the left hand, is the Decollation. Salome receives the head. On the right, she presents it to her mother at the table of Herod. (Old German print—Israel von Mechenen.)

17. St. John beheaded in Prison—called properly the 'Decollation.' The death of St. John took place in the fortress-palace of Macheronta, where Herod was celebrating his birthday. Here John had been confined for several months, for Herod feared to put him to death.

In general there are only three figures. The dead body of John lies prostrate, and the executioner, generally a soldier, one of Herod's guard, presents the head to Salome, or, by a stroke of delicacy in some painters, not Salome herself, but an attendant, receives the head, and bears the dish before her mistress.

In general, however, she carries the dish herself, and the executioner holds up the head by the hair. She turns away, sometimes

---

[1] A story is told of Shah-Abbas, that on a certain occasion a woman danced before him with such exquisite grace, that he, being intoxicated, promised to grant whatever she would ask. She set the price so high, that the next morning the vizier remonstrated, and Shah-Abbas was glad to redeem his promise by the payment of an enormous sum.

A. J.] with an expression of pity, sometimes merely as a fine lady would turn her eyes from an unseemly or disagreeable object.

Single figures of the daughter of Herodias, bearing the charger and the ghastly head, are very frequent. Here are three examples, all contrasted.

Salome. Figure three-quarters, wearing a tunic of green velvet; face seen in front, with long golden hair, bound with a fillet of rich jewels; holds before her with both hands the silver dish containing the head. Her expression is sad, regretful, almost bitter—the head more pathetic than ghastly. This is the most beautiful picture of the subject I have ever seen, the most poetical and suggestive, and exquisitely painted.[1]

In the strongest contrast is the picture by Rubens, in which the bold, exulting, voluptuous beauty of the daughter of Herodias is perhaps more true to character than the last, and in shocking contrast with the bleeding, ghastly head—all painted with true Rubens-like vigour.

Very different from both is the picture by Guido, in which Salome, in a jewelled turban and light blue embroidered tunic, with delicate features and a soft pensive expression, seems to have nothing in common with the horrible task awarded to her. She holds up the dish, looking out of the picture.

In the picture by Carlo Dolce, famous for the number of copies and engravings made from it, Salome holds up the head as far from her as possible, and turns away her face, which is seen almost in profile. There is more power in this picture, and the beauty of Salome is of a more energetic kind than is usual with Carlo Dolce.

Such representations appear to have derived much of their popularity and frequency in churches and private chapels, from two circumstances. There is a tradition that the head of John the Baptist was brought to Europe after the taking of Constantinople in 1204, and the possession of this precious relic was an honour claimed by several churches, both in Italy and France. The severed head became an object of great veneration, and seems, in itself, to have represented, not unfrequently, the *personalité* of the saint. Another reason was the great number of those who bore

[1] A picture in the Dresden Gallery answers to this description.

J. J.] his name. I cannot, however, remember any very early picture in which Salome appears as a single half-length figure, presenting the head on the dish. There are many examples in which we have the ghastly head alone, lying in the dish—one by Correggio (marvellously painted), one by Murillo, and one by Andrea del Sarto, equally fine, may be mentioned; another, by an excellent Spanish painter, was in the gallery of Lord Northwick; and another, I remember, where the head, lying in the silver charger, is lamented by little angels, one of whom closes the eyes. Very pathetic and fine.

The two subjects of the Banquet and the Decollation are often combined in the same picture, which enhances the horror. In the centre Herod is feasting at table, Salome dancing before him; on one side, separated by a wall or partition, the body of St. John, prone and bleeding, lies on the ground, while Salome receives the head in a basin, or a silver dish; on the other side, Herodias is seated on a throne, and Salome, kneeling, presents the head to her. It must be remembered that the three scenes all took place under the same roof, and about the same time.

But the variations of this terrible and dramatic subject are innumerable. I will mention only one or two of the most remarkable.

The daughter of Herodias, crowned with myrtle and flowers, stands in a crimson tunic, over which is thrown a mantle bespangled with gold, which she sustains with her left hand; with her right she commands the soldier to place the severed head in a charger, which is placed on a table. (Luini.) In this and in other instances, Salome is not supposed to be present at the execution, but to receive the head. The Decollation is in the background; in front, a slave presents the head in a dish, and she smiles a cruel smile. She places herself the head in a dish, which is held by a female attendant. When Salome is attended by a maid or an old woman, the subject has been mistaken for a Judith; but the accessory of the silver dish, so expressly mentioned in Scripture, distinguishes them. (Guido.)

I have seen the Decollation represented, by a mistake of the artist, as taking place in a landscape under a tree. The dead body lies in the foreground; behind it Salome is seen crowned with flowers and running away, as if in terror; her maid, carrying the

A. J.] head in a dish, runs after her. But for the dish and the executioner, this might be a Judith.

Luini. She points to a golden vase which stands on a table, and half averts her face; the executioner, with a frightful expression, holds up the blood-dropping head by the hair; behind Salome the head of an attendant. Figures half-length. Supremely elegant.[1]

It is a tradition that when Herodias received the head she treated it as Fulvia treated the head of Cicero—piercing with her needle or her knife the tongue which had testified against her. In some

118 Burial of Baptist. (Andrea Pisano. Doors of Baptistery, Florence.)

instances, where Salome presents the head to her mother, this action is indicated.

18. The disciples of St. John receive his head and reverently bury him. [We take our illustration (No. 118) from the series by Andrea Pisano. Here, though the body apparently lies in one piece, the evident care of the head shows its severed condition.] This is in general the last subject as a series. There is a legend

[1] Tribune, Florence.

[I. J.] to the effect that Herodias would not give up the head of the saint, but, after insulting the sacred relic, carried it off and buried it in her own palace, lest John should come to life and rise from the dead to reproach her with her sin. On the silver diptych at Florence we have one more subject.

19. The discovery of the head in Palestine by two priests, who being informed in a vision of the exact locality, dig it out of the ground.

In a Greek series, the Emperor Theodosius carries the severed head from Chalcedonia to Constantinople, but this never occurs in Western Art.

The two following subjects are very uncommon, but I have seen them on a triptych in the Academy of Siena.

20. John the Baptist descends into Hades.

His death took place two years before that of our Lord, and, according to the old Greek legend, he descended into Hades (the place of departed spirits), to remain there with the prophets and patriarchs till the day of the Crucifixion should bring them redemption. St. John bears to the imprisoned spirits the glad tidings of their approaching deliverance, whereat they all rejoice, while the devils gnash their teeth. This poetical legend, which I have seen on a triptych in the Academy at Siena, may be found in the Apocryphal Gospel of Nicodemus (chap. xix.)

21. John is received into Paradise by our Lord and the Virgin, and is seated on the left hand of Christ.

Having described separately, and at length, the subjects from the life of St. John the Baptist, I will now give some celebrated examples of the story treated as a series, comprising a certain selection, in number more or less, from the incidents enumerated, but seldom complete.

Giotto. Painted in the Carmine at Florence, on the wall of the Chapel of the Baptist. These valuable frescoes were destroyed when the church was nearly consumed by fire in 1771; but an English painter, Thomas Patch, had previously made sketches from them, which were engraved. Some fragments remain, cut out of the ruined walls: two heads of saints, once Mr. Rogers', which used to hang in his breakfast-room, as I well remember. They appear to have belonged to the disciples who are burying St. John, and bending over the body

A. J.] with devout sorrow—they are certainly not St. Paul and St. John, as they have been called. These belong to figures about four feet high. In the fragments at Liverpool, said to have belonged to the same series, the figures are not more than fourteen inches high.

Andrea Pisano. The series on the West doors of the Baptistery at Florence, and comprising all the subjects enumerated except the two last, in small lozenge-shaped compartments.

Taddeo Gaddi. A large altarpiece, consisting of a triptych and predella, dedicated in honour of St. John. In the centre, the Baptism of our Lord. In the wings, St. Peter and St. Paul. In the predella, five historical subjects :—The Apparition of the Angel. The Birth of St. John. The Banquet of Herod. The Decollation. Salome presenting the Head to her Mother.

Attributed to the same painter is a curious predella in the Louvre, evidently part of an altarpiece dedicated to St. John. In the centre, the Crucifixion, with St. Longinus conspicuous. On the right hand, the Banquet of Herod, with St. John in prison and Salome presenting the head to her mother. On the left hand, the Decollation. Christ and St. John seated together on a throne, before which death presents a malefactor attended by demons. This I believe to represent the punishment of Herod Antipater. In the catalogue this figure is styled Judas Iscariot, because of the rope round the neck; but the rope was the common sign of a malefactor. All the historical subjects belong to the life of St. John, and I do not see what Judas Iscariot has to do with them.

In the centre of a predella, the Crucifixion is always mystical— the *Sacrifice*.

Greco-Italian or Byzantine Art. An altarpiece (a triptych) dedicated to St. John. In the centre, the Baptist as patron saint, enthroned. He wears a coronet of gold and a rich robe; both have been formerly studded with large jewels, of which the orifices remain. The right hand is raised in benediction; in the left he holds a globe, or circle, out of which springs a lily or a reed cross, it is difficult to say which. Two angels hover above. In the side compartments are twelve historical subjects, very curious from the following uncommon *motifs* :—

1. The Vision of Zacharias.
2. The Meeting of Mary and Elizabeth.

1. J.] 3. The Birth of John.
4. Elizabeth presents her Infant Son to Christ and the Virgin Mary, and seems to dedicate him to their service.
5. An Angel carries the Child John on his Shoulders into the Wilderness.
6. John, meditating in the Desert, sees a Vision of the Messiah in the Heavens.
7. He is questioned by the Levites, and bears witness to Christ.
8. He baptizes our Lord.
9. The Decollation.
10. Salome appears with the Head at the Banquet of Herod.
11. John descends into Hades with Good Tidings.
12. Christ and the Virgin Mary, seated on golden Thrones, receive him into Paradise. The whole very quaintly treated, yet not without a certain grace.

The font in the baptistery at Siena, executed for the Sienese by the greatest artists of the time. It is of bronze gilt, with six sides, and on each is an historical scene in bas-relief, and in the style of the famous gates at Florence. 1. The Vision of Zacharias. (Donatello.) 2. The Birth of John. (Della Quercia.) 3. The Preaching of John. (Della Quercia.) 4. The Baptism of our Lord. (Ghiberti.) 5. John reproves Herod. (Ghiberti.) 6. The Banquet of Herod. (A. Pollajuolo.)

Fra Filippo Lippi. A series in the Cathedral of Prato, which is dedicated to St. John the Baptist and St. Stephen. The history of the two saints is painted on the walls of the choir. On the right hand is the story of the Baptist in three longitudinal compartments, one above the other, and each containing several groups. In the Birth of St. John, a woman is kneeling on one side, and while her companions are engaged with Elizabeth and the child, she seems lost in meditation on his wonderful destinies: 'What manner of child shall this be!' (Luke i. 66).

But the most beautiful group of all is that in the next compartment—St. John as a Child taking Leave of his Family before his Departure to the Wilderness. His father gives him his blessing; an old servant stands by in sympathy and admiration; but the mother bends over her son with one hand round his neck, and rests her cheek upon his head as she presses him to her, with an action the most expressively mournful and maternal (woodcut, No. 119). Fra Filippo was never at fault when he had to express the natural affections, but he was, in spite of his sacred calling, an abandoned profligate. It was while painting at Prato that he seduced and carried off from her convent a young novice, Lucrezia Buti, and his son by her, afterwards the famous Filippino, was born while he was painting on these frescoes. It is a tradition at Prato that he has represented Lucrezia Buti in the figure of

119   Baptist taking leave of Parents.   (Fra F. Lippi.   Cathedral, Prato.)

Salome; but I do not know that there is any authority for this supposition, which in any case would have been the reverse of a compliment.

Besides the individuality of expression and strong homely feeling, there is another characteristic of the style of Fra Filippo

J.] which distinguishes these frescoes. No painter of his time equalled him in the grand, large, yet graceful disposition of his draperies, and it is thought that he owed this merit to his captivity among the Moors, and to his familiarity with the ample flowing robes of the Eastern costume, such as he has represented here.

Ghirlandajo. The series in S. Maria Novella at Florence. The Blessed Virgin and John the Baptist are the joint protectors of Florence, and in the choir we have on one side the history of the Madonna, on the other the history of the Baptist. The first I have already described at length. The arrangement of the opposite pictures is similar. They will be found enumerated by name in Vasari, and in Murray's Handbook, and in almost every guide for Florence. You begin with the lowest compartment.

1. The Vision of Zacharias. This is in the centre, on the summit of a flight of steps, while lower down on each side are spectators, most of them portraits of celebrated persons of the time, and therefore especially valuable; the most interesting are those of Poliziano and Marcilio Ficino.

2. The Meeting of Mary and Elizabeth, each with their attendants; behind Elizabeth is the beautiful female figure celebrated as the portrait of Ginevra de' Benci. Above these, 3. The Birth of John. 4. The Naming of John. Several figures, among them the two majestic females on the right, are especially remarkable. 5. Above these, the Preaching in the Wilderness. 6. The Baptism of our Lord. Over all, the grand scene of the Banquet of Herod, and the Dance of the Daughter of Herodias, containing at least thirty-five figures.

Rogier van der Weyden. A small altarpiece; a triptych of the most wonderful beauty, dedicated to St. John the Baptist, as usual. In the centre, the Baptism of our Lord. Two angels hold His garments, while the 'Padre Eterno,' a half-length figure of the colour of flame, appears above, sending forth the dove. On the left-hand wing is the birth of John; the Virgin Mary, clearly characterised, presents the child to Zacharias. On the right-hand wing is the Decollation. Salome receives the head from the executioner. Behind this group, two disciples of John lament the fate of their master, and in the distance, through an opening, is seen the Banquet of Herod. Over each of these divisions is painted a

A. J.] Gothic arch *en grisaille*, of the richest tracery work, on which are represented, as in sculpture, minute representations of other scenes in the history of St. John, and the statues of four Apostles, in as many Gothic niches, twelve in all. The nature, the truth, the individual character of every head, the delicate, finished execution of every detail, the vivid colour in the living groups, and the perfect execution of the architectural ornaments, render this little altarpiece a miracle of Art: one cannot examine it without thinking that it must have taken half a man's lifetime, and more than human patience, to produce it.

Andrea del Sarto. The series in Lo Scalzo at Florence. There existed in ancient times, in this city, a religious and charitable congregation, styled 'La Compagnia di San Giovanni,' especially under the protection of the saint. This society had a house in the Via Larga, before which was an open court surrounded by an arcade, a sort of miniature cloister (*chiostrino*). The members decreed that on the walls of this arcade should be represented the life of their tutelary saint, and that Andrea del Sarto, then at the height of his fame, should be the artist employed; but as they were not rich, it was agreed that the subject should be painted only in grey and white (*a terrella*). Andrea prepared his cartoons, and began his task with the principal subject, the Baptism of Christ, which is opposite to the spectator on entering; but after finishing this and two others, between 1514 and 1518, he was summoned to France by the king, Francis I., and the community, despairing of his return, commissioned his friend and pupil, Franciabigio, to finish the work. Andrea, however, did return in the following year, and resumed his labours in the Scalzo, which were not completed till 1526, twelve years after the commencement; one of the last and the finest of all being the Birth of St. John. As the series now exists, they must be taken in the following order:—1. The Vision of Zacharias. 2. The Meeting of Mary and Elizabeth. 3. The Birth of St. John. 4. St. John departs for the Desert. 5. Christ and St. John meet as Children in the Wilderness. 6. The Preaching of St. John. 7. The Baptism of Christ. 8. St. John baptizing the Multitude. 9. St. John reproves Herod. 10. St. John in Prison. 11. The Banquet and the Dance. 12. The Decollation, and the Head presented to Herodias.

These frescoes have suffered much, particularly those on the right hand, which have been most exposed to damp. The court is now roofed in, and everything done, too late, to preserve them, for they seem perishing daily. Their great beauty consists in the simplicity with which each story is told, with the fewest number of figures, in striking contrast with the exuberant crowded compositions by Ghirlandajo. It is a usual characteristic of Andrea to employ few figures. Here, in chiaroscuro, a crowd of figures undistinguished by difference of colour would have been perplexing.

Andrea Sacchi. I shall mention one more series, painted in the Baptistery of the Lateran (San Giovanni in Fonte), when that antique edifice was restored by Urban VIII., about 1644. The Pope entrusted the decoration of the interior to Andrea Sacchi, who, naturally cold-blooded and lazy, disliked the trouble of fresco painting, and turned over most of the work to his pupils and assistants. He left them to paint the history of Constantine, and only executed himself the eight panels in oil above the pillars, representing eight scenes in the life of St. John:—1. The Vision of Zacharias. 2. The Meeting of Mary and Elizabeth. 3. The Birth of St. John. 4. The Parting from his Parents. 5. The Preaching. 6. The Baptism of our Lord. 7. The Decollation.

There is nothing to be said of them in praise or in blame—correct in drawing, mediocre in composition, and heartless in sentiment and expression. It is a good lesson in Art (and in Nature too) to place before us the engravings after Ghirlandajo, Andrea del Sarto, and Andrea Sacchi, and observe how these three artists, each famous in his turn, have represented the same scenes.

THE TEMPTATION IN THE WILDERNESS.

Ital. Nostro Signore tentato nel Deserto. *Fr.* Notre Seigneur tenté par le Diable.
Germ. Die Versuchung Christi.

Matt. iv. 1 ; Mark i. 12 ; Luke iv. 1–13.

A. J.] THIS subject, most difficult to deal with, has been very rarely treated by the early painters, and is often omitted in an (otherwise) complete history of Christ. It seems to have been avoided as a church picture, lest it should shock the pious and the ignorant to see the Saviour of the world in such near propinquity with the Demon and author of evil.

'Three forms of temptation were placed before our Saviour. The first was upon the instances and first necessities of nature : " *Command that these stones be made bread ;* " for Christ, having fasted forty days and forty nights, "was," as the Evangelist says, "afterward an hungred." The second temptation was to pride and presumption : "If thou be the Son of God, cast Thyself down." An invitation to no purpose, save only as it gave occasion to this truth, that God's providence secures all His children in the ways of nature, and while they are doing their duty, but loves not to be tempted to acts unreasonable and unnecessary. And, also, we are desired to observe that Satan tempts our Lord to cast *Himself* down ; knowing that though he may persuade us to fall, he cannot precipitate us without our own act.'[1] The third temptation which Satan placed before our Lord was that which had ruined himself, namely, ambition. He proffers Him all the kingdoms and treasures of the world : ' All these things will I give Thee, if Thou wilt fall down and worship me.' The first of these temptations, being the most obvious and intelligible, is usually chosen for representation ; but they are often found all three in the same picture. It has been well observed, that if the artist were to follow the text of Matthew iv. 3 : ' Command that *these* stones

[1] Bishop Taylor's Life of Christ.

1. *J.*] be made bread,' and represent the demon as pointing to the rocks scattered in the wilderness, it would convey a more sublime impression to the mind than by making him present a single stone: 'Command *this* stone that it be made bread'—as in Luke iv. 3.

It seems to have been a question with the old painters whether they should represent Satan with all his horrible and bestial deformity, or clothe him in some alluring disguise; 'seeing that Jesus was not a person of those low weaknesses to be affrighted or troubled by an ugly phantasm.' It seems, however, to have been impossible in the old times, especially among the old German masters, to attempt this subject without some unconscious irreverence or absurdity. I remember a little miniature in which Christ is set down on a high mountain, where a demon, with wings at his shoulders and his feet, who has carried Him thither, supports Him; another stands before Him, pointing down to the kingdoms of the world beneath them, and holding a scroll on which is written in Latin, 'All this will I give Thee if Thou wilt fall down and worship me.' And Jesus answers in a like scroll, 'Thou shalt worship the Lord thy God.' The devils are without any human lineaments, with eagles' claws, dragons' tails, heads like vultures —more fit to scare than to allure.

And there is another example, about the same date, in an old German print, wherein the demon is made as horrid and as monstrous as possible.

Milton describes the tempter as approaching our Saviour under the disguise of an aged peasant, 'clad in rural weeds,' at once attracting confidence by his venerable appearance, and disarming suspicion by his simple attire. And this idea, though not precisely in the same form, has been adopted by all the later artists, even when they have otherwise sinned in taste.

Raphael has not treated this subject, nor Albert Dürer, that I know of.

Tintoretto. In a mountainous landscape, the two figures of our Lord and the Evil Spirit are treated as accessories, but in a manner the most original and picturesque.

Titian. (?) Two figures only, half-length. The demon, as a young man, holds the stone. Both heads look like portraits, and the whole conception is a mistake, and too coarse for Titian.

A. J.] There is an exquisite little print by Dirk van Staren, with only the two figures, and Christ, turning His back on the demon, just glances round at him, as if with scorn (1515). Bartsch, viii. p. 28.

Two representations of this subject are by two celebrated artists, both of whom have conceived the subject in a peculiar manner. The first as a vision, the last as a mystery.

Botticelli. In the second of the large frescoes, on the right-hand wall of the Sistine Chapel, is represented in the foreground the High Priest, in front of the Temple, sacrificing before the assembled multitude. Far off in the centre of the picture Christ is seen with the tempter standing on a pinnacle of the Temple. On the left hand Satan, in a black mantle drawn over his head, stands before our Lord, pointing to some large stones lying on the ground: 'Command that these stones,' &c. On the right hand our Lord is seen again on the summit of a rock, from which the tempter falls headlong, while the angels approach the Saviour to bear Him up, and at the foot of the mountain are seen again, ministering and adoring. This fresco was executed for Pope Sixtus IV., about 1480. It has been often criticised, because Botticelli has placed his accessory figures in the foreground, and given to them more prominence than to the subject itself; but I think he may have so arranged his composition as a matter of taste. The subject commanded was *The Temptation;* and had he placed the principal group in the foreground, the enormous size of the figures and the prominence of the Evil Spirit as an actor in the scene would have inspired horror. I have often considered this fresco, and made up my mind that it is better as a matter of taste that it should be as it is.

Perugino. The Temptation is one of the four mystical subjects painted at the four corners of the ceiling in the Sala del Incendio in the Vatican, and which Raphael refused to destroy to make room for his own works. It is a curious conception, altogether poetical and unreal in arrangement, but very beautiful. On the left hand stands the majestic figure of our Lord, as one reproving, but gently. Opposite to Him the tempter, in form of a venerable man with horns, but without the cloven foot, presents the stone. Both are sustained on clouds, or in mid air, as in a vision. In the background, within a glory of light, is seen the mild figure of our Lord; on each side is a ministering angel, one bearing fruit, the other a vase. A multitude of angels and cherubim surround the whole.

Lucas van Leyden. One of his series of prints from the New Testament, of which we give an illustration (No. 120). On the

120   Temptation.   (Lucas van Leyden.)

left, Christ is seen standing near a rock, on which he leans; one hand raised as if in rebuke. The demon, under the form of an old bearded man, with a long robe trailing behind, yet not quite con-

A. J.] cealing the Satanic hoof, stands opposite; his head is covered with a cowl, with a long pointed end, hanging down his back so as to resemble a tail, and terminating in a serpent: extremely fantastic.

Joachim Patinier. Christ is standing, and opposite to him the demon, like an old monk, with a cowl half concealing his face, and a long robe which does not quite hide the clawed feet. In the background is the pinnacle of the Temple, with Christ and Satan standing on it, and in the distance, on one side, Satan is seen departing; on the other, two ministering angels are approaching.

The Angels minister to our Lord in the Wilderness.

Ital. Cristo a mensa nel Deserto.

A. J.] This beautiful subject is seldom treated in a series of the history of Christ, because perhaps it is merely the second scene of the Temptation; but some examples in the later schools, in which it appears as a separate representation, are worth notice.

L. Carracci. Jesus, a very noble and dignified figure, washes His hands in a vase which an angel, kneeling, holds before Him; other angels approach from behind with fruits and refreshments. (Musée, Lyons.)

Vasari. A very pretty small picture; one angel holds a vase before Jesus, another pours water on His hands (in the Oriental manner on preparing to eat).

G. di San Giovanni. A table prepared and spread with viands; six angels minister, and Christ blesses the meal. (Etruria Pitture.)

> They in a flowery valley set Him down
> On a green bank, and straight before Him spread
> A table of celestial food—divine
> Ambrosial fruits, fetched from the tree of life—
> And from the fount of life celestial drink,
> . . . . And as He fed, angelic quires
> Sung heavenly anthems.

Lebrun. A large picture. Jesus is seated at the foot of a tree. Four angels in adoration before Him. One kisses His feet; an angel places near Him a large vase and dish, and another, hovering, brings a basket of fruit.

THE MONEY-CHANGERS EXPELLED FROM THE TEMPLE.

Fr. Le Seigneur chasse les Vendeurs hors du Temple.
Germ. Christus treibt die Verkäufer aus dem Tempel.

Matt. xxi. 12; Mark xi. 15; Luke xix. 45; John ii. 15.

A. J.] THIS is another subject which is comparatively uncommon. It has never been popular as a church picture, and for obvious reasons. Our Lord is here seen filled with a just indignation against those who had desecrated the house of His Father; but expressing it with a vehemence most difficult to represent without in some degree departing from the mild and tranquil dignity which we associate with His face and figure.

It is true that the sheep, the cattle, and the doves, which were brought within the precincts of the Temple for sale, were ostensibly there for the purpose of furnishing sacrifices, and that the money-changers were allowed to have their counters there for the advantage of those who came from a distance to worship. But the whole arrangement had degenerated from its original object—altercations ensued between buyers and sellers, quite inconsistent with the sacredness of the place; therefore we are told that when our Lord beheld this motley and noisy assemblage, disgracing His holy Temple, 'He twisted a scourge of small cords,' and drove them forth. According to the usual chronology of the Gospels, this event took place soon after the Baptism, and when Christ went up to Jerusalem to keep the first Passover following the commencement of His ministry. It is therefore remarkable that two great artists, Giotto and Albert Dürer, should have placed it after the triumphant entry into Jerusalem, just before the last Passover and the Crucifixion. The scene is mentioned in all the four Gospels, but the circumstance of the *scourge* only by St. John. It has, however, been rarely omitted by the painters. I shall now give some examples.

Albert Dürer. In the centre stands our Lord, turning to the right and brandishing a scourge. Before Him one of the traders

A. J.] lies on the ground; stools and benches, overthrown, are scattered around, and the terrified people seek to escape out of the doors. One of the small series of the Passion.

Bonifazio. Our Saviour towering in the midst—a most dignified figure, severe, and yet not agitated by displeasure—just raises His hand armed with the scourge. The crowd of people fly hither and thither in consternation; one, standing before a magnificent table heaped with gold and silver, tries to gather it up and escape with it. The architecture of the Temple is seen in the background; the numerous figures agitated by different passions—amazement, terror, anxiety for their possessions—the fine, vigorous, truly Venetian colour—above all, the fine expression in the head and attitude of Christ, render this perhaps the masterpiece of Bonifazio. It was presented to the Venetian Republic, when Venice was a republic and a nation of traders and merchants and money-changers, by one of the noble Contarini family, and still, not without a certain significance or propriety, hangs in the Palazzo Ducale, near the entrance of the chapel.

Rembrandt. Jesus stands in the middle of the foreground. He has overturned one of the tables of the money-changers, who is endeavouring to secure a bag of money while he looks up with terror at the scourge in the hand of our Lord; a woman with a basket of doves on her head, and many others, seek to escape; some of the traders on the right hand are thrown down by the sheep and cattle; all are hurrying away as in a fright. In the background is seen the splendid architecture of the Temple, with numerous pillars, and a chandelier suspended from the roof; in the far distance the High Priest with his attendants.

The whole scene, though on so small a scale, is full of expression, variety, and movement, and is one of the finest works by Rembrandt.

Bassano. The principal figure, as is too often the case, is quite a failure, and almost vulgar in expression. Market women with baskets of eggs and doves, men with sheep and cattle, crowd the foreground, all delineated with Bassano's usual homely truth and animation, and coloured with his usual warmth and brilliancy. The subject was one peculiarly suited to Bassano, as it gave him an opportunity of introducing his favourite objects—cattle, sheep, dogs, fowls, and market-people—without impropriety.

Christ as Teacher.

'The Son of man is come to save that which was lost.'

A. J.] It was not difficult, comparatively speaking, to represent in His merely human capacity, and under His human lineaments, the Divine Redeemer of mankind, in the general character of Preacher and Teacher, as addressing His disciples and the people with earnest gesture and mildly speaking eyes, while the reverent listeners round Him are seen in various attitudes of attention, and with all the diversities of age, sex, and character. Thus far painting could go; but to express the exact theme of His exhortation, or the exact doctrine to be impressed, this was beyond the capabilities of Art. Accessory figures or objects with a visible significance, or an inscription placed underneath, or (as in old Byzantine Art) a scroll over the heads or in the hands of the figures, indicated the exact sense. Thus, when our Saviour was intended to say, 'Feed my sheep,' He pointed to some sheep near Him. When He says, 'I am the bread of life,' He holds ears of corn in His hand. When He says, 'I am the good shepherd,' He bears the weak and the weary of the flock on His shoulders; and for the same reason, I suppose that in a modern picture, where Christ says, 'I am the light of the world,' He carries a lantern in His hand. But I have already treated of these symbolical accessories, as suitable only to ideal and devotional figures.

When Christ is not only the heavenly Teacher, but in the act of teaching men on earth—not merely the 'light of the world,' but occupied in enlightening the world—then the Spiritual *Word* becomes visible in form, the whole representation assumes a dramatic cast, and requires an entirely different treatment not beyond the reach of Art. As He taught in various places—in the Temple, in the Synagogue, in the habitations of men, on the mountain, in the valley, by the lake shore; as His exhortations were sometimes addressed to one or two persons especially—sometimes to multitudes, who in His presence were moved to forget even the want of food; as the subject of His discourse varied—sometimes being full of sadness, sometimes denouncing the sinner, and sometimes encouraging the penitent, sometimes full of hope—so, in the attempt to convey thus far a general impression, the locality selected, the number of attendant figures, the gesture and expression of the principal personage, might be varied in accordance with the sentiment to be conveyed. But this was all that the highest Art, in the most accomplished hands, could effect, and any attempt to particularise the text or theme became artistically a failure. A certain nobleman once came to Sir Joshua Reynolds, and requested him to paint a picture of the reply which the Earl of Bedford, the father of the murdered Russell, made to James II., 'I had *once* a son who might have assisted your Majesty!' Sir Joshua in vain endeavoured to explain to his friend and patron that Art has its limits, and that he was requiring what Art could not accomplish.

But though it cannot do all that words can do, yet within its proper limits Art can do much more than words; and I cannot convey a better idea of what its legitimate objects ought to be, and its natural and necessary limits must be, than by selecting a few examples of the attempts made by various artists, with various success, to express in silent forms the divine teaching of Christ; it may not only be a lesson in artistic criticism, but edifying in a far higher sense.

Matt. v.; Luke iv. 18; Isa. lxi. 1.

The Sermon on the Mount—called, from the first ten verses of the sermon, the 'Mount of Beatitudes.'

I believe this to be represented in a very beautiful print by Karolus, after Lambert Lombard, quite Raphaelesque in taste and style. Our Lord stands on an eminence under a tree, in an expressive attitude, 'as one teaching with authority,' and yet with gentleness. In front many persons, and among them several women; one very graceful figure reclines, listening devoutly, with a child in her arms; five disciples stand behind Christ; in the distance, landscape, ruins, and a group of men and women bearing water.

Claude has painted the subject in a landscape; a high woody eminence, in the centre of which our Saviour stands, surrounded

A. J.] by His disciples; a multitude of people ascend the hill, or stand round it in groups; beyond, on either side, the sea of Galilee—one of Claude's largest compositions, in the Grosvenor Gallery, the subject being merely accessory, while the landscape has beautiful aerial effects of light and distance. We are told of an old lady, whose admiration for this picture was such, that she offered a former possessor a handsome annuity for the loan of it during her life.

Peter Breughel. An extraordinary little picture, in his usual elaborate and exquisitely-finished style, with a crowd of figures, round a wooded eminence.

By Sebastian Ricci and Lebrun, large compositions in the late style of Art.

Parmigianino. A picture much praised by Lanzi, not only because compositions of many figures by this painter are extremely rare, but as in itself most beautiful—'*un vero gioiello.*'

C. Reverdino. A fine print. Christ is teaching on an eminence. On His right hand a group of devout listeners, in a broad light; on the left hand a group of men, overshadowed with darkness, who retire averting their faces, and which Zani supposes to be an allusion to the words of our Lord—Matt. xi. 25. This print is styled, 'The Sermon on Mount Tabor,' which by some ancient writers was supposed to be the scene of the Sermon on the Mount; but the true locality is pointed out in a most interesting passage of Dr. Stanley's 'Sinai and Palestine,' p. 360. The Greek word, which in Luke vi. 17 is mistranslated 'plain,' should, he says, be *platform*, a level place on a height.

'The eight Beatitudes,' with which our Lord opens His divine exhortation, have been treated in Art. There is a curious example in the famous enamelled chandelier which the Emperor Frederic Barbarossa the First suspended as an offering over the tomb of Charlemagne, at Aix-la-Chapelle; the bronze circle is surmounted by eight lights, and under each light is one of the beatitudes allegorically represented, and executed in enamel and gold.

'Then came to Him the mother of Zebedee's children with her sons (James and John), worshipping Him. . . . And she saith unto Him, Grant that these my two sons may sit, the one on Thy

4. J.] right hand and the other on the left, in Thy kingdom' (Matt. xx. 20, 21). In Mark x. 35, where the same story is told, the two young Apostles make this request for themselves. The painters have taken the first version, wherein the petition is at least more excusable. The most beautiful example is by Bonifazio, in which our Lord is seated in a house, the Apostles, apparently, are on either side, and the mother, veiled, kneels in front. Without knowing the story, we cannot of course guess the nature of her petition, except by the expression in our Saviour's countenance, which is approving, not compassionate. The picture is most beautiful in sentiment and colour, and has never, that I know of, been copied or engraved. The same scene, by Paul Veronese, serves as the altarpiece of the family chapel in Burleigh House—not very good, according to Dr. Waagen, and the picture by Tintoretto appeared to me vulgar. These are all the instances I have met with, and all of the Venetian school, in which the domestic scenes of the Bible were especially popular.

CHRIST TEACHES IN THE TEMPLE (OR THE SYNAGOGUE).[1]

Christ, in the centre, is arguing with four Pharisees—He is in the attitude of one demonstrating divine truth. The contrast between the serene beauty of the head of our Lord and the coarse acute faces of the Jewish doctors, is admirable. This picture, in the National Gallery (woodcut, No. 121, over leaf) has been styled, by mistake, 'The Dispute in the Temple;' but our Lord is here a grown man, not a boy of twelve years old. It is supposed to be painted by Luini from a cartoon by Leonardo.

Raphael. A lofty flight of steps leading to a portico in the classic style, under which Christ is seated, His hand raised as teaching or preaching. On the left hand Martha is leading her sister Mary up the steps to present her to Jesus; four disciples are behind Him, and on the steps, and below many others listening or meditating.[2] The engraving by Marc Antonio, from the precious original drawing in the Louvre, is celebrated.

[1] The locality is not discriminated.
[2] See in Sacred and Legendary Art, vol. i., the story of Mary and Martha, where this composition is given.

121   Christ Teaching. (Luini. National Gallery.)

CHRIST PREACHING FROM THE SHIP.

[A. J.] The locality and accessories sufficiently distinguish this subject, of which there are few examples.

The sea-shore. Christ in a small bark, with His disciples, addresses a crowd of people who listen on the shore. There are at least fifty figures in all. This composition, finely engraved, has been attributed to Raphael, but is by one of his scholars.

There is also a fine large woodcut after Titian, with at least thirty figures, but I am unacquainted with the original picture.

The Tribute Money.

Ital. Il Cristo della Moneta.   *Fr.* Le Denier de César.   *Germ.* Der Zinsgroschen.

Matt. xxii. 15; Mark xii. 14; Luke xx. 22.

4. *J.*] The finest example of this subject is without doubt the celebrated picture by Titian. It contains only two figures, not quite half-length; yet the story, without the aid of words, could not be more perfectly rendered—and no words, certainly, could have brought before us, at a single glance, the mild, refined, contemplative, yet intellectual and penetrating head of the Saviour in immediate contrast with the powerful but vulgar and cunning face of the Pharisee who tempts Him.

I think the moment chosen is just after Christ has asked the question, 'Whose image and superscription is this?' He points with His well-formed delicate finger to the piece of money held in the coarse hand of the Pharisee.

In the picture by Titian, in our National Gallery, there are three figures—our Lord and two Pharisees—and the sentiment is different. Our Lord, raising His hand to heaven, is uttering the words, 'Render unto God,' &c.; and the same moment is expressed in the third example by Titian, containing five figures, but neither of these can be compared to the Dresden picture.

There is a fine though rather coarse version of the subject by Rubens, containing nine figures, half-length, in which the significance is the same.

I remember another by Van Dyck—three figures, in which the physiognomy of Christ is singularly noble and penetrating. (Genoa—Brignole Palace.)

And there are others by Caravaggio, and by Valentin, in which one of the Pharisees peers at our Lord through a pair of spectacles—a similar anachronism is in the picture by Antonio Arias in the Madrid Gallery (242); but I do not find among my notes one

[*A. J.*] example before the time of Titian. I think the subject may have derived some importance and popularity from the contests between Charles V., as Cæsar, and the Roman Church. I must not omit to mention the exquisite and most effective little etching by Rembrandt, containing about sixteen figures. Christ, placing one hand authoritatively on the arm of the Pharisee, raises the other to heaven. The significance cannot be mistaken: 'Render unto God the things which are God's.'

The Pharisees inquire of Christ why His disciples do not wash their hands before going to meat (Matt. xv. 2). This subject would be unintelligible, but for the explanatory text and the situation. It is, or was, a small fresco, over the lavatory in the now ruined convent of S. Michele in Bosio, near Bologna. (Tibaldi.)

The disciples standing before Christ exhibit to Him two swords (Luke xxii. 38). Raphael. This small composition is under the fresco of jurisprudence in the Vatican; and it should seem that Raphael intended to express, not allegorically, but historically, that divine as well as human justice may sometimes wield the sword.

A series of three engravings, expressing the doctrine of Christ.
He bears witness to His Father.
He discourses to His disciples concerning the efficacy of His sacrifice.
He teaches His disciples to avoid the false prophets, here represented by the Pharisees and the dignitaries of the Romish Church, which shows that the artist, Daniel Hopfer, had embraced the Lutheran faith. These curious designs are accompanied by long inscriptions, or the subjects would be unintelligible. In the same manner, the denunciation of our Lord against the Pharisees, 'Woe unto you, Scribes and Pharisees, hypocrites!' is applied to the Roman Church in a curious set of eight small subjects—rarely met with.

By the same quaint artist we have five verses of the 10th chapter of St. Matthew, from the 34th to the 38th inclusive, expressed in five small subjects on the same plate. It should seem that he intended to indicate the public contests, the family divisions, and the suffering of all kinds which followed on the religious dissensions of his time, from 1490 to 1527. Little is known of this Daniel Hopfer, but as the most distinguished of a family of artists and engravers who lived and worked at Augsburg.

Christ teaches Philip (John xiv. 8, 9). Bonifazio.[1] I have described this picture in the story of St. Philip the Apostle. It is a signal instance of a beautiful picture, which, without the accompanying inscription underneath, would have been scarcely intelligible except as representing in a general way the Teacher and the disciples.

Christ instructing Nicodemus. 'There was a man of the Pharisees named Nicodemus. . . . The same came to Jesus *by night*' (John iii. 1). This subject is more easily represented, and there are several examples.

Tintoretto. Both seated in earnest converse. A servant brings a torch; four other figures behind listening.

A. van Vost. Both seated at a table, on which are a candle, books, &c.; two figures only, three-quarters—engraved by Peter de Jode.

Another, in which Christ is seated, and Nicodemus stands before Him in an attitude of respect, better expresses the relative position of the two personages.

Nicodemus visits Christ by night. A powerful half-length group by Rubens, and a fine effect of light by Rembrandt.

CHRIST IN THE HOUSE OF MARTHA AND MARY.

I HAVE so fully described this subject, and the relations of Christ with the two sisters, that I can add nothing here.[2]

In the interpretation of mediæval Art, it is necessary to accept the mediæval legends which identify Mary, the sister of Martha and Lazarus, with the penitent woman who wept at the feet of Jesus, and whose sins were forgiven her. The visit of Christ to Martha and Mary does not usually form one of the cycle of Gospel subjects, and when separately treated is almost always seen in the

---

[1] Sacred and Legendary Art. Third edition.
[2] *Ibid.*, vol. i. p. 365. Third edition.

A. J.] legendary or the *genre* style, not as a Scriptural incident, or a religious lesson.

There is a picture in the Berlin Museum, which is curious. Our Lord, seated on a high dais or throne between His Mother and St. Peter, points to Martha, who with a dish of fruit in her hand reproaches Mary, seated in a meditative attitude at His feet. Their brother Lazarus is seen in a suit of armour (to express his military character). Marcella, the handmaid, with a vessel of wine, and three disciples are also present, and the votaries who dedicated the picture—a man, his wife, and two children—appear kneeling below.

This large altarpiece, strictly a devotional picture, is interesting as being one of the authentic works by Suor Plautilla Nelli, the Domenican nun, who was a scholar of Fra Bartolomeo. She, who united in herself the working capabilities of Martha and the devout humility of Mary, must have had pleasure in painting this picture. The drawing, as might be expected from a secluded nun, is rather feeble, but the arrangement is elegant, the conception of character and the heads of the female figures lovely, and the whole bears out the praises given to her by Vasari and Lanzi. Vasari, who styles her 'questa veneranda e virtuosa suora,' says, that if she had had the advantages of study, allowed to artists of the other sex, she would have done wonders, and painted men as well as she painted women. As it is, her apostles and warrior-saints give one the impression of women disguised as men—which probably was the fact.

There is a picture in the gallery at Vienna, in which the subject is treated, not devotionally, but with much elegance. Christ is seated, and Mary at His feet looks up, devoutly listening to His words; on the other side is a table spread with fruits. Martha, while preparing the feast, looks round reproachfully at her sister. Marcella is drawing water from a well.

Of the manner in which Bassano has treated the subject, we may judge from the fact that it forms one of a series of three compositions, known as 'Le tre Cucine' (The Three Kitchens), engraved by Sadeler.

We give an illustration of this subject by the French painter Jouvenet (woodcut, No. 122).

122   Jesus in the House of Martha and Mary.   (Jouvenet.   Louvre.)

A. J.]   Christ teaches His disciples how to pray ('Le sette Dimande del Paternoster')—in seven subjects.

Christ blessing little Children.

A. J.] It seems, at first view, extraordinary that this most beautiful and touching incident in the life of our Saviour should have been so seldom treated in the early Italian schools, and never, that I know of, in Spanish Art. The cause may be the same which, in other respects, has influenced the selection of religious subjects for church pictures—namely, the particular views and predilections of the theologians and ecclesiastics who patronised Art, and who professed celibacy. The natural instincts pleased themselves later in the perpetual iteration of the Holy Families, and of those scenes in which the Christ, as a beautiful infant, descends from heaven to caress in beatified visions the ecstatic monk or nun. These I have described in the 'Legends of the Madonna,' and in the stories of St. Francis, St. Antony, the two St. Catherines, and others; but the human children brought to Christ that He might make their parents happy by blessing and encouraging them, was a theme comparatively avoided, and I have often wondered why two among the greatest painters, who seem in their works to have revelled in the delineation of childhood—Titian and Murillo—should never have represented a scene so congenial; but among their works I find no example, nor in those of the tender Raphael, nor the prolific Albert Dürer.

In Greek Art as in Western Art, the subject is comparatively modern. On the sarcophagi, and in the mural paintings in the Catacombs, there occurs frequently a group which has been supposed to represent this subject. Christ, standing in the usual classic costume, and generally beardless, lays His hand on the head of a child.

On the famous embroidered Dalmatic preserved in the sacristy of St. Peter's, a *chef-d'œuvre* of Byzantine Art,[1] there is a group in one corner, which Lord Lindsay supposes to represent Abraham

---

[1] It is described with just enthusiasm by Lord Lindsay. Christian Art, vol. i. p. 138.

A. J.] with a child on his lap, laying his hand on the head of another, and with four others near him.

I think it represents Christ with the children—the representation of Abraham would be out of place in a composition which in every part is dedicated to the glory and beneficence of the Saviour. On the other hand, as the principal subject above is our Lord as Judge of the world, it may represent Abraham receiving the souls of the just.[1]

In modern Art we find, among the earliest painters who treated the subject, the famous Lucas Cranach, and he has repeated it several times—so often, indeed, that the novelty as well as the charm of the subject seems to have rendered it popular. There is great *naïveté* and beauty in some of the *motifs*—the mothers and the children, in the old German costumes, are, if not very pretty, full of expression, and there is a beautiful touch of nature in the figure of a young girl, who looks on the principal group with feminine sympathy.

In the Esterhazy Gallery at Vienna—in the church at Naumberg—in the Pauliner-Kirche at Leipzig—in the Church of St. Anna at Augsburg—and in several private collections, there are repetitions, varied, of this favourite group; in the picture at Augsburg is the inscription, 'Ein Vater über Uns Allen' (one Father over us all). An original drawing of the subject is in the collection of the Grand Duke of Weimar.

I remember a beautiful Italian woodcut of the 16th century, in which the benign Redeemer stands with one child in His arms, His hand on the head of another—five mothers, seven children, and two Apostles are looking on; which is the earliest Italian example I have seen, but there may exist examples of earlier date.

Rottenhammer. A small, elegant, and most delicately-finished picture.

Van Winghen. A very beautiful composition, engraved by Johann Sadeler, and his masterpiece.

Rubens. At Blenheim is a picture in which Christ blesses a family of children—evidently portraits. The mother and father, in rich Flemish costumes, present their children to Him. He lays

---

[1] See further account of this Dalmatic, vol. ii. p. 357.

.1. J.] His hand on the head of a boy, behind whom is a little girl. The mother holds an infant in her arms, and three Apostles are seen behind Christ.

Rembrandt (of which we give an illustration, No. 123). Christ

123   Christ blessing little Children.   (Rembrandt.)

seated on a bank under a tree, bends down with a look of tenderness as He draws towards Him with one hand a little girl, and lays His right hand on her head as in benediction; the child turns away shyly, with her finger in her mouth, looking up at her mother.

4. ./.] who pushes her on, holding at the same time an infant on the other arm; behind our Saviour, a father lifts up a child to be noticed, and behind him is St. Peter. There are ten figures in all, life-size, and the heads, excepting that of our Saviour, are all of the coarsest Dutch type; but the picture is quite wonderful for the intense truth of expression, the animation of the grouping, and the fine execution. (Gallery of Count Schönborn, Vienna.)

THE WOMAN TAKEN IN ADULTERY.

Ital. L' Adultera. *Fr.* La Femme adultère. *Germ.* Die Ehebrecherinn vor Christo.

John viii. 3–11.

A. J.] THERE remain two incidents connected with the ministry of our Lord, which place before us the divine character of His moral teaching under the most beautiful aspect—those in which He inculcated, by act and word, reverence for childhood and mercy towards the guilty, respect for the innocence of the child and compassion for the fallen woman. It happens that both these incidents are capable of the most dramatic and the most picturesque treatment, and that the significance of both is at once sympathetic and intelligible. Hence we find that it is since the time when religious Art ceased to be conventional and doctrinal, and became dramatic, picturesque, and what we term *sentimental*, that the most beautiful examples of both these subjects occur. Neither of them, however, have been frequently included in a religious series of the life and works of our Lord.

It was while teaching in the Temple that the Scribes and Pharisees brought before Jesus the frail guilty woman. 'Moses in the law commanded us that such should be stoned; but what sayest Thou?' I think it unnecessary to give the whole passage, because it may at once be referred to; but we may imagine the unhappy creature standing in the midst of her accusers—the old and stern, who had outlived all pity, and who stood there for law—the young, according to their creed of man's strength and impunity and woman's weakness and responsibility, ready to condemn, 'lest they cause scandal in Israel'—and the cunning, who, without caring either for law or pity, came there to ensnare, even through His own mercy, the merciful Redeemer, who, at first stooping down, wrote with His finger on the ground, 'as though He heard them not,'[1] and then, raising His head, spoke as one having authority to bind or loose—'He that is without sin among you, let him first cast a stone at her.' This, in general, is the moment chosen for representation, as being the most intelligible. I will now give some examples.

The earliest in date I have met with is a mere fragment of a fresco, by Vitale di Bologna (1340), in which our Lord, after stooping down, has just raised His head; the woman stands on the left with hands bound, and there are vestiges of about six other figures.

Titian has repeated this subject several times.

1. A composition of twelve figures, less than life and rather more than half-length. Christ is seated; the two Apostles behind Him are portraits of Venetian senators. The accusers stand opposite—one of them, an old bearded Rabbi, looks very stern and grand; but in the luxuriant beauty of the woman there is not much contrition, and in the expression of our Saviour but little dignity. (Grosvenor Gallery.)

2. Another similar, but much finer in sentiment; the head of Christ, like that in the 'Cristo della Monetà,' noble, grave, and mild. The woman, modest and contrite; behind her, five accusers, with eager, malicious faces.

3. A large picturesque composition in a landscape. Our Lord and His Apostles appear to have just come out of the Temple on the left hand, and meet the woman and her accusers. This is a departure from the local truth, as the scene took place *within* the Temple.

4. In the Church of St. Afra, at Brescia, a most beautiful picture, in arrangement like the two first; the figures half-length; the grave and dignified compassion of the Saviour, and the wonderful loveliness and downcast looks of the guilty woman, and the rich colour, are all in his best manner. The picture appeared to me in fine preservation—perhaps untouched.

In the picture by Paul Veronese, the moment chosen is when

---

[1] The tradition is that He noted down their sins, and that of such power was that writing that each of them knew it to contain his own sins. S. Bonaventura, in his Life of Christ, mentions this tradition as from the older commentators.

A. J.] Christ utters the words of pardon, 'Neither do I condemn thee,' and the accusers are seen stealing off through the doors.

In Bonifazio's picture, Christ looks up, pointing to the words He has written on the ground: extremely fine. In Varotari's, a Scribe appeals to the book of the Law, 'Moses hath said,' &c. Ten figures, also fine. By Palma Vecchio, Tintoretto, Pordenone,

124   The Woman taken in Adultery.   (Mazzolino da Ferrara.   Pitti.)

Romanino, and Giorgione (so called), other examples. All these are Venetian, showing a decided predilection for the subject in that school of Art.

Mazzolino. A small exquisite picture. Five accusers; one, stooping down, tries to read what Christ has written on the ground; another, crestfallen, tries to steal away (woodcut, No. 124).

Lucas Cranach. A small picture; many figures. One of the

A. J.] Pharisees, with a malicious countenance, has a stone in his hand, ready to throw at the unhappy culprit.

By Rubens, a celebrated picture, and one of his finest. Five figures in the foreground, and seven behind, rather above a lifesize; perhaps because the picture was to be seen from a distance. The woman stands in the centre, a full-formed, luxuriant Flemish beauty, with downcast eyes. Our Lord on the right hand, more refined and dignified than is usual with Rubens. On the left hand, the accusers; among them one of a horribly vulgar expression, and a meagre-looking Pharisee with cunning malicious eyes. There is a tradition, without the slightest foundation or likelihood, that Rubens intended in these two heads to represent Luther and Calvin.

Rembrandt. The woman has just been brought before our Saviour, and one of the accusers is in the act of removing her veil. She weeps bitterly. Christ stands with joined hands, calmly listening; St. John behind Him. Very fine. (Blenheim.)

In another beautiful little picture, by the same painter, we have the interior of the Temple. The woman, surrounded by her accusers, kneels before our Saviour at the foot of a broad flight of steps leading up to the high altar. For expression, and for the peculiar effect of light, of wonderful beauty. Fifteen figures. (National Gallery.)

Giulio Romano. The scene is a splendid portico, like the 'Beautiful Gate' in Raphael's cartoon. Between the two central pillars stand Christ and the woman. She looks down, drawing her drapery round her—not very graceful, nor very penitent. He turns to her, as if asking, 'Hath no man condemned thee?' and points to the accusers, who are hurrying away to the right and the left. In the foreground are two lame beggars. About twenty-six figures. The large engraving by Diana Ghisi of Mantua, in an admirable style, is celebrated as the *chef-d'œuvre* of this fine engraver. It is dedicated to Leonora of Austria, Duchess of Mantua, in 1575.

N. Poussin. The scene is in a public place with rich architecture. Christ stands in front, surrounded by the Scribes and Pharisees, and the woman kneels before Him, weeping. Three

A. J.] persons on the right are stooping down to read the words which Christ has traced on the ground. Twelve figures. (Louvre, 427.)

Agostino Carracci. Christ looks at the accusers, and the sentiment is evidently, 'Whoever is without sin,' &c. The woman is most lovely in expression and attitude, and the execution of the whole picture exquisite for finish and delicacy. The fault, and it is a *great* fault, is, that the head of Christ is of a feeble type. (Milan—Brera Gallery.)]

CHRIST AND THE WOMAN OF SAMARIA.

Ital. Nostro Signore al Pozzo.   *Fr.* Le Christ avec la Femme samaritaine.
Germ. Christus am Brunnen.

[A. J.—THIS beautiful and picturesque subject was, in the most ancient times, and in the most primitive forms of Christian Art, used only in a symbolical and devotional meaning, and in reference to the words of our Lord, 'I am the living water; whoso

125   Christ and the Woman of Samaria. (Ancient sarcophagus.)

drinketh of the water that I shall give him, shall never thirst.' In this sense, and as a sacred symbol, we find it on the sarcophagi, but not often; only two instances are cited, and I give one (No. 125). Christ and the Woman of Samaria stand on each side of a draw-well; both ideal forms, in a classical costume. The woman has drawn up the bucket, which has the shape of the antique bronze buckets we see so often in the collections of antiquities, and Christ extends His hands as one speaking. The subject has

[J. J.] not often been included in a series of the history of Christ, but has very frequently been treated by the later painters as a separate picture; more, perhaps, from its picturesque capabilities than from its profound mystical significance as a doctrinal lesson. When thus treated as an event only, it is necessary to bring before our minds the locality and the peculiar circumstances of the scene. Jesus, on His way from Judæa into Galilee, must needs go through Samaria; and He came to a city of the Samaritans named Sychar, near to that parcel of ground which Jacob gave to his son Joseph. Now Jacob's well was there, and Jesus, being weary with His journey, sat down on the brink of the well. 'There cometh a woman of Samaria to draw water. Jesus saith unto her, Give me to drink.' But the woman does not, like Rachel or Rebekah, hasten to give the Stranger drink; she hesitates, and asks how it is that He, being a Jew, asks drink of a woman of Samaria. 'Little knew the woman the excellency of the Person who asked so small a charity; neither had she been taught that a cup of cold water given to a disciple should be rewarded; but she spake as a Samaritan. At that time, between the Jews and Samaritans, there reigned an animosity so great, that they would have no dealings with each other. It arose out of a religious dispute which had arisen as far back as the days of Alexander the Great. The Samaritans averred that their priesthood were the true successors of Aaron, and their place of worship on Mount Gerizim holier than Jerusalem. From whence, the question of religion grew so high, that it begat disaffections, anger, animosities, quarrels, bloodshed, and murders, not only in Palestine, but whenever a Jew and a Samaritan had the misfortune to meet; such being the nature of men, that they think it the greatest injury in the world when other men are not of their minds, and that they please God most when they are most furiously zealous, and no zeal better to be expressed than by hating all those whom they are pleased to think God hates. Hence, when the woman heard the Stranger (whom she perceived to be a Jew) ask her courteously for drink, she wondered, and her wonder became amazement when He told her "all the things that ever she did."'[1] The locality, the true character of the Wayfarer, and of the woman, and the extraordinary colloquy between them, have

[1] Bishop Taylor's 'Life of Christ.'

A. J.] evidently been in the minds of the best artists who have treated this subject.

I will now give a few examples.

Michael Angelo. A composition which has been executed by his scholars—a rich landscape with a large tree in the centre, the dark massive branches overshadowing Jacob's well. (Devonshire House. Engraved by Beatrizet.)

Garofalo. The attitude and expression of the seated Christ unusually fine, the woman perhaps too elegantly dressed ; rich heathen sculpture on the well and vase; in the distance the city of Sychar on a hill, and the disciples approaching.

Bronzino. Our Lord is seated on the well. The woman, holding her vase with both hands, listens intently ; a child, seated at her feet, leans on a vase; in the distance the disciples approach with provisions.

Annibale Carracci. A fine landscape, with Jacob's well beneath a shady tree. Our Lord seated, and the woman standing reverentially. The expression uncommonly fine and dramatic, and the whole picture most beautiful.

Lucas Cranach. The well fills the centre and foreground ; Christ leans on the well in the attitude of one speaking earnestly: 'I am the living water.' The woman stands opposite, holding her bucket and listening ; a water vase in front; in the distance the Apostles are seen coming over a hill from the city of Sychar.

By Rembrandt there are two beautiful etchings, differently conceived. In the first, which is arched at top, our Lord is seated on the left hand, rather behind the well, leaning with His right arm over a slab of stone; the woman stands opposite to Him, leaning on her bucket, which rests on the well, and listening; on the steps of the well a pitcher : the disciples are seen approaching from the city of Sychar in the distance. In the second there is a draw-well with a beam, pulley, and chain ; the woman, who has her hand on the chain, seems to be arrested by the earnest words of the Saviour, who is seated on the other side of the well ; the disciples approach from the city, and the whole is expressed in a small compass, with great simplicity and animation.

THE TRANSFIGURATION.

Ital. La Trasfigurazione.   *Fr.* La Transfiguration.   *Germ.* Die Verklärung Christi.

A. J.] WE give this name to the glorified apparition of our Lord, with Moses and Elijah talking to Him, when 'His face did shine as the sun, and His raiment was white as the light,' as He was manifested to the three most beloved of His disciples, Peter, James, and John.

It appears from the words of St. Matthew, xvi. 13, that Jesus had inquired of His disciples what men thought of Him, and then what they themselves thought. To which Peter responded, with eager faith, 'Thou art the Son of the Living God;' but afterwards, when Jesus spoke of His destined suffering, that He should be taken and killed by the Pharisees, Peter seems to have been scandalised: 'Be it far from Thee;' and therefore, argued some of the early Fathers, this manifestation of His divine character, this testimony from above, was vouchsafed, that these disciples might entertain no doubt of His heavenly mission and His identity with the expected Messiah. It has been well observed, that while Christ appeared among men as a man—poor, lowly, despised—that was in fact the real transfiguration; whereas when He displayed Himself to the astonished and dazzled Apostles, with a face radiant as the sun, and clothed with ineffable glory, *this* was but a return to the real and superhuman character which He had quitted for a time only. We are told that the interlocutors in the vision, Moses and Elijah, talked with our Lord 'of His decease' (the word in the original does not mean *death*, but *departure, transit*) which should be accomplished at Jerusalem; thus further preparing the minds of the Apostles for that time of deepest and sublimest suffering which was so soon to follow on this wondrous testimony to eye and ear of His divine and immortal nature, 'and then they, Moses and Elijah, having finished the embassy of death which they had delivered in forms of glory,' departed from Him.

A. J.] This vision took place on a high mountain, not expressly named in any of the Evangelists, but it has been a constant tradition that this was Mount Tabor in Galilee.]

The Transfiguration is an early subject in Christian Art, and has gone through different phases. It is given in the mosaics of S. Apollinare in Classe, at Ravenna (6th century), in that reticence of form and emblematical character significant of classic Art. By the uninitiated the subject would not be readily deciphered. In the centre of the domed apse is a large jewelled cross, in the middle of which is the head of Christ. This represents the Lord. On each side are bust-lengths of Moses and Elijah, while below are three sheep, emblems of the three disciples.

Another form is seen in early miniatures—for instance, in a magnificent Evangelium preserved in the cathedral at Aix-la-Chapelle. Here Christ is seen with three rays above Him; at His side are the full-length figures of Moses and Elijah; below are the three disciples—two crouching low in terror, while Peter raises himself, saying, 'Lord, it is good for us to be here,' &c.

The next form is that given by early Byzantine artists, of a very formal and conventional character. Christ is in the mandorla, from which five rays of glory proceed. These five rays touch the prophets at His side, and the disciples, all three crouching low at His feet. We see Giotto scarcely emerging from this convention in his series in the Accademia.

Fra Angelico has a more fanciful representation. The Christ has His arms extended, as a type of the death He was to suffer on the Cross (woodcut, No. 126, over leaf). The disciples retain the traditional Byzantine positions. At the sides are the mere heads of the prophets, while the painter's adoration of the Virgin, and his homage toward St. Domenic, the founder of his Order, are shown by their attendant figures.

[*A. J.*—It must be allowed that there could be no more daring or more difficult undertaking in Art than to represent by any human medium this transcendent manifestation of the superhuman character of the Redeemer. It has been attempted but seldom, and of course, however reverent and poetical the spirit in which the attempt has been made, it has proved, in regard to the height of the theme, only a miserable failure. I should observe,

126. Transfiguration. (Fra Angelico. S. Marco, Florence.)

A. J.] however, that the early artists hardly seem to have aimed at anything beyond a mere *indication* of an incident too important to be wholly omitted. In all these examples the representation of a visible fact has been predominant, the aim in the mind of the artist being to comply with some established conventional or theological rule.

Only in one instance has the vision of heavenly beatitude been used to convey the sublimest lesson to humanity, and thus the inevitable failure has been redeemed nobly, or, we might rather say, converted into a glorious success.

When Raphael, in the last year of his life, was commissioned by the Cardinal de' Medici to paint an altarpiece for the Cathedral

J.] of Narbonne, he selected for his subject the Transfiguration of our Lord.

Every one knows that this picture has a world-wide fame; it has, indeed, been styled the 'greatest picture in the world;' it has also been criticised as if Raphael, the greatest artist who ever lived, had been here unmindful of the rules of Art. But it is clear that of those who have enthusiastically praised or daringly censured, few have interpreted its real significance. Some have erred in ignorantly applying the rules of Art where they were in no respect applicable. Others, not claiming to know anything, or care anything about rules of Art, insisting on their right to judge of what is or is not intelligible to *them*, have given what I must needs call very absurd opinions about what they do not understand. It has been objected by one set of critics that there is a want of unity, that the picture is divided in two, and that these two parts not only do not harmonise, but ' mutually hurt each other.' Others say that the spiritual beatitude above, and the contortions of the afflicted boy below, present a shocking contrast. Others sneer at the little hillock or platform which they suppose is to stand for Mount Tabor, think the group above profane, and the group below horrible. Such as these, with a courage quite superior to all artistic criticism, and undazzled by the accumulated fame of five centuries, venture on a fiat which reminds one of nothing so much as of Voltaire's ridicule of Hamlet, and his denunciation of that 'barbare,' that 'imbécile de Shakespeare,' who would not write so as to be appreciated by a French critic.

I hope that, throughout these volumes, I have clearly explained and sufficiently reiterated that distinction between devotional and historical representations as one to be constantly kept in view, the first being the expression of an idea, or of some doctrinal or moral truth, and the latter of a fact, action, or incident, as it may be supposed to have occurred.

Now, in looking at the Transfiguration (and I hope the reader, if the original be far off, will at least have a good print before him while going over these following remarks), we must bear in mind that it is not an historical but a devotional picture—that the intention of the painter was not to represent a scene, but to excite

A. J.] religious feelings by expressing, so far as painting might do it, a very sublime idea, which it belongs to us to interpret.

I can best accomplish this, perhaps, by putting down naturally my own impressions, when I last had the opportunity of studying this divine picture.

If we remove to a certain distance from it, so that the forms shall become vague, indistinct, and only the masses of colour and the light and shade perfectly distinguishable, we shall see that the picture is indeed divided as if horizontally, the upper half being all light, and the lower half comparatively all dark. As we approach nearer, step by step, we behold above, the radiant figure of the Saviour floating in mid air, with arms outspread, garments of transparent light, glorified visage upturned as in rapture, and the hair uplifted and scattered as I have seen it in persons under the influence of electricity. On the right, Moses; on the left, Elijah; representing, respectively, the old Law and the old prophecies, which both testified of Him. The three disciples lie on the ground, terror-struck, dazzled. There is a sort of eminence or platform, but no perspective, no attempt at real locality, for the scene is revealed as in a vision, and the same soft transparent light envelopes the whole. This is the spiritual life, raised far above the earth, but not yet in heaven. Below is seen the earthly life, poor humanity struggling helplessly with pain, infirmity, and death. The father brings his son, the possessed, or, as we should now say, the epileptic boy, who ofttimes falls into the water or into the fire, or lies grovelling on the earth, foaming and gnashing his teeth; the boy struggles in his arms—the rolling eyes, the distorted features, the spasmodic limbs are at once terrible and pitiful to look on.

Such is the profound, the heart-moving significance of this wonderful picture. It is, in truth, a fearful approximation of the most opposite things; the mournful helplessness, suffering, and degradation of human nature, the unavailing pity, are placed in immediate contrast with spiritual light, life, hope—nay, the very fruition of heavenly rapture.

It has been asked, Who are the two figures, the two saintly deacons, who stand on each side of the upper group, and what have they to do with the mystery above, or the sorrow below? Their

1. *J.*] presence shows that the whole was conceived as a vision, or a poem. The two saints are St. Lawrence and St. Julian, placed there at the request of the Cardinal de' Medici, for whom the picture was painted, to be offered by him as an act of devotion as well as munificence to his new bishopric; and these two figures commemorate in a poetical way, not unusual at the time, his father, Lorenzo, and his uncle, Giuliano de' Medici. They would be better away; but Raphael, in consenting to the wish of his patron that they should be introduced, left no doubt of the significance of the whole composition—that it is placed before worshippers as a revelation of the double life of earthly suffering and spiritual faith, as an excitement to religious contemplation and religious hope.

In the Gospel, the Transfiguration of our Lord is first described, then the gathering of the people and the appeal of the father in behalf of his afflicted son. They appear to have been simultaneous; but painting only could have placed them before our eyes, at the same moment, in all their suggestive contrast. It will be said that in the brief record of the Evangelist, this contrast is nowhere indicated, but the painter found it there and was right to use it— just the same as if a man should choose a text from which to preach a sermon, and, in doing so, should evolve from the inspired words many teachings, many deep reasonings, besides the one most obvious and apparent.

But, after we have prepared ourselves to understand and to take into our heads all that this wonderful picture can suggest, considered as an emanation of mind, we find that it has other interests for us, considered merely as a work of Art. It was the last picture which came from Raphael's hand; he was painting on it when he was seized with his last illness. He had completed all the upper part of the composition, all the ethereal vision, but the lower part of it was still unfinished, and in this state the picture was hung over his bier, when, after his death, he was laid out in his painting room, and all his pupils and his friends, and the people of Rome, came to look upon him for the last time; and when those who stood round raised their eyes to the Transfiguration, and then bent them on the lifeless form extended beneath it, 'every heart was like to burst with grief' (*faceva scoppiare l' anima di dolore a ognuno che quivi guardava*), as, indeed, well it might.

A. J.] Two-thirds of the price of the picture, 655 'ducati di camera,' had already been paid by the Cardinal de' Medici; and, in the following year, that part of the picture which Raphael had left unfinished was completed by his pupil Giulio Romano, a powerful and gifted but not a refined or elevated genius. He supplied what was wanting in the colour and chiaroscuro according to Raphael's design, but not certainly as Raphael would himself have done it. The sum which Giulio received he bestowed as a dowry on his sister, when he gave her in marriage to Lorenzetto the sculptor, who had also been a pupil and friend of Raphael. The Cardinal did not send the picture to Narbonne, but, unwilling to deprive Rome of such a masterpiece, he presented it to the Church of San Pietro in Montorio, and sent in its stead the Raising of Lazarus, by Sebastian del Piombo, now in our National Gallery. The French carried off the Transfiguration to Paris in 1797, and, when restored, it was placed in the Vatican, where it now is. The Communion of St. Jerome, by Domenichino, is opposite to it, and it is a sort of fashion to compare them, and with some to give the preference to the admirable picture by Domenichino; but the two are so different in aim and conception, the merits of each are so different in kind, that I do not see how any comparison can exist between them.

The Miracles.

A. J.] The miracles performed by our Lord during His short manifestation on earth, either before His disciples, or in sight of assembled multitudes, form a large portion of the events chronicled in the Gospels, and, as artistic representations, have a peculiar importance; for which reason, and for the better understanding of the variety and significance of the treatment, they are placed together here as a series.

The distinction I have been careful to perceive throughout this work, between the devotional and the historical representations of all sacred events, must be especially remembered in reference to the miracles. It is clear that, in the most sacred examples which exist, those on the sarcophagi, the object of the artist was to convey the idea of superhuman beneficence and power, in the expression, as simply as possible, of a certain action—it was to be a miracle, and nothing more. Take, for instance, the transformation of the water into wine, as it appears on the sarcophagi of the 3rd, 4th, and 5th centuries. Christ, as a single figure, in classical drapery, stands before three vases (the antique Hydria), and with a touch of the wand which He extends towards them, the water is supposed to become wine (woodcut, No. 127). The divine power of our Lord, and

127 Conversion of Water into Wine.
(Ancient sarcophagus.)

the object on which He exercises that power, are alone present; there is no attempt to express any locality, or any attendant circumstances. It is the idea merely, suggested rather than repre-

A. J.] sented. But in the later works of Art we have the Marriage Feast at Cana in Galilee, in which the transformation of the water into wine is indeed the principal circumstance, but only one of the circumstances ; we have the banquet and the guests, the bride and bridegroom, the astonishment of the master of the feast, as he puts the miraculous beverage to his lips, and, in short, the full dramatic scene, such as Paul Veronese has given it to us. To feel the full force of the contrast, it is sufficient to compare the ancient bas-relief, with its single majestic figure, with the sumptuous picture in the Louvre and its 150 figures, where we look about for some time in vain for the chief personage.

But the most important of all the miracles in the early religious cycles, and the one most frequently repeated, is the Raising of Lazarus. In the Catacombs, and on the sarcophagi, it was especially significant ; it was not only a miracle testifying to the divine character and mission of the Saviour, it was understood as a symbol and pledge of the resurrection of the body in the general sense of the Christian dogma, and likewise as figuring the resurrection of our Lord, which at that time was considered a subject much too awful to be treated in Art, with a direct and personal application to the Saviour Himself. There exists innumerable ancient remains in sculpture and in the mural paintings, in which this subject is repeated with slight variations. Christ wearing the classical toga, and generally beardless, stands before a tomb or niche, to which there is an ascent by several steps, wherein the figure of Lazarus, swathed like a mummy, is placed upright, in the Egyptian fashion. Sometimes our Saviour holds a wand, with which He touches the dead man—'Lazarus, awake!' Sometimes He has no wand, but merely stretches forth His hand ; very frequently, one female figure kneels at His feet, which expresses the previous moment : 'Lord, if thou hadst been here, my brother had not died.' In some instances that I have seen, the tomb is not a building, but a hollow in a rock. In one example, it is a sort of open grave, like a box ; Lazarus does not appear, and our Lord touches the edge with His wand, as if saying, 'Lazarus, come forth.' Then, again, there is an instance in the Catacombs in which there is no tomb, but the figure of Lazarus,

.l. J.] swathed in linen, and only the head uncovered, stands upright before Christ, who extends His hand.

Dr Münter observes that in these ancient symbolical representations we never find the story of the daughter of Jairus or the widow's son at Nain—it is the resurrection of Lazarus which has been invariably chosen to express 'the first fruits of them that slept,' and the belief in the resurrection of the dead.

The multiplication of the loaves and fishes is also often repeated on the ancient Christian remains, in manner similar to the changing of the water into wine. It is not the feeding of the four or five thousand people, upon whom Jesus had compassion because they continued with Him three days, 'and had nothing to eat'— it is simply the *miracle*. Our Lord, with His wand extended, touches three or more baskets of bread, which stand at His feet; near Him is a youth, with two small fishes on a plate. In other examples, Christ stands between two men, one holding a basket of bread, the other a basket of fish. I remember one of these groups on a sarcophagus, treated with singular elegance. In another instance we find the *seven* baskets at the feet of our Lord: the bread is generally round, and marked with a cross, like our Easter buns. There are examples in which Jesus is attended by Peter or one of the other disciples, but always there is the

128   Miracle of Loaves and Fishes.
(Ancient sarcophagus.)

same simplicity, the expression of the *idea* only: the wand, which is like the wand given to Moses, and which is placed in the hand of Jesus in so many of these antique groups, gives Him too much the air of a magician.

This miracle, as recorded in Matt. xiv. and xv., is twice repeated; but the two events, though distinguished in the Gospel, are

A. J.] not in any way discriminated in works of Art, ancient or modern, that I know of. The circumstances were so nearly similar, only the number of people and of the loaves being different on each occasion, that it was not worth while to make two representations where one sufficed to convey the idea.] By the 13th century the miracle of the Loaves and Fishes, which occurs in most illustrated Bibles, was treated as realistically as before ideally. Our illustration (No. 129) is taken from one of the same size in a psalter belonging to Mr. Holford, of about A.D. 1300. Here our Lord is rather the dispenser of bounty than the worker of a supernatural

Miracle of Loaves and Fishes. (MS. A.D. 1310. Mr. Holford.)

event. For the miracle is over, the basket is full, and is already in the hands of the Apostles, while Christ Himself gives both loaf and fish to a cripple.

[*A. J.*—The healing of the sick, blind, and infirm, were also

A. J.] favourite groups, selected by the early Christians to express the tender mercy as well as the miraculous power of the Redeemer. When the general action of healing is expressed, Jesus lays His hand on the head of the suppliant; when the blind are healed, He touches the eyes of the figure before Him (woodcut, No. 130).

Of this last miracle, we are told that it was one of those sometimes embroidered on the garments of the early Christians; of one of the groups on the sarcophagi, Bottari remarks, that the blind man wears his tunic without a girdle, which, with the Jews, was a sign of mourning

130   Christ healing the Blind.
(Ancient sarcophagus.)

Luke viii. 43. The healing of the diseased woman is simply expressed by a veiled female figure kneeling at the feet of Christ, and touching the hem of His robe as He extends His hand over her (woodcut, No. 131), while the Canaanitish woman, who cried to Him for mercy on her afflicted daughter, is kneeling with outstretched arms, and our Lord has the roll of the Scriptures in His hand, as if He were quoting from it: 'It is not meet to take the children's bread,' &c. (Matt. xv. 22-28). But, in general, it is hardly possible to distinguish between these two subjects, they are so alike.

It is, however, the story of the

131   Christ healing the Woman.
(Ancient sarcophagus.)

A. J.] paralytic man which we find most frequently repeated to express, in a general way, the beneficent and miraculous power of healing:

132   Christ healing the Lame.
(Ancient sarcophagus.)

'Take up thy bed and walk.' The divine command and its fulfilment is the moment chosen. Christ stands, as usual, beardless, and in classic drapery, with His hand extended. The paralytic man—in general a diminutive figure—carries his bedstead on his back (woodcut, No. 132; see also illustration of ceiling of Catacombs, woodcut, No. 3). In some examples, Christ is attended by Peter or by John; but there are seldom more than the two figures, and no attempt to express the locality, whether the Pool of Bethesda or the dwelling-house.

There exists an ancient bas-relief, in which the representation of this miracle is more complicated and dramatic than is usual. The composition is divided into two compartments, an upper and a lower, both of which exhibit the interior of an hospital, with various sick and afflicted, lying or sitting. Between these two compartments is the representation of water—perhaps intended for the Pool of Bethesda. In the lower compartment the paralytic man is seen lying on his couch, his hand to his head (the usual attitude to express pain); in the upper compartment he has taken up his bed, and carries it away.

Our Lord walking on the sea does not appear on the sarcophagi or in the Catacombs; but it may be found on two antique gems, with Peter about to sink, and the bark with the three disciples beyond.

In describing the antique theological and symbolical cycles, I have shown how frequently certain of the miracles occur as expressing the Christian's belief in the divine power and benefi-

A. J.] cence of the Saviour, and the hopes through *Him* of eternal life.
I have now said enough of the separate subjects to render them intelligible and interesting in the simple forms adopted in the earliest Christian monuments, and proceed to show how they have been represented in the more complex and picturesque style of the revival of Art.

The Marriage at Cana of Galilee.

I HAVE noticed this subject in the 'Legends of the Madonna' with reference to her, because it so frequently forms an important scene in the life of the Virgin Mother as well as in that of her Son, and I have not much to add here. In modern Art, the personages considered necessary for the proper representation of the story are our Lord as chief actor; His Mother, at whose request the miracle was performed; the bride and bridegroom, the master of the feast, and the guests more or less in number. The four Apostles, who at that time had been called to follow our Saviour —Peter, Andrew, James, and John—are supposed to be present, and are generally to be distinguished from the other guests. Servants are bringing in pitchers of water, and emptying them into the wine-jars. Jesus stands by, directing them, or, more frequently, He is seated at the table, and, with uplifted hands, blesses the vessels of water placed before Him. I am aware that the date of the marriage is placed before the calling of Peter and Andrew in some chronologies; but St. John expressly says that both Jesus was called and His disciples to the marriage. The opportunity has been seized by the later painters to introduce many accessories, as vases of gold and silver, with viands and fruit, rich dresses, flowers, and groups of musicians—all which are conspicuous in the pictures by Paul Veronese, Bassano, and Tintoretto, all containing a number of figures, and all full of animation, movement, and splendid colour. We must observe, however, that the first painter who treated this subject after the revival of Art, namely, Giotto, was also the first to dramatise it. He has introduced the governor of the feast as a fat *gourmand*, drinking off a goblet of the wine, with equal wonder and enjoyment. In this composition, the Virgin Mother sits next to the bride, as is the case in Bassano's beautiful picture; but, in general, I think our Lord and His Mother are seated together, and in Tintoretto's splendid composition of forty-nine figures they are at the head of the table—the men are all seated to the right, and the women to

A. J.] the left. Paul Veronese made the subject popular as a banquet scene for refectories; he painted it five times on a large scale, varying from thirty to one hundred and fifty-nine figures, and the finest though not the largest example is the picture in the Dresden Gallery (No. 277), which, for dramatic expression and harmonious and glowing colour, is unparalleled—a perfect delight to the eye, yet hardly satisfactory if considered as a religious picture. I have mentioned that of Luini, as the finest in conception I have ever seen.

By Carlo Bononi of Ferrara (1627), an immense composition of forty-four figures, and his masterpiece. Here the Virgin stands, which is unusual, and seems addressing her Son, to show that it is near the end of the feast; the bride gracefully washes her mouth (*la sposa, che con grazia ripulisce i denti, fa veder il finir della tavola*). In splendid colour and effect, this painter comes near to Paul Veronese, and, like him, is celebrated for his Scriptural banquet scenes, with which it was the fashion at that time to decorate the refectories of the rich convents.

Jan Steen has several pictures of the Marriage at Cana.

Neither Raphael nor Albert Dürer have painted this subject, and, considering its capabilities for colour and sumptuous treatment, it is still more surprising that it has not been treated by Rubens.

The Raising of Lazarus.

A. J.] Of all the beautiful Gospel histories, there is not one which leaves a more vivid, a more indelible impression on the mind, than the story of Lazarus. Even considered apart from its profound and wonderful significance as a manifestation of divine power, what an exquisite tenderness and simplicity in the narrative, what a pathetic beauty in the details! Nowhere does the character of the benign Redeemer beam upon us with a more attractive light; and, as an important incident in His earthly history, it is scarcely ever omitted in any series which comprises the events previous to the Passion, unless the object be the glorification of the Virgin Mother, or the series of her joys and sorrows, in which case the Marriage at Cána, where she was present, is preferred to the Raising of Lazarus, where she was not present.

As a separate subject, we find it embellishing altars, cemeteries, and oratories, where the dead were especially remembered (as formerly it was conspicuous on the sarcophagi), though the Entombment and Resurrection of our Lord have been in later times more generally preferred for this purpose. It must also be borne in mind that the passionate devotion for Mary Magdalene in the Middle Ages, to which I have elsewhere adverted, gave additional importance to this representation. The popular legends identified the penitent Magdalen with Mary the sister of Lazarus, as she was certainly the same woman 'which anointed the Lord with ointment, and wiped His feet with her hair' (John xi. 2). Therefore it is that in works of Art consecrated to her honour, we find the Raising of Lazarus seldom omitted. I do not think it necessary to enlarge here on the connection of Mary Magdalene with this subject, because I have fully treated it in a former volume of 'Sacred and Legendary Art' (vol i. p. 336; third edition).

To these sources of interest must be added the wonderful capabilities of the story for picturesque representation—the principal figure arrayed in all the majesty of divine power, yet touched with the softest human sympathies; the grief contending with faith in the two sisters; the mourning friends and the people 'who wept with them;' the Apostles looking on, and all these of different ages and character, animated with various expression; and then the ghastly dead man wakening to life in their presence, and emerging from the shadow of the tomb! It must be acknowledged that such materials for character and picturesque effect were here as seldom fall to the choice of the painter within the verge of simple historic truth; the more extraordinary is it that so few of the great painters have treated it—that in almost every instance, however fine, the power of the artist has, in some respect or other, always fallen below the beauty and greatness of the theme, and that the nearest approach to what we require of solemn and sublime feeling in the general conception of the scene has been made by that inspired Dutchman, Rembrandt. But this is anticipating.

The personages necessary for the treatment of the story are first our Lord and the dead man, who are of course indispensable. Then, one or both the sisters, and, as the design is amplified, the Apostles—especially Peter and John, and the friends and mourners, few or many. The locality is near a city, and the tomb a cave with a stone laid upon it.

Of the Byzantine or Greek formula, there exists a very perfect specimen in the small mosaic diptych preserved in the guardaroba of the Baptistery at Florence. Here, the Raising of Lazarus is portrayed with eight figures only. Christ stands with upraised hand, as summoning the dead man to come forth. The two sisters kneel at His feet. Lazarus rises, swathed in his graveclothes, and three Apostles are behind.

Giotto, in the series in the Arena Chapel at Padua, has closely adhered to the Byzantine formula, with, however, a certain freedom in the treatment; and as it happened that every *motif* adopted or invented by Giotto was immediately repeated by his scholars, with slight variations, but with no attempt at originality, we find the same distribution of the figures and the accessories prevalent in all the examples that could be cited down to Angelico da Fiesole. In Giotto's composition, our Saviour stands to the left, in front of two or three of His disciples; His countenance

A. J.] beautiful, His attitude noble, His right hand held up with the gesture at once of command and blessing; at His feet kneel Mary and Martha, side by side; to the right, in front of the cave, stands Lazarus between two Apostles, swathed up, pale and cadaverous, hardly yet alive. The lookers-on do not hold their noses, as in later repetitions of the subject (in allusion to John xi. 39), but they have wrapt their robes tightly over the lower part of their faces. We take an illustration from Fra Angelico (No. 133).

133   Raising of Lazarus.   (Fra Angelico. Accademia, Florence.)

I find no example of this fine subject among the works of Raphael, or Perugino, or Fra Bartolomeo, or Albert Dürer, or Titian, or Andrea del Sarto. All the greatest artists of the beginning of the 16th century seem to have neglected it, with one exception—but that is indeed a grand exception.

A. J.] It is a well-known story that, when Michael Angelo entered into competition with Raphael, he did so, not in his own person, but by assisting his friend Sebastiano del Piombo in the famous Resurrection of Lazarus, now in the National Gallery.

I take the description of the action from Ottley's Catalogue.

'The point of time chosen is after the completion of the miracle. Lazarus is represented sitting on the stone coffin which had contained his body, supported by three men, who, having been employed to remove the lid from the sepulchre, are now relieving him from the grave-clothes with which he was enveloped. Jesus, standing in the midst, appears to be addressing him after his return to consciousness, in words as may be supposed, not unlike those which He had before used to Martha and Mary : " I am the resurrection and the life; he that believeth in me shall never die;" or, as others have interpreted the action, He is appealing to His heavenly Father to bear witness to His divine mission : " I knew that Thou hearest me always; but because of the people which stand by, I said it, that they may believe that Thou hast sent me;" or, according to others, He is uttering the command : " Loose him, and let him go " '—which last appears to me the right interpretation. It seems a curious thing that people should be so impressed by their own peculiar associations and conceptions, as to differ wholly with regard to the meaning of an attitude or the expression of a face. But there is some excuse in this instance, for the figure of Christ is undoubtedly the weakest part of the picture.

Martha, standing a little behind, turns away her head, fearing, sickening at what she most desires; the other sister is gazing up at the Saviour—all faith, hope, and gratitude; and herein the characters of the two sisters, as well as their deportment on the occasion, are finely discriminated. The distance represents a view of Jerusalem and a river traversed by a bridge, on the banks of which is seen a group of women washing clothes. A striking effect is produced in this part by the bridge and the arched entrance into the city being represented in shadow, while the houses and banks of the river appear through them illuminated by sunshine. As to the execution in detail, it is inconceivably fine. The hands, feet, draperies, heads, features, are all modelled with the utmost care, and are worthy of the closest observation and study. The kneeling

A. J.] figure of Mary, and the foreshortening of her hand and arm, which seem to project from the canvass, are very striking.

Though the Raising of Lazarus has not been popular in the Venetian school, there are some remarkable examples; for instance, the fine composition by Tintoretto in the Scuola di S. Rocco at Venice, and by Bonifazio a smaller but beautiful picture in the Louvre, once in the San Luigi at Rome, but the unequivocal disgust expressed by two of the Jews, one of whom turns away his head, and the other stops his nose, is a fault in point of taste.]

Rubens has painted this subject. It is a small picture in the Berlin Gallery (No. 785). The expression of the principal figures is very fine; but instead of both sisters turning in adoration to Christ, as the highest and most engrossing feeling, which is stereotyped in all early representations, one of them is turning to Lazarus.

[*A. J.*—There are two compositions by Rembrandt, etched by himself; one small—beautiful in its way, that is, in *his* way; the other larger, altogether different, and incomparable for scenic and poetic effect. This is a large arched piece finely executed, and the chiaroscuro produces a great effect. Our Lord, who is placed a little to the left, and turned to the right, is represented standing in a dignified attitude on a stone, which appears to have been a part of the tomb of Lazarus. His left hand is extended above His head, and His right rests upon His side; behind Him is a group of six figures, two of whom, with uplifted hands, appear terrified at the prodigy. At the feet of our Lord appears Lazarus, in the action of just rising above the tomb; his death-like countenance is admirably expressive of his late situation. On the right are several figures; one of them, probably intended for his sister, stretches out her arms, and seems in haste to receive him; above her a man (his head covered with a cap) starts back with terror and amazement. Above our Lord are some folds of drapery that form a kind of funeral canopy, within which, in the background, hang the turban and sword, the bow and quiver of Lazarus, in allusion to his military vocation. The legend which describes Lazarus as a soldier, I have already given at length in 'Sacred and Legendary Art.'

The two analogous subjects, the Resurrection of the Daughter of

A. J.] Jairus, and the Resurrection of the Widow's Son at Nain, have very seldom been treated—which is unaccountable, considering the artistic and dramatic capabilities of both.

Of the Daughter of Jairus, I remember one in the Belvedere Gallery (marked Old Florentine School). There are too many figures—sixteen; Jairus wears a rich dress, as becomes the ruler of the Synagogue. The best example for expression is the composition by G. Muziano, containing merely the personages mentioned in the Gospel: 'He suffered no man to follow Him, save Peter, James, and John. . . . And when He was come in . . . . he taketh the father and the mother of the damsel, and them that were with him. . . . And He took the damsel by the hand . . . . saying, Maid, arise. And her spirit came again, and she arose and walked, and they were astonished with a great astonishment.' The references on the engraving are Mark v. 37, &c. This picture is known by the very fine engraving by Beatrizet.

The Raising of the Widow's Son at Nain is one of the most beautiful and pathetic of all the Gospel incidents, and so surrounded by picturesque associations, that we are surprised not to find it more frequently treated. The finest I have seen is by Agostino Carracci, a famous picture originally painted for Prince Giustiniani. I remember being struck by the wild look of the youth as he starts to life. As is usual with Agostino, the story is told with as few figures as possible, and the gate of the city of Nain forms the background.

There are two other compositions which have a certain degree of celebrity, and make an impression by their size and multifarious composition, rather than by the pathos of the sentiment and expression of character. That by Zucchero contains more than forty figures—here, too, the face of the youth and the look of bewildered terror as he raises his head, have been much admired; but I do not think in either case that the expression is appropriate—the youth should meet the eye of our Saviour with another feeling. The mother, of course, is always conspicuous, full of rapturous gratitude and faith.

MIRACLES OF HEALING.

.I. .I.] THOSE representations of our Lord as the Divine Physician, as healing compassionately the sick, the lame, the blind, the possessed (or insane), such as were afflicted with maladies and infirmities incurable by any human means, were often of great beauty: accompanied by the various picturesque incidents and accessories described in the Gospels, they were more easy to the artist, and more successful, because more within the capabilities of Art, than those which attempted the more Godlike impersonation of the Divine Teacher and Preacher. The dramatic action (by which I mean the external relations between the persons of the scene) were more direct, more obvious to human senses and human sympathies, than the hidden spiritual influences of mind addressed to mind. In Western Art we do not find these miracles of healing often introduced into a series of the history of Christ. To express the miraculous power, a more important or more significant miracle was chosen, as the Marriage at Cana, or the Raising of Lazarus; but as separate pictures, the Healing of the Sick generally or in individual instances, as that of the Blind Man, the Lepers, &c., were often placed in hospitals and charitable institutions, or in the churches and chapels attached to them, either as appropriate decorations or as offerings of gratitude and devotion. I think most of the pictures now scattered about in various galleries and collections have had this origin, though it cannot always be traced with certainty.

'Medicine receives great honour from the works of our Saviour, who was Physician both to soul and body, and made the latter the perpetual subject of His miracles, as the soul was the constant subject of His doctrine.'[1]

I will now give some instances of the treatment of such subjects, confining myself to the most remarkable.

'And they brought unto Him all sick people that were taken with

---

[1] Bacon, 'Advancement of Learning,' book iv. c. 11.

A. J.] divers diseases and torments, and those which were possessed with devils, and those which were lunatick, and those that had the palsy; and He healed them' (Matt. iv. 24).

Jouvenet. Large composition painted for the Chartreuse at Paris. Christ heals the sick on the shore of the Sea of Galilee. (Mark iii. 7, 8.)

Rembrandt. Christ heals the sick. This is the *chef-d'œuvre* of the painter, one of his largest and most effective etchings. Our Lord is seen in front with a large glory surrounding His head; He is leaning upon what looks like a fragment of masonry, the left hand raised, and the right hand extended towards the people. A woman who has been brought before Him is lying on a mattress; near her is an old woman, who stretches out her shrivelled hands, as if in supplication. Another woman approaches with a sick child. To the right are other sick and afflicted persons—one has been brought in a wheelbarrow; then there is an aged woman leading an aged man. On the left hand, again, are seen several persons who appear to be disputing about the miracles performed in their sight; and they said, 'When Christ cometh, will He do more miracles than this man hath done?' In the background is seen an Ethiopian with a camel, to denote that many who were present had come from a great distance, led hither by the fame of our Saviour.

Jesus withdrew Himself with His disciples to the land of Gennesareth, and when the men of that place had knowledge of Him, they sent out into all the country round about, and brought unto Him all that were diseased, and He healed them (Matt. xiv. 34, 35; Mark iii. 7).

JESUS HEALS THE DAUGHTER OF THE WOMAN OF CANAAN.

'A CERTAIN woman, whose young daughter had an unclean spirit, heard of Him, and came and fell at His feet: The woman was a Greek' (that is, a Gentile), 'a Syrophenician by nation' (in Matthew she is called a Canaanite—xv. 21). . . . 'Jesus said unto her, Let the children first be filled; for it is not meet to

A. J.] take the children's bread, and to cast it unto the dogs. And she answered and said unto Him, Yes, Lord: yet the dogs under the table eat of the children's crumbs' (Mark vii. 25-28).

It is clear that nothing can be more difficult than to convey, in representative Art, a scene of which the chief interest consists in a speech of our Saviour and the reply of the woman. When she kneels at His feet, it is difficult to express that the appeal is not for herself but for another, and that her daughter who was absent was made whole from that very hour.

There are two pictures, however, of this subject, both comparatively modern, and both celebrated; one by Annibale Carracci, painted for Prince Giustiniani. Here the significance of the group is made apparent by the presence of a dog, to which the woman points expressively and appealingly.

This picture had a great celebrity, and Malvasia styles it 'La Cananea famosa:' it came to England with the Lucca Gallery in 1842.

The other picture alluded to is by Drouais, painted when he was only one and twenty. It is quite classically treated, and for power and colour almost equal to Poussin. It contains eleven figures.

CHRIST HEALS THE CENTURION'S SERVANT.

Matt. viii. 5; Luke vii. 2.

WHEN He entered into Capernaum, a certain centurion's servant, who was dear to him, was sick and ready to die; and the centurion came unto Him, beseeching, and saying, 'My servant lieth at home sick of the palsy, and grievously tormented.' And Jesus said, 'I will come and heal him.' And the centurion answered and said, 'Lord, I am not worthy that Thou shouldest come under my roof: but speak the word only, and my servant shall be healed.' This story is very effectively represented in a picture by Paul Veronese —Dresden Gallery, No. 281. The centurion bends before our Lord in an attitude of the deepest humility; he is a fine, manly, and military figure, attended by two soldiers, and a page who carries his helmet. Although, as is usual with Paul Veronese, the figure and face of Christ are not very refined or majestic, yet the contrast between the military group on the right and the peaceful Redeemer is very striking.[1]

Paul Veronese. The woman afflicted for twelve years with an incurable infirmity. The scene takes place, as described by the Evangelist, before the entrance to the house of Jairus, the Ruler

134   Christ healing Woman. (Paul Veronese.)

of the Synagogue, on a flight of marble steps leading to a portico. Our Lord, who is about to enter the house, turns round suddenly, holding back His robe, as if aware that He had been 'touched,' 'Somebody hath touched me, for I perceive that virtue is gone out from me,' and He looked round to see who 'had done this thing.' The woman kneeling and looking up with a most expressive gesture, opening her arms, acknowledges the truth. She is richly dressed,

[1] The catalogue tells us that it was painted for Guglielmo Gonzaga, Duke of Mantua, a prince by no means warlike, but perhaps to commemorate some especial family incident. It is not mentioned in Ridolfi.

A. J.] and supported by two attendants. Immediately beyond our Lord, on His right, is Jairus, who holds up his hand as if reproving the woman, while Peter in front leans over the balustrade, watching her with interest. Behind are James and John; below the steps, in the background, are the sick who 'thronged Him.' This is a small but exquisitely beautiful picture; not only for the picturesque arrangement, sentiment, and colour, which we expect from Paul Veronese, but for more refinement and propriety of conception than he usually exhibits. It combines, in short, all his finest characteristics in a small compass.

Parmigianino. The ten lepers are healed. Our Lord in the act of saying, 'Go show yourselves to the priest.' This is a beautiful print in chiaroscuro—one of the finest works of Vicentini. (Bartsch, xii. p. 39.)

G. Genga. The same subject; a small beautiful picture, in treatment very like Poussin. (Crozat Gallery.)

Paul Veronese. Our Lord heals the mother of Peter's wife. The scene is under a kind of portico. The sick woman lies upon a sumptuous couch with a canopy, and is supported by a young girl. Our Lord standing near her, touches her hand with His. The Apostles are around.

Lucas van Leyden. The blind men restored to sight.

Van Dyck. The paralytic man healed. A composition of five figures, three-quarter life-size. The Saviour, whose figure and attitude are exceedingly fine, is in the act of saying, 'Take up thy bed and walk.' The man bends in adoration and gratitude before Him. This, for dramatic power and vigorous execution, is one of Van Dyck's finest works. I believe the subject to be taken from Matthew ix., where they bring 'a man sick of the palsy, lying on a bed,' and our Lord, after reproving the Pharisees for their evil thoughts, commands the infirm man to take up his bed. For there was another occasion in which they let down the sick man through the roof of the house, and laid him at the feet of Jesus, which I have seen in a picture, though I cannot remember where. These, however, must be discriminated from the next subject, in which our Lord commands the man to take up his bed and walk —which is far more important, and requires an entirely different treatment.

The Pool at Bethesda.

A. J.] 'Now there is at Jerusalem, by the sheep market, a pool, which is called in the Hebrew tongue Bethesda, having five porches. In these lay a great multitude of impotent folk, . . . waiting for the moving of the water. For an angel went down at a certain season into the pool, and troubled the water: whosoever then first . . . stepped in was made whole. . . . And a certain man was there, which had an infirmity thirty and eight years. . . . Jesus saith unto him, Wilt thou be made whole? The impotent man answered Him, Sir, I have no man, when the water is troubled, to put me into the pool. . . . Jesus saith unto him, Rise, take up thy bed, and walk' (John v. 2–8).

This has been a favourite subject for hospitals, and there are some beautiful and celebrated examples: very few early ones, I believe, for I can remember only one—an ancient half-ruined fresco in the series of the history of Christ, painted in the Church of S. Maria di Mezzaratta, near Bologna, and attributed to Jacopo Avanzi and Lippo d'Almasio. There are eleven figures visible. An angel stirs the waters, in which we see a sick man praying. The helpless paralytic man lies on the edge of the pool, addressed by the compassionate Saviour, 'whose countenance,' says Lord Lindsay, 'is particularly sweet and holy.'[1]

Parmigianino. A very beautiful chiaroscuro woodcut from a drawing.[2]

And by Ludovico Carracci, a picture now in San Giorgio at Bologna, which Malvasia praises with a heap of epithets—'così vasta la invenzione, propria e viva l' espressione, inarrivabile il costume e il decoro, profondo il disegno, gagliardo il colorito,' &c. It was painted in friendly rivalry with Annibale, and I am obliged to add, that though I have seen this picture, I do not remember it. I *do* remember seeing a picture of the same subject, appro-

---

[1] Description of these frescoes in 'Christian Art,' vol. iii. p. 212.
[2] Bartsch, xii. p. 38.

priately placed in the hospital at Siena, by a late mannerist, Sebastian Conca, which has sufficient merit to fix attention.

There is also a fine picture by Nicolas Poussin. But all these are surpassed, eclipsed, by the wonderful picture by Murillo, a large grand composition, 'formerly in the Hospital of Charity at Seville, whence it was stolen by Marshal Soult.' Our Lord, three Apostles, and the lame man, are seen in front; the head and attitude of the Saviour most impressive for beauty and benignity —the finest in point of character ever painted by Murillo. In the background is seen the Pool of Bethesda with its portico (its five porches, as described), and above it, in the sky, hovering in a blaze of glory, is seen the angel, as if about to descend and trouble the waters. For grandeur and poetry, for the sober yet magical splendour of the colouring, for its effect altogether on the feelings and on the eye, there are few productions of Art that can be compared to this; and till I saw it, I think I was rather inclined to underrate the Spanish school generally. Murillo himself has never equalled it, that I am aware of: but then I have never been to Seville. I have a vivid recollection of the occasion on which I first beheld this beautiful picture, and something, perhaps, may be allowed for the associations connected with it. I had breakfasted with Mr. Rogers, and when the other guests had departed, he took me to see it. It was then in a back room in a house on Carlton Terrace, looking out on gardens quite still and bright with summer sunshine. It had been raised only a little from the ground, so that the heads were not much above the eye, only sufficiently so to make one look up—as one would instinctively have done before that divine presence. Then, when we had contemplated for a time the beauty of the painting, which really struck me into silence—for the colour seemed to affect us both in the same manner, like tender, subdued music from many grand wind-instruments, all breathing in harmony—we sat down opposite to it. He pointed out the rich violet-purple colour of the robe of our Saviour as peculiar to the Spanish school, and contrasted it with the conventional red tunic and blue mantle in the Italian pictures. He speculated as to how Raphael would have treated the same subject, and we compared it with the Cartoon of the 'Beautiful Gate,' and the crippled beggar in that picture with the poor disabled paralytic man before us; and we gave the preference to Murillo in point of character and living expression. The porches of Bethesda did not equal the wreathed columns of the Gate called—how justly!—the 'Beautiful.' But then, how soft, how translucent the aerial perspective, and how the radiant angel comes floating down! Goethe used to be provoked when comparisons were made between two characters, or two artists, or two productions of Art, the true value of which rested in their individuality and their unlikeness to each other; but a large portion of the pleasure we derive from Art, and from Nature too, lies in the faculty of comparison, in the perception of differences and of degrees of qualities — in the appreciation of distinct aims, and of the wondrous variety with which Nature reveals herself to the souls of men. If we were forced to choose between Raphael and Murillo—who was the master of the great and the graceful—we must turn to him who created the Heliodorus, and the School of Athens; but, luckily for us, we are neither obliged to compare them, nor to choose between them, since God has given us both. Something like this did we say on that summer morning, sitting before that marvellous picture; and since then, I cannot bring it before my mind without thinking also of the dear old poet, whose critical taste was at once the most exquisite and least exclusive that I have ever known.

Let me add, that the sight of that picture awakened some thoughts which were perhaps deeper and more mournful than the painter intended. How many of us might well, metaphorically, have laid ourselves down for years by that Pool of Bethesda, and no angel have come down from heaven to trouble it with a divine power, or infuse into its waters a new spiritual life. Or, if it were so, yet were we prostrated by our own infirmity, and there was no human sympathy near to help us down into its healing and reviving waters, no aid in man or angel, till Christ comes to say, 'Take up thy bed and walk.'

'Mais parler de la couleur en peinture c'est vouloir faire sentir et deviner la musique par la parole' (G. Sand).

The Blind are Healed.

A. J.] 'And as they departed from Jericho, a great multitude followed Him, and behold, two blind men sitting by the wayside. . . . And Jesus had compassion on them, and touched their eyes' (Matt. xx. 29–34).

N. Poussin. Christ heals the two blind men at Jericho. The scene is outside the gate of the city. Our Lord, who is attended by the Apostles Peter, James, and John, touches the eyes of one of the two blind men kneeling before Him, the other extends his arms towards the Saviour, behind whom is a man stooping down to observe the wonder. On the left is a group of women and children.

'And as Jesus passed by, He saw a man which was blind from his birth' (John ix. 1).

L. Bassano. Christ heals the blind man who was blind from his birth. Our Lord is here attended by eleven Apostles.

L. Carracci. The Blind Man healed at Bethsaida, 'outside the town.' He is here an old blind fiddler, led by a boy.

Christ feedeth Five Thousand Men with Five Loaves and Two Fishes.

Matt. xiv. 13; Mark vi. 32; Luke ix. 10; John vi. 10.

In contrast to the antique symbolic group of one or two figures, the modern painters, in treating this subject, have tasked their powers to crowd as many personages into their canvas as possible —to express, in short, the greatness of the miracle by the greatness of the multitude. It does not often appear in a series of the history of our Lord. The large composition attributed to Raphael, and engraved under his name, is not his apparently, but is ascribed by Passavant to one of his scholars.

A. J.] It was a subject frequently chosen for refectories—for which it was appropriate in its significance, and fitted by its extent to cover a large wall. One feels, too, that it was better for this purpose (the decoration of an eating-room) than the Last Supper of our Lord. There exists a vast composition in the suppressed convent of San Lucchese at Poggibonsi, near Florence, which is curious as one of the few accredited works of Gerino di Pistoia, one of the Perugino school. Lanzi cites, with strong expressions of admiration, the great fresco of this subject by Bernardino Gatti (1552), painted on the walls of the refectory of the 'Canonici Regolari Lateranensi,' in Cremona, adjoining the splendid Church of San Pietro al Pó; Tintoretto's great picture in the Scuola di San Rocco at Venice is also remarkable. But, without doubt, one of the finest examples of all is the colossal composition by Murillo, not painted for a refectory, but as one of the illustrations of the works of charity ('Feed the Hungry') in the Church of the Caridad at Seville. (Stirling's 'Artists of Spain,' ii. 859.) It forms the companion to the 'Moses striking the Rock.' Our Lord is seated on the left hand, on a fragment of rock, surrounded by the Twelve Apostles; one of them places before Him the five loaves, which He blesses with uplifted hand, and St. Peter is about to take the two fishes from the hand of 'the lad'—a very perfect specimen of an Italian *gamin*, and probably painted from the same model as his famous Beggar Boys. On the right hand is a group, principally of women, who are anxiously watching the performance of the miracle—altogether about twenty figures in front. Between these two groups is a view of the valley, where, in the distance, the assembled multitudes seem countless in number, and melt away into an accumulation of indistinct forms.

The beautiful small sketch for this enormous composition is in England.

Mr. Stirling mentions a repetition of the Seville picture as being once in the Soult Gallery. I remember a beautiful picture at the sale of this collection in 1852, but it was attributed to Francisco Herrera the younger. I do not know where it is now. We sent commissioners to this sale, who committed the extraordinary and ridiculous mistake of purchasing, at an exorbitant

A. J.] price, a third or rather fourth-rate Titian, and overlooking some of the finest examples of Herrera, Zurbaran, Roelas, and Alonzo Cano.

Most of these went into various public galleries, particularly into those of Dresden and Berlin, so that such an opportunity will never again occur.

THE MIRACULOUS DRAUGHT OF FISHES.

THIS miracle does not occur on the early monuments of Art. In later times we find it frequently used in a symbolical sense as denoting the conversion of the heathen, or the gathering of the Gentiles into the Church of Christ. The fish, it will be remembered, is the ancient emblem of Baptism and Christianity. In this sense I have seen this miracle in the Jesuit missionary churches and elsewhere. I remember an especial instance in the Jesuit Church at Traunstein, in which the pulpit was hung round with a net carved in wood, in which a multitude of fishes were seen heaped together, shining with gold and silver scales, with Peter and Andrew standing at the corners to haul in the net. The preacher stood between.

Of Raphael's famous cartoon at Hampton Court, I need hardly speak here; it is so well known from innumerable engravings, and so near at hand. The locality is the Sea of Gennesareth. On the right, our Saviour is seated in a small boat; He is seen in profile, with a most refined head and face. Peter has fallen on his knees before Him: 'Depart from me, O Lord, for I am a sinful man;' to which our Lord calmly replies: 'Fear not; henceforth I will make you fishers of men.' Behind Peter is Andrew, with his hands outspread as in astonishment, and the boat is full to overflowing with fish. Farther off, in another boat, James and John are drawing up their nets, so miraculously laden. The great black cranes which are flapping their wings on the shore in the foreground have been often criticised, but well defended by Hazlitt. 'They are,' he says, 'a fine part of the scene; there is a certain sea wildness about them, and as their food was fish, they contribute mightily to express the affair in hand.' It may be added, that they contribute to the general effect of the whole composition, by throwing the boats farther into the distance and by breaking the horizontal lines. These and the fish were admirably painted by Giovanni da Udine; the rest of the cartoon is by Raphael's own hand. In the tapestries this subject is not one of the series of the history of Christ, but of the story of St. Peter as head of the Catholic Church.

The next in celebrity is the fine altarpiece by Rubens in the Church of Notre Dame at Malines. It was painted for, and dedicated by, the guild of Fishmongers, and used to hang in their chapel on the right of the nave; it is now placed behind the high altar. The whole is full of vigorous life and light, and the piles of fish lie glittering and tumbling about like nature itself. On the interior of the wings we have, on one side, the tribute money found in the fish, and on the other, the story of Tobias and the fish—everywhere fish! Beneath this altarpiece there was once a predella composed of three small pictures. In the centre, as usual, the crucifixion. On one side, the story of Jonas thrown into the sea and saved. On the other side, Peter, about to sink, is saved by our Lord. On the exterior of the wings, we have the four Apostles who were fishermen, Peter, Andrew, James, and John.

The appropriate choice of these subjects, and the manner in which they were combined to express a certain significance, render this picture very interesting in itself, and it is throughout wonderfully executed.

THE CALLING OF THE TWO FIRST APOSTLES, PETER AND ANDREW.

A. J.] 'AND Jesus, walking by the sea of Galilee, saw two brethren, Simon called Peter, and Andrew his brother, casting a net into the sea: for they were fishers. And He saith unto them, Follow me, and I will make you fishers of men. And they straightway left their nets, and followed Him' (Matt. iv. 18-20).

Ghirlandajo. A fine landscape with a lake. In the foreground, Peter and Andrew kneel before Christ; behind Him are eight persons, and behind Peter and Andrew, about fifteen others. In the distance, on the left hand, the two Apostles are seen leaving their nets at the call of Christ, and, on the right hand, James and John, the sons of Zebedee, who are on board a small bark, prepare to leave it when called by Jesus. I must observe, with regard to this beautiful picture, one of the large frescoes in the Sistine Chapel in the Vatican, that the incidents are poetically, rather than historically, brought together, and that the great number of figures introduced is unnecessary to the simplicity of the story; but so fine are the characters, heads, and draperies, that we cannot wish them absent. It is not said in the Gospels that a great multitude were present on the occasion; but in Luke v. 1 it is said, that as He stood by the lake, 'the people pressed upon Him to hear the word of God.'

Barroccio painted a picture of this first calling of these Apostles, but he made St. Andrew, not St. Peter, the principal person. He kneels on the shore with open arms extended towards the Redeemer, while St. Peter in the distance is seen getting out of the boat to follow Him. St. Andrew is here the principal person, because it was painted for the confraternity of St. Andrew, at the request of the Duchess d'Urbino, 1580; but, when finished, the Duke d'Urbino sent it as a present to Philip of Spain, because St. Andrew was the protector of the order of the Golden Fleece.

The Parables of our Lord.

4. *J.*] It may be truly said, that when our Lord taught the people in parables, He taught them in pictures. There is hardly one of these divine allegories which does not afford, in dramatic action, or in the expression of character, admirable subjects for representative Art—subjects to which the most scrupulous could not object; for no passages of Scripture could be so easily rendered with so little detriment to the original words, and in a manner so calculated to instruct and delight the people, to exercise the reflective faculties, and to touch and awaken the religious feelings; and yet the parables have been rarely treated by the best artists, in the best period of Art, and have entered but little into the schemes of architectural church decoration. For this there were several reasons: in the first place, the most munificent patrons of Art were ecclesiastics, and some of the most distinguished architects and painters were themselves ecclesiastics. Hence it followed, perhaps, that the subjects chosen by them for instruction were in general theological and doctrinal. The miracles of Christ, which were not only part of His history, but the visible proofs of His divine character and mission, were preferred to His parables, which were fictions and allegories, not events. I believe, also, that the ecclesiastical authorities who planned the decorations of the churches might be influenced by a fear, analogous to the fear of idolatry in our days, lest these beautiful allegories should be mistaken for real histories. I know that I was not very young when I entertained no more doubt of the substantial existence of Lazarus and Dives than of John the Baptist and Herod; when the good Samaritan was as real a personage as any of the Apostles; when I was full of sincerest pity for those poor foolish Virgins who had forgotten to trim their lamps, and thought them—in my secret soul—rather hardly treated. This impression of the literal, actual truth of the parables I have since met with in many children, and in the uneducated but devout hearers and readers of the Bible: and I remember that when I once tried to explain to a good old

A. J.] woman the proper meaning of the word parable, and that the story of the Prodigal Son was not a fact, she was scandalised—she was quite sure that Jesus would never have told anything to His disciples that was not true. Thus she settled the matter in her own mind, and I thought it best to leave it there undisturbed. I do not know certainly that any scruples prevailed with regard to the representations of the parables in the mediæval period of Art; but in the 14th and 15th centuries they occur but seldom in church architectural decoration, and I think never in separate pictures. It is worth remark that we owe to the Reformers in the beginning of the 16th, and to the Jesuits in the beginning of the 17th century, the adoption of the parables in prints and pictures to aid in the moral and religious instruction of the people. Of course it is not to be inferred that before this time religious prints were unknown, but they have been chiefly used—as, indeed, they are now used throughout the greater part of Italy—as a vehicle to set forth the sanctity of some particular saint, or the importance of some particular festival; and thus it has happened that so many of the fine old religious prints and moveable pictures are figures and miracles of St. Francis, or St. Domenic, or St. Bernardino, or St. Catherine, executed for the ecclesiastics of certain convents and churches to be distributed to the people. It appears, on a comparison of dates, that it was just about the time of that religious ferment in Germany which accompanied the Reformation there, without imparting to it that destructive tendency and those cruel and vulgar impulses which disgraced the same movement in England and Scotland, that the fine 'Old German masters,' as they are called, began to invent and publish religious representations, tinctured more or less with the new ideas, while in Italy the reaction against the materialism, the scepticism, and the paganism of the *cinquecento* produced the later Bologna school, and inundated the whole population with the religious prints published by the Jesuits. These were usually in the exaggerated and affected taste of that period of Art, and distinguished by their far-fetched unintelligible mysticism, but sometimes also of great beauty in the conception, and well adapted to attract and instruct the people—especially those which represented the humble childhood of our Lord, His obedience to His earthly parents, His

A. J.] industry in His adopted trade, His beneficence to the suffering and poor, or the domestic and maternal virtues of His Mother.

These I have already described, and it is among these early German and later Italian works of Art that we find the parables of our Lord (more particularly those of the Good Samaritan, the Prodigal Son, the Rich Man and Lazarus, and others of easy comprehension) employed for the purpose of conveying popular instruction.

But, returning to the earlier ages, we must bear in mind that when the parables were introduced into a Gothic or Byzantine system of decoration, it was only with reference to their second or mystical interpretation, and not to that which was apparent. To this double signification our Saviour Himself alludes, when He vouchsafes to give His disciples the explanation and hidden meaning of one of His most beautiful similitudes—that of the Sower (Mark iv. 14).

Now, in Western Art, the parables are represented literally as our Saviour had uttered them, and the religious application was either left to the comprehension of the observer, or expressed in accessory groups, or explained in an inscription; while in genuine Byzantine Art, or in the decoration of the Greek churches, it is not the literal text of the apologue, but the mystical sense and theological interpretation which is placed before the people, so far as it can be done in painting. For the better comprehension of what I mean, I will give one or two instances.

In the parable of the Good Samaritan, we are accustomed to understand, and in its artistic expression we naturally expect to find, a divine lesson of mutual compassion—we are told to go and do likewise; but in Greek Art it is different, the obvious significance being merged in one of the profoundest mysteries of our faith. In the man who fell among thieves is figured Adam and his progeny, *i.e.*, the personified humanity, tempted, betrayed by the powers of evil, stripped of his pristine glory, 'left for dead.' And the Good Samaritan is Christ, who comes to rescue, heal, and redeem. He presents Himself to Adam and Eve, who stand naked, wounded, and shivering before the closed gates of Paradise; at His word the gates fly open, and He offers them baptism and the sacramental bread.

A. J.] The Prodigal Son is treated in a similar manner. It is not the relenting human father who receives with joy the repentant son. The second and mysterious significance of the apologue is at one glance revealed before us. It is Christ who stands on the threshold; the repentant sinner kneels before Him, and receives from His hand the Bread of life and the Sacrament of reconciliation; while angels sound their silver trumpets, and sing allelujahs. Very finely imagined, but, as it seems to me, not coming home to the heart like the lesson of human forgiveness in that simple representation of the offended father who folds in his arms his erring, long-lost son, and commands to kill the fatted calf: 'For this my son was dead, and is alive again; he was lost, and is found.'

The same application of the apologue of the Good Samaritan may be found on a window of Bourges Cathedral. The traveller goes down from Jerusalem, the city of the blessed, to Jericho, the city of the accursed; and the double meaning is expressed by the lateral subjects, which form a commentary on the literal story painted in the central compartments; the same arrangement may be found on a window in the Cathedral at Sens, still more finely executed in regard to character and composition.

In the usual treatment of the Rich Man and Lazarus, our compassion for the wretched Lazarus divides our feelings with a natural horror for the selfish sin of the Rich Man; but in Greek Art, and in the older representations, the attention is concentrated on the terrible doom of the Rich Man, which becomes a type, a foreshadowing, of the fate of the wicked in the day of judgment. Didron describes a picture which he brought from Greece, of the death and punishment of the Rich Man, which I forbear to translate.

It appears that some similar impression of the real personal existence of Lazarus and Dives prevailed in the Middle Ages. Lazarus was regarded as a saint, and became the patron saint of diseased beggars, and the places of refuge or hospitals dedicated to him were thence called *Lazar-houses*. In France he was St. Ladre.

In Italian Art it should seem that the Venetians were the first who treated the parables as separate pictures, and in a popular manner, as domestic scenes—perhaps after the example of the Germans, with whom they were in constant relation.

It is well known that the old Da Ponte family (old Bassano

A. J.] and his sons) had at Bassano a sort of manufactory of religious pictures, not only for the convents and churches, but for sale to the merchants who carried them to the chief cities of Italy, to the yearly fairs, whence they were dispersed over all Europe. Among these were many of the parables, several times repeated. Ridolfi enumerated nine parables, painted by old Bassano. The similitude of the 'Good Shepherd,' which is not properly a parable, but rather a personal symbol, which Christ has clearly identified with Himself —' I am the Good Shepherd '—will be treated of in the second volume. I will only add here, that this similitude, as carried out in John x. 1-14, has been curiously treated on two of the carved oaken doors of a church at Rouen, attributed to Jean Goujon. There we see, on one door, the sheepfold on the right hand surrounded by hurdles; the robber, who attempts to climb over, instead of entering by the door, is cast out. The shepherd, wearing the papal tiara, with St. Peter, stands before the entrance: 'He that entereth by the door is the shepherd of the sheep.' The carving on another door refers to v. 11-14. In the uppermost compartment is the hireling, 'who seeth the wolf coming, leaveth the sheep and fleeth; and the wolf catcheth them.' In the lower compartment, the Good Shepherd defends His flock, and attacks the wolf with His sheep-hook, ready to give His life for His sheep.

The Rich Man and Lazarus.

Luke xvi. 19-31.

In this subject, the *motif*, however varied in arrangement, when represented in one composition, is generally the same. In the front, or on one side, the beggar Lazarus lies extended before the door of the Rich Man, the dogs lick his feet; in the background, or above, the Rich Man is seen feasting with his guests.

Giacomo Bassano. The beggar lies in front, with outstretched hands, as if appealing for food. The dogs lick his feet; an attendant approaches, as if to drive him away—we may suppose, by order of the cruel Rich Man. He carries a dish, and wears a

A. J.] peculiar high cap, made of the long flakes of sheep's wool, dyed crimson, such as is worn to this day by the peasants of the Friuli, in the neighbourhood of Bassano. Beyond this group, and a little raised, is seen the Rich Man feasting at table. I used to admire this picture when in the possession of Mr. Rogers, and it is certainly one of Bassano's finest works—dramatic in feeling and conception, and resplendent in colour. He has repeated it several times with variations; one is in the Florence Gallery, where a kitchen is seen behind with glittering gold and silver plate. In a picture by Domenico Feti, the sideboard, heaped with vessels of gold and silver, is also conspicuous. Lazarus stands at the side, appealing; the Rich Man and his wife and companion, by significant gestures, motion him away.

Domenico Feti. By this painter, who had, as we shall see, a particular predilection for the parables, there is a small finished picture.

Jan Steen. While the Rich Man is seen feasting within, Lazarus, extended before the door, looks up beseechingly to a woman who is shaking out a tablecloth, 'desiring to be fed with the crumbs which fell from the rich man's table.' This is a stroke of humour quite characteristic of the painter, and the picture is fine in his way.

The Doom of the Wicked Rich Man.

He is seen wallowing in fire and flames, and tormented by all sorts of grotesque and horrible demons; far off, in heaven above, he sees Lazarus lying in the lap of Abraham. (Attributed to the younger Palma.)

Teniers. The scene is a rocky cavern. The Rich Man, dressed in velvet and furs ('purple and fine linen'), is dragged down the road to hell by a crowd of demons, miscreated, fantastic, abominable things, such as Teniers liked to paint. (Sir Robert Peel.)

Hans Schäufflein (about 1510). Below and in front Lazarus is seated at the gate; the dogs as usual. Above him, in a balcony, the Rich Man is seen feasting at table, a flaunting woman at his side. Far off in the sky, on the left hand, Lazarus is reposing in the arms of Abraham. On the right hand Dives in flames begs for a drop of water.

Sometimes we find the various scenes of this apologue treated in a series for the edification of the people—for instance, by that quaint old German, Heinrich Aldegrever—in five subjects:—1. The Rich Man is feasting sumptuously, and making merry. 2. Lazarus, crouching before a gate, implores food in vain. 3. The death of the Rich Man. The Devil seizes his treasures. 4. He is dragged down to hell by several demons. 5. 'And being in torments, he lift up his eyes, and seeth Abraham afar off, and Lazarus in his bosom.'

There are other instances, by George Pencz, and by Heemskirk, in three or four different scenes, in which the fate of the cruel Rich Man is always prominent; but no one has exhibited him as praying in behalf of his brethren, that they may be converted, 'lest they also come into this place of torment.'

In conclusion, I will only observe that, when this parable is introduced into Gothic sculpture, it is sometimes placed significantly and conspicuously on one side of the church-door, where the rich enter and the beggars congregate; for instance, the whole story is treated on one of the magnificent windows at Bourges. In the last and highest pane, Abraham is seen with Lazarus in his lap, or rather, as if he were holding him in a white napkin.

The Prodigal Son.

Ital. Il Figlio prodigo.   *Fr.* L'Enfant Prodigue.   *Germ.* Der verlorene Sohn.

A. J.] We can easily understand how this parable became more popular as a subject of Art than any of the others. As related in the simple words and with the divinely persuasive tenderness of the Redeemer, it touches every heart. Taken in its mystical sense, it is a lesson of faith and hope; in its more obvious sense, it is a lesson of hope and charity, at once a comfort to the erring and a rebuke to the self-righteous.

The moment usually chosen for artistic representation, when the story has to be told in one scene, is the return of the Penitent to the house of his Father, for that certainly is the chief point in the religious moral. This was the incident told in early Christian Art, as embodying the ideas of Repentance and Forgiveness.] We give this quaint illustration, of the 14th century (No. 135), from Mr Boxall's Speculum. It has a tender grace of its own. The youth of the Prodigal is conspicuous here—he is 'l'enfant prodigue.' An attendant stands by, holding the raiment. [*A. J.* —But sometimes we have the moment of self-abasement, where he is reduced to feeding swine, and perishing of hunger; or, much more rarely, we have the scene in which he is wasting his patrimony in riotous living.

Of the first subject, the instances are so numerous, that I can only mention a few of the most remarkable. Its picturesque capabilities in expression, character, and costume, and in the contrast between youth and age, have rendered it a favourite Scriptural piece with the later painters and designers, as its familiar and tender significance, and intelligible grouping, have made it a favourite with the people.

We have here Bassano again in great force. It was just one of those subjects in which his genius revelled—homely, natural, strong feeling, with all the accessories of domestic furniture—preparations for a feast, animals, and these painted with an evident *gusto*, and all glowing with life and colour.

135   Prodigal Son.   (Italian Speculum. 14th century.)

. J.] Annibale Carracci. The Prodigal Son, kneeling before the door of his father's house, in ragged garments, weeps and wrings his hands in an agony of sorrow and repentance. The aged father, standing on the threshold, bends down with open arms, in act to pardon and to bless. The contrast between the venerable tenderness, and long sumptuous robes of the old man, and the nakedness and anguish of the young man, which are not without a certain elegance, as reminding us of his first estate, are as fine as possible. In the distance is seen the elder brother, who appears to be expressing his displeasure, and farther off is the slaughter of the fatted calf. And that the religious application of the subject may not be forgotten, the symbolical figure of the 'Padre Eterno' appears in the sky above, surrounded by a glory of angels, with His hand extended in benediction. I must observe that when the slaughter of the fatted calf is introduced, as in this and many

A. J.] other instances, it has reference to the sacrifice on the Cross, through which our sins are forgiven. The fame of this picture, painted for the Zambeccari family, rendered the subject popular in the Bolognese school.

Guercino. The father clothes his repentant son with a new garment. Life-size figures, rather more than half-length—a composition frequently repeated by this painter—and suited to his style when only the natural domestic feelings were to be expressed.

136.   Prodigal Son.   (Guercino.)

Lord Cowper has a beautiful specimen, Lord Lansdowne another. We give an illustration by this painter (No. 136).

Murillo. The aged father stands on the threshold of his dwelling, his arms thrown round his son, who kneels before him, looking up in his face, eager, suppliant, deprecatory, his sinking form half embraced, half sustained in the arms of his father. On the right hand a woman stands behind, watching the scene with sympathetic looks. Three attendants approach with the apparel—the shoes and the ring (Luke xv. 22). On the left hand a boy leads forward the fatted calf, followed by a man who carries an axe. The dog leaping up and recognising the penitent (as in our

A. J.] illustration from Guercino) is a touch of nature characteristic of Murillo. This is one of his largest and most important works, containing nine figures, above life-size. It was one of the celebrated series of eight large compositions, expressing Charity and Mercy, which he painted for the 'Caridad' at Seville, and one of the four carried off by that 'plundering picture-dealer, Soult,' from whom it was purchased by the Duke of Sutherland. 'I know not any picture whatever which can go beyond this in heartfelt nature and dramatic power. The execution, too, is as fine as possible; the drawing so firm, the colours so tenderly fused, the shadows so soft, the effect of the whole so in harmony with the sentiment and the subject, that I consider it a rare example of absolute perfection of its class.'[1]

The Penitence of the Prodigal, as a separate subject, is not so common; by far the most remarkable of those I have seen is the engraving by Albert Dürer. The Prodigal Son, having spent his patrimony, is seen on his knees, with clasped hands, near a trough, at which several pigs are riotously feeding, and which are so humorously expressed, that our attention is distracted from the principal figure—the portrait of Albert Dürer himself. Altogether a masterpiece.

Salvator Rosa. In a fine landscape the Prodigal Son kneels with clasped hands in the midst of a herd of sheep, oxen, goats, as well as swine.

Rubens. The scene is in a farm stable, with several cows and horses, and men busied about them; a woman is feeding some hungry pigs, who rush towards the trough, near which the Prodigal Son, on his knees, looks up imploringly at her. The sentiment is, 'How many hired servants,' &c. (v. 17). The expression of misery in the Prodigal Son, the animation of the animals, and the spirited yet careful execution, render this picture particularly interesting. It was brought to England in 1823, and is now at Narford Hall. (Andrew Fountaine, Esq.)

The scene in which the Prodigal Son wastes his substance in riotous living has been treated principally by the Dutch painters. I do not know a good Italian example.

Teniers. The scene is in front of an inn, where a table is

---
[1] Private Galleries, p. 191.

.1. J.] spread, and the Prodigal is feasting with two courtesans; a wretched old woman, leaning on a stick, approaches to beg an alms —perhaps intended to foreshadow the probable fate of the ladies at table. On the left hand, a page is filling a glass with wine; on the right, a servant is approaching with a dish, and a woman casting up the reckoning; behind are two musicians; quite in front, on the left hand, are the cloak, plumed hat, and sword of the Prodigal, lying on a bench. On the right are flagons of wine, cooling and drinking vessels, and in the far distance a landscape, in which the Prodigal Son is seen kneeling by a trough with swine around him. This small picture is, in the style of the painter, a *chef-d'œuvre*, exquisite for finish and expression. (Louvre, École Allemande, 512.) It was purchased in 1776 for 29,000 francs.

Holbein. In the foreground the Prodigal is feasting with his mistress, and gambling with a sharper, who is sweeping the money off a table; in the background are the more important scenes. He is driven out and stripped by his profligate companions; he is feeding the swine, and he returns to his father. (A small spirited picture, in the Liverpool Museum.)

Jan Steen. The scene is a garden before an inn. At a table plentifully served, the Prodigal Son is feasting with women and attended by servants; a man is playing the guitar, and two children are blowing bubbles — an allegory of the transient pleasures of the spendthrift. This is in the painter's homely coarse style of conception, and of admirable execution.

Treated as a series, the story of the Prodigal Son has been extremely popular. The earliest, as well as the most complete, I ever met with is on one of the magnificent windows in the North transept of the Cathedral of Chartres. The artist, however, has somewhat amplified the original narrative. To read the subjects in order, it is necessary to begin with the lowest pane on the left hand :—

1. The Prodigal Son requires from his father his portion of goods. 2. The father takes money out of the strong box and gives it to him. 3. The Prodigal mounts his horse, and, attended by a valet on foot, leaves his father's house. 4. On the road two courtesans tempt him to enter their dwelling. 5. He is seen feasting with them. 6. The two women crown him with flowers and caress

A. J.] him. 7. The Prodigal, lying on his bed, is gambling with two sharpers. 8. The sharper and the courtesans strip him and beat him. 9. One of the women drives him out of the house with a stick. 10. He weeps and laments outside the door. 11. He offers himself as servant to a rich man. 12. He is feeding the swine, shaking down the acorns for them. 13. He repents of his fault: 'I will arise and go to my father.' 14. He appears before his father's door, who receives and embraces him. 15. His father clothes him in a new robe. 16. The fatted calf is killed, and the feast prepared. 17. The eldest son stands before his father with a ploughshare in his hand, and expostulates with him (v. 29). 18. The father seated at table with his two sons. One servant presents a cup of wine, others play and sing. At the summit of the window is seen our Saviour with His hand raised in benediction; on each side are adoring angels.

On a window of the Cathedral of Bourges, the arrangement of subjects (seventeen in number) is much the same. In the highest and last compartment, the aged father is seen between his two sons, holding a hand of each, as if reconciling them. The series in the Cathedral of Sens, also on a window, has fewer subjects, but is peculiarly elegant in design and treatment.

By the old German engravers are several series: one of them (anonymous, 1543) in twelve scenes; one, very beautiful (by Hans Beham), in four; others in four, five, or six scenes. Some of these are full of character, and others curiously grotesque in design and costume, but well calculated for their purpose.

Murillo. Four small beautiful studies, apparently intended for large pictures. 1. The Prodigal Son receives his patrimony. 2. He leaves his father's house. 3. He is feasting with courtesans. 4. He is kneeling repentant in the midst of the swine.[1] Of the return to the house of his father, that wonderful picture in the Sutherland Gallery, there is no sketch, I believe.

[1] Madrid Gallery. Copies or duplicates were in the collection of Louis-Philippe, and sold at Christie's, May 28th, 1853.

The Good Samaritan.

A. J.] To understand the full force of this beautiful apologue, we must remember the bitter feuds which then existed between the Jews and the Samaritans, and that they would not even speak to each other; yet our Lord, who was Himself a Jew, makes the hero of His tale a Samaritan. When the story is told in one picture, the moment chosen is always that in which the Good Samaritan ministers to the wounded man.

Giacomo Bassano. A woody landscape, with a road. The Jewish traveller lies on the ground 'half dead,' the Good Samaritan is binding up his wounds. The ass from which he has alighted stands near; the Priest and the Levite are seen in the distance, 'passing by on the other side.' A beautiful picture, full of character, while the colour has the depth and transparency of gems. This, which is now in the National Gallery, was in the collection of Mr. Rogers —the companion picture to Dives and Lazarus. There is a repetition at Berlin (314), and another, quite different and of wonderful beauty, at Vienna. (Belvedere Gallery.)

Paul Veronese. The same group, life-size, in a most lovely landscape. (Dresden.)

Rembrandt. Before the door of an inn, two persons have assisted the wounded traveller from a horse, and are about to carry him into the inn, while a boy holds the horse. On the right hand, the Good Samaritan is seen on the steps, with his purse in his hand, and speaking to the host: 'Take care of him, and whatsoever thou spendest more, when I come again, I will repay thee.' From the window of the inn three persons are observing what passes; in the distance, a landscape, a bridge, and a city, meant perhaps for Jericho. (Louvre.)

There is a celebrated etching by Rembrandt of this subject, with fewer figures, and with a well introduced, from which a woman is drawing water. This otherwise most expressive and touching scene, incomparable in execution, is disgraced by the introduction

A. J.] of a dog. I remember seeing a first impression of this etching, for which the possessor had paid eighty guineas.

A. Vandervelde has painted it as a night-piece. The Good Samaritan arrives at the door of the inn with his wounded charge, and the host appears with a candle.

The story forms an interesting and popular series, of which there are several examples.

H. Aldegrever. Four scenes, treated like the history of Dives and Lazarus. 1. The thieves attack the traveller, leaving him half dead. 2. The Good Samaritan pours oil and wine into his wounds. 3. He places him on his mule. 4. He brings him to the inn. These have often been copied.

THE WISE AND THE FOOLISH VIRGINS.

A. J.] THIS striking parable has never, that I know of, been represented dramatically, except by the very late schools of Art, and then generally in the worst taste. In the earlier times it was constantly employed in the decoration of the Gothic cathedrals, and other religious edifices, in its mystical signification, as symbolising the Last Judgment. The righteous, who watched and prayed, and entered not into temptation, are accepted, and enter into Paradise. The unrighteous, careless, and sensual, are rejected, and the doors are closed against them. In the old ecclesiastical monuments, the representation is but slightly varied. In some instances, the figures are mere lifeless conventional types; in others, they have some degree of sentiment and personality. The costume, too, varies with age, but the arrangement is nearly the same in all. The five Wise Virgins are on the right, bearing their lamps upright and flaming, the five Foolish Virgins on the left, with their lamps extinguished, and held upside down, to show that they are empty of oil.

At Chartres, on the vault of the North lateral door, the five Wise Virgins are seen modestly veiled, holding up their lamps, while the Foolish Virgins, with long floating hair, and crowned with flowers, carry their lamps upside down.

And there is another instance on the South façade of the same cathedral, where, after the Martyrs, but separated from them, appear the two processions of Virgins, as a *résumé* of the fate of those who watched and toiled, and those who slumbered and took their pleasure.

At Strasburg, the Ten Virgins are figured in ten statues larger than life; at Rheims, the statues are less than life; at Amiens, they are on each side of the principal door; at Nuremberg, in that beautiful porch leading into the Church of St. Sehaldus (the entrance fitly called the 'Braut's Thor'—the Bride's Door), the Ten Virgins stand on each side. These figures are remarkable for

A. J.] the simple elegance of the conception and for the sentiment conveyed—the Wise Virgins solemn and serene, and the Foolish Virgins sad and penitent, with drooping heads and lamps reversed.

Fribourg. The ten statues are, if I remember aright, almost colossal, and an angel, hovering between the two processions, has in his right hand a scroll, on which is written, in Gothic letters, *Vigilate et orate;* in the left hand, a scroll inscribed, *Nescio vos*—' I know ye not.' On the great West portal of the cathedral at Berne, they appear in a procession under the Last Judgment. These figures, which are of much later date (1474) than in the old French and German cathedrals (1200–1350), are very elegant.

With regard to the treatment of this parable in pictures, I have never met with any instance in the great old masters of the Italian school. I remember an old Flemish picture of the Last Judgment (Vienna, Belvedere Gallery), in which, beneath the usual group of our Saviour as Judge, St. Peter stands on the right hand, and receives into Paradise (of which he keeps the keys) the five Wise Virgins, and a number of other holy women, while on the left hand stands St. Paul, rebuking and rejecting the five Foolish Virgins, who also have a crowd of followers. The archangel Michael stands between the two groups, with a crown of laurel in his right hand and a flaming sword in the left. This is a late picture of the 16th century.

I have said enough to render this subject intelligible and interesting when it is met with, but, before I conclude, will mention two late but fine examples.

Martin Schön. The five Wise Virgins, five separate prints, all moving to the right, all crowned with flowers, holding up their drapery with one hand and their lamp with the other; but no two are exactly alike. And the five Foolish Virgins, each holding her lamp reversed or extinguished, with her garland on the ground, and her hair dishevelled. These figures have that peculiar mingling of the quaint and the graceful which distinguishes Martin Schön, and the series, which is rare and valuable, has often been copied.

Gottfried Schalken. The five Wise and the five Foolish Virgins

A. J.] are seen by night hurrying to the door of a palace. On the side of the Foolish Virgins, the only light is from the waning moon. The other side of the picture is lighted by the procession of the Wise Virgins with their flaming lamps. This picture, beautiful in itself, is remarkable also as the masterpiece of the painter in his peculiar style of excellence; the treatment of artificial light is here most appropriate.

137   The Wise and the Foolish Virgins. (Speculum. M. Berjeau.)

Sanredam. Five large prints. 1. The Wise Virgins, grouped together, are reading the Scriptures, and meditating. 2. The Foolish Virgins are dancing and amusing themselves. 3. The Wise Virgins rise in the middle of the night to trim their lamps, while the Foolish Virgins are seen fast asleep. 4. The Wise Virgins, having their lamps lighted, are received by the Bridegroom with festal rejoicing. 5. The Foolish Virgins, with their

A. J.] empty lamps, find the door shut against them, and weep and wring their hands in despair. On reading over this description, we cannot but feel how well the subjects are selected for dramatic expression, and how beautiful they might be if treated by a religious and imaginative painter; unhappily, though drawn and executed with much cleverness, the conception is in the worst style of Art, intolerably mannered and affected.]

The parable of the Wise and Foolish Virgins takes its place in the 'Speculum Salvationis' as a type of the Last Judgment. We give an illustration (No. 137) from the Speculum facsimiled by M. Berjeau. The Wise Virgins are here seen with their lamps burning, and ascending the steps of a building, where they are welcomed by Christ and by an angel. The Foolish Virgins, whose lamps are reversed, are descending the steps on the other side, directly into the jaws of hell.

THE HOUSEHOLDER WHO HIRED LABOURERS FOR HIS VINEYARD.

Matt. xx. 1.

A. J.] THE interpretation of this striking parable, as given in Greek Art, is so extremely curious, that I must notice it here, though perfectly unknown among us.

Christ, as the master of the vineyard, is standing in the midst of His Paradise, and the Patriarchs of the early times, Enoch, Noah, Abraham, Moses, &c., point to the Apostles, seated on thrones near the Saviour, and expostulate, saying, 'These last have wrought but one hour, and Thou hast made them equal unto us, which have borne the burden and heat of the day.' And Christ answers them as in the text, 'Friend, I do thee no wrong,' &c. In the only examples I know of, the subject is treated without any reference to this double signification, and in a manner the most literal and prosaic. There are two beautiful little pictures by Andrea del Sarto in the fine collection at Panshanger: in the first, the householder is hiring the labourers; in the second, he is paying them, and one is counting the money with a dissatisfied air. These pictures, from their shape and style, appear to have ornamented a piece of furniture—perhaps a money-chest or coffer. It was the custom among the Florentines to decorate with painting, as well as carving, their household furniture, such as beds, chests, presses, cabinets, &c., and often to employ for this purpose the most distinguished artists—on which point I shall have more to say elsewhere.

Dr. Waagen attributes these pictures to Franciabigio, but I must observe that the original drawings, which exist at Vienna, in the collection of the Archduke Charles, have always been attributed to Andrea.

There is also a sketch by Titian. The lord of the vineyard stands in the middle of the picture. On the right hand is the vineyard on a hill, and labourers at work; on the left two

A. J.] labourers come to be hired—those, apparently, of the eleventh hour. Farther in the distance, the master is seated at a table, paying his labourers, and, as we may suppose, expostulating with them. The companion picture is 'The Unjust Steward.'

The long shape of these two pictures, ten inches by two feet six, shows that they have formed part of a *cassone*—possibly a money-chest.

A landscape and a group of labourers asleep; in the background the evil spirit is sowing tares, as in the large print engraved by Matham after A. Bloemart.

Bassano. A rustic scene, with peasants and cattle reposing in front, and a woman with milk-cans. Behind is the 'sower that went forth to sow' (Mark iv. 3).

The same subject by Battista Fontana.

Quentin Matsys. The Unjust Steward is seen through a door or window, trafficking with the creditors of his Lord, who stand before him with their accounts. In an old Flemish picture in the Munich Gallery, apparently an imitation (not a copy) of this, the Unjust Steward has a most comically cunning expression, as if rejoicing in his knavery.

The Unjust Steward is also treated in a sketch by Titian. (Berlin Gallery.)

The Unmerciful Servant.

The king forgives the servant who is his debtor to a vast amount, and the same servant thrusts into prison a debtor who owed him only a hundred pence (Matt. xviii. 23–35).

This parable has been treated by Bassano, and by Rembrandt in a very fine picture in Lord Hertford's gallery. The king, wearing a turban, and in red drapery, is seated behind a table with papers; three persons stand before him—the culprit, the accuser, and the soldier about to take charge of the culprit. Dr. Waagen thinks that this picture is the Unjust Steward, but, looking to the expression, it appears to me to represent the Unmerciful Servant.

THE BLIND LEADING THE BLIND.

A. J.] 'IF the blind lead the blind, they shall both fall into a ditch.'

Dietrich. In a beautiful wooded landscape one blind man is leading another, and both are about to fall down a precipice. (Munich Gallery, No. 170.)

THE TREE WHICH BORE GOOD FRUIT AND THE TREE WHICH WAS BARREN.

'EVERY tree that beareth not good fruit shall be cut down and cast into the fire.'

We find this similitude in Gothic sculpture, where it is used as a symbol of the Last Judgment, as on each side of the grand portal of the Cathedral at Amiens. On the right hand is the good tree, laden with fruit, and with lamps suspended from the boughs. On the left hand the barren tree, leafless, and with an axe stuck into the trunk.

THE MERCHANT WHO BUYS THE PEARL OF GREAT PRICE.

'THE kingdom of heaven is like unto a merchant man seeking goodly pearls,' &c. (Matt. xiii. 45).

Bassano has represented this parable in his picture of the Jeweller.

In Greek Art the interpretation is very expressive. Christ stands in the midst in an attitude of benediction; around Him crowns, treasures, idols, royal robes, lie broken and scattered on the ground. The sages and heathen philosophers of Greece look on, and a prophet points to our Lord, saying, 'Behold the pearl of great price!'

There is a series of eight small pictures by Domenico Feti, representing eight parables. 1. The Prodigal Son. 2. The Good

A. J.] Samaritan. 3. Labourers in the Vineyard. 4. The Blind leading the Blind. 5. The Lost Sheep found. 6. The Lost Piece of Silver. 7. The Unmerciful Servant. 8. The Blind and the Lame are bidden to the Feast. (Dresden Gallery, No. 76–86.)

138   Lost Drachm. (Domenico Feti. Pitti.)

These little compositions are, in execution, light, spirited, and well coloured, but conceived in the most literal and prosaic style. For instance, in the sixth parable—the Lost Drachm (woodcut, No. 138)—the scene is the interior of a hovel; a woman, groping with a lamp (or a candle, I forget which), after seeking everywhere for her piece of silver, finds it between the chinks of her floor. In the Greek picture of the same parable, the scene is Paradise. The angels, archangels, and saints, are seated on golden thrones, but one throne is empty; below this, Christ descends into hell in search of the lost sinner; in another part of the picture He ascends again into heaven, holding Adam (*i.e.*, the human race) by the hand, and there is joy in heaven, and the angels sing hallelujahs.

This may be deemed far-fetched, but the other extreme seems to me worse, and the attempts to render literally that which is a mere metaphor have been sometimes grotesque and even profane. I remember an anonymous German print of the 16th century, in which we have the parable of the Camel and the Needle's Eye (I believe an old Oriental proverb, applied by our Saviour figuratively). A rich man is trying to enter a narrow gate leading into heaven; behind him three of his servants, with whips and sticks, are trying to force a camel through the eye of a needle, held by a celestial hand. Nothing can be worse in point of taste or more absurd than this.]

END OF THE FIRST VOLUME.

www.ingramcontent.com/pod-product-compliance
Lightning Source LLC
Chambersburg PA
CBHW051740300426
44115CB00007B/642